The Bobbed Haired Bandit

Stephen Duncombe & Andrew Mattson

The Bobbed Haired Bandit

A Story of
Crime and Celebrity
in 1920s New York

Random House Trade Paperbacks ⬤ New York

2007 Random House Trade Paperback Edition

Published in the United States by Random House Trade Paperbacks,
an imprint of The Random House Publishing Group,
a division of Random House, Inc., New York.

RANDOM HOUSE TRADE PAPERBACKS and colophon are trademarks
of Random House, Inc.
MORTALIS and colophon are trademarks of Random House, Inc.

Originally published in hardcover in the United States
by New York University Press in 2006.

ISBN 978-0-8129-7735-6

Library of Congress Cataloging-in-Publication Data
Duncombe, Stephen.
The bobbed haired bandit : a story of crime and celebrity in 1920s
New York / Stephen Duncombe and Andrew Mattson.
   p. cm.   Includes bibliographical references and index.
ISBN 978-0-8129-7735-6
1. Cooney, Celia, 1904–1992.   2. Cooney, Edward, 1899–1936.
3. Brigands and robbers — New York (State) — New York — Biography.
4. Robbery — New York (State) — New York.   I. Mattson, Andrew.
II. Title.
HV6653.C66D86   2005
364.15'52'09227471 — dc22   2005020720

Printed in the United States of America

www.mortalis-books.com

9 8 7 6 5 4 3 2 1

Contents

Cast of Characters

This is not an exhaustive list of characters, but only the players who have important roles in the drama of the Bobbed Haired Bandit.

CELIA COONEY: The Bobbed Haired Bandit

EDWARD COONEY: Husband of Celia and her "tall male companion" in crime

KATHERINE COONEY: Celia and Ed's first and short-lived child

PATRICK and EDWARD COONEY: Celia and Ed's sons

DANIEL J. CAREY: Police captain in charge of all detectives in Brooklyn and Queens

WILLIAM J. CASEY: Brooklyn detective who arrests Celia and Ed in Florida; later describes the case in *True Detective*

JOHN D. COUGHLIN: Inspector and chief of detectives for entire New York Police Department (NYPD)

CHARLES DODD: Brooklyn district attorney in charge of the Bobbed Haired Bandit case

RICHARD E. ENRIGHT: Police commissioner of New York City

FRANK S. GRAY: Casey's partner on the pinch in Florida

WILLIAM RANDOLPH HEARST: Media mogul, publisher of Celia's serialized memoirs in the *New York American*

HARRY C. HONECK: Warden of Raymond Street Jail in Brooklyn where the couple are held during their sentencing

THOMAS C. HUGHES: Brooklyn assistant district attorney (ADA) under Charles Dodd

JOHN F. HYLAN: Mayor of New York City

TOM W. JACKSON: Humor writer for the *Brooklyn Standard Union*

BENJAMIN JOSPEY: Drugstore proprietor and frequent female bandit victim

WILLIAM J. LAHEY: Chief inspector and head of all uniformed forces of the NYPD

SAMUEL S. LEIBOWITZ: Lawyer who tries to represent Celia and Ed

WALTER LIPPMANN: Editor for the *New York World* who writes an influential piece on Celia and society

MARIE MAHON: Probation officer who investigates and reports on Celia's childhood and past life

GEORGE W. MARTIN: Brooklyn county judge who sentences Celia and Ed

NATHAN MAZO: Nabisco Biscuit Company cashier shot in the derrière

JOHN MCCLOSKEY: Police captain and head of all Brooklyn detectives; Carey's immediate subordinate

HELEN QUIGLEY: First of many girls wrongly arrested as the Bobbed Haired Bandit

WILLIAM BUEHLER SEABROOK: Celia's ghostwriter for her serial in the *New York American*

JACOB SHIENTAG: Sam Leibowitz's law partner who later wins a cash settlement for Ed's accident

Preface

Is a crime less reprehensible because it is a classic?
However that may be, the adventures of the original
bobbed-haired bandit are entitled to be ranked among
the minor masterpieces of outlawry, worth a thousand
hold-up pot-boilers.   —New York Herald-Tribune
                                        January 1, 1924

"I want a magazine with detective stories in it," Celia Cooney told the reporters. "The monotony is getting on my nerves. If you can't get me one of those, get me one with real live stories in them — shooting and all the rest." It was a long trip north from Jacksonville with nothing to do but look out the window at the rain and the crowds gathered along the tracks to catch a glimpse of them. Sometimes she waved her free hand, but usually she pulled down the shade.

Detectives Casey and Gray were nice. They hadn't roughed her up when they smashed through the rooming-house door two nights ago. Best of all: they didn't give any lectures. "That was pretty tough about your baby dying last Saturday," one of the detectives said almost tenderly. Celia's usual quick smile and gay spirit disappeared whenever she thought about Katherine.

The Brooklyn detectives could afford to be nice. After all the press ridiculing the police department, it was they, William Casey and Frank Gray, who had finally pinched New York's most famous gungirl. On the train they took off her cuffs, she found some cards, and they all played hearts. They even let Celia order the Pullman porter around: "Mose, you make up that upper birth for me," she told him. Then they let her sleep.

Edward Cooney, Celia's husband and partner in crime, sat next to her, but he wasn't saying much. "Sullen" is what the newspapers would call him. The detectives kept handcuffs on him, probably because he was a man, six feet tall, and built like a pugilist. Celia was small, just over five feet. She seemed bigger with her automatic.

It all seemed ages ago. Before the last botched holdup, before the getaway, before getting caught. Now she and Ed were sitting in a Pullman car guarded by two armed detectives. Celia found something to smile about—here she was, riding home in a private compartment on the Florida Limited like a debutante on her way back from Palm Beach. The working girl saw the irony: "Us and all the rest of the swells come up from Florida together," she said to an *Evening Post* reporter, "but we leave the swells at the station. We go to jail. No use whinin' is there? We're caught and we're goin' to laugh about it."

As the train pulled toward Pennsylvania Station, Celia got serious. She looked at a glass set into the wall of the Pullman compartment and thought to herself that she "didn't look so good. Hair all straggled and messy. No color. I looked a sight."

Answering a question from a *New York American* reporter, she put on some powder and lipstick and combed her hair with a half a white pocket comb borrowed from Detective Casey: "Don't ask me whether I'm afraid of pistols. My mind is on my make-up now. In a few minutes I'm going to make my entrance in New York City."

RIOTOUS THRONGS BLOCK PATH OF BOBBED BANDIT;

FISTS FLY, MEN SHOUT, AND WOMEN SCREAM

A crowd so dense and so determined that it almost crushed her to death greeted the bob-haired bandit when she returned to New York at 3 o'clock this afternoon from Florida. . . .

Only drastic action stopped the crowd. A score of policemen, charging like football players, smashed into the swaying crowd, some of whom were in danger of falling to the tracks. Fists flew, men shouted and women screamed. And the air became murky with magnesium powder from upset flashlight stands of photographers.

With the detectives grasping each of her arms a diminutive woman was shot through the press of humanity. All that could be seen of her was a little pink hat, pulled tightly around her head and a fur collar which completely hid her face. . . .

Station attendants said they had never seen such a crush on the platform, adding that the arrival of President Coolidge this morning did not begin to cause such excitement as that of the bob-haired bandit this afternoon.

As she emerged upon the taxi platform, Mrs. Cooney, her hat lifted slightly back and her fur collar down, smiled broadly to the newspaper photographers and winked as a battery of flashlight "guns" exploded.

It was the spring of 1924; New York City was aroused by the exploits of the Bobbed Haired Bandit, a smartly dressed woman armed with a "baby automatic." Since the first week of the New Year the gungirl's stickups had captured newspaper headlines and New Yorkers' imaginations. What hadn't been captured was the bandit herself. For three and a half months she and her male accomplice had eluded what was claimed to be the largest manhunt in New York City's history, humiliating the police with daring crimes and taunting notes. With each false clue and every fruitless roundup, the press roasted the police and their political bosses, using the Bobbed Haired Bandit as evidence that the administration of Mayor John Hylan was powerless to stop the lawlessness of Prohibition-era New York. Their capture in Florida ended the chase, as the *Daily News* reported: "The spectacular career of the most-advertised woman desperado and her tall male companion was ended — they are through."

As bandits they were finished, but as icons they were not. Mobs crowded the courtrooms and jails where the Bobbed Haired Bandit appeared, snatching up newspapers that claimed to have exposed the real woman behind the bandit's mask. Who was she? Why did she turn to a life of crime? Dozens of editorials were penned on the "gun miss," while readers gushed, sympathized, and raged in letter after letter to the editors. *True Detective* magazine published a series of breathless articles, renowned writers such as Ring Lardner and Walter Lippmann posted copy, and gangsters and psychiatrists were solicited for their expert opinions. In a media coup, William Randolph Hearst's *New York American* paid Celia one thousand dollars to write her memoirs, serializing the "Bobbed-Hair Bandit's Own Story: The strangest, weirdest, most dramatic, most tragic, human interest stories ever written." Hearst's King Features Syndicate distributed the story to papers across the nation. The gungirl was a celebrity.

Six months before, Celia Cooney was a laundress standing over a hot mangle in Brooklyn. Pregnant, she wanted to give her baby a better upbringing than she herself had been given. She dreamed of adventure, celebrity, and the good life she saw all around her in movies, magazines, and the shop windows of New York. Banditry bought her the good life; she stuck her way up to more cash than she had ever seen. As glamorous as a motion picture star and as romantic as the heroine in a detective serial, she became a celebrity in her own right. Infamous, she was "someone" . . . at least for the spring of 1924.

Seventy-five years later we found Celia in the pages of a New York City newspaper. As is often the case, the discovery came by chance. Digging through yellowed clippings in a scrapbook at the New York State Library in Albany, we came across a criminal with an intriguing moniker: the Bobbed Haired Bandit. With so much type set on her behalf, she was hard to miss. What drew us to the story were the same things that grabbed readers and writers at the time. The Bobbed Haired Bandit was as thrilling as any heroine in *True Story* magazine.

Celia Cooney's story entertained us, but what held our interest as historians and scholars of the media were the many ways in which the story was told. Seemingly everyone had their own tale to tell about her. To reporters, the gungirl was an assignment, a news item to bang out on deadline, adding a little zest here and there if it helped the story; to progressive newspaper editors, Celia Cooney was an example of what happens when a community does not protect its children; to conservatives, the flapper bandit was a symbol of a permissive society that coddled its criminals and gave too much freedom to the young, poor, and female; to the writers of pulps and plays and popular songs, the sassy, smart bandit was an anti-heroine come to life; to the mayor, the police commissioner, and all their minions, the story was dynamite. If handled well it could be parlayed into publicity and promotion, if told badly: humiliation. The Bobbed Haired Bandit was even a character to its own leading lady; with the attention of the mass media turned her way, Celia spun out her own breathless narrative.

We, too, are writing the story of the Bobbed Haired Bandit. Our story is a story of stories.

The sheer number of accounts made writing a book about Celia Cooney difficult. For any given event, we found anywhere from two to twenty competing and often conflicting reports. With each instance we tried to determine what actually occurred. First, did a majority of sources agree on one version? Second, was there an obvious bias in the news source that might explain an event being recorded (or misrecorded) in a certain way? Third, and this is where our years of research on this story and the decade helped us, did the description simply make sense? That is: did what was being reported jibe with what we knew about the case, the people, and the period? And finally, all else being equal, we asked ourselves which account was told in the richest vernacular and promised the most lively and interesting story. There were times, however, when accounts could not be reconciled. All the players were dead, and the record was crumbling and spotty; the facts of any incident were shadows at best. Factual reconciliation, however, was not our only goal. As concerned as we were in getting to the "truth" about the Bobbed Haired Bandit by carefully examining and rigorously comparing all the stories told about her, we were just as interested in how and why the stories differed.

There is no "true" crime story of the Bobbed Haired Bandit. We are *not* saying that there is no truth, or that it doesn't matter; what we are arguing is that the importance of the Bobbed Haired Bandit does not lie in what *really* occurred during her string of petty crimes. What is important is the way what happened was interpreted, recorded, instrumentalized, and mobilized. For it is in the multiplicity of these competing stories that we can discern the tensions of the times and begin to understand how the historical record comes to be. The stories told about the bandit were used to explain the world, to wage cultural battles, to further political interests, and above all, to sell newspapers. Her significance increases as she becomes fictionalized.

It is the play of stories that makes up the heart of our book. Different newspapers recording the same scene and using the same sources came up with radically different descriptions of what happened. For instance, where the *New York Times* saw a hard-boiled criminal return from Florida, the *New York Sun* witnessed a broken-hearted, grieving mother, as each played to the sympathies of their own class of readers. Larger political and economic agendas shaped the contours of the Bobbed Haired Bandit narrative. For example, Police Commissioner Richard Enright, facing political pressure to appear in control of law and order in the city, soft-pedaled the story of Brooklyn's gungirl. Newspaper editors opposed to Mayor Hylan used the story as a vehicle to attack his administration and his police commissioner. Meanwhile, most of the city newspapers, looking to boost circulation with the tried and true formula of controversy, outrage, and a pinch of fear, sold the story as a contest between a wily female bandit and the Keystone Kops; it was evidence of the latest crime wave in a city out of control. And finally, Celia made sense of her own life using the romantic themes of pulp magazines and Hollywood fantasies as she transformed herself into the character of the Bobbed Haired Bandit.

To capture the richness of these narratives and convey the tenor of the times, this book is built of primary sources. Our analysis of the period, although informed by the work of current historians, is rooted in our analysis of the archival record: newspaper reports and editorial cartoons, magazines and journal articles, popular songs and jokes, fiction and memoirs, advertisements, movies, and the records of the courts, prisons, social service agencies and the census bureau. We privilege the voices of that time, letting them lead the reader though the city of 1924. We rely on these sources, not just to tell the story but to interpret the material as well. Their interpretations tell us something valuable about the period and the way people saw their own times. It is hubris to think that the historian of today is always more insightful than the astute analyst of 1924.

Most research on the Jazz Age in New York City bypasses Celia and Ed's social world entirely, focusing instead on the upper classes and their flapper daughters or, more recently, the artists of the Harlem Renaissance — the worlds of F. Scott Fitzgerald and Langston Hughes, respectively. This myopia is understandable: the middle and upper classes, as well as artists and writers, leave copious records of their existence behind to read, see, hear, and interpret. With rare exceptions, working-class women from Brooklyn do not. Luckily for us, Celia Cooney was an exception.

The story of Celia and Ed is a snapshot of a time and place: a world of great wealth and poverty; of immigrants and debutantes; of crime, fast cars and Prohibition; of corruption and luxury; of politics and class antagonism, sex and morality. The working-class girl with her bobbed hair and shiny automatic was a magnet for the fears and desires of the 1920s. It was an exciting, anxious time. The old ways were shaken, and the new ways of modernity were not yet fixed. With the Bible and tradition no longer providing a universal and resolute answer for everyone, many people turned for guidance to what they increasingly had in common: mass culture. The press became a forum in which to work out social and moral issues, constructing narrative frames with which to make sense of the world.

This book is built on those frames. We begin our tale with the heroine's own version of how her criminal career began, printed at the time in the *American*. Her account is quickly layered by innumerable press accounts of what happened, and we shall see how her account, just like all the others, is subject to revision. Indeed, the Bobbed Haired Bandit was so intensely popular at the time precisely because she could be cast in many different ways. The story was told and interpreted, pushed and pulled, to fit the morality and politics of the writer and reader. She was a feminist heroine *and* a wanton vamp. She was symptomatic of a permissive society that coddled its criminals *and* the unfortunate product of the slums and the factory, an argument for law and order, *and* a call for progressive social reform. She was a desperate mother who stole for the sake of her unborn child *and* a spoiled flapper looking for kicks and cash to buy luxuries for herself. The Bobbed Haired Bandit was as much a symbol to be fought over as she was a woman. And most important, she was a good story.

Introduction

It is a new region the world is in. Many of the old land-
marks have disappeared. Strange forests and new hills
rise ahead. The questions to be faced have multiplied. . . .
1924 promises to be as stirring a year as any that has
arrived.
                                              —*New York Tribune*

It was a wet New Year's in New York City as 1923 passed
into 1924. The weather was raw: rain, sleet, and snow, with the temperature hovering just around freezing. A low fog sat on the city, and the
damp crept past fur coats and felt hats and seeped into partygoers'
bones. But it wasn't the weather the city's newspaper reporters were
writing about when they called this New Year's the wettest in years.
The city was wet with booze.

By law the United States was dry. The New Year celebrated the
fourth anniversary of Prohibition, inscribed in the Eighteenth Amendment to the Constitution and enforced through the Volstead Act. Even
after four years of trying to wean the gin out of what was becoming
known as the Gin Age, the forces of law and order were still publicly
optimistic, voicing all the go-go boosterism of one of Sinclair Lewis's
provincial Rotarians. According to New York Prohibition Enforcement Division Chief R. Q. Merrick, this year "was to be the driest
New Year's in history" as "one hundred and fifty Federal agents are to
be sent out from prohibition headquarters to interrupt the 'yo-ho-ho'
and confiscate bottles of rum" on the "White Way" of the Times
Square district of Broadway. But this was F. Scott Fitzgerald's New
York City, not the small-town America satirized by Lewis.

On New Year's Day, the city's newspapers ridiculed Merrick's
claims. FATHER TIME REELS OUT ON A JAG crowed the *Daily News*
headline, continuing: STORK'S GAIT UNSTEADY AS HE DROPS BABY
NEW YEAR. The *New York American* took up the refrain, proclaiming
on page one that "Liquor Flows in Torrents at 'Parties' in All Quarters
of the City," adding that "Rum raiders . . . might as well as have, like
King Canute, bid the waves of the sea to retreat, or attempt to bail out
the Hudson with a punctured tablespoon." The *American* concluded

that "no one who wanted a drink last night, seriously or casually, had to go without one, and this applied equally to the best restaurants, corner saloons and second story hooch mills."

New York wasn't the only city on a jag. Chicago reported her "wettest New Year's since 1919," while 1924 in San Francisco "was born with a corkscrew in his mouth and a pint flask on his hip." Since Prohibition, the per capita consumption of alcohol across the country had dropped, but you wouldn't know it from observing New Year's celebrations in the nation's major cities. All that Volsteadism had done here was boost the allure and cost of booze, providing a steady stream of revenue for showy bootleggers and shady public officials.

Prohibition made breaking the law an everyday occurrence for half of the population and a cause for concern for the other half. It also demonstrated, perhaps unfairly given the magnitude of the problem, the ineptitude of law-enforcement agencies. While Merrick's Prohibition agents were enforcing the law of the land, the rest of New York seemed intent on ignoring it by celebrating the New Year with flask in hand. Even Merrick, who promised to lead the effort himself, was quoted by the papers saying that he "may catch some of my own friends" on his New Year's raids.

Despite the miserable weather, the mood across the city was buoyant. Crowds massed on the streets and packed the fashionable new urban institutions called "night clubs." For some Americans 1923 had been a good year, a very good year, and 1924 seemed to promise even better. Only a few years before, there had seemed little to celebrate. Following the Great War, the country had sunk into a serious economic recession. Prices fell, unemployment rose, and a hundred thousand businesses went bankrupt. But since 1922 the economy of the United States had grown steadily. Production and consumption of goods was rising, the real estate and stock markets were booming, and by the end of the decade corporate profits would nearly double. A man who would famously (or, perhaps infamously) intone that the "business of America is business" was in the White House, and Calvin Coolidge's cabinet was full of men dedicated to cutting taxes and increasing the wealth of wealthy Americans.

On New Year's Day the newspapers quoted Andrew Mellon, the Secretary of the Treasury and one of the richest men in America, saying he "had confidence in a prosperous 1924." Secretary of Commerce Herbert Hoover, at the same New Year's press conference, added that "taking the country as a whole, we never in history have enjoyed a higher standard of living and comfort, nor so great a degree of commercial and industrial efficiency as today, or so wide an understanding of the forces which control the ebb and flow of business." In retrospect, Hoover's claims to understand the forces that control the economy seem laughable, but in 1924 the future looked assuredly bright.

It was a sparkling time to be rich. The *Tribune*'s New Year's Day headlines celebrated the flowing wealth almost as much as the flowing gin: "PROSPEROUS BROADWAY POURS OUT ITS RICHES TO GREET 1924 . . . / BANK ROLLS BULGING . . ." Meanwhile, *American* columnist Cholly Knickerbocker reported on the New Year's activities of high society, inviting the reader into the city's elite gatherings and lavishing the most attention, understandably, on the party thrown at the Ritz-Carlton Hotel by his boss, Mr. William Randolph Hearst. After being received by Hearst and his wife, guests strolled into the ballroom of the "popular hostelry," which had been transformed into a Japanese garden with hundreds of imported palms and countless Japanese lanterns. At four large tables decorated with cut flowers and titled nobility (duchesses, marquises, marchesi, counts, countesses, lords, ladies, and at least one heir apparent to a duke), more than two hundred of New York's notable and wealthy supped and then danced to the music of the Paul Whiteman Orchestra.

The newspapers also described in titillating detail the holiday whirl of balls and dinners in more favorable climes, with the most space given over to the "fashionable colony" of Palm Beach as "undoubtedly the most favored winter retreat of the socially elite of that most aristocratic peninsula, Florida." Speculation was rife, and real estate prices were skyrocketing on the coast of Florida. Society people had been arriving early this year. The shops were open, the golf club houses and links were ready for visitors, and the "cottages" were almost full. So much space was given over to the lives and loves and fashions of Palm Beach in New York City's newspapers that an unsuspecting observer might be led to believe that it was the sixth borough. Yes, 1924 was a good time to be rich.

It was not as good a time to be poor. The economic downturn of

1920 hit the working classes hard, with the number of blue-collar, manufacturing employees declining by twenty-five percent between 1920 and 1922. Demobilized after the war, men returned to fewer jobs and an aggressive anti-union campaign waged by employers looking to erase gains that workers had made during the war years when labor was scarce. Even after the recession was officially over, the poor were still poor. The *New York Evening Post*, citing a New York State Department of Labor inquiry, had recently reported that thousands of women were working for under ten dollars a week, while tens of thousands of men labored for less than sixteen.

By the end of 1923, however, things were looking a bit better in the working-class neighborhoods of New York. Although pay packets were still thin, working-class wages had risen since 1922, beginning what would eventually be a twenty-five percent increase before the decade ended. Production was also increasing, raising the nation's gross national product by thirty-nine percent by 1929. This meant more jobs and more substantial wages. It also meant more products to spend those wages on.

Outstripping the advances of factory workers' still meager wages and clerks' slowly growing salaries was the striking increase in their material aspirations. Americans were buying into "the good life." Whereas consumerism had been a relatively elite affair before the In-

PEOPLE WHO PUT YOU TO SLEEP—NUMBER FORTY-ONE.

LISTEN, GIRLS - I HAVE A FRIEND WHO IS VERY CLOSE TO ONE OF THE BIG FILM PRODUCERS AND HE TELLS ME EVERYTHING ABOUT THE MOVIE STARS. DO YOU KNOW THAT DOUGLAS FAIRBANKS ONLY TAKES ONE LUMP OF SUGAR IN HIS COFFEE FOR BREAKFAST IN THE MORNING ? AND MARY PICKFORD DOESN'T CARE FOR ARTICHOKES - A VERY BIG MAN TOLD MY FRIEND IN THE GREATEST CONFIDENCE THAT CHARLIE CHAPLIN LIKES BLONDES EQUALLY AS WELL AS BRUNETTES - I HEARD THAT CORINNE GRIFFITH AND PAULA LA MARR EACH GET OVER $5000 A WEEK - HAROLD LLOYD HAS HIS NECKTIES MADE TO ORDER AND NITA NALDI LIKES BEAN SOUP - THOMAS MEIGHAN MIXES HIS OWN SALAD DRESSING AND GLORIA SWANSON OWNS 68 FUR COATS - LEW CODY WEARS A NUMBER 7½ SHOE - I HEARD . . . .

AS IF ANY BODY CARED!

THE GIRL WHO KNOWS MORE ABOUT THE MOVIE STARS THAN THEY DO ABOUT THEMSELVES.

McNaught Syndicate, Inc. N. Y.

dustrial Revolution, it had since made its way down through the classes. The increased efficiency and output of industrialization in the United States resulted in a ready supply of new products, and these commodities demanded a mass market of consumers. The creation of this market was helped along by the expansion of easy credit, so that by the 1920s consumer credit allowed the working classes to live like the middle classes, the middle classes to ape the upper, and the upper classes to inhabit the stratosphere.

"Just Charge It" advised an advertisement for women's coats in the *Daily News*, and credit was available for the smallest to largest consumer items. Seventy-five percent of all radios and sixty percent of all cars were paid for in installments during the decade. HAS OUR GREAT COUNTRY GONE INSTALLMENT MAD? the *New York Herald* wondered in 1924, arguing that "the $1 down and $1 a week habit seems to have gripped every class in proportion to income" and wringing its hands over this "sin of extravagance." With easy credit, American consumers (and, as it turned out, American corporations and financial institutions) were building fantastic lives on mountains of debt.

This mass marketplace was displayed in all its abundance in the newspapers marking the first day of 1924. After a page or two of news on the revelries of the night before, the column inches were pushed to the side, or off the page entirely, by quarter-, half-, and full-page illus-

By RUBE GOLDBERG

Rube Goldberg, "People Who Put You to Sleep—Number Forty-One," *New York Telegram and Evening Mail*, May 6, 1924.

trated advertisements of New Year's sales. Stern Brothers advertised their "semi-annual sale of FINE FURNITURE" featuring a walnut dining room suite available for only one hundred ninety-eight dollars and fifty cents, and a few pages later Stewart and Co. on Fifth Avenue hawked Hudson Seal (dyed muskrat) coats starting at two hundred ninety-five dollars. While such a coat cost nearly half a working girl's yearly salary if bought in cash, credit meant buying now and worrying about the payments later. In the words of "Wile's House of Honorable Credit" in Brooklyn: "Why Wait?"

Aspirations for a better, or at least richer, life were helped along by the relatively new advertising trade, which had recently discovered that selling lifestyles was far more effective than selling simple products. In 1923 celebrities like "beautiful photoplay star" Viola Dana promised that Maybelline was a "miracle worker," implying that the eyeliner might just make a plain Jane into a photoplay star herself. Meanwhile the "'best dressed' woman on any stage," Florence Walton, offered what was "formerly . . . the Beauty Secret of only a Few," Youthglow facial clay, for the democratic price of only one dollar. Amid all of this ad-speak, Chesterfield sold its cigarettes silently, without copy, only a simple illustration of an elegantly clad woman holding out a light to a dapper man in evening dress, smoking, presumably, a Chesterfield cigarette. The image said it all. Through the promises of advertising, Americans were learning they could become whoever they wanted to be, or rather, become who they currently were not.

A popular, commercial culture also fueled aspirations for a different, richer life. In the pages of pulp magazines, "true stories" told the tales of love, fame, and fortune suddenly found. And on the silver screen motion picture gods and goddesses like Rudolph Valentino and Clara Bow lived lives of adventure and unimaginable wealth, parading the dreamable before the public in the new, ornate "movie palaces" that were replacing the shabby nickelodeons.

The stars of stage and screen were a running feature in New York newspapers. Their faces graced front pages, as well as amusement sections, and lucky readers of the *Mirror* were even treated to a revealing picture of Valentino's buttocks and naked back as he bent over to demonstrate an exercise routine. With you-are-there series like the *Daily News*'s "Me in Hollywood" ("Everybody is interested in Hollywood"), and "news" stories with headlines like WHAT STARS REALLY MAKE ("Norma Tallmadge Tops List with $10,000 a Week"), newspaper readers were transported, at least for a little while, someplace warmer, more exciting, and certainly wealthier than where they were.

Brooklyn wasn't warm and, as Manhattan's more proletarian relation across the river, it wasn't all that wealthy, but on New Year's Eve whatever the borough lacked in these two areas was well compensated for by an excess of excitement. The *Brooklyn Standard Union* reported "clubs and dance halls filled to overflowing with revelers" and that "church bells, factory whistles, [and] sirens on water craft mingled with the raucous din and clatter of the merrymaker's horns and cowbells in the streets." While more sober citizens spent their New Year's at special midnight church services or imbibing with their fraternal fellows at Elks, Rotary, or Masons clubs, the younger and rowdier elements of Brooklyn took to the streets, brawling and firing off guns in the air (the falling bullets injuring five by night's end). "Something of the Elizabethan spirit seemed to move the crowds of Brooklyn revelers who throng the streets with flask and gun and continued their merriment to the ringing of chimes in farewell to the old year," reported the *Brooklyn Citizen*. Knickerbocker bluebloods may have been in short supply at the street parties, church services, and Elks Clubs of Brooklyn, but the borough held its own with hooch: "Although there were crowds and horns in great plenty," the *Citizen* reassured their readers "there was more than enough to drink," adding sardonically: "No one remarked on a shortage of either wine or lead."

Women made the news on New Year's Day as they had, with increasing frequency and some concern, throughout the decade. Of special interest to the New York newspapers — and apparently their readers — were stories on the part that women were playing in New Year's partying. Some applauded the new sexual freedom and equality. Reports of Manhattan's upper crust in the *New York Tribune* complimented the generosity (and fashion sense) of women whose "well filled flasks" were concealed in "the new style 'under-the-arm' bags carried by numerous of the lady guests." The ladies' willingness to share their contraband "provided a fair quota of evidence to establish the case on behalf of the good sportsmanship of the fair sex."

Elsewhere on the pages of New Year's papers, the image of the flask-toting, free-drinking woman was under attack. The *Herald* worried openly about the sullied reputation of the formerly "fair sex," saving the bottom of page one for the comments of the recently arrived (and today largely forgotten) British novelist and playwright Major Ian Hay Beith. Interviewed as he docked in New York, the writer and former war hero decried the state of the "flapper class" of young women today. Speaking of women on both sides of the Atlantic, Hay Beith warned that "the privileges that young women have enjoyed since the war have reduced the happiness that life holds for men, and men of today lack the old fashioned reverence for women that was the most sacred thing in life." The major concluded with the New Year's advice to his fellow man that "we should not take women to night clubs and give them drinks."

Good sportsmanship or the fair sex's fall from grace? This difference in opinion regarding women and alcohol was less likely a matter of ideological disparity between the editors of the *Herald* and *Tribune* than the result of their desire for distinction within a competitive market (in fact, the two papers would merge into the *Herald-Tribune* before year's end). Hard-drinking women, whether for or against, made for good copy. But the articles were not just about drinking. Drinking was a New Year's Day angle on a longer-running story: women's proper place.

The status of women was undergoing a seismic shift in the Twenties. Women had finally won the vote with the passing of the Nineteenth Amendment in 1919. Since the Great War, more women were at work, too: a quarter of all women worked outside the home throughout the 1920s (for married women this number was twelve percent). With political rights and ready cash came power, and Americans — male and female — were struggling with what this meant.

Should a woman sit on a jury, run a business, or work at night? Would she preach in a Methodist church or pack a pistol as deputy sheriff in Staten Island? Could she smoke a cigarette in a smoking car, use her own name at the library, or bob her hair without permission from her father or husband? Story after story in the city's newspapers wrestled with the new woman and her new roles. Headlines proposed that PRETTY GIRLS DREAM OF VAMPING WORLD'S RULERS and called A CAR, WOMAN'S EMANCIPATOR. They wondered if there should be an "Equal Rights Amendment to the Constitution," sug-

gested that WOMEN IN POLITICS LOSE
CHARM, and then asked: ARE OUR MOD-
ERN WOMEN BECOMING MORE BAR-
BARIC? Finally, there was the *Brooklyn
Eagle* header that called the question:
WHAT'S THE MATTER WITH THE
WOMEN? ("Nothing Very Much Says
W. Somerset Maugham"; "F. Scott
Fitzgerald Says That All of Them
over 35 Should Be Murdered").

While the stories and their headlines were
often humorous — designed to ridicule
women's new aspirations as much as
explore them — behind this levity lay
serious public anxiety. The tight-laced
corset of the Victorian woman was being un-
done, and questions about who or what was stepping out of the closet kept reporters' keys clacking
and cartoonists' pens scratching. One such highly
visible and all-too-definable creature to dance her
way out of the Victorian closet was the "flapper."
With her furious drinking, fast driving, frantic dancing, and free flirtation, the flapper was celebrated,
decried, and endlessly caricatured by the press
and in popular culture. F. Scott Fitzgerald had
deemed the flapper passé by 1923, but the newspapers and their readership still couldn't get
enough of them, even finding "flappers" in
the South Seas and writing feature stories
about "Fanny, the Flapper Troutess" at the
1924 National Outdoor Sports Show (it was
claimed that the trout was a shameless flirt).

THE FLAPPER
THROWS IN
A WINK
WITH HER
SMILE,
JUST TO
SHOW HOW
TERRIBLY
WICKED SHE WANTS
PEOPLE TO THINK
SHE IS.

A. Russell, "Flapper Smile,"
Brooklyn Daily Times, April 1924.

Of all the features of this "modern girl," it was her bobbed hair that
generated the most interest — and controversy. Her shorn locks were
blamed for breaking up marriages. They were a symptom of the
"mentally-defective," or an unnaturally strong female will. Bobbed
hair was the sign of youth gone wild and the decline of civilization.

Conversely, bobbed hair and the flapper style was just a fad, a passing fancy. In any case, it was a style embraced by more and more respectable females. So widespread was the discussion of the flapper and her coif that the *Brooklyn Eagle*, with confidence that their audience would appreciate the humor, posed the question: "to bob or not to bob," as THE GREAT NATIONAL QUESTION of 1924. In an increasingly image-conscious age, the flapper with her bobbed hair, lithe profile, and devil-may-care attitude became an immediately recognizable silhouette, a stand-in to represent the shifting status of women and the changing morality of the younger generation.

Worry over women and youth was not the only concern of the time. Right below the shiny surface of the prosperous nation's New Year's party was a murky underbelly of crime and corruption. Shady "get-rich-quick" schemes and tales of stock market swindlers running "bucket shops" to fleece the public filled the papers. Cartoonist Winsor McCay illustrated the point with a savage top-hatted tiger mauling unwary investors fleeing the "Catchem & Cleanem Bucket Shop." Sandwiched between the front page news of New Year's parties and the economic optimism of Mellon and Hoover was a story on the widening investigation of the "Wood affair," a scandal involving the sons of the well-known Major General Leonard Wood, who were accused of using the standing of their father — with or without his knowledge was still the subject of speculation — to sell worthless oil stock to soldiers. This story played to a public used to government corruption. For months, the Teapot Dome scandal had been making news and selling papers. Public oil reserves, including the Teapot Dome in Wyoming, had been leased to private oil companies by President Warren Harding's secretary of the Interior, Albert Fall. Fall's bribery by the oil barons — and their money — came to light after President Harding's death in the summer of 1923, and the scandal gave the public a focal point for their anger at (or resigned acceptance of) what was perceived to be widespread corruption at all levels of the government. "Democracy: Government of the people, by the people, for the oil speculators" was how the editors at the humor magazine *Life* summed it up.

Some of that corruption oozed up from the local level. Few newspaper readers could fail to appreciate the irony of stories reporting public drunkenness running cheek by jowl with Prohibition boss Merrick's

Winsor McCay, "The Wildcatter," *New York American*, May 7, 1924.

The caption reads: Satan: "I see by the papers that you boys have been doing wonderful work lately. Fine! I congratulate you. Keep everlastingly at it and if the political situation ever gets too hot for you, just come down here and cool off." Art Young, "At the Go-Getters Conference," *Life*, May 8, 1924.

proclamations that this was the driest New Year's in history. The singular failure of law-enforcement agencies to stem, much less stop, the consumption of alcohol meant that either the police were incompetent or they were on the take — or perhaps a bit of both. A thorough reader, one whose eyes could still focus after the night before, would have read a short piece on New Year's Day in the *New York Times* about New York Police Commissioner Richard E. Enright's MINOR SHAKE-UP at the police department as he transferred captains and demoted detectives for an unspecified, to quote the commissioner, "good of the service."

Playing to the more cynical reader, the *Daily News* humorously proposed that the prohibition forces and the bootleggers were all part of the same racket. A New Year's editorial proposed a pair of matching resolutions for "any bootlegger" and "any ardent dry":

Any bootlegger: I resolve to work heart and soul for the retention of the Volstead law and against legalizing manufacture and sale of light wines and beers — because I am getting richer as things are.

Any ardent dry and any prohibition enforcement agent: We resolve to show more consideration for bootleggers — because we don't want to work ourselves out of soft jobs.

While drinking on New Year's Eve was an offense for many New Yorkers to laugh about, other crimes reported that night were not as humorous. Vandals looted three churches in Brooklyn, and modern-day "river pirates" tied up a watchman and stole one hundred thousand dollars in Turkish opium from a docked steamship, among other felonies.

The press kept track of the city's mortality; in the *Daily News*, the "Hands of Death" barometer, "which registers daily the chief medical examiner's records of death by moonshine, guns and autos" on a grim three-handed dial, marked the year in violent death. On December 30, 1923, the Hands of Death showed autos in the lead with 884 fatalities, followed by bad liquor with 271. Motorcars always crushed the opposition; New York was a dangerous city for pedestrians. Alcohol barely edged out

This barometer registers daily the Chief Medical Examiner's records of death by moonshine, guns and autos in all boroughs of New York City from Jan. 1.

The "Hands of Death," New York Daily News, December 30, 1923.

the city's gunmen, who finished with 270 killings. Those numbers would change on New Year's Eve in a last flurry of liquor, lead, and drunken driving. The Old Year closed out with a last murderous holdup shooting. The *Daily News* headlined:

"New York's Red Terror." Stickup men and crime waves were a favorite topic of editorial cartoonists in the early 1920s. (Rollin Kirby Collection, Museum of the City of New York)

1923, GUNMEN'S YEAR
PASSES WITH KILLING;

JEWELER IN BRONX SLAIN
FIGHTING FOUR THUGS

New York's year of crime, outstanding for the number and daring of brutal assaults against life and property was finished yesterday in a blaze of murderous viciousness with the killing of Barnett Brown. . . . Four bullets, digging into Brown's body at a range close enough to set fire to his clothing, ended a heroic struggle on his part to defend his property. The crime was a dramatic climax to a year of bold murders.

And, it might be added, a year of bold headlines.

The day after New Year's dawned fair and cold in the city. New Yorkers returned to their everyday work and their everyday lives, maybe a bit worried about the changes of the present, probably optimistic about the shape of their future, and perhaps still a little bleary from the excesses of the night before last. New Year's Eve in New York's newspapers passed on to other news in the routine march of mass media amnesia. At the *Daily News*, the Hands of Death would be reset to zero in preparation for a new year of fatalities. New stories eclipsed old, but all of them still telling and selling much the same story: crime, corruption, and the dramatic — or dramatizable — lives of both famous and infamous.

PART I

Woman with Gun

1

It was a bitterly cold evening in January, the fifth day of the New Year. It was the first Saturday night of 1924. Ed Cooney left his wife, Celia, sitting at the kitchen table while he went to borrow a car just a couple of blocks away on Atlantic Avenue. They had big plans for the evening.

The young couple lived in a furnished room at 53 Madison Street in the Bedford section of Brooklyn. It was a mostly white, working-class neighborhood full of first-, second-, and third-generation immigrants from Ireland, Italy, Germany, and England, sandwiched between what is now called Bedford-Stuyvesant and Prospect Heights. The couple had only moved to Madison Street three months before, but neither of them was new to the neighborhood. Now twenty years old, Celia had lived in the area since she was eighteen. And Ed, except for a stint in the Navy, had spent all of his twenty-five years in Bedford. Down the street from their little room was the Church of the Nativity of Our Blessed Lord, the Catholic church where they were married the previous spring. A few blocks south and west, over on Fulton Street, was the motion picture and vaudeville theater where the two had met the year before.

Celia remembered that meeting vividly. It was a Saturday evening and she was lonely. "I thought I'd blow thirty cents," she later wrote, taking in a show and hoping to run into some friends. So she walked down to the Fulton Theatre and settled in for the night's entertainment.

When the lights went up she spotted her friend Joe, a nice enough guy whom she had gone out dancing with a time or two before. But it was the man next to him that really drew her eye. He was a tall, blond, blue-eyed man who looked a little like the famous boxer Jack Dempsey. Celia herself was small and dark, with black hair and black eyes, barely over five feet tall. "They say people fall in love with their opposites and I expect it's true." Celia was smitten.

Edward and Celia Cooney's wedding photo, May 18, 1923. (Library of Congress)

She was also savvy enough to play hard to get. She walked over to Joe. "Oh, hello Joe, you here alone?"

"No, shake hands with my friend, Mr. Cooney."

Ed smiled as he put out his hand. "He's Irish," Celia recalled, "you know, real Irish and he's got a wonderful smile." She looked over his sharp coat with the belt in back, his brightly striped silk shirt and "nifty cap," and thought that he "carried himself swell."

The three of them went out to a local chop suey place where they could eat and dance. Celia made sure to dance mostly with Joe; she didn't want to overplay her hand, and Ed didn't dance much anyway. But he did offer to walk her home. It was a pretty night. On her doorstep Celia turned to him and said, "Well, good-night Mr. Cooney."

"You haven't said when I was going to see you again," Ed replied.

"Just like that, as if it was all made up that I would see him again," Celia remembered.

Celia and Ed "kept company" for several months, then Ed bought Celia an engagement ring with a solitary red stone. By May they were married and living together in a furnished room. Celia held a job nearby at the Ostrander Company, earning twelve dollars a week, and Ed took home thirty dollars each week working in a garage.

As Celia later recalled:

> I had never been so happy in my life. But we weren't saving a cent. Ed kept insisting on my buying myself some nice clothes. He took a lot of pride in my looks and the clothes he wanted me to wear cost money. . . . It seemed so wonderful to me to be loved and worried about. So we spent our money that summer almost as fast as we made it.

Their most extravagant purchase was a fancy sealskin coat. According to Celia, "Eddie wouldn't rest" until she'd bought herself a fur coat for the winter. "I had always longed for a real fur coat," Celia later explained, "and always known it was impossible. But Eddie was different than me: when he wanted anything, he went right after it." As the weather turned colder the couple went over Manhattan, "to a big fur place on Fifth Avenue." Celia remembered being scared: intimidated by the luxuriousness of the store. But with Ed on her arm, she walked right in, "like I was used to buying myself a swell fur coat every other day in the week":

> I came out wearing a sealskin coat that made me feel like a million dollars. . . . My weekly wages were spent for months in advance; but I didn't seem to care. I was drunk — with the exultation of spending — of having nice things — with Eddie's pride in me.

In September Celia and Ed found out they were expecting a baby. Celia was thrilled, but also worried: what kind of life were they going to give their child? She remembered looking around their solitary room and exploding: "I can't *stand* this room!" Her husband "had never seen her hysterical before." He assured Celia that they would move to another room, asking her where she wanted to live. The mother-to-be let him know that he was missing the point:

> "I don't want a room!" I cried wildly. "I want a *home*! I'm not going to have my baby raised in a little two-by-four hole like I was. He's going to have a home — a *decent* home!"

Ed promised Celia that they'd get a real home for their baby. But how?

Ed worked as a welder for a man named Paul Horgan at his automotive repair shop on Atlantic Avenue. While the pay wasn't great, the job had some perks. Horgan left a couple of cars locked up in the garage there. The Cooneys could not afford a car of their own, so Ed borrowed one of his boss's motorcars from time to time — usually an old Oldsmobile. This was the car that Ed drove Celia around in while they were "keeping company" on Saturday nights.

The shop was Ed's first stop the evening of January 5th. He walked around the corner from their furnished room to 1057 Atlantic Avenue, a block lined with automobile repair shops, warehouses, and factories. Twenty years before, the garages had been stables. Ed had the keys to the garage; he was a trusted employee, having worked there for six days a week for almost twelve years. He went to work every morning at seven to open the shop and get the furnace going before the boss arrived. Mr. Horgan knew he borrowed the car sometimes, but not for what Ed had in mind this Saturday night.

Ed had prepared for this evening. He had used his welding skills to doctor up a couple of phony license plates to mislead the police. New

York State alternated colors every other year: one year it was yellow on black, the next black on yellow. By cutting a couple of 1922 plates in half and then welding them to a pair from 1924, Ed created a set of plates with a 1924 stamp but a new number that couldn't be traced back to Horgan's garage. After bolting these on to one of the cars in the garage, he drove back to pick up Celia.

Back in their room Celia sat at the kitchen table with three guns laid out before her. One was a .25 automatic that Ed had owned since before they were married. She didn't know where Ed had gotten it, but the fact that her new husband owned a gun hadn't worried Celia. "Lots of fellows had pistols," she reasoned. "There were lots of hold-ups in Brooklyn, and who knows when we might have got held up and robbed?" One small gun had been enough for protection but not for armed robbery, so Ed had made a visit to the Bowery to buy a couple more. He didn't have any luck in any of the pawnshops that lined Manhattan's skid row, but in one of the stores a "negro" overheard what Ed was looking for and followed him outside. Drawing him into a doorway, the man sold Ed two guns for three dollars each, and gave him a handful of bullets. Stuffing the guns and bullets into his pockets Ed came home.

"We staged a little hold-up that night," Celia remembered:

> I put on my hat and coat and put the little automatic in my pocket. We had made up our minds we'd try a store first. So we moved the table over, and Ed stood behind it like he was a clerk and I pretended to walk in and ask for a dozen eggs, and he pretended to give them to me and as he was handing them, I backed off and pulled the gun out of my pocket and said "Stick 'em up quick!" Just like I'd read in a magazine.

Celia loved reading. And the scene, the gun, the language — it all seemed like something out of the detective magazines and cheap pulp novels she voraciously consumed. A story come to life. "I had been reading magazines and books about girl crooks and bandits and it began to seem like a game or play acting after Ed really came home with the guns. It was more exciting than anything I thought I'd ever do."

Now the night they had planned for had come. She felt "all excited and happy and gay" and couldn't sit still. She jumped out of her chair and danced, singing "a sort of song that had no sense to it, about pink leather shoes for baby and to —— with the laundry now. Wasn't it silly?" But her mood swung suddenly:

> And then I cried. I was all so happy and strange inside me, and warm, that I couldn't help crying. And I picked up one of those big pistols and kissed its handle, where Ed's hand had been.
>
> Then all of a sudden I sort of slumped, and cold shivers went all over me, and I got plain scared, sitting there by myself. It seemed like it all wasn't so. That it couldn't be. It seemed like I didn't know myself, like some other girl had promised to do this, and then gone off and hid, and left me to pretend I was her, and do it in her place.
>
> I got up and screamed. I said "Ed, I can't do this. I can't do this. I am scared." Of course Ed wasn't there.

Celia felt better when her husband returned with the motorcar. Climbing into the car, they returned to Atlantic Avenue, cruising the major Brooklyn thoroughfare, "all fixed up with guns and a car and everything, just like real bandits":

> Ed was driving and saying nothing. I was beside him on the front seat. I put my arm behind his shoulder and cuddled up close to him and he must have felt me sort of shivering.
>
> He put one hand over on my knee and patted me and I said Ed, are you sure it's all right?" and he said, "Sure, it's all right, kid; you're not losing your nerve, are you? And I said, "Of course not, Ed, you know I'd do anything with you."

It was nine-thirty, dark and near freezing. Atlantic Avenue was busy with traffic, but the cold kept people off the sidewalks. Ed and Celia figured that there would be a lot of money in the tills late on a Saturday night, and they had waited until there wouldn't be so many customers in the stores. As they rode along, Celia began to "feel fine" again: "I was proud of Ed and proud of myself and ready for anything."

Ed turned the car slowly onto Seventh Avenue, where they had spotted several grocery stores. Driving close to the curb, they peered through the windows looking for a nice quiet shop. There on the corner of Seventh Street and Seventh Avenue in Park Slope was the Thomas Roulston grocery, an outpost of one of the grocery store chains that were taking over mom and pop shops across the country in the Twenties. It was open late on a Saturday night.

The block was quiet, and through the big windows of the grocery store they saw that there were no customers, just the clerks in their white coats. Ed eased up to the curb, leaving the engine running. The Cooneys "had it all figured out like clockwork." They had practiced at the kitchen table at home. Celia was to enter first and ask to buy something, while Ed kept watch outside. If it was all clear, Ed would enter and Celia would start the holdup.

Ed looked up and down the street. As they got out of the car together, she thought she "looked pretty nice — seal coat, beaded grey dress, black shoes and stockings and a cunning tam. I had dolled up like I was going to a party in everything I had." Celia Cooney wanted to look her best when she went out robbing. Now it was time to show herself off:

> I walked into the store, cold as a cucumber, with both my hands in my fur coat pockets, and one hand holding the butt of the little automatic hidden in my pocket. The store was lighted up as bright as day, and there were six men, six clerks, in white coats, standing around or fiddling around with the stuff on the counters.

The sight of the six male clerks gave Celia a shock. Some of them were as big as Ed, and their white coats in the bright light were an imposing sight. Celia felt "about two feet high." She thought, "Gosh what a simp I am. They'll laugh at us and throw us out on our necks in the street." Inside, she was all nerves, scared, "but outside, I tell you, I was cold as ice, not scared cold, but cold like a person walking smooth and steady in a dream."

Celia walked right up to the man at the cash register; she thought he was the manager because he handled the money. None of the other clerks paid any attention to her.

"Yes, Miss?" he said, "as nice as pie." She asked him for a dozen eggs, please. The manager turned and walked behind the counter to fill her order. He returned with the eggs and began to wrap them up for her, tying the pasteboard box with string: "All of a sudden I had the funniest thought. I thought, 'what am I doing; I haven't got a nickel to pay for these eggs!' Then I remembered."

Ed walked in quietly, and Celia knew the time had come. Just as the manager was laying the package of eggs on the counter before her with both hands, she took two steps backward and pulled the gun from the pocket of her fur coat:

> "Stick 'em up! Quick!" Just like that. For a second I thought he wasn't going to do it. But it was only because he was so surprised and scared he couldn't move. Then up they went, both arms together, like one of those monkeys you buy on a stick with a string at the ten cent store. I thought, "Gee, that would make a pretty toy for my baby."

Celia snapped out of her little reverie. She didn't know what to do next. She turned just a little to glance at Ed:

> It was fine. There he stood flat-footed with his legs spread a little apart, his cap down a little over his eyes, looking big and strong as Jack Dempsey, and a lot handsomer. A big gun was in each hand, held low, with his elbows bent a little, covering the whole back store.
>
> "Get to the back, all of you, quick," he calls, and it was a sight to see. Honest, they were exactly like sheep. They went where we told them, and they stood in a line, with their mouths gaping, and their eyes popping, looking so silly, it made me want to laugh.

As they moved to the back of the store, none of the clerks had their hands up; even the manager began to lower his. It didn't matter; they weren't going to do anything. When Celia "got wise to that," she thought, "it gave me a grand thrill. For once in my life I was boss. Here were six of them, afraid to move, afraid to do anything except what I told them. And they were so big and me so little."

Ed told Celia to "hold 'em back." He had to work quickly. Sticking both guns in the pocket of his overcoat he "poked" at the register; "no sale" popped up, and the bell rang as the drawer sprang open. He grabbed the bills and stuffed them in his pants; he scooped the change into his overcoat pockets where it clinked against the guns. Ed noticed the corner of an envelope sticking out of a little safe under the counter; bending over, he grabbed it and stuck it in the breast pocket of his coat. It was full of fives, tens, and twenties.

Ed stood up. When he jerked the guns from his pocket, change fell out, quarters and pennies rolling on the floor as he backed to the door. He didn't stop. "Don't make a move!" he yelled; "if you want your head blown off just try to follow us out." Celia went to the door and pulled it open, while Ed covered the cowering clerks. Out she went, followed by her husband. The sidewalk was clear, the engine was running; Celia hopped in first, and Ed hopped in over her. He put his foot on the gas, threw the car into gear, "and off we went, smooth, without a bobble."

Ed turned left at the corner and made two more quick turns without either of them speaking a word. They passed a cop, but he didn't seem to notice, the first of many that they would pass in their getaways. "Gee!" mused Celia, some nights the cops were "so close you could reach your hand out of the car and touch them, but they never guessed a thing."

As they drove away, Ed was silent. "I wanted him to kiss me or something," thought Celia, "but I guess that was foolish." She whispered: "Was it all right, Ed?" "And he put down one hand from the wheel — Ed was a grand one-armed driver — just like he did before and patted me on the knee and said: "Sure kid, you're a peach."

That made Celia happy. "Ed, how much do you suppose we got?" Ed thought it might be more than a thousand dollars. There were "big bills in it," he said, "that big envelope is thick, feel it." Celia reached through his coat and felt the bulge; it was thick. They returned to Atlantic Avenue, driving back to Paul Horgan's garage between Classon and Franklin Avenues. Ed parked the car and turned out the lights in the garage. Celia kissed him. She asked him again if everything was all right. They shut the door, locked it, and walked home.

Nervous and excited, they opened the door of their room on Madison Street. Before they even took off their coats, they locked the door and jammed a straight-backed chair under the knob. Ed shut the torn window blind, but there was still a hole where someone could peep through. Celia got an old shawl and pinned it up so that no one could see into their lair: "Then Ed listened at the door. Of course nobody was there, but now that it was quiet and all over, I think we were both more scared and nervous than when we were in real danger." Satisfied that they were alone, Ed walked to the bed and began to empty the contents of his bulging pockets:

Holy Cat! What a thrill when Ed dumped all that money out on the bed — nickels, dimes, pennies, quarters, half-dollars — like one of those pictures of a treasure chest opened by pirates you sometimes see on the front cover of a magazine.

I was glad that there were pennies, for some of them were bright and shiny like gold. And my the bills! Some greasy and old and torn, some crisp and new, some green and some yellow backs, all mixed together, except those in the envelope, which were sorted together and fastened in packages with thin strips of paper.

Ed started counting, got mixed up and started again. Celia had never seen so much money at one time; the most that she ever brought home in a pay envelope was fifteen or sixteen dollars. Ed received only twice that every Saturday night for his week's work welding at the garage. "Now we had hundreds!" recalled Celia.

When Ed finally finished counting, there were more than six hundred dollars stacked on the bed. Finding a hiding place was tough in their "little two-by-four room with nothing you could lock but the door." Ed folded the guns in a shirt and stuck them under some clothes in the bureau drawer. All the silver went into the coffee pot, and the bills were stuffed between the pages of the three or four books they owned. One of the books was an old catalog. In her *New York American* confessional, Celia recalls that she used to pass the time looking wistfully at the pictures of cribs and baby carriages for the baby growing in her belly. Now she had money, big bills stuck between the pages of her Sears and Roebuck wish book.

With the money and guns safely squirreled away, Celia and Ed made ready for bed. "Ed got in bed first." It took Celia a little longer. She "rubbed some cold cream" on her face, "switched out the light and jumped in beside him":

> I had been all peppy and jazzed up. When the lights went out I seemed to sort of "go out" too. Ed put his arm out to pet me, but I said, "No Ed; I'm tired." Pretty soon he heard me crying. He tried to make me tell him what was the matter, but I didn't know myself. Just felt all let down and sort of shot to pieces.

Celia fell asleep but she had an "awful dream" that still gave her "the cold chills" thinking about it months later as she wrote it down for the newspaper. "It began pretty enough, but God! How it ended":

> There was my baby that was not yet really born, sitting on a high chair, happy and so sweet and pretty, with a great big laundry basket at its feet!
>
> And there I stood beside the basket with a pistol, and there came a long procession of men in white coats, dumping money into that basket for my baby. First they looked like the clerks we held up at the grocery store.
>
> Then the white changed, and they were green, sort of like the color of dollar bills, and then their clothes turned blue, and they were cops, with shiny pennies sewed on for brass buttons.
>
> And they kicked over the basket, and two of them grabbed me, and one picked up my baby by the dress behind its neck, like you'd carry a kitten or a rabbit, and I fought and tried to kick and scratch and scream.
>
> I must have really screamed, for Ed grabbed me . . . and jumped out of bed and turned on the light, and said "For God's sake, what's the matter kid?" I blinked at him and couldn't believe I was back there in our little room. And then it all came to me. And I said, "Oh, nothing, I just had a bad dream." But I was afraid to tell him what it was for fear he'd think I was crazy.

The next morning was Sunday; Ed went out to buy the papers. He found a story about their stickup in the *Brooklyn Eagle*. There were two brief items in the Brooklyn papers and nothing in the major New York dailies. The *Eagle* reported that a WOMAN WITH GUN HOLDS UP SIX MEN, describing a "startling holdup" of the Thomas Roulston grocery. A "richly-dressed" woman in a fur coat stole six hundred eighty dollars. She was "good-looking, about 5 feet 5 inches in height, of dark complexion, with bobbed hair." Her male accomplice was not deemed worthy of a physical description. The *Eagle* described him as having "sneaked in behind the woman." The *Eagle*'s competitor, the *Brooklyn Citizen*, opened their account of the "woman bandit," with "Six Employees in Grocery Held Up by Pretty Girl," Celia's sex being the key theme of the story.

What made the story stand out amid the other everyday holdups was its novelty value: WOMAN WITH GUN. According to Celia's account, when the manager of Roulston's grocery got up the nerve to call the police, they "wouldn't believe a girl had done it—said it must have been a man dressed up in girl's clothes." And when Ed returned to work on Monday, a fellow mechanic whose cousin was a detective reported that his cousin said, "who the —— ever heard of a girl bandit except in the movies." Celia Cooney was a movie villain come to life.

The Brooklyn newspaper writers and editors thought so, too. They knew they were on to a story that could compete with the celluloid product pumped out by Hollywood. Accordingly, they cast Celia in the role of tough-talking, hard-boiled woman bandit. In the *Eagle*'s version, Celia boldly commands the clerks: "Get to the rear, you fellows. And move quick, you sons of guns. If you try any steer I'll pump you full of lead." The newspaper goes on to report that the clerks and the manager obeyed meekly, moving to the back room under the watch of the woman bandit's automatic. As she left, the woman waved her revolver menacingly at the cowed group of clerks with a parting warning: "If you move less than fifteen minutes after we're gone your families will have a nice funeral to go to."

Character outlines were being drawn. According to Celia's memoir, it was Ed who did the tough talking. But in the newspaper accounts, supposedly based on eyewitness testimony, it was Celia who barked out the orders. Who was the boss?

The papers decided early on who carried the big gun in the Cooney family. A tough-talking Celia made much better copy than yet another stickup man with a female accomplice. Gun molls were not uncommon at the time. Girlfriends often acted as look-outs, sometimes with special pockets sewn into their coats as they toted weaponry for their gunmen, and sometimes even getting behind the wheel for a modern motor getaway. A bandit queen who called the shots and was a "'Boss' over Men" (as a later subhead put it) was a novelty, an escalation in the battle of the sexes, an arms race even. The bossy woman with a gun upset the balance of power, an idea that made Celia's own pulse quicken, not to mention putting the lead back in the pencils of crime reporters all over town.

"Well, Ed, what do we do now?" Celia asked at breakfast the morning after their first successful robbery. Ed replied, "The first thing we'll do, as soon as we can, is to get out of this lousy dump and get a decent place to live in." Celia's pride as homemaker was wounded. She hated the little furnished room as much as Ed and would be even happier than he to be out of it, but she kept it clean enough; it was just a little cramped and bare.

Ed took a half day off from the garage on Monday to find a new place. He didn't have far to look. Just a half dozen blocks from their old Madison Street digs, around the corner from Horgan's garage on Atlantic Avenue, and a block from his mother's house on Dean Street, Ed found Celia a new home. An old two-story frame house stood at 1099 Pacific Street, with a pretty, young landlady who occupied the top floor. Ed rented the parlor floor and the basement, making a "duplex home" for his bride.

The pleasure of having money to spend really began for Celia the next day. On Tuesday, January 8th, Ed took another half day off from work and the two of them "went out to buy furniture and stuff." They arrived at John A. Schwartz's big furniture store at 1319 Broadway in Brooklyn. The Cooneys told Schwartz that they were bride and groom, which was not far from the truth; they had, after all, been married less than eight months. "We're going to be married and we want the best," said Celia. The proprietor, she remembered,

> was nice to us, and we had a grand time of it, picking out a real dining-room set—think of us having a dining room! Ed wanted fumed oak, but I liked the dark red shiny stuff best, like mahogany, almost black, and so slick you could see your face in it. It was more refined. And that's what we had.
>
> There was a sideboard with a big looking glass, and drawers and a cabinet underneath, and a table, and six chairs. And then we went to it. Bedroom set, and rugs, and a sofa and lamp for the parlor, just like the pictures of a man and his wife in the advertising part of the magazines, and pots and pans, and dishes, and so many things you couldn't think of them all.

"Gee, I was surprised when I found that it came to more than $1,000," thought Celia. But she was not finished shopping:

> There was a crib for the baby that was going to be born in the last of April or the first of May with shining brass rails, and I wanted some

other stuff. But Ed said, "No, there's plenty of time for that," and it was all right with me, for I knew he'd let me have everything I wanted when the time came.

Ed was ready to put a lot of money down, but Celia stopped him. She knew better. On the installment plan she could hand over only two hundred dollars now and agree to pay the rest off at fifty dollars a month.

The furniture was delivered the next day when they moved into their new home. While Ed went to work, Celia waited to receive the goods:

> They brought it all in trucks, and I was proud, and the men that delivered it called me "Lady!" and said "Where do you want this and where do you want that?" And I gave them fifty cents.

The lady of the house "had the time of her life fixing the place up." She didn't think about where the money came from. She went around singing and daydreaming about "how grand it would be for the kid when it came." At nineteen years old Celia had what she wanted: "a home of our own." Celia remembered when she was a little kid her "mama at the wash-tub, doing big piles of clothes," told her: "Celia, you go out and play in the street." Those days were gone as long as they had money. To complete this rosy picture of middle-class prosperity, Celia went out to buy something special for Ed's dinner. She bought a porterhouse steak to surprise him when he came home. She tried to fix French fried onions to go with the steak, but they didn't turn out right. Ed pretended not to notice. "Hot dog!" thought Celia, "We're sitting in our own dining room, and my baby will never play in the street."

2

BOB-HAIR BANDIT ROBS 2 MORE SHOPS
—New York Telegram and Evening Mail

In less than a week the six hundred eighty dollars from the Roulston job was depleted. It cost a lot of money to live like the "pictures of a man and his wife in the advertising part of the magazines" that Celia admired. Porterhouse steaks, their new higher rent, and the fifty-dollar installment payment for the trappings of the good life added up to more than Ed's thirty-dollar salary could bear. Their haul of "pirate treasure" had only sunk them into debt. Since Ed had decided that his pregnant wife shouldn't work, that left only one option:

> Later that same week, Ed said to me one night, "Look here, kid, this is pretty soft, ain't it, but we got to think now."
> I said, "Think, what?"
> I don't want to pass the buck to Ed. I knew almost right away what he was talking about. I had been thinking too, that thirty dollars a week wouldn't run this swell place we had now.
> He said, "You saw how easy it was. But we didn't get enough. We got to do it again. Maybe we can get a big roll, and then we'll quit and be square."
> I said, "Sure, Ed, it's all right, whatever you say."

They decided to think it over, but that didn't take long. As Celia recalled, "it's too easy, once you get started" to just "keep going." Having made up their minds, the couple figured they had better familiarize themselves with the tools of their new trade:

> We went down to the cellar and Eddie set up a board at one end and we practiced shooting. The [small calibre shots] didn't make any noise to speak of and I got so I was pretty good. We practiced every day that week. And I couldn't wait for Saturday to come.

That Saturday night Celia didn't want to sit at home waiting for Ed to get the car: "It makes me nervous sitting at home, waiting." So together they walked around the corner from their new home on Pacific Street to Horgan's Atlantic Avenue garage.

"I wasn't half as scared as I was the first time," Celia recalled. They "cruised around a bit," trying to decide which store to stick up. Looking through windows, it didn't take long for Ed to choose one to rob. "This'll do," he said as they slowed to a stop in front of the Atlantic and Pacific chain store at 451 Ralph Avenue in the nearby neighborhood of Brownsville. Ed left the engine running, and they walked up to the store together. "Let's make snappy," he said.

Ed stepped inside the door as Celia strode to the counter. "This time I was bold," she remembered. There were a man and a woman, as well as four clerks, in the store. One clerk was waiting on the couple. "Gimme a dozen eggs," said Celia to the man behind the register. He hardly looked at her, just wrapped up the order and put it on the counter with an "anything else, please?" He appeared to be "sort of absent-minded," thinking of something else, "but it couldn't have been bandits for when I shoved the gun in his face and said, sort of low, 'Stick 'em up and be quiet,' he jumped like he'd already been shot and first turned red and then white as a sheet."

Ed stood behind her brandishing two guns, covering the store. He had instructed her to always be careful of the manager behind the register because if there was a gun in the place it would be under the counter where he could reach it. Always wait to see both his hands above the counter before you pull anything, Ed had warned her. Ed quickly saw that this one wouldn't be a problem. He yelled, "Get to the back, all of you, and turn your faces to the wall."

The woman customer, Mrs. Gibbons, didn't put up her hands when Celia said "stick 'em up." Instead she turned to her husband, who had already hoisted his hands, and asked, "Hey, what is it? What do they want?" Celia thought the guns should have given the lady a clue.

Mr. Gibbons turned to his wife, "My God! They're robbers, don't you understand! Put your hands up like they tell you or we'll both get killed!"

"Oh," she said and stood there with her hands still at her sides, "her chin stuck in the air." "Well, it's plain this is no place for me. I'll never trade at this store again. Come on, John." And she turned for the door.

Ed didn't know what to do. He let his arms fall, guns pointing toward the floor. Celia thought for a second that he was going to let the woman leave, but then he lost his temper, jerked the guns back up, and cursed loudly: "For —— sake, lady, won't you PLEASE get to the back? This ain't a joke. Beat it now to the back." Mrs. Gibbons halted, then moved slowly back to her husband, "grumbling and mumbling," all the way, "something about it oughtn't to be permitted and where was the police."

Later Celia remarked that women were more of a headache than men during the robberies: "It's not that they fight, but they talk and argue and won't do what you tell them, and sometimes they're liable to scream." Men "act like sheep when you get them at the point of a gun, but you can't never tell what a woman will do." Celia reasoned that if "all the managers and clerks were women you could hardly get away with robbing a store at all."

Celia held the unreasonable Mrs. Gibbons and the rest at bay while Ed went to the cash register. Then, according to an account published in the *Telegram and Evening Mail* and other papers, they had a visitor:

> As the three men and woman retreated slowly to the rear of the store be-
> fore the menacing muzzles of the two guns, a negro opened the front
> door and started in, evidently to make a purchase. He stopped with the
> door swung half-way back, instantly sensed the situation and with dis-
> creet diffidence silently withdrew, closing the door silently behind.

Ed finished with the cash box, and delivering a parting "keep the change," the couple backed leisurely out of the store and then hurried quickly to the car idling at the corner. All told, they'd been in there for only a couple of minutes; it had almost been "snappy." After a couple of quick turns to make sure they were safe, Ed took his foot off the gas.

"Kid," he said, "we didn't get much that time — less than a hundred dollars." Ed was still raring to go: "We got plenty of time and every-thing's set. Let's try another." "Sure," said Celia. "It was getting to be fun and didn't seem to be much danger." Away they drove into the night, cruising onto Brooklyn Avenue out of Brownsville and back into the Bedford section of Brooklyn. At the corner of Lincoln Place there was another chain grocery store, this one belonging to the H. C. Bohack company. They looked into the windows and up and down the street. It was quiet. In they went.

There were a couple of male customers and a few clerks in the store, but "nobody made any trouble"; they all did as they were told and filed to the back. Celia summed up this uneventful robbery with an almost blasé bravado. The Bohack job was a little better money-wise than the A&P because they got two hundred fifty dollars instead of less than one hundred. But money wasn't everything. "Gee!" she thought, "This don't amount to so much after all. It's like any other work, except that it pays better; but where's the excitement?" For Celia, a young woman who had been a robber for all of a week, banditry had already changed from "danger" to "fun" by the second robbery, and now—a veteran of three stickups—she wearily called it all routine, just another job with better pay.

But soon Celia found out "where all the excitement was, all right." Sunday morning the Cooneys slept late on Pacific Street. Celia awoke and "slipped on an apron over [her] nightie and made some coffee and boiled some eggs." Ed stepped out for the papers. When he returned he threw a stack of Sunday papers onto the bed. The two hard-boiled crooks ate their eggs in bed while they looked at the funny pages—a typical Sunday morning. Celia had gone to clean up when Ed called her back to the bedroom:

"Great cripes, come here and look what they've done!"

There he was with two or three of the papers all spread out at their front pages and smeared all the way across the top of the page in letters so big that they would knock you for a goal, was "Bobbed Haired Girl Bandit Terrorizes Brooklyn." And "Pretty Girl Robber Raids Stores," and a lot more stuff of the same kind that I can't remember.

Gee! Who'd have thought they'd get so excited. We read on down the columns. The cops had been kiting around Brooklyn with flivvers and motorcycles all night long chasing us, while we were home asleep in bed.

And, Gosh! What they said about me. Right away some wise guy had pulled that line about how I must have been a dope fiend, and leader of a band in the underworld. I had to stop and laugh at that.

I said: "Here, Ed, wait a minute while I take a shot in the arm and play you a tune on the slide trombone. Pipe your little wifie. See who I am! I am the Bobbed Haired Bandit! I am a dope fiend and the leader of a band! Don't you just love it?"

But he didn't think it was so funny. I danced around the room. Who'd have ever thought that little Cecilia Cooney, working in a laundry at $12 a week, would be all over the front pages of the newspapers like that! Gee! I felt big! And I couldn't see why Ed sat so sore, still bent over the papers.

The robbery may have been routine, but celebrity was exhilarating. The new bandit was making her newspaper debut. The *Daily News* called Celia "Brooklyn's Girl Robber." But the *Telegram and Evening Mail* came up with a catchier name. In homage to Celia's hairdo, the *Telegram* called this new gun-wielding girl the "Bob-Hair Bandit." A name was born. Soon it — or some variation — would be adopted by the other newspapers, the police, and even Celia herself.

The police description had her in "black bobbed hair and a gray coat," but she had several key accessories: an automatic, an automobile, and the male accomplice to complete the ensemble. In the *Eagle*, the woman bandit was "armed with a powerful automatic and accompanied by a male companion." It was the "armed woman" who "directed the robberies, ordered those held up about in a gruff manner, and flourished her gun at the least provocation." The *Telegram and Evening Mail* noted — erroneously — that it was the woman behind the wheel of the getaway car. As in their reports of the first robbery, the newspapers played up this novel twist in the roles of the sexes.

"The woman was plainly in command," according to the husband and wife in the A&P. When Mrs. Gibbons balked at the order to stick up her hands, it was Celia who pointed the pistol "threateningly" and "snapped": "You're not dumb, are you? . . . that means you too!" The initially acquiescent Mr. Gibbons found his courage later, telling reporters afterward that he would have tried to "grapple" with the bandit, but "she waved the revolver at his slightest move." And while the *Telegram* had Celia in the driver's seat, the *Eagle*'s version of the getaway was far more dramatic: "Warning the four in the store that an outcry would mean 'being filled full of lead,' the man was ordered by the woman to run for the car, [while] she backed out of the store and darted onto the running board as it gathered speed."

"All of a sudden," while reading these newspaper accounts of their exploits, Celia thought she'd figured out what was making Ed "so sore":

> There was hardly a thing about him in the headlines and only down in the small type they spoke of him once or twice as my "male companion." And once they called him a "confederate." That seemed foolish, for I thought confederates were rebel soldiers who fought in the Civil War. Ed's only a couple of years older than me. He was barely old enough to get in the Navy last war. But I've found out since what confederate means.
>
> Anyway, I thought Ed was sore, because the papers had sort of left him out, and I started to rib him about it.

Likely Ed *was* a bit sore about playing second fiddle to his wife, but that's not what was bothering him right then:

> "Aw, Celia, cut it, you don't seem to understand what we've been doing. Look here."
>
> And he showed me a place in the newspaper where it said the police had been given orders to shoot to kill us on sight.
>
> I said, "Why that's awful. You don't think they mean it, do you? They haven't got any right. They wouldn't do that, would they?"
>
> He said, "Well Celia, they have done it with others; I guess they've got the right, all right."

Celia got sick to her stomach and vomited. And then she cried.

⊙ 3

> Get the news. Get it first. Spare no expense. Make a great
> and continuous noise to attract readers; denounce
> crooked wealth and promise better conditions for the
> poor to keep readers. INCREASE CIRCULATION.
>   —William Randolph Hearst

After the robberies of the A&P and Bohack stores on Saturday, January 12, the Cooneys were no longer just another pair of bandits in a local Brooklyn crime story. Their crimes caught the attention of reporters and editors across the city who recognized a good story when they saw one, and the contours of the Bobbed Haired Bandit story fit well within the new terrain of New York newspapers in the 1920s.

New York City, since the nineteenth century, was America's great newspaper town. It was here that arch moralist Horace Greeley's *Tribune* was born and his more disreputable competitor James Gordon Bennett launched the *Herald*. Benjamin Day pioneered the popular "Penny Press," publishing his *Sun* from Newspaper Row down by City Hall, while across the East River in the then still separate city of Brooklyn, the *Eagle* counted among its writers and editors a young local poet by the name of Walt Whitman. (Richard Adams Locke, famous for his "Moon Hoax" at the *Sun*, was also a later editor at the *Eagle*.) Joseph Pulitzer's *World* and William Randolph Hearst's *Journal* developed their signature style of sensationalist "yellow journalism" in New York, and the city was where their starch-collared counterpart Adolph Ochs brought a new professionalism to the industry with his "paper of record," the *New York Times*.

By the turn of the twentieth century all these newspapers were publishing in New York City. And they were not alone: in 1890 New York City boasted fifteen English-language dailies represented by twelve owners, and the years 1910–1914 marked the high point for the number of newspapers published in the United States. Following the Great War, the monopoly capitalism that characterized the steel and oil industries, as well as the "chain" model of supermarket and drugstore ownership, came to the newspaper business. The 1920s were the beginning of the long march to the concentration and consolidation of media we are familiar with today. During the Bobbed Haired Bandit's spree in 1924, New York City was served by eleven dailies and Brooklyn by four; today the city has three.

All the big chains were represented in the New York newspaper market in the Twenties: Hearst (*American, Journal, Mirror*), Pulitzer (*World*), Scripps-Howard (*Telegram*), Ridder (*Journal of Commerce*), and Gannett (briefly, the *Brooklyn Eagle*). Now that newspapers were organized more like businesses, the business of profit and loss became increasingly important. No publisher embodied this new ethos better than newspaper magnate Frank A. Munsey. In the first quarter of the twentieth century Munsey bought, sold, or destroyed seven New York City newspapers: the old *Daily News* and the *Press*, *Sun*, *Herald*, *Evening Telegram*, *Globe*, and *Mail*. Munsey merged the *Press* into the evening *Sun* and the morning edition of the *Sun* into the *Herald*, killed the *Globe*, melded the *Mail* into the *Telegram*, and when the owners of the *Tribune* wouldn't sell their newspaper to him, he sold them his *Herald* to create the *Herald-Tribune*. "My work of amalgamating newspapers," Munsey told reporters in 1924, "has been as sound a piece of economics as the amalgamation of competing lines of railroads or banks or manufactures." Others were not as impressed with his sound economics; press historian Frank Luther Mott called him the "Grand High Executioner." Munsey's newspaper slaughter only ceased when he died in 1925. For that occasion William Allen White, the celebrated populist editor of the Emporia, Kansas *Gazette*, wrote this epitaph:

> Frank Munsey the great publisher is dead. Frank Munsey contributed to the journalism of his day the talent of a meat packer, the morals of a money changer, and the manner of an undertaker. He and his kind have about succeeded in transforming a once noble profession into an 8 percent security . . . may he rest in trust.

The scramble for the eight (or greater) percent profit margin that the new business trusts demanded heated up New York's already scorching circulation wars. William Randolph Hearst's advice to his editors that begins this chapter gives a sense of the temperature. Each paper scrambled to get *the* story and get it first. If they couldn't get it first, they pumped up what they had to Hearst's "great and continuous noise." Then they put a spin on the story to make it appeal to a given market, a certain demographic. Ochs's *Times* aimed for the professional upper-middle classes, while Hearst's *Journal* and *American* looked for its readers in the lower-middle and working classes. Each tailored their news accordingly. In modern business speak, it was product differentiation.

In 1919 Captain Joseph Patterson introduced a new and different news product to New York City and America: the tabloid. Modeled on the *London Daily Mirror* he had read overseas during the war, Patterson's *Illustrated Daily News* brought a new style of news to New York, one that was well suited to the frantic rhythms of the Jazz Age. The tabloid was small, half the size of a traditional paper, and convenient to read on the subway or in transit. Its front page was made up entirely of photographs, and its screaming headlines made it easy to discern the feature story at a glance. Its articles were short and snappy, written in punched-up vernacular and focused on the attention-grabbing topics of crime, sports, and sex.

The entry of the *Daily News* into the New York newspaper market immediately put it up against Hearst's *New York American* and *Evening Journal*, as each paper fought for the eyes and hearts of New Yorkers. Soon the *News* would face battle on its own terrain as other tabloids hit the streets of the city, but already by 1924 the smashing financial success of the *Daily News* had spawned imitators in style, if not format, and the other New York newspapers were drawn to the drama of Brooklyn's gungirl.

The Bobbed Haired Bandit attracted press like a magnet: it was a perfect story for the cutthroat competitive newspapers, all looking for that next big scoop. A gun-toting, smartly dressed, female bandit whom the police couldn't catch had all the right ingredients: drama, thrills, conflict, morality, and a unique "man bites dog" gender role reversal that made the story special.

At the same time that the press was discovering the Bobbed Haired Bandit, there was another — related — story in the making: all the publicity the daring girl bandit received translated into bad press for the police department, and this meant bad news for New York mayor John F. Hylan's police commissioner, Richard E. Enright.

Traditionally, New York's police commissioners were selected more for their political connections than their policing experience. Theodore Roosevelt, police commissioner between 1895 and 1897, moved straight from the New York State Legislature to the position of top cop and then eventually up to the presidency of the United States. Richard Enright was different. He was the first police commissioner in the history of New York who was selected from within the ranks of the New York Police Department (NYPD), promoted up from lieutenant by Mayor Hylan in 1919.

His rise from the ranks kept Enright loyal to the cop on the beat, and in his eight years on the job he succeeded in improving working conditions for the men on the force. But his rank-and-file lineage also meant that Enright had no power base outside the police force and his patron, Mayor Hylan. With no other protection, he often bore the brunt of the all-too-frequent charges of favoritism and inefficiency, incompetence and corruption leveled against the mayor and the police force. In 1921 his police force was investigated by a grand jury and a legislative investigating committee for corruption, and newspaper editors and the Citizens Union asked for his removal. Weathering that storm, Enright was publicly blasted the following year for his inability to stop the latest "crime wave." Set upon by hostile politicians and a hungry news media, Enright was understandably sensitive to public image and political pressure. He was convinced that the city was beset not by a crime wave but by a manufactured wave of bad publicity.

In 1921 the police department published a pamphlet titled *No "Crime Wave" in New York City: Police Commissioner Richard E. Enright Replies to His Critics*, within whose pages the cop with "a fighting jaw, a pair of clear, unwavering eyes and a gift of straightforward talk" spun the story on crime in the big city. "Crime wave? There is none" was Enright's succinct and unsurprising conclusion. The "transcriber" of this "interview" was none other than George Creel, a one-time newspaperman, recently the director of the Committee for Public Information (the United States' propaganda bureau during the Great War), and presently an agent for hire in the new and burgeoning field of public relations. Enright had engaged the master propagandist to help him fight off the bad press of a "crime wave" with his own publicity campaign. The modern police commissioner of 1924 fought crime *and* the newspapers in a battle for law, order, and public opinion.

Enright could have used Creel's help in the opening weeks of 1924. New York's wet New Year's revels had left the police department with a hangover. The public's perception was that New York City was a center of vice where liquor ran in the streets. Police enforcement of Prohibition was seen as ineffective, incompetent, or worse. On December 27, 1923, Rear Admiral Charles Plunkett, the commandant of the Brooklyn Navy Yard, went so far as to declare that the neighborhood surrounding the Navy Yard was a "restricted area," off limits to his sailors. The *Brooklyn Eagle* commented that under Plunkett's order,

"Conditions Don't Seem to Have Improved Much Since Our Forefathers Fought the Indians," *New York Tribune*, April 3, 1924.

"a large section of this community rests under a ban that classes it with the more objectionable areas of Asiatic cities from which sailors are barred," the implication being that parts of Brooklyn were too dangerous even for sailors.

After the Navy's opening salvo from the Brooklyn Navy Yard, the Marines landed in Philadelphia. War hero Brigadier-General Smedley Darlington Butler had been granted leave from the U.S. Marine Corps by President Coolidge to become Philadelphia's director of public safety. His job was overseeing the city's police who, like their New York counterparts, were widely recognized as being too corrupt or inept to stem the tide of illegal liquor, vice, and banditry. The general quickly had the city under near martial law in his campaign to eradicate the criminal element.

After an intensive forty-eight-hour "marine-style" sweep of the "moonshine valley" section of the city to shut down the saloons, disorderly houses, and vice resorts, "Hell Devil" Butler turned his attention to banditry. A shoot-to-kill order was reportedly issued. Like good war correspondents, New York reporters relayed the general's battle plans to defeat banditry in Philadelphia: BUTLER MAKES QUAKER CITY ONE BIG BANDIT TRAP, read the headline of the New York Tribune.

Butler planned to place Philadelphia's bandits under siege. He would surround the city with a series of sentry outposts on every road in and out of the city. His forces would be coordinated by radio and telephone and notified at once when a robbery occurred. "There will be no rest at the outpost," the general was quoted as saying:

> At each of these outposts will be stationed an armed motor car, detectives with sawed off shotguns, motorcycle policemen and a permanent sentry. The sentry will see to it that not a car leaves the city without inspection. . . .
>
> Director Butler also explained that each booth will be equipped with arrows and colored lights of green, red, blue and yellow. These lights will be operated from City Hall. Whenever reports of a hold-up, bank robbery, or any other big crime reach City Hall, the lights in the booths will be flashed.

The general's cockamamie scheme seemed to get results — or at least the New York papers were reporting that it did. One Brooklyn paper wrote that Butler's raiders were so successful that they FAIL[ED] TO FIND A SUSPECT; NOT A BOOTLEGGER LEFT IN ONCE NOTORI-OUS DISTRICT. Moonshine valley was dry: "The force chalked it up as a victory for the general, for the district had been the notorious home of poison hooch. His crusade apparently has the moonshiners frightened." Back at the general's office, there was a stack of applications from five hundred ex-Marines looking to be deployed on the Philadelphia police force.

The front page of the *Brooklyn Standard Union* reported that an alderman from Queens had the temerity to send a letter to the mayor's office, suggesting that he request that General John J. Pershing of the U.S. Army be sent to New York to take charge of the police department. The alderman concluded that "if it takes the commanding general of the Marines to clean up a quiet town like Philadelphia it will take at least the commander of the armies of the U.S. to make New York spotless."

The drama of Butler's campaign in Philadelphia was big news in the New York press, and the papers played it for all it was worth, culminating in scare stories that warned that every pickpocket, confidence man, and gunman was on his way to Gotham. So pervasive was the story of Butler invading Philadelphia that a *Tribune* editorial poked a little fun at the general's imperial pretensions, while at the same time praising his results:

> Of course there had been a lot of plain "bunk" in the adventure of the General in the City of Brotherly Love. The business of a forty-eight hour clean-up, the silver stars on the shoulders of the Director, the "shoot to kill" background, were a bit funny, but it cannot be denied that cussedness in Philadelphia has suffered a severe jolt and that complacency in the midst of lawlessness has been unseated....
>
> The marines accustomed to iron-handing the little brown men of the East and making the black free States of the Indies feel a little less free, had at least caused Philadelphians to turn a shade whiter.

Butler's apparent success was so embarrassing to Enright that the New York police commissioner was forced to take bold action. On January 12, the very same Saturday night of the Cooneys' second and third holdups, Enright raided his own house. Stung with charges of corruption and incompetence, Enright made "sweeping accusations," charging thirteen of New York City's twenty-two police inspectors with "neglect of duty," primarily for "failure to suppress speak-easies." This promised to be "a sweeping shake up such as the department had not seen for many a day," reported the *Brooklyn Citizen*, which predicted that "New York is in for a housecleaning such as that to which 'Old Gimlet Eye' Butler is treating the City of Brotherly Love."

New Yorkers were accustomed to the police being accused of incompetence and corruption, but rarely did such accusations come from the police commissioner himself. Reporters smelled blood. It was an easy time to make the police department look foolish, and the newspapers were on to a new story that could do just that. Sandwiched between the Sunday *Brooklyn Citizen*'s front page declaring Enright's new WAR ON LIQUOR and ENRIGHT CHARGES 18 INSPECTORS WITH NEGLECT OF DUTY was another headline: GIRL BANDIT GETS $113 IN HER WEEKLY STORE HOLDUP. News of a new bandit—and a *woman* bandit at that—made for even more bad publicity for New York's tarnished finest.

That Sunday's reporting of the girl with a gun was both a legitimate news story and an attraction. The big-city press used sensational crime and human-interest stories, of which the bandit girl was just the latest, to boost circulation and profit in a competitive market. Their editorial pages justified this coverage by lamenting the sad state of the modern world; crime stories were spun as so many tawdry cautionary tales and modern morality plays. The gender twist broke up the almost monotonous recounting of yet another stickup by another masked man. And the girl bandit stories swelled the crime wave that was breaking on the Hylan administration in the pages of the press. This pressure goaded the police force to silence their critics and restore the appearance of law and order to the pages of the daily papers with some decisive action.

This new female crime problem was solved by Commissioner Enright and the New York City Police Department with stunning efficiency on the very next day. On Monday, January 14, the police captured the Bobbed Haired Bandit.

PART II

Get Girl Bandit Dead or Alive

⊙ 4

BOBBED HAIRED GIRL CAPTURED. —*New York Herald*

EX-CHORUS GIRL ARRESTED AS CHAIN STORE BANDIT
—*Brooklyn Standard Union*

SQUEAL TRAPS GIRL IN THEFTS —*New York American*

"South Brooklyn merchants, terrorized the past few months by a girl robber and her male escort, may breathe easier hereafter," reported the *Daily News*. The Brooklyn police had arrested the gungirl, "a wisp of a girl, slim and scarcely five feet tall."

The events leading to the arrest of the Bobbed Haired Bandit began early Monday morning, January 14th. Patrolman John Peters was walking his beat on Ninth Street and Fifth Avenue in Brooklyn when he observed a tall young man who "didn't look as if he ought to be out so late." This was enough for Officer Peters to arrest him and take him down to the Fifth Avenue station, where he was interrogated by half a dozen detectives.

The man was Vincent "Apples" Kovaleski, a tall and well-built nineteen-year-old. Apples matched the description of one of three men who held up a nearby grocery store the day before. After a "severe grilling," the police finally "wrung" a confession out him. When Kovaleski started talking, it seems he couldn't stop. He confessed not only to holding up the grocery store the day before but also to the three robberies that Celia and Ed had committed. The detectives pressed him for the name of his bobbed haired accomplice. Apples "came across"; he gave the girl up: her name was Helen Quigley. "In the vernacular of the Police Department," Vincent "Apples" Kovaleski "is said to have 'squealed.'"

Helen Quigley lived with her father, a seventy-year-old cigar salesman, at 63 Eighth Street in Brooklyn. She was twenty-three years old, the youngest daughter of eight children, and her mother was dead. She had left school after seventh grade and worked as a saleswoman in a bakery, and later had a job in a clock company. But the papers found her latest vocation the most interesting. Helen dreamed of being an actress. The papers, however, were quick to tag her with the more titillating title of "chorus girl" because a couple of years previously she had a job with the Parisian Whirl, a touring burlesque troupe. She left the stage when the show swung round the circuit and finally reached Brooklyn, quitting because she didn't want her friends to see that she was still stuck in the chorus when she had set out to be a star. So she moved back in with her widowed father and became his housekeeper.

After breaking Kovaleski, detectives from the Fifth Avenue Precinct in Brooklyn went and picked up Helen Quigley. The suspected Bobbed Haired Bandit came to the door wearing a kitchen apron. She calmly asked if she could finish drying the supper dishes before they brought her in for questioning. Helen was a tougher nut than Apples.

"Powders Her Nose as Police Grill Her" read the *Brooklyn Citizen*'s subhead:

> While the ring of detectives fired question after question at her the girl sat back calmly in a chair and quietly denied everything. When questioned as to whether or not she was the girl who had barked commands at store clerks while she pointed an automatic revolver at them she merely shook her head.
>
> "But your name has been mentioned as the girl who played the lead in these jobs," the detectives said. The girl shook her head.
>
> "'Not me," she answered smoothly.
>
> After more than two hours of cross-fire examination during which the girl maintained her outward calm and even stopped to powder her nose and chin with the aid of a purse mirror the detectives gave up the task of trying to break her down.

Since the local dicks couldn't make Helen talk, she was taken down to Brooklyn police headquarters on Poplar Street, where the man in charge of all detectives in Brooklyn and Queens, Captain Daniel J. Carey, spent several hours trying to "break" the girl. Carey knew his business. He was a thirty-year veteran of the NYPD and had just been named acting captain a year earlier. In order to hold the rank, Carey knew he needed to close a high-profile case. The Bobbed Haired Bandit looked like it might be that case.

Grilled by Carey, Quigley admitted that she knew Apples, saying that she met Kovaleski in a Brooklyn speakeasy and that she was supposed to have a date with him on Saturday night the 13th of January, the same evening the Bobbed Haired Bandit robbed the A&P and Bohack stores. But, she insisted, she did not keep the date. She told Carey that Kovaleski was "a dirty rat and a squealer," that he had framed her as a way to get back at her for standing him up.

Carey, however, was not convinced. Witnesses were assembled for a lineup and brought to the big room at the Poplar Street headquarters of the Brooklyn police. The *Standard Union* described it this way:

> Helen Quigley, who it is said, formerly graced the boards of the burlesque stage, faced the strangest audience in her career to-day.
>
> Fifty masked men gazed intently upon her. There was no applause or cat calls. For the audience, it seemed as if the last curtain had fallen, but throughout the performance, in the detective's room at Poplar street headquarters, the principle character never lost her bearing.
>
> When the masked men — detectives — filed out their place was taken by a score or more of small storepeekers [*sic*], victims of the numerous hold-ups staged within the past few weeks. Several identified the young woman, who is only twenty-three years old, as the bobbed-haired bandit for whom the police have been searching.
>
> "You've got me wrong," emphatically declared the well dressed prisoner. Then she smiled.

"Smilin' Helen" Quigley, as the papers soon named her, recounted a very different version of what happened that day at the lineup. The identification at the lineup was "fishy," she said:

> The officers took an old tam-o'-shanter I discarded a few years ago and a fur coat of my sisters which was all ripped inside from the house when they grabbed me.
>
> When I came in in my own clothes the man they had shook his head. He couldn't identify me. Then they had me put on those rags I ain't worn for years and made me come in. He just looked doubtful then, and the police whispered to him and he nodded.

Appearances were everything in this case, not just to the police but to the press, who readily described the suspected gungirl to their read-

hier hone, Seahman 2000 NEW YORK AMERICAN—*A Paper for People Who Think*— WEDNESDAY, JANUARY 16, 1924

"*That Is the Girl Who Held Us Up!*"

She is pretty, the flush of youth is on her cheeks, she wears the bobbed hair of a flapper and she isn't much bigger than a minute, as Mark Twain would say. Yet the Brooklyn police declared yesterday that the case of Helen Quigley, former chorus girl, accused as having gone a-banditing with a .45 caliber revolver and the daring of a Jesse James, was one of the most problematical in all their experience.

Hours of grilling by detectives failed to obtain a confession from Helen that she robbed several grocery stores at the point of her gun, and even when she was positively identified by two of the store clerks, Bernard Kennedy (left) and Leslie Loudon—who declared "There is the girl who held us up"—Helen merely powdered her nose and asked, "How do you get that way?"

She became angry only when her alleged male accomplice, Vincent Kovaleski, was mentioned to her as having confessed, calling him "a squealer."

"Girl Bandit's Detention Fails to Halt Holdups in Brooklyn"

Less than twenty-four hours↓Brooklyn, the girl arrested Monday↓forcible language ·and in other

Helen Quigley. The caption reads: "She is pretty, the flush of youth is on her cheeks, she wears the bobbed hair of a flapper and she isn't much bigger than a minute, as Mark Twain would say. Yet the Brooklyn police declared yesterday that the case of Helen Quigley, former chorus girl, accused of gone a-banditing with a .45 caliber revolver and the daring of Jesse James, was one of the most problematical in all of their experience." "That Is the Girl Who Held Us Up," *New York American*, January 16, 1924. (Harry Ransom Humanities Research Center)

ers on the day following Helen's identification, questioning, arrest, and arraignment. The *Daily News* was the most succinct in declaring her to be "bobbed haired and pretty." The *American* elaborated: "She's pretty, the flush of youth is on her cheeks, she wears the bobbed hair of a flapper and she isn't much bigger than a minute." And the *Brooklyn Standard Union* gave her the full once-over:

> Attired in a short sealskin coat with a large beaver collar, black and white striped dress, flesh colored stockings and brown pumps, she

looked more like a society debutante than a bandit. Her face was continually wreathed in smiles and her eyes snapped. The small black velvet hat, trimmed with silver ornaments and worn jauntily on the back of her head, displayed her brown hair, cut in the latest mode of the flapper.

Helen was finally a star, but she insisted it was not her part. She was not the Bobbed Haired Bandit, and she barely knew Apples.

"Housewife and bandit! Miss Helen Quigley, bobbed haired blonde, admits the first and denies the second," the *American* reported, continuing: "She folds her arms in defiance and flashes indignant glances from her bright blue eyes." She protested her innocence loudly, "They framed me. . . . Before my maker, I am willing to take punishment for anything I ever did. I'm no angel. But steal! Me steal! Never." "I'm not foolish enough to go around robbing people, and if I was I'd know better than to take a kid [like Apples] along." "Why I'm so afraid of a gun that I can hardly look at one," she added, "and the only occasion I ever use a knife is when I am eating."

Less than two days after the arrest of Helen Quigley, the press was already beginning to doubt that the police had grabbed the right woman. On January 16, the *Evening Post* relayed Helen's side of the story, repeating her claim that she was not the "daring woman sought by the police but the spite victim of a man with whom she failed 'to keep a date in a Brooklyn speak-easy.'" But the police were not listening. As far as the detectives were concerned, once Helen had been picked out of a lineup the case was closed. The police congratulated themselves on ending the crime spree and quickly packed her off to the Fifth Avenue magistrate's court for arraignment: "Capt. Dan Carey, in charge of the Brooklyn and Queens detectives complimented the detectives who so efficiently worked up the case and closed it." His praise would prove premature.

The alleged bandits were arraigned together in the Fifth Avenue court before Magistrate James O'Neill. Helen Quigley did not have a lawyer. Her family tried to defend her by claiming that she was "simple minded" and "easily led." Papers reported that Helen liked to drink and stay out late at night and that her widowed father, unable to control his daughter, had even taken Helen to an observation ward at

Kings County Hospital and then to a psychiatrist to have her watched for signs of insanity. The diagnosis was "mental weakness," but she had not been committed.

That criminal — or even headstrong — behavior in a woman was a sign of mental illness was not an uncommon belief among law-enforcement and mental-health professionals in the 1920s. The Brooklyn district attorney, Charles Dodd, requested another mental examination for Helen. "If she is a mental incompetent she should be treated as such," Dodd explained, "and provision made that will save her from herself and the evil influences of others."

The Brooklyn DA was new to his job but old to the ins and outs of politics and prosecutions. The Brooklyn-born Dodd got his start in politics as a city assemblyman. Well connected in the Democratic Party, he had been appointed by one mayor to a municipal court judgeship; another seated him as city magistrate. In 1921 Mayor Hylan reappointed Dodd to the magistrate's court, and then a year later he was elected DA in a special election. This wasn't Dodd's first high-profile stickup case. In 1923 he prosecuted four men for the sensational murders of two bank messengers, sending three of the defendants to the chair and one to life in prison. Dodd was reelected as Brooklyn district attorney the same year. The DA had learned the value of a successful prosecution of a public case. He was careful, making sure he covered all the bases on Quigley's case.

Sitting in court, oblivious to the politics of it all, Helen was not amused. All this talk about her insanity made her angry, and demonstrating a degree of mental alacrity, she commented that "they say I'm weak-minded and say I did a stickup that was darn clever. I don't get it."

Based primarily on the identifications made by the two clerks from the Bobbed Haired Bandit's Roulston robbery, Helen and Apples were formally charged with assault and robbery and held on ten thousand dollars bail each. Kovaleski was also charged with the grocery robbery involving three men. Over the vehement protestations of Kovaleski's lawyer, who in open court accused the judge of being incompetent, the two were led back to the detention pen. As the pair was led away,

Helen's father turned to Apple's mother, "saying that the whole affair was a 'frame up' and that the boy had been beaten into submission by the police."

The Cooneys, like the rest of New York, read about the capture of the Bobbed Haired Bandit in the newspapers the day after her arrest. Celia and Ed "thought that was fine." The two didn't believe the police department and the DA's office could hold the ex–chorus girl long, and "while they were finding out that she wasn't the right one it would keep suspicion off of us." In "The Bobbed-Hair Bandit's Own Story" in the *American*, Celia speculated as to why the police had arrested poor Helen:

> The Brooklyn papers began to say rough things about the police and to ask was this the Wild West or a peaceful city, and could one girl buffalo the whole force.
>
> I guess they just had to arrest somebody, and they couldn't catch us, so what did they do but rope in some poor simp with a pretty face by the name of Helen Quigley, that had never done anything worse than dance in a burlesque show.

The Cooneys read that Helen Quigley was positively identified in the police lineup, but Celia didn't believe that the witnesses were lying to frame Helen Quigley:

> I don't believe for a minute they were trying to crook her. People say that she does look a little bit like me, though I can't see it, and she is about my size. And I guess they were so scared at the time they couldn't remember very well — so busy maybe looking at the automatic that they didn't pay much attention to my face.

Celia knew that the inability of witnesses to agree on what they saw was what had kept her from being identified. "The only thing they all got right was the fur coat. Most every girl wears a fur coat in cold weather, so that didn't make much difference."

Celia's interest in the fate of Helen Quigley did not extend to Vincent Kovaleski, who was about to take a fall for Edward in the role of the "male companion." Even though Apples was also falsely accused, Celia seemed to agree with Helen that he was a rat: "Some Russian by the name of Kovaleski gave them a bum steer to square a private grudge," was all Celia had to say on the subject.

While Celia and Ed certainly weren't going to turn themselves in to save Helen Quigley, Celia knew that she couldn't just sit tight and let Helen take the fall:

> I may be a bandit, but I'm not the kind of a girl that would do a dirty thing like seeing someone else get sent to the penitentiary, innocent, and me to blame. . . .
>
> When I saw how things were going for Helen Quigley, I said: "Ed, we got to do something to get this girl off."
>
> He said: "I guess you're right, but it's pretty dangerous for us to mix in on a thing like that."
>
> I said: "Well, we can write a note to the police saying she is innocent, like they do in detective stories."
>
> Well we talked about it awhile, and he agreed; and I sat down and wrote a note that said:
>
> "To the police: You are wrong on Helen Quigley. Let her go. She is not the girl you want. The Bobbed-Haired Bandit."
>
> Ed looked at it a while and said:
>
> "Say, I got a better idea. They've been saying we are a professional gang — that we are professional crooks, thugs, underworld stuff and all that. Well let's write a different sort of note and make 'em think it's so."

Celia thought it was "one of the swellest ideas Ed ever had." So they "doped it out together" and wrote out a new note for the cops.

There's no reason to doubt that Celia felt compassion for the wrongly accused Helen Quigley, but she may have had another motive for writing the note. After all, ever since the discovery of Smilin' Helen, the detective story she and Ed had been starring in suddenly had a new leading lady. The working-class housewife from Brooklyn was learning to like her notoriety. A well-timed note could turn the attention back to the *real* Bobbed Haired Bandit.

Whatever their motivations, the very day they read about Helen Quigley's capture in the papers, the Cooneys went back to work. Ed and Celia had decided to "get away with another holdup or two. After all, it was pretty easy money. And we liked the excitement." They knew that the police had been posting plainclothes men at the chain stores and groceries in Brooklyn expecting them make their weekly hit on a Saturday night, so they decided to try something different to "fool them."

That night, Tuesday, January 15th, was bitterly cold. The Cooneys were back behind the wheel, "driving slow and looking through windows," trying to make up their minds. It wasn't easy. During the week many businesses closed early: "Pretty much everything was closed up tight except the drug stores and cigar stores." Cruising through the Clinton Hill section near Pratt Institute, they turned onto Ryerson Street. On the two hundred block at the corner of Dekalb Avenue they looked in the window of the Weinstein drugstore and knew that they had found the place. It "looked like it was just waiting to be robbed — not a soul in it but a couple of clerks, and nobody walking in the whole length of the block."

Ed didn't want to wait outside because of the cold, so they entered the drugstore together. Standing behind the counter at the cash register was Louis Hecht, one of the two clerks. Celia described him as "one of those slick little fellows, all dolled up like Rudolph Valentino." Celia Cooney clearly preferred her men to look more like Jack Dempsey than the oily sheik of the movies. She was a boxing fan; Ed was no "Rhubarb Vaselino."

Ed pretended to look for something in one of the showcases as he edged toward where the store manager, Leo Greenburg, was standing. Celia wanted one of the employees to open the register because Ed had had trouble opening the one back at Bohack during their previous holdup, so she asked the clerk-cum-sheik for change for the phone:

> I plunked down my quarter on the counter with my left hand, keeping the right in my coat pocket all ready to pull out the little automatic, and waited until Louis Hecht had taken the quarter and opened the register. Before he had time to close it I said: "Say wait!" as if I was going to ask him for something else or maybe buy something.

The clerk turned his head toward Celia. Celia stopped. She couldn't see his hands. Ed had instructed her not to act until the victim's hands were in full view: "You don't need to watch a man's face so much, but don't ever pull a gun unless you can see exactly what he's doing with his hands." Ed had it all "doped out," so she "hesitated, to give the bird a chance to turn more around." When the clerk turned to face her with only the change in his hands, Celia pulled her gun

> and jammed it at him and his mouth jumped open as if he was going to yell, and I said:
>
> "No noise, please."
>
> I heard Ed behind me. I guess he'd got a hunch from what I said that they might be going to let out some sort of yap, for he called out sharp to Greenburg:
>
> "Keep your trap closed, too."

They forced the pair out from behind the high counter and toward the back of the store. Celia held them back there with the point of her automatic. Ed rifled the register, turning up a measly fifty dollars. He looked in the money order booth, but there wasn't much there, either. Ed finished quickly and began to back toward the door. Celia reached into her left coat pocket and pulled out the note. She put it down in front of Hecht and said, "Here kid! Give this to the police."

It read:

> You dirty fish-peddling bums, leave this innocent girl alone and get the right ones, which is nobody else but us, and we are going to give Mr. Hogan, the manager of Roulston's, another visit, as we got two checks we couldn't cash, and also ask Bohack's manager did I ruin his cash register. Also I will visit him again, as I broke a perfectly good automatic on it. We defy you fellows to catch us.
>
> The Bobbed-Haired Bandit and Her Companion

The contents of the Cooneys' note defying the police was reprinted in almost all of the papers, but the exact wording varied from paper to paper. The *Eagle* even ran a facsimile reproduction, complete with grammatical and spelling errors, but missing any reference to the robbery at Roulston's or to Mr. Hogan, the store manager. It's unclear if the variances in wording were the result of some police tactic or the consequences of reporters and editors who were not about to let specifics get in the way of a good story — or graphic layout.

YOU - dinty - FISH- PEDDLING- BUMS

LEAVE- THIS - INNOCENT- GIRL-ALONE

AND-GET-THE-RIGHT-ONES- WHICH

IS- NOBODY-ELSE- BUT-US-

ALSO-ASK-BohAKS-MANAGER-DID

I- RUIN-HIS- CASH- REGISTER-ALSO

I WILL -VISIT- HIM-AGAIN -AS-I

BROKE-A PEFFECTLY-Good-AUTO-

MATIC-ON-IT- WE-DEFY- YOU

FELLOWS- TO-CATCH-US-

THE
BOBBED-HAIRED
BANDIT
AND
COMPANION

Celia and Ed's note to the police. The note was transcribed differently in the various papers. "Defiant Note Left for Police by Girl Bandit Who Declares Helen Quigley Is Innocent," *Brooklyn Eagle*, January 16, 1924.

Whatever its wording, the note had an effect in the shops of Brooklyn, even those the Cooneys had already robbed. The *Evening Post* reported that "the employees of the Roulston grocery stores are not feeling their easiest just at present. Whenever the door opens the half dozen clerks turn their heads in unison toward it, on the lookout for the girl bandit who wrote a note to the police accepting responsibility for the robbery and promising to return because she had broken a perfectly good automatic pistol while in the store."

The press was thrilled with this new development; the plot was thickening. But there was also a bit of confusion. How many girl bandits were there? Was this *the* Bobbed Haired Bandit? Or was it a NEW GUNWOMAN, as the *Eagle* headlined. The *Evening Post* worried that there "May Be Two Girl Bandits Operating in Brooklyn." According to the *Eagle*, this additional bandit "has thrown a pair of monkey wrenches into the mental machinery of Captain Carey of the detective bureau." But the police and the press were not the only ones confused by the number of Bobbed Haired Bandits.

It must have been quite a surprise to Celia and Ed when they woke up the next morning and read in the papers that they had committed not one but two drugstore robberies the night before. They had attempted to clear one falsely accused girl bandit, only to be usurped by the exploits of yet another female bandit. Girl bandits, it seems, were multiplying in New York.

The same night that Celia and Ed were sticking up Weinstein's, another Brooklyn drugstore was robbed by yet another bobbed haired bandit. At around seven o'clock in the evening, a blonde and bobbed girl entered Samuel Grant's drugstore on the corner of Rogers and Lefferts Avenues. She was "good looking and fair of hair and complexion. Her height is about 5 feet 6, her nerve as equable as a summer's day," recalled a witness. She pretended to shop for perfume until two armed men burst in and carried out the robbery while she stood by the front door and kept a lookout. The men were described as wearing belted overcoats and being "foreign." "They were dark and appeared to be Latins," according to the *Eagle*. The girl did not carry a gun (although one account described her as suggestively keeping her hand in her right coat pocket during the robbery) and, unlike the *other* bobbed gungirl, she did not use what the Brooklyn paper delicately referred to as "forcible language."

This was a problem for the police and an opportunity for the press. The arrest of Helen Quigley was supposed to end the career of the woman bandit. Now the police had one woman, Helen Quigley, locked up in the Raymond Street Jail, another "bobbed-haired brunette" robbing Weinstein's drugstore, and — for anyone paying close enough attention — a third unknown blonde bandit sticking up yet another drugstore. The *Brooklyn Standard Union* summed up the situation clearly:

> The expected lull in the wave of banditry, anticipated with the arrest of Helen Quigley, suspected girl bandit, has failed to materialize.
>
> On the contrary, a new wave of crime, in which at least one other young woman, and possibly two, enacted stellar roles, has given the police an enigma difficult of solution.

The story was spreading from the news pages to the editorial and opinion sections of the paper; the bandit's defiant note and police bewilderment over the identity of the bobbed haired girl left the department open to editorial attack and even ridicule. In just a few days, the triumphal newspaper announcement of the capture of a wanted criminal had been usurped by the well-publicized taunts of a female bandit and reports of a "new wave of crime." The same newspaper publicity machine that had pushed police into making a quick arrest and claiming an easy victory was now forcing them to concede that the case was not completely tied up. The police stuck to their story of the capture of the Bobbed Haired Bandit, but they also leaked that Captain Carey was having "misgivings" and acknowledged that there was at least one other female bandit on the loose. The woman hunt would continue — and so would the jokes.

On the day after Celia and Ed's dramatic note to free Helen Quigley was published in the papers, the prisoner was brought back again before Magistrate James O'Neill in the Fifth Avenue court. But Miss Quigley was not set free; instead, the judge doubled her bail — which she already couldn't pay — from ten to twenty thousand dollars. She was remanded to a cell in the Raymond Street Jail. No matter how loudly the prisoner claimed frame-up from her cell, the note left by an anonymous bandit was not considered exculpatory evidence. The note "bothered Captain Carey not a little" — but not enough to set poor Helen free.

5

STILL SHE PROGRESSES.
The girl with the bob
Is right on the job
And, in the Holdup Clan
She has proved that she
The equal can be
Of any bandit man.
　　　　　　—Tom W. Jackson, *Brooklyn Standard Union*

The Bobbed Haired Bandit struck on Sunday, January 20th, only five nights after her last robbery at Weinstein's drugstore. Not long after eleven o'clock that night, a "pretty young woman, bobbed-haired and clad in a sealskin coat" and a small hat walked into a drugstore on New York Avenue at the corner of Union Street. There were only two people left in the store: the owner, Benjamin Jospey, was in the rear making up a prescription, and his mother Rose was sitting near him, waiting for him to close up and go home. When he heard the door open, Mr. Jospey went forward to greet his customer. She asked for a bottle of talcum powder: "She moved quickly as he turned. Jospey felt the muzzle of a pistol pressing against the small of his back and obeyed without hesitation the girl's instruction to 'Get 'em up!'"

"Put up your hands and shut up," commanded Celia. As Ed entered with his guns drawn, Celia started backing the druggist toward the rear of the store.

"Now just keep quiet and keep your hands up and back over to where the old lady is," said Ed.

Mrs. Jospey "jumped up as if to interfere." Celia waved her gun at the feisty, sixty-five-year-old Rose. Benjamin Jospey stepped between them. Celia later remembered that Jospey was the "worst scared man we ever held up, but it wasn't for himself, it was for his mother." When Celia pointed her gun at his mother, Jospey "took one look at us and screamed almost like a woman: 'For God's sake don't shoot. Don't point those guns at her. Take what you want and go — please!' "

The *New York Herald* reported the exchange differently, giving Celia's patter an even harder edge. When Rose "started to make an outcry," Celia reportedly retorted:

> "Shut your mouth or I'll shoot you," said the flapper bandit.
> "Take what you want," said Jospey, "but don't shoot her."
> "You shut up, too," said the woman with a gun. "Where's your tin?"

A big part of banditry in Brooklyn seemed to be getting the victims to shut up. In the version printed by the *Citizen* and the *Standard Union*, it went this way:

> "Mind your own d—— business," the bandit snapped. "We know what we want, and we'll take it. Another peep out of either of you and you'll stop gassin' forever."

Mother and son cooperated. Celia held them in line with her automatic, while Ed took the money from the register. At his signal she began to back toward the door, keeping her gun on the Jospeys.

Ed slipped around Celia and opened the door, making a break for the car idling at the curb. The druggist raised his head. Celia saw him and, according to the *Citizen*, said: "Raise that dome just a couple of inches more, and I'll put a hunk of lead in it — where your brains ought to be." Cowed, Jospey dropped back to the floor. Celia stopped:

> "Say," she told Jospey. "Look here a minute. This thing's for the bulls. Tell 'em I left it with my compliments."
>
> She dropped a sheet of notepaper on the counter, then backed to the door, felt behind her for the knob, then turned it, whirled suddenly and ran to the edge of the curb, climbing into the automobile. It sped away the instant before Jospey reached the door.

After the gun-wielding couple was safely gone, the druggist went to the telephone and called the Atlantic Street station. When the detectives arrived a few minutes later, Jospey gave them the Cooneys' second note:

> Well, I'm certainly having a fine time with you bulls. Isn't that so? Give it up, boys, because you will never get me, because I'll kill you off one by one if you start after me. Be careful now, that is my advice to you. We are using the money we get to good advantage, so now you fellows be decent and don't try to make us spend it on a lawyer. So long, boys, but don't forget. You'll hear from me during the week.
>
> The Bobbed Haired Girl and her Tall Companion

This second note bolstered the bandit's reputation as a "Bobbed Haired Desperado" intent on toying with the police. The front page of the *Standard Union* described her as "the note-writing, bobbed haired girl bandit, who scoffs at police and displays the daring of a cowboy," and the press portrayed the police as the Keystone Kops chasing around Brooklyn after a modern-day Jesse James. "Detectives working on the case," the newspaper reported, "admitted to-day that they are completely baffled by the courage displayed by the girl bandit." According to the *Eagle*, the detectives from the Atlantic Avenue station "expressed amazement at the boldness of the robbery because every available man, it was said, has been on patrol during the past week to guard against just such a thing happening." The *Post's* headline said it all: GIRL BANDIT TAUNTS POLICE AND ESCAPES.

Jazzed from their much-publicized bravado, Celia didn't want to wait for the weekend for their usual robbery but wanted to "pull another job right away." Ed agreed. Celia later saw this as evidence that both of them were changing: "A few days before he wouldn't have agreed," she wrote. "Now we were both scornful of the police — and I guess our heads were swelled a little by the newspapers and the publicity we were getting. Everybody was talking about us."

Meanwhile, the police had still not given up on poor Helen Quigley. They were loath to release someone who had been positively identified by eyewitnesses as *the* Bobbed Haired Bandit. Their latest theory was that there were two girl bandits, Helen Quigley being the first, and this new girl bandit who is "trying to weaken their case against Helen Quigley." The case against Quigley got a little weaker when two days after the Jospey robbery Celia and Ed struck again:

GIRL BANDIT ADDS ANOTHER
TO LONG LIST OF HOLD-UPS

The elusive girl bandit — she of the shorn locks and pretty face — made another move last night in the game of checkers she has been playing with the police for a month past. Accompanied by her steady companion, the mysterious tall young man, she went into a grocery store at 341 Albany avenue, held up Abraham Fishbein, the proprietor, and a woman customer who happened in, and then escaped.

Tuesday, January 22nd, was a very cold day in Brooklyn, and the *Standard Union* quipped: "If this weather keeps up the girl with the bobbed hair may try her luck in getting away with a red hot stove." That night Celia and Ed did try their luck; their last few robberies had netted considerably less than their first big haul, and it would take more than a red hot stove to keep them warm.

At ten o'clock, the couple borrowed a car from Horgan's garage and drove around, looking for a store to stick up. Celia was feeling "gay that night and laughed and sang" as they rode along the streets of Brooklyn. According to Celia, this worried Ed: "It seems like those days I was always either laughing or crying, and he couldn't make me out."

They found a likely store just three blocks from their last job: a small grocery store at the corner of Albany Avenue and Union Street. Ed left the motor running when he pulled up next to the curb. The car was facing west on Union with the front wheels turned toward the center of the street, ready for a quick getaway. Celia went in first, while Ed kept an eye on the street. Not a soul was in sight.

Abraham Fishbein was standing alone behind the counter of his corner grocery store when Celia entered. He seemed glad to see her and "rubbed his hands together and bowed," just like she was a regular customer. There was something about him that made Celia want to laugh.

Celia asked him for "a cake of Ivory soap, please." As Fishbein turned to pick a cake of soap from the shelf behind the counter, Celia was distracted. Her memory of this moment is quite vivid:

> As he was going to get it I spied a big dirty barrel of dried mackerel or herring or something, all yellow, brown and black they were. That sort of fish disgusts me. I can't stand the sight or smell or taste of it. But all of a sudden I got an idea that I wanted to eat a lot of those fish. They were really nasty to look at, but it seemed I had to have them and eat them, and they looked beautiful.
>
> I said, "Hey Mr. Man, these fish here, they're ???" and he was so glad to maybe make another sale that he said, "Yes, lady, they're herring, finest quality and cheap too," and bent down over the barrel to show me.

Nearly five months pregnant at this point, Celia found her attention shifting from larceny to maternity and she was suddenly consumed by a craving for the dried herring:

> I had forgot all about being a bandit. I was for those fish. My mouth watered and I was going to eat one. Ed stopped me. And I sort of woke up. The man was still bending over the barrel and I pulled my gun and jabbed it against his ribs. He was soft, and I poked it in and sort of tickled him with it.
>
> But he wasn't tickled when he saw what it was. He spread out his arms so that his hands waggled in the air, and his knees began to wobble too; and he caught his breath and then got it again and began like a person praying in church.
>
> He said, "Oh lady, lady, please don't shoot!" and if he said it once he said it a dozen times."

The *Daily News*'s headline, BROOKLYN'S FAIR GUNMISS MERRILY PURSUES CAREER, captures the general insouciant tone of the coverage. The *Brooklyn Citizen* covered the Fishbein robbery in the greatest dramatic detail. The papers reported, or supplied, the hard-boiled bandit patter that Celia either didn't remember, didn't wish to remember, or — just as likely — never actually said:

> "Keep your mouth shut or I'll blow a hole through you," the girl said sharply.

Fishbein's eyes widened when he looked down and saw the gleaming barrel of a small revolver.

"Don't open your gap. Move back," the girl ordered.

With her gun, Celia moved Fishbein behind a partition dividing the store. Ed, who had slid into the store while his pregnant wife was ogling the fish, went over to the register and rifled it for fifty dollars. Then, all of a sudden, a woman from the floor above bustled in and asked for Mr. Fishbein. Ed stood there, unsure what to do with this new complication. "What does she want?" Celia asked from behind the partition. The upstairs neighbor, thinking that Celia worked at Fishbein's, asked for a pound of butter. That was enough for Ed. They were robbers, not stock clerks. He pulled out his revolver and leveled it at the woman. "To the rear!" Ed barked at her, and Mrs. Phillips took her place beside Mr. Fishbein. Celia checked with Ed to make certain he'd gotten all the money, and they made ready to leave. Turning to her victims she said, "We're on our way, now," then added threateningly: "If you (pointing to Mrs. Phillips) scream or if you yell (to Fishbein) I'll knock your nut off with a couple of bullets."

On the way out the door Celia had a parting shot for the police. According to a Brooklyn *Citizen* reporter, she said: "Tell the cops, when they get out of their sleep . . . that I didn't have time to scribble a love note for them." She turned to the woman customer and smiled: "I've got a date on for to-night."

◉ 6

There isn't any bobbed-haired bandit. That's only a myth.
—Mayor John F. Hylan, quoted in the *New York Herald*

The reporting of the Tuesday night robbery of Abraham Fishbein's grocery store played up the image of the taunting bandit. The *Brooklyn Citizen*'s headline read BOBBED-HAIRED GUNWOMAN DERIDES POLICE AS SHE ROBS GROCERY. The press developed this tension between the irreverent bandit and the police into a dominant theme. Celia's parting taunt to the police may well have been the creation of an imaginative reporter rather than the actual utterance of a herring-craving bandit. But it didn't matter: conflict between cops and robbers sells papers.

The Cooneys did not leave what the newspapers were now referring to as their "usual note" for the police. The press expected another note, and its absence had to be explained. Noting that "the girl failed to leave behind one of the mocking notes as in the other robberies, the *Brooklyn Standard Union* observed, "All attempts to give a humorous touch to her transgressions against the law were abandoned in this instance. She was just a bandit pure and simple."

Though the Bobbed Haired Bandit hadn't left a note with her latest grocer-victim, the *Standard Union* saw fit to reprint on their front page a taunting note sent to their paper that *might* have been written by her:

To the Editor of the Standard Union:

I must say we have a wonderful police force. They must be all asleep. cold night are best to stick people up. the cops and the bulls have hang outs. and are always in on cold and wet nights. I passed 2 cops and a bull standing on fulton street and Bedford avenue Saturday night. I asked one of them where keeney's theatre was and they directed me. I almost laughed in their face, to think they were talking to the one they are looking for, and can plainly see they are blind or asleep. am leaving this city Thursday for jersey. I think the pickings are better there. you must give me credit. I am tired writing notes. guess I will have them tipe written.

THE BANDIT AND HER PAL.

P. S. — Would call on you for a chat, but am afraid you would hand me over to the bunch of bull cops. they are not clever enough for me. they walk around asleep.

Wrote this in the post office on broadway near roebling st. a cop is writing a card along side of me. he looked at me several times and went out. he to is asleep.

It's unlikely that Celia penned this note. She later denied writing it, but more importantly, it doesn't fit her modus operandi: the note was not dropped at a robbery, and the grammar and spelling are almost artfully tortured. The Bobbed Haired Bandit's celebrity was spawning copy-cat notes as well as crimes.

Even the editors of the *Standard Union* may have recognized this missive as a phony; they quickly dropped this "third" note and picked up on another angle on the cops and robbers contest: the gungirl was taunting the police with the very pattern of the robberies themselves. Out of all the stickups committed by the bandit pair thus far:

> Strangely, it would seem, five of these have been perpetrated in the Atlantic avenue police precinct, within the confines of which live Commissioner Richard E. Enright and Capt. Daniel J. Carey, who is in charge of the detectives of Brooklyn and Queens. In fact, the Enright home is in rather close proximity to the places robbed.

The *Standard Union* was right: Celia and Ed's robbery spree was taking place in Commissioner Enright's backyard, encircling the commissioner's home on Saint Marks Avenue. The pattern was a coincidence. Celia and Ed were actually robbing stores in their *own* backyard. Commissioner Enright just happened to live less than ten blocks away from Celia and Ed's newly furnished duplex on Pacific Street. While this encirclement of Enright's home was by chance, not design, to the press it was another example of the girl bandit getting the commissioner's goat. The papers had succeeded in framing the story as a personal challenge to the police commissioner's competence and manhood.

Commissioner Enright had faced criticism before, and he had demonstrated that he was not afraid to dismiss, demote, transfer, and even indict his subordinates. There were those in the press, however, who believed that Enright's well-publicized housecleaning of the previous couple of weeks had been just a bit of grandstanding for publicity. The *New York Tribune* reported that none of the twelve police inspectors who had been very publicly accused by the commissioner of neglect of duty would be dismissed or even demoted unless it could be proven that the neglect was "glaring and willful." The *Tribune* concluded that the "whole police upheaval was involved with politics." In other words, it was all for show. The commissioner's drastic order "had been developed as a means of giving Mr. Enright, the City Administration and Tammany Hall an alibi for the next State and National campaigns." Enright needed an alibi, the *Tribune* reporter continued, "to meet the accusations that New York City was 'lawless.'"

Confronted with this allegation, as well as the well-publicized exploits of a taunting Bobbed Haired Bandit, Commissioner Enright was reeling. And to make matters worse, his political patron was packing his bags to leave the city.

Mayor John F. Hylan was born in Brooklyn. He was a former railroad motorman with a full head of bright red hair. Hylan had a fondness for populist rhetoric and angry invectives against conspiratorial "interests." His supporters called him "Honest John"; his detractors used words like corrupt, incompetent, stupid, and, more recently, absent.

The mayor had collapsed during his regular jaunt to Saratoga Springs in August of 1923, catching the flu while staying at his summer cottage. (Putting a patriotic spin on the event, Hylan blamed a cold he had caught at President Harding's funeral.) Soon he was diagnosed with influenza, then double pneumonia and pulmonary problems; finally, he was confined by doctors to bed rest in Saratoga. Returning to New York City on crutches, he was still too weak to resume his duties. Fortunately, it was almost time for his annual sojourn to the fashionable winter resort of Palm Beach. So the mayor — on well-publicized doctor's orders — announced that he would finish his convalescence with the other snowbirds in the warm Florida sunshine.

Fortunately for Commissioner Enright, John Hylan was loyal to his friends. On the eve of his departure for Palm Beach, the mayor came to his police commissioner's aid. On January 23, the day after the Fishbein robbery, when New Yorkers were busy reading headlines about the gunmiss's merry career, the *Tribune* published excerpts from a letter written by Hylan for a dinner celebrating Enright's sixth anniversary as the biggest man in blue.

"The office of Police Commissioner of the City of New York is no bed of roses," wrote the mayor. "Thorns are plentifully scattered by those who would like to discharge the incumbent from his berth. The vice, gambling and criminal interests would prefer to have some one in that place who would be amenable to their influence." Mayor

Hylan made it clear who was scattering the thorns for these unnamed "criminal interests":

> It has always seemed to me a very regrettable feature of life in New York that some of the newspapers, as well as individuals high in official place should, consciously or unconsciously, aid in attempts to dislodge a fearless Police Commissioner. The sounding of a hue and cry through the columns of the press, and the mouthings of publicity mongers in legislative halls and elsewhere, while intended to embarrass and possibly remove the Police Commissioner, tend toward the even more serious possibility of creating in the minds of the people the entirely false idea as to the honesty and efficiency of public servants and as to the real plane on which law and order is here maintained.

Hylan's message was clear: the real enemy was bad publicity and a hostile press. Much of the New York City press had it in for Mayor Hylan and his police commissioner. Newspapers are run by wealthy men, and wealthy men have political interests, some of which brought them into conflict with the ex–working class Tammany Democratic mayor and his handpicked commissioner.

Enright agreed: crime was not the problem; the press was. In his introduction to the *Annual Report of the Police Department* of 1924, Commissioner Enright referred to the "perennial, irrepressible attacks of the press" that spread "malicious and designing falsehoods," lamenting the valuable police time "diverted to the dissection of venomous canards." One doesn't need to look far to find evidence of Enright's diversion: a few pages further on in his *Annual Report* are facsimiles of letters of refutation and complaint he wrote to editors of the *Tribune*, *World*, and *Brooklyn Eagle*. The commissioner bore a special grudge against the Brooklyn paper. In twelve closely typed pages, he details and corrects instance after instance of "falsehoods" involving the police department that the *Eagle* had published over a five-month period. This foray into media criticism was not Enright's first. His 1922 report included examples and analysis of editorial cartoons which created, so he claimed, the perception that New York was a "thieves' carnival." In November of 1923, the *Brooklyn Citizen*, a paper that featured holdup after dramatic holdup on its front pages, had criticized

Enright for leaving "on a three weeks vacation to Bermuda leaving the city in a carnival of crime."

The mayor also saw dark designs behind the press coverage his administration had received. In 1923 Hylan had bitterly attacked the New York press at the meetings of the National Editorial Association:

> Newspapers have fallen into the hands of banking groups and are the incessant apologists for their financial backers and so are more prone to pursue corporate favors than public approval. It marks the decadence of independent journalism and the centralization of the power of the press too often in the hands of those who use this power to hoodwink the people they are exploiting.

He singled out the "newspaper grabbag" Frank Munsey, owner of the *Herald* and the *Sun* among other papers, condemning him as a "Republican Wall Street Financier." Hylan attacked all of the major publishers except for one: William Randolph Hearst and his papers, the *American* and *Evening Journal*.

Hylan and Hearst were political allies. Hylan's enemies claimed that the mayor was Hearst's lackey. Both Hearst and Hylan claimed to be men of the people and had a common populist cause: public ownership of utilities and the transit system. (Preservation of the five-cent subway fare was the ex-motorman mayor's political grail.) Hearst had been thwarted in his own race for New York City mayor in 1905, but in a deal with the powerful Democratic Party machinery of Tammany Hall, Hearst backed Hylan's successful run for the office in 1918 and his reelection in 1922. Hylan rewarded his patron by appointing Hearst's wife as chairwoman of the Mayor's Committee on National Defense in 1918. Later that year, in a more surreptitious move, the mayor also did a favor for Hearst's girlfriend, the former Ziegfeld Follies girl and aspiring actress Marion Davies, appointing her father to a city magistrate's job worth a generous annual salary of seven thousand dollars. But the red-haired mayor and the philandering media mogul were more than just political allies. The *Daily News* caught Hylan and Hearst lightheartedly posing in cowboy duds on a dude ranch, and while recuperating down in Palm Beach the mayor was a frequent guest at the Hearst's Florida estate.

William Randolph Hearst used his papers to support his friends.

Publisher William Randolph Hearst (*standing*) and Mayor John F. Hylan dressed as cowboys, *New York Daily News*, July 7, 1924.

The *Journal*'s front page gave the mayor credit for reforming the police: N.Y. POLICE SHAKE-UP DIRECTED BY HYLAN. The accompanying article described a diligent and hands-on mayor directing the police department's "greatest shake-up in its history," while neglecting to mention that Hylan was planning an extended trip to Palm Beach in two weeks' time.

When it came to the question of publicizing the daring crimes of the Bobbed Haired Bandit, however, the *American* and the *Journal* were as vigorous as the other New York newspapers. In fact, it was Hearst's own news syndicate that would later pay for Celia's serial autobiography, and it was the *American* that ran it. There may have been dark forces purposely spreading thorns — even paranoids have enemies — but a better explanation for the "hue and cry" of the newspapers over the latest crime wave and the inability of the commissioner to stop it was that a crime wave made for good news in a competitive market. It was simply too entertaining a story *not* to cover.

"Every now and then there occurs the phenomenon called a crime wave," explained the great muckraking journalist Lincoln Steffens in his 1931 autobiography: "New York has such waves periodically . . . and they sweep over the public and nearly drown the lawyers, judges, preachers and other leading citizens who feel they must explain and cure these extraordinary outbreaks of lawlessness." He then admits: "I enjoy crime waves. I made one once."

Steffens goes on to explain how he once reported on a burglary of a well-known Wall Street broker, which involved the unwitting assistance of a beat officer. It was a good story. So good that Jacob Riis, his friend and fellow journalist at a competing newspaper (as well as author and photographer of *How the Other Half Lives*), was called into his editor's office with the question of why *he* hadn't gotten the story. Riis then went out and found his own burglary to report on. The next day Steffens was called in by his editor, who showed him Riis's copy and demanded that he top it. And so it began, with Steffens and Riis and soon other journalists from other papers scrambling around the city chronicling crimes that had always happened but rarely been reported. Finally, as Steffens tells the story, Police Commissioner Teddy Roosevelt stepped in, showed his friends Steffens and Riis statistics demonstrating no increase in reported crimes, only an increase in newspaper reports of crimes, and asked them to knock off their competition. "Thus the crime wave was ended to the satisfaction of all."

In his letter defending Commissioner Enright, Mayor Hylan resurrected Roosevelt's solution: a dramatic end to these stories about the bold crimes of the Bobbed Haired Bandit could help to dispel the image of New York as the "den of wickedness one would imagine it to be from the stories circulated in some of the metropolitan dailies and copied by the press of the country," and perhaps even begin to restore people's faith in law and order itself.

"There isn't any bobbed-haired bandit. That's only a myth," Mayor Hylan went so far as to proclaim in a later interview in the *Herald*:

> It's mostly newspaper talk; the imagination — and creation — of newspaper writers. True, occasionally a girl may commit a larceny, but there's surely no occasion for the scare heads about girl bandits, nor for moralists to say the town is infested with them.

Rein in the reporters and the problem would disappear. Unfortunately, Hylan didn't have friends like Steffens and Riis, and those friends he had in the newspaper world — like Hearst — were unwilling to risk losing precious readers in a time of cutthroat circulation by passing up stories about this newest female crime wave.

"Scare heads about girl bandits," and sometimes even crime waves themselves, were a product of newspaper writers' imaginations, but there was still a very real girl bandit on the loose, and with Celia and Ed still on the job so were Enright and his police department. By the end of January, Captain John McCloskey, Captain Carey's immediate subordinate and head of all Brooklyn detectives, had assigned every one of his men to the "task of running down the bandit and her companion," the *Standard Union* reported: "In groups of twos and threes the sleuths have virtually patrolled the business section of the precinct searching for the prey that they are confident will eventually be theirs."

But law and order doesn't sell newspapers, crime does, and reported sightings of the bobbed one began to multiply. Any bobbed haired girl who got in a bit of trouble made the headlines of the papers, like this smattering from January 25th:

BOBBED HAIRED GIRL FIGHTS DETECTIVES ON BUS

NEW BOBBED-HAIR BANDIT MAULS MAN

NEW GIRL BANDIT, A BLONDE,
HELPS KIDNAP TRUCKLOAD OF
SUGAR; TWITS CHAUFFEUR

Standard Union columnist Tom W. Jackson noted sardonically that "the Bobbed Haired Girl Bandit appears to be one of the features of the permanent crime wave." A new genre or subcategory of crime — or at least crime reporting — seemed to be blossoming: the bobbed-haired crime beat.

◉ 7

BOBBED HAIR IN TROUBLE —*New York American*

For twelve days after the stickup at Fishbein's grocery, Celia and Edward Cooney lay low. In Washington, Woodrow Wilson was dying, and the press kept New Yorkers posted on his slow decline. Also in the news from the capitol was the political corruption that followed Wilson under the Harding and Coolidge administrations. The Bobbed Haired Bandit stepped back onto the front pages on February 3rd:

"BOBBED HAIR" GIRL BANDIT IS AGAIN ON JOB

The bobbed-hair girl bandit came back last night and added another cleverly-executed "stickup" to her lengthening list. And at last reports, the police, like the villain in the ancient melodrama, still pursued her.

It was Saturday night in the H. C. Bohack chain store at 320 Lafayette Avenue. There were four or five clerks and three customers in the combination butcher shop and grocery. "Just at 10 o'clock a pretty girl, wearing a sealskin coat and a saucy turban trimmed with fur sauntered in." During a lull in business, the bobbed haired girl approached the counter where Peter Kossman, the head butcher, stood.

She asked for a chicken. Mr. Kossman "smiled engagingly. 'Nice chicken. Certainly.'" He entered the refrigerator to fetch the order. The *Standard Union* reported:

> As he turned to get the bird, the young woman shoved a revolver against his ribs.
>
> "One peep and you're a dead butcher," she said.

In the *Telegram and Evening Mail*, Kossman was still holding the cold chicken when he turned to find "himself gazing into the muzzle of a very convincing pistol."

> "Get 'em up!" the girl commanded. Peter "got 'em up." The chicken dropped with a thud.
>
> The girl whistled. The tall, well dressed young man, who is inevitably present whenever the girl bandit decides to do something, entered, a revolver in his hand. Flourishing it, he backed the clerks — four of them — and the customers — three in number — to the rear of the store.

Celia held a gun on the clerks and customers while Ed opened the registers, pulled out one hundred fifty dollars, and stuffed them in his pockets. Threatening to shoot anyone who made a move on them or cried out to the police, the couple backed out of the store and leaped into the Ford waiting outside. Ed threw it into gear and stepped on the gas. The people in the store rushed to the window and watched the bandits as they sped down Grand Avenue in the "flivver." "Police were on the scene in a few minutes in a high-powered automobile and 'mopped up' the neighborhood carefully, but the bandits had left no trace."

Four days later, on a rainy Wednesday morning, New Yorkers awoke to the "muffled boom of guns sounding faintly though the winter haze from the coast defenses." Woodrow Wilson had died. At three-thirty precisely, all business in Washington and New York was to come to a halt. Telephone and telegraph instruments were to be stopped, the stores closed, and trolley cars halted; pedestrians were to stand bareheaded, and "drivers of taxicabs [were] to stop their cars, shut off their engines, alight and stand at attention for two minutes."

All of the solemn stoppages for a fallen president did not slow the police in their hunt for the girl bandit. These national stories of oil scandals and mourning had to share the front page with the news that the police had made dramatic progress in their fight against crime. In addition to posting plainclothesmen around stores that might interest the pair, the department had embarked on a series of raids all across the borough to capture the elusive bandit. This "Brooklyn Gunmiss Hunt," as the *Daily News* named it, netted not one but two suspects in the girl bandit case.

The first suspect was a young, dark-haired woman by the name of Mary Cody who was keeping house for her boyfriend and two stickup men. Besides her company, the only thing connecting Cody to the Bobbed Haired Bandit was her sex, a sealskin coat, and a cerise hat. When the bobbed bandit's victims failed to identify her, Enright's men had to release her.

It was another sealskin coat and pink hat that helped to land a second young woman — a teenager named Rose Moore — in jail that very same day. Rose had been picked up by a Brooklyn detective working the street on a tip. She was wearing all the trappings of the girl bandit, and, more damning, she resembled a photograph that had been posted at the precinct. The detective, the *Eagle* reported, was "satisfied in his own mind that Rose Moore and the notorious bobbed-haired bandit, wily and defiant, [were] one and the same."

Rose Moore *did* resemble the picture hanging in every New York precinct house. No surprise: it was her picture. Rose was a runaway teenager from Canarsie whose relatives had given the police a photograph that was then distributed to every precinct in the city with a request to "pick her up on sight." It was bad luck for Rose that Leo Weinstein, the druggist from the Ryerson Street robbery, had seen the picture of the missing girl earlier and commented to the police that she resembled the famous Bobbed Haired Bandit.

The suspect was taken to the Poplar Street headquarters "for a more thorough grilling" by the captain of detectives, Daniel Carey himself. A squad of detectives was immediately dispatched to round up robber victims for a lineup.

Unfortunately for Carey, this girl, like the others before her, was not the one. When she stood in the lineup on Poplar Street the eyewitnesses rounded up by the detectives failed to finger her. Benjamin

Jospey, the drugstore owner from the New York Avenue robbery, was the one exception. He thought she might be the girl bandit, but this lone identification didn't satisfy the detective captain, and he let young Rose go home.

"The young woman," the *Brooklyn Eagle* observed, "was a victim of the close surveillance the police have been exercising over bob-haired girls out without an escort." Given that the Bobbed Haired Bandit had always been spotted *with* a male escort, the police surveillance of girls without escorts seems—at face value—a bit curious. But the furor over the girl bandit was never just about Celia; it was also about a generalized fear of female independence. After Rose was released into the custody of her family, her brother had this analysis of her ordeal:

BAD, BOLD, BOBHAIRED BANDITS ARE ABROAD IN THE LAND THIS SPRING. DON'T LET THEM GET YOU,

> As Capt. Carey told me, any girl on the street after twelve o'clock is being watched with suspicion now, and it's a good time for girls to stay home, where they belong. No bob-haired girl on the streets at night is safe from suspicion. My sister is young and likes a good time, and I owe it to her to make it clear

A. Russell, "Character Sketches," *Brooklyn Daily Times*, May 4, 1924.

that I, not the police, was searching for her. She's safe at home and this will be a little lesson to her to stay there.

In the dark, a bobbed haired miss was at the very least a potential delinquent, if not the gungirl herself. Rose's brother told her story as a cautionary tale: good girls stayed home, safe from suspicion; girl bandits, in contrast, did not.

◉ 8

FORGET SEX—SHOOT!   —*Brooklyn Eagle*

Benjamin Jospey was seeing more than his share of Bobbed Haired Bandits. He thought he had gotten a good look at her when Celia robbed his drugstore on January 20th. Then, three weeks later, he saw the gungirl again, picking Rose Moore out of a lineup at Brooklyn Police headquarters. The druggist didn't have long to wait for another sighting. The very night of Rose's lineup a bobbed haired bandit robbed poor Jospey again:

> As if to chide Brooklyn police for their mistaken statements yesterday that they had captured the borough's famous gunmiss, that mysterious individual last night participated in the holdup of the drug store of Benjamin Jospey. . . . It was her second looting of the store.

The girl bandit was AGAIN BUSY IN BROOKLYN.

It was around eleven o'clock in the evening, just before closing, and there were only two people left in Jospey's drugstore, the proprietor himself and Benjamin Weiss, a salesman who lived around the corner. The druggist's mother was not waiting in the back for her son to close up this time. Jospey and Weiss were chatting quietly at the end of the counter when the door opened, and "a short nattily dressed youth entered. He asked for a cake of soap." When Jospey went behind the counter to get the soap, two other young men walked in "and the druggist turned to find himself staring into the muzzles of two revolvers."

The armed trio forced Jospey and Weiss to the rear room, the very "same room in which Jospey and his aged mother were held at the point of a gun by the girl bandit" three weeks before. The male bandits emptied the register and the pockets of the two men:

> Warning the victims that they would be shot to death if they made an outcry, the three bandits backed toward the door and the street. On Union Street, close to the curb, stood a small automobile with engine running, bending over the wheel and looking eagerly toward the drug store was a young girl, with black bobbed hair. Her sealskin coat was thrown up to muffle her face almost to the eyes. On her head, saucily set, was a tam-'o-shanter.
>
> A moment later the bandit quartette was whirring down the street in an automobile which had been awaiting them, and Jospey was excitedly telephoning the police, with some heated observations as to their sleuthing ability and the protection accorded honest druggists.

The following morning the newspapers were abuzz with the story that the Bobbed Haired Bandit had made good on the threats leveled in her first note, fulfilling her promise to return to the stores that she had robbed earlier. "Girl Hold Up Artist Keeps Return Date to Rob Brooklyn Drug Store," the *American* reported. The *Post* explained that the gungirl "returned last night and robbed a store as she promised to do when she held it up the first time three weeks ago." The press coverage dramatized the episode as a bit of swashbuckling bravado. According to the *American*, this was "one more example of the audacity and versatility" of the Bobbed Haired Bandit.

There was only one problem with this stirring story. Celia and Ed had never promised to rob Jospey a second time. The note the newspapers were referring to was the one that Celia and Ed had left during the Weinstein robbery on January 15th. In that note the couple threatened to return to rob the manager of the Roulston chain store, who gave them checks that they couldn't cash, and the Bohack's on Brooklyn Avenue, where they claimed to have broken a perfectly good automatic on the cash drawer. But no mention was made of Jospey. There was a good reason for that: they wouldn't rob the luckless Jospey until five days *after* leaving the note swearing revenge on the others. The competitive New York press were not about to let facts stand in the way of a dramatic hook for the story.

There were other discrepancies in this crime to overcome as well: if this was the real Bobbed Haired Bandit, then why was she driving the getaway car and not holding a gun? The *American* printed a novel explanation: she was doing it for professional development. "This time," the reporter explained, "she did not wield the revolver, but as if to display her proficiency in all branches of the hold up profession, contented herself with remaining as 'lookout' outside." With this latest robbery, the now gun-less girl qualified as a bandit "expert" because "her experience as a 'lookout' last night served to demonstrate that she has attained full graduation in metropolitan banditry."

On top of this, the *American*, in a jab at the police, ascribed an ulterior motive to the robbery. The bandit girl was sending yet another message to her bumbling pursuers: "To deride the police for their inability to catch her she took part in her latest robbery but a few hours after detectives said they felt sure that one of the two young women they had arrested must be the 'bobbed haired bandit.'" The reporter snidely added that the police were finally "convinced last night that they were *somewhat* in error."

The woman who helped rob the Jospey drugstore the second time around was not Celia Cooney. She was just a lookout for another band of Brooklyn stickup men. But for the police, the press, and the public the Bobbed Haired Bandit had struck again.

Back at the Poplar Street headquarters, the *Herald* announced, the BOBBED HAIRED BANDIT WORRIES DETECTIVES. The paper was quick to rub it in:

> The Sheriff of Nottingham had no more worries than the police at
> headquarters in Brooklyn. The mysterious bobbed-haired Robin Hood,
> or Dick Turpin, or whoever she may be the reincarnation of still eludes
> capture and continues to rob, always accompanied by her tall
> companion.

According to the *Herald*, the police resented these attacks on their abilities and "hoped to capture the romantic couple within twenty-four hours." New tactics were required: "Boarding houses have been requested to watch suspicious clients who stay in all day and go out all night. All bobbed haired girls in automobiles should be noted, together with the license plate of the car." In addition, "young married couples who suggest the bobbed haired robber and her six foot accomplice" should also be "scrutinized." Driving while bobbed was now officially suspicious.

As the man in charge of all the detectives in Brooklyn and Queens, Captain Carey was forced to explain why the police had been unable to apprehend this Robin Hood in skirts. "One reason we haven't caught her," Carey explained, "is that we have an insufficient number of uniformed policemen to patrol the streets of Brooklyn." Carey gave another reporter another reason: "She has taken care not to leave fingerprints or to remain long enough to permit victims to recover from their surprise and fright sufficiently to retain a good description of her." After interviewing several police sources, a writer for the *Brooklyn Citizen* noted that "she has eluded police traps and police bait with consummate ease" and concluded: "The fact is being borne in upon them that they are opposing a super-criminal." The police themselves were building up the Bobbed Haired Bandit's reputation as a way of salvaging their own.

As Celia's reputation increased, the reputation of the police department suffered. In order to stem the criticism and humiliation, Enright announced he would personally take charge of the investigation. The *Brooklyn Standard Union* dramatically set the scene of the duel between the commissioner and the bandit:

> Police Commissioner Richard E. Enright is going to match wits with Brooklyn's will-o'-the-wisp bobbed haired girl bandit. Where others have failed he will now try his hand at the effort to land her behind bars.
>
> It became known to-day that Commissioner Enright has taken personal charge of the pursuit of the romantic, but nevertheless thoroughly adept and daring highwaywoman. He has become aroused, apparently, by her taunts and mockery over the futile efforts to capture her.

That Saturday morning, February 9th, the aroused Enright began his campaign by calling a "special headquarters conclave" of every detective in the department. One hundred fifty first-grade detectives arrived at police headquarters at ten in the morning, and seven hundred second-grade detectives followed at half-past noon. This secret assembly of the detective division established a "precedent in the annals of police history," according to the *Brooklyn Eagle*. Although Enright kept the proceedings of his meeting hushed up, hundreds of ears meant that word soon leaked out to the press. The commissioner complained that there had been more crime during the month of January 1924 than in any other month of his tenure: "There is entirely too much crime and it has to be stopped." There was also one criminal singled out by name; the assembled detectives were read the riot act over their failure and were told that their "first order of business" was to catch the Bobbed Haired Bandit.

SHAKEUP SEEN FOR DETECTIVES OF BROOKLYN reported the *Citizen*, and one of the ways that Enright planned to "shake up" his detectives was to dangle the threat of their replacement. The commissioner was reported to have brought in one hundred fifty new detectives, "fresh from training school, where they have been thoroughly initiated into the methods of hunting criminals," and given these "school detectives" the opportunity to work on the case, while busting many of the old-timers back to street duty in uniform. In other words, it wouldn't just be top brass inspectors who were disciplined this time around. According to one detective, unless "some results are shown in the immediate future every precinct in Brooklyn will be cleaned out, and done thoroughly."

It was Dan Carey's job to carry out the commissioner's directive. That very evening the detective captain marshaled his troops. He sent them out to get the gungirl with the following (no doubt, dramatized) command:

"Get the bobbed hair girl bandit."

"Get her — dead or alive."

"Shoot, and shoot to kill. Don't hesitate, and shoot straight at the first sign of resistance. It may be your life or hers."

The *Brooklyn Eagle*'s headline trumpeted FORGET SEX — SHOOT! ORDER IN NEW WAR ON GIRL BANDIT. "The sex of this bobbed haired bandit be forgotten," Carey went on to say. "If occasion arises, shoot her! Shoot her as quickly as you would any dope-saturated gunman; she is just as dangerous, probably more so!"

The police mobilization that Saturday night was dramatic. In addition to the two hundred fifty plainclothes detectives ordered onto the streets of Brooklyn, there was the regular force of patrolmen beefed up with new probationary officers from the headquarters training school. The one hundred fifty new recruits from the detective school also provided fresh blood. They were "ambitious, every one of them, and the bobbed haired bandit will have to elude an extra 150 pairs of unusually searching eyes to-night."

The Atlantic Avenue precinct, in the vicinity of which most of the bandit's raids occurred, was packed with plainclothesmen who "loitered in convenient areaways and at nearby corners until the last bolt of each establishment was shot." And there they stayed until the chain stores closed at eleven, some lurking in all-night cigar stores until dawn. On top of all the manpower, "a fleet of high-powered automobiles were waiting at precinct stations and various strategic places in the borough — all after one little girl bandit with bobbed hair."

The maneuver was a decisive failure. All of Enright's detectives, schooled and unschooled, and even the fleet of fast cars did not deter Brooklyn's bandits that evening.

As the *Brooklyn Standard Union* described it the next day:

"SHOOT TO KILL" EDICT FAILS;
GIRL BANDIT STRIKES AGAIN

With two hundred and fifty detectives under orders to shoot her on sight — and shoot to kill — Brooklyn's bobbed-haired girl bandit emerged from hiding last night and once again figured in the holdup and robbery of a chain store.

A girl bandit had stuck up a chain store. But which bandit was it? The press had made up their mind. The *New York Herald* subhead read "Bobbed Hair Girl Eludes 500 Police in New Robbery." This time "the victim of the girl bandit" was the manager of another Roulston chain store located on Fulton Street and Carlton Avenue in Brooklyn. Just before closing, two men with guns entered the grocery "and drawing guns forced him to throw up his hands." They stole three hundred dollars from the register and backed out of the store, "revolvers in their hands." According to witnesses, "the men jumped into the car and the girl laughed as she put on the speed and darted away." A dozen policemen sped to the scene in just a few minutes, but no trace of the car or the bandit crew was to be found.

Here was an image certain to arouse Enright: a woman at the wheel of a "red sedan" speeding from the scene of a crime, laughing as she darted away through the dark streets of Brooklyn with an army of police on her tail. Under the headline BOB HAIR GIRL BUSY, the *Brooklyn Standard Union* reported that the holdup "became public much to the consternation of the sleuths" who had been warned earlier that every precinct would be cleaned out, unless the "criminal element was driven out." Well, the criminal element did drive away, but that is not at all what Enright and Casey had intended.

The bad press did not let up for a week. On Thursday, the 14th of February, the *Brooklyn Standard Union* printed a front-page headline announcing CRIME WAVE RAMPANT. The "Latest Outbreak of Stick-Ups Alarms Public," the headline writer claimed, as these robberies were "more brazen than in the past" and the "ease with which thugs have been holding up storekeepers and getting away with it is undermining confidence in the police."

Was there really a crime wave? Or was it all, to use that phrase of Mayor Hylan's, "mostly newspaper talk"? The record is unclear. While it was reported that Enright was concerned about a crime spike in January, he also insisted elsewhere that crime was on the decrease overall. At the beginning of the year, the administration-friendly *Evening Journal* carried the commissioner's claim of a forty percent cut in crime in New York City over the past decade. And at the end of 1924, in the Police Department's *Annual Report*, the commissioner trotted out arrest records to demonstrate a further decrease in most categories of major crimes between 1923 and 1924. But these were police reports and, even then, reports based only on arrests, so it's hard to know for sure whether crime was on the decrease or increase. However, ever since the 1830s, when the *New York Sun*'s founding editor, Benjamin Day, hired an unemployed printer named George Wisner as the first full-time reporter and sent him off to record the drama of the New York police court, it's been understood that crime sells newspapers.

On the same day that the *Standard Union* declared a rampant crime wave, newsboys were shouting out the story of "two middle-aged women with bobbed hair and revolvers" who held up a furrier on Flatbush, threatening to "plug him" if he made a "false move." They escaped with cash, the furrier's ring, and two fur coats, one of them a pricey Hudson seal, the same coat that all the bobbed haired bandits were wearing this season. The furrier, it was reported, was dumbstruck by the appearance of two women bandits in the flesh; he had also been "cautious enough, about two months ago . . . to take out hold-up insurance for he feared that some of the bobbed-haired bandit sisterhood would visit him and he wanted to protect himself."

In the midst of this paper crime wave, the real Bobbed Haired Bandit had dropped out of sight. While the press attributed as many crimes as they could to the Bobbed Haired Bandit in order to keep a successful story going, they also seemed aware that there was only one genuine article and that she had not struck for weeks. On Saturday, February 16th, two weeks after Celia and Ed Cooney had robbed the Bohack store on Lafayette, the *New York Evening Post* seemed almost concerned about this:

> Has that phantom-like young adventuress who stole her way into the police records as the "Bobbed Hair Bandit" tossed her trusty pistol into her work basket and decided to take a vacation with her "tall" companion?

Was she "retired" or "only resting"? It was a "new mystery," wrote the *Post*.

The "rumor factory ground out so many stories" about the girl bandit that the *Post* sent a reporter to ask Captain Daniel Carey for the facts. "There has been much written and said about this so-called 'Bobbed Haired Bandit' that is without foundation," the captain insisted, saying little else.

The *New York Telegram and Evening Mail* sent their reporter Elizabeth Smith to Captain Carey to get more answers about the girl bandit. Women reporters, especially those covering crime stories, were uncommon in the 1920s. But the gender angle of the Bobbed Haired Bandit story opened up opportunities for a few women like Smith who might otherwise be sequestered to the society pages. Smith's sex also got her name on the byline — men reporters, as a rule, remained anonymous.

Faced with this female rarity, the captain was polite but again not responsive. Smith came away from her mostly one-sided interview convinced that the police were not willing to admit the magnitude of their problem. "When the police of Brooklyn had only the male sex to keep in the strait and narrow path of the law," the *Telegram* reporter wrote, "they had it comparatively easy sailing. Now it's different." This woman bandit had the "Brooklyn boys of brass and blue . . . running in circles":

> And do the Brooklyn police admit it?
>
> They do not, and thereby hangs a story.
>
> According to their tale, all Brooklyn bobbed girls are as innocent as a cup custard.
>
> Their story is that no Brooklyn girl would carry a gun any more than a Follies girl would carry a lipstick.
>
> In their opinion, it's as obvious as an Elks watch chain that it's all a hatched up story about Brooklyn's girl bandit, anyway, and those who spread the tale are only seeking to injure the reputation of Manhattan's perfectly respectable country cousin across the bridge.

Smith asked Carey a lot of questions about the girl bandit, for "all the good it did." Captain Carey had little to offer on that particular topic, but he did hand the reporter "an official typewritten account of the confession" of a young holdup man. She read it. The confession contained not a word about bobbed haired girls. Smith was puzzled. Carey then explained its importance. In his confession, the gunman said "he'd been reading how easy it was to stick up people. He had read it in the newspapers."

This was the detective captain's justification for not discussing the girl bandit's exploits with a newspaper reporter: "No girl would get any feminine bandit ideas from reading interviews with Captain Carey if he could prevent it." Carey then clammed up and passed the reporter off to another officer, who passed her off to still another. Smith gave up. If the police would not provide her with the facts, she could always do exactly what Carey feared and fill her newspaper column with speculation:

> In the meantime, Princess Paprika — for such might be the name of the bobbed hair one — is doubtless chuckling over the hold-ups in which she had taken part. . . .

Princess Paprika of the bobbed locks has been described as dark and light; short and tall; as wearing a sealskin and a plush coat; as wearing a turban and a tam 'o shanter.

Who she is, or why she is, none knows.

It may be that she is some brave daring soul whose sense of adventure could not be satisfied with merely lighting the breakfast fire with kerosene each of the seven mornings. It may be she is purely and cussedly bent on deviltry.

At any rate, she is, in the patois of the proletariat, some girl, even if the Brooklyn police don't know much about her.

Although written as entertainment rather than analysis, Elizabeth Smith's light-hearted piece was one of a number of newspaper stories that opened up the topic of Celia's character in mid-February. Was she an adventurous soul? Was she bent on deviltry? What were her motives for these crimes? This speculation as to who the Bobbed Haired Bandit really was became a crucial element of Celia's newspaper coverage in the weeks and months that followed, allowing her to become — even if often only through a reporter's imagination — a sympathetic character; in Smith's words: "some girl."

Tom W. Jackson also lauded the girl bandit in his wry "Periscope" column for the *Standard Union*:

STILL ON THE JOB

Yes, I've got to hand it
To the Bobbed Haired Bandit.
Said druggist in his store
And right on the spot
Oh I would be shot
Once, or twice, maybe more.

I, too, must hand it
To the Bobbed Haired bandit,
Chain store grocer said —
For she has a gun
And it is no fun,
To be filled up with lead.

> We'd like to hand it
> To the Bobbed Haired Bandit
> Enright Detectives say—
> But she of the bob.
> Is still on the job
> And laughs at the cops all day.

The flip side to this complimentary character development of the Bobbed Haired Bandit was the denigration of the police force. Lacking any new information about Brooklyn's girl bandit, the newspapers lambasted Enright and the force for any old stickup that happened in the borough. The *Brooklyn Eagle* was a vocal critic of Mayor Hylan and his police commissioner. The Sunday *Eagle* published a day-by-day list of fifty-seven "crimes of violence," including murders, stabbings, affrays, and holdups, that had been committed during the preceding two weeks in Brooklyn, providing a blow-by-blow account of what they too were calling "a carnival of crime." The *Eagle* even claimed that their figure was actually too small because it did not include "numerous crimes, news of which has been suppressed on order of Police Commissioner Enright." The commissioner now stood accused of conspiring to keep the public from knowing the extent of the crime wave sweeping Brooklyn and the rest of the city.

An *Eagle* cartoon showed a towering list of holdups and burglaries dwarfing the city skyline like a skyscraper of felonies. It was not just the number of violent incidents that troubled the *Eagle*; this "epidemic of thievery" was a sign of an anarchic collapse of respect for legal authority in the city. While Enright would blame the press for creating this climate of disrespect for authority, the press turned the blame back on the police force. Adding insult to injury, the *Eagle* went on:

> Not only do the crooks operate with an almost unrestricted freedom but they have fallen into the habit of jeering at the police by kidding telephone calls and insulting messages left at the scene of operation. . . .
>
> It is a standing joke in Flatbush that the natives of that section should appeal to the Governor to post a guard of State Militia around the police station for fear some enterprising gangsters should be seized with a sudden desire to haul it away.

The newspaper demanded a response from the police department. New York's newspaper readers did not have to wait long for results. The raids began that very evening.

The dragnet yielded quite an unsavory catch in the early morning hours of February 18, "including 32 of the worst desperadoes known to the New York police." The roundup was run from the top of the police department. Enright's Deputy Police Commissioner John Daly, in charge of Brooklyn, Queens, and Staten Island, came to the big trial room at Brooklyn headquarters to watch the lineups. Witnesses were collected and brought to Poplar Street. All of Daly's inspectors, captains, and acting captains were assembled there to watch the detectives question the prisoners and put them through their paces in front of the eyewitnesses. The *Eagle* described the scene:

> Squads of self-confessed thieves were lined up and their victims walked before them. Some of the complainants were too much under fear of the thieves to make an identification. One man who had been robbed walked the entire line and then declared to the detective who had charge of him that he could not pick out any in the group who had robbed him.
>
> "Try again," he was told.
>
> Again he walked past the line, and again he nodded a negative to the observing officer.
>
> "Why," exclaimed one of the prisoners, "that's one of my men. I stuck him up in Queens."
>
> "Oh, yes," returned the shy one, "I remember you now."

"The matter of identification was a bit difficult," the *Eagle* also reported, "for some of the prisoners had been subjected to the 'third degree' and were scarcely fit for exhibition."

Thirteen prisoners were paraded in the lineups that day at the Poplar Street headquarters. They represented five or six different holdup gangs, "all young men, and all of whom had some confession of banditry to make when questioned." No doubt the "third degree" helped loosen their lips. The police believed that these gangs were responsible "for at least 90 percent of the stick-ups that have been continuing daily in Brooklyn for months." According to the *Eagle*, "Acting Capt. Daniel Carey looked on them with satisfaction, for he believed that the round-up would put a stop to a major portion of his daily worries."

But the police were not taking any chances, and the "bandit roundups" continued as the detectives scoured Brooklyn for suspected holdup men for a second day. One of the suspects netted this time around was charged with robbing a drugstore just a block away from the Grand Street police station. He may have been stupid, but he did have a bit of style: on his way out the door with the money, the bandit turned to the proprietor and doffed his cap saying, "See, I've got red hair, I'm the pal of the 'bobbed-haired' bandit, she is waiting for me outside." This bit of showmanship may have cost him his freedom, for not an hour later a clerk from the store recognized him as he stood on a nearby corner, and he was arrested.

The very next day another mass lineup was held on Poplar Street. This time twenty-seven suspects were led before more than forty witnesses. Two of the suspects were women who had the misfortune of being married to two of the alleged criminals swept up in the early morning raids.

The first, Mrs. Lillie Licausi, a "beautiful young woman," was arrested in possession of a gun, which she carried for her husband Louis Licausi. Women carrying guns for their bandit men were a tradition in the city where a man was much more likely to be stopped and searched on the street than a woman. To act as a lookout and transport the guns was the traditional subordinate role that a gun moll played in gang life. Fortunately for Mrs. Licausi, she had long hair.

The second female suspect swept up seemed to better fit the description of Brooklyn's girl bandit. Her name was Jean Scharfman, she was twenty-one, and she was picked up with her husband, John, "known to the police as 'Detroit Red.'" Suspects detained in the previous day's sweep fingered the bobbed haired Mrs. Scharfman as the driver for a gang that "frisked the occupants" of Bill Yarrington's saloon at the corner of Albany and Atlantic.

Jean Scharfman worked in a shirtwaist factory. She and her husband were taken from their furnished room on South Ninth Street and subjected to an "all-night grilling." The latest bobbed-hair prisoner indignantly denied that she "ever ran an automobile" or that her husband owned or drove one. There was "nothing in her life," she stated, "to justify the police in arresting her."

Scharfman's denial did not satisfy Detective Captain Carey. He had her paraded before witnesses who had seen the Bobbed Haired Bandit. Leo Weinstein and his clerks "looked long and hard at her" but could not identify her as the bandit who left a note after robbing his drugstore. Benjamin Jospey, the irate druggist from New York Avenue who'd seen far too many bobbed haired bandits already, could only shake his head and tell the detectives that he did not recognize her. Despite the fact that Carey could not connect Jean Scharfman to any of the Bobbed Haired Bandit's robberies, he was reluctant to release her, so he had her locked up on a charge of assault and robbery until more witnesses could be summoned to headquarters. Meanwhile, Helen Quigley, the "bobbed haired bandit" pinched by Enright's cops after being fingered by a worked-over Vincent "Apples" Kovaleski, still languished in jail unable to raise her twenty-thousand-dollar bail.

"The challenge of the bob-haired bandit was accepted by Police Commissioner Enright," the *Post* reported, describing the most recent sweeps as the latest move in Enright's contest with the Bobbed Haired Bandit after she had "defied his detectives." And even though the dragnet hadn't snared the famous gungirl, the police optimistically "asserted they had come closer to the flying skirts of Brooklyn's bob-haired bandit than at any time since the young woman and a half dozen imitators began to terrorize small shopkeepers nearly two months ago." This was wishful thinking. The new wave of sweeps, crackdowns, and lockups had brought Enright's men no closer to the "phantom-like young adventuress."

PART III

Mystery of the Bobbed Haired Bandit

This faceless figure illustrated George Spelvin's "The Mystery of the Bobbed-Haired Bandit," *True Detective Mysteries*, May 1924.

9

THE MYSTERY OF THE BOBBED-HAIRED BANDIT
For daring banditry this unknown girl rivals the sensational villainy of Eighteenth Century road agents. Who is
she? Why does she taunt police? Is she twins? Is she an
organization of bobbed-haired girls? Is she a man in
disguise?   —George Spelvin, *True Detective Mysteries*

While Enright was trying to shut down the city's carnival
of crime, press speculation on the nature of the Brooklyn's own criminal ringmistress continued to open up. The questions of who she was
and what type of a person she was made news at a time when the gungirl herself—apparently on vacation—did not.

BOBBED-HAIR GIRL BANDIT KEEPS THE TOWN GUESSING announced the headline of the *Brooklyn Standard Union* on February
11th, more than a week after her last robbery. Asking, "What type of
individual is the elusive bobbed-haired girl bandit?" the writer
continued:

> Is she a young woman of refinement who has been reared in a good en-
> vironment who is merely committing the depredations for the thrill and
> excitement to be obtained by this type of outwitting the police?
>
> Is she the type to be found among habitués of cheap dance halls and
> cabarets, ever seeking good clothes and so-called amusement?
>
> Is she a girl addicted to the use of drugs, or is it that she is in love with
> her tall male companion in crime and the latter has her under his con-
> trol, influencing her by some mysterious hypnotic power to do his
> bidding?

Seeking answers, or at least some titillating speculations, a reporter
for the *Standard Union* interviewed a number of detectives to learn
their "personal opinions of the girl." Most of them agreed on one
point: she *must* be addicted to drugs. The detectives said they could
not conceive that a young woman, "no matter what the environment
in which she was reared," could commit holdups in such a "brazen
manner, displaying unlimited courage and carrying out her plans

calmly and coolly," knowing all the time that the police were hunting her down, without some sort of narcotic assistance. One detective's response to the question "What type of individual is this girl?" was quoted at length:

> It is my honest opinion that she is a coke fiend and we will have a great deal of trouble taking her. . . . You know this girl has shown more grit than our boldest hold-up men of the past. . . . It is my personal opinion that the "cop" who gets her will have to either get a good drop on her, or wound or kill her, before she will submit to arrest.

Detectives were not the only experts in crime consulted. A later item in the *New York World* asked the opinions of a "Reformed Underworld Leader," luring readers in with cryptic references to a "Strange Phase of Modern Feminism" and an illustration of a flapper bandit, complete with a cutaway to show the hidden automatic she has stored under her coat in a ruffle around her waist. One ex-gangster told the *World* that there are many bobbed haired bandits out there and there always have been. They start out as gangsters' girlfriends: holding their "gats" as a "gun-toter," acting as lookouts, or driving getaway cars—always taking the orders of their male "general." But then, he explained, the female sidekick gets crossed:

> She has been promised a percentage, plus everything from new shoes to a new evening gown, swell times and automobile rides. She gets the promise, and that's about all. . . .
>
> Slowly but surely these girls learn how the jobs are done. The girl who has been double-crossed is out for revenge. She wants to show that she can pull off a job too. She has graduated from being a girl bandit who has been "bobbed" time and again into a bob-haired bandit.
>
> Now, instead of standing lookout for a male companion, she has them stand lookout while she does the job. She is going to be sure that what she gets is HERS!

Another thug, "a formerly well-known member of underworld gangs in the west side," had a different take. Dismissing the explanation that hell hath no fury like a woman scorned, he explained that the volatile mix of poverty, fashion, and consumerism were to blame. "I am positive," he asserted, that

The GUN
IS IN A POCKET
of The DRESS
CONCEALED by
A RUFFLE
AROUND The
WAISTLINE
WHICH HANGS
DOWN OVER
The POCKET.
+
The GUN
IS ALWAYS
DRAWN with
The RIGHT
HAND from
The LEFT
SIDE

SKETCH SHOWING HOW BOB-HAIRED BANDIT
CARRIES HER WEAPON

"Sketch Showing How Bob-Haired Bandit Carries Her Weapon," *New York World*,
April 13, 1924.

the bob-haired bandits are all poor girls. They would like to make an honest dollar, but they can't get jobs. Result, no new dresses like their friends have who are working. . . . She does not go out to kill, although she gets a revolver. She goes out to get enough to buy a new dress.

Still more frightening than the figure of a feminist coke addict seeking revenge or just an out-of-work girl looking for a new frock was the idea that the Bobbed Haired Bandit could be invisible: look like us, talk like us, and walk among us without our knowledge. For this theory the *World* reporter left the underworld and returned to the law. An unnamed police source (possibly Captain Carey) posited: "She is a female Dr. Jekyll and Mr. Hyde, a stenographer meekly taking dictation by day and a bandit giving orders, pistol in hand, by night." The anonymous source explained his reasoning: the notes the Bobbed Haired Bandit had left for the police seemed deliberately misspelled, "the work of an educated woman trying to simulate ignorance." This theory may have resonated with a male readership that feared that their own wives and daughters, or stenographers and secretaries, possessed secret lives and secret thoughts residing just below the surface of traditional subservience.

The Bobbed Haired Bandit's bold actions and independent character didn't jibe with traditional notions of feminine passivity. Therefore, a more radical explanation was floated to explain the character of the gungirl. *She wasn't a girl at all.* After all, how could a member of "the weaker sex" take charge, intimidate men, and cuss like a sailor? Rumors were circulating. The *Brooklyn Eagle* addressed the question directly: could the Bobbed Haired Bandit be a man?

The enigma of the hour in the Police Department is: Who is the bobbed-hair bandit who pens such defiant and sarcastic notes to the police after a holdup, who wields a gun with the easy nonchalance which another woman displays in using a knitting needle?

The latest suggestion, one that the police have devoted more than a little attention to, is that the pert bandit with the black half-portion hair is not a girl at all but a young man masquerading in girl's clothing.

In support of this theory it is recalled that in a recent instance in the West a bandit persistently reported as a girl turned out on apprehension to be a man. It would be comparatively easy for a slimly built youth to successfully counterfeit a girl and a sealskin coat might readily be stowed away in the tonneau of the bandit car to be slipped over the shoulders as the occasion required.

The *Eagle*, however, also had reservations about this theory and offered "evidence" that the Bobbed Haired Bandit was all woman after all:

HER FEET ARE FEMININE.

[The police] have threshed over at length the possibility that the evasive letter writer may be a cleverly disguised man, but it sticks in their memory that certain women witnesses who have seen her describe the bandit's feet and shoes as typically feminine and her walk as characteristic of the weaker sex.

But if the gungirl truly was a girl, then she was also a new and different model:

Weak the bandit certainly is not. In the more than half a dozen holdups in which she has figured she has carried out the harsh domineering role of a thoroughly "hard boiled stickup" to perfection. Her ready gun has not wavered ever so slightly in her hand and the language she uses in ordering her hapless victim into a back room would awaken boundless envy in the heart of a deep-sea sailor. It is unprintable and torrid.

Like the *Eagle*, other New York newspapers would raise the issue of the bandit's gender and bat it around a little, only to dismiss it again based on witness testimony and the police's conclusion that she was indeed a woman. One of Celia's male victims was quoted as telling the police: "She's a peach and, to tell you the truth, when she first came into my store I tried to 'make' her." Evidence of softness and kindness was also offered as proof of her femininity. In an account sharply at odds with the initial reports of Celia's brusque demeanor and rough patter, it was claimed that the woman who entered Abe Fishbein's grocery store in the middle of the Bobbed Haired Bandit's robbery was "patted on the back, comfortingly, by the girl, who said in a soft tone: 'Don't worry, dear, we won't harm you; just get inside and keep quiet.'" She was a "Jekyll and Hyde" with a voice that could be "soft" and "smooth" or "coarse" and "ordinary." The Bobbed Haired Bandit presented a complicated character that didn't fit neatly into traditional molds of women and men.

Neither did the various bobbed haired bandits picked up in the following weeks by Enright's police force. On Friday evening, February 29th, a "bobbed-haired shoplifter" was arrested by a store detective in Orbach's department store, on Forty-eighth Street in Manhattan. He was, the papers gleefully revealed, "a man disguised as a woman." Dressed in "full feminine garb" he sported a black, bobbed wig and a fur coat. Stuffed up under that plush fur coat were two expensive evening gowns. The store detective summoned the police to take custody of the "flapper robber."

When they arrived, the police realized that the thief in feminine apparel looked remarkably like descriptions of the Bobbed Haired Bandit, and he was taken down to headquarters for identification. The suspect's name was Raymond Stanley. He was twenty-six years old, worked as a waiter, and lived in a lodging house on the Bowery. This was not his first arrest for shoplifting.

Behind the Georgian facade at police headquarters down on Centre Street in Manhattan, Inspector John D. Coughlin, head of the entire detective division of the NYPD, decided that the shoplifter's resemblance to the famous gungirl called for a lineup, so he summoned the Bobbed Haired Bandit's victims from Brooklyn. When the witnesses looked Stanley up and down in the lineup, they saw a man who under his black bobbed wig had long blond hair and a face that was "well made up with rouge and powder." He was still "attired in an expensive burnt orange afternoon frock, black plush coat, black turban, grey suede slippers, flesh colored hosiery and cheap jewelry." The witnesses failed to identify Stanley as the Brooklyn gunmiss. He made a "vehement denial that he is the famous bob-haired bandit," and after confessing to the theft of the two fancy frocks from Orbach's, Raymond Stanley was sent to the Tombs.

This ripple of transvestite banditry was about to crest the very next day with the arrest of two more men in bobbed-haired wigs. BOB HAIR HID SHAVEN NECKS; COUPLE CAUGHT NEAR BROOKLYN GROCERY STORE USED ROUGE INSTEAD OF RAZOR read the headline of the article in the *New York American*. The action took place back "in the heart of the bob-haired bandit's favorite territory." At ten past eleven on the first of March, a taxi carrying two women and a driver pulled up to the Butler chain store on the corner of Lafayette Avenue and South

Elliot Place. The driver got out of the vehicle and entered the store. He approached the counter and asked the clerk for change for a ten-dollar bill. The clerk told him that there wasn't enough money in the till to make change. The chauffeur turned to the car and motioned to the two women sitting in the back of the taxi. Then, empty-handed, he exited the store and spoke briefly with the two young women. The passengers got out of the vehicle and walked toward the store as the driver sped away: "When the clerk saw this and noted the bobbed hair of the occupants of the cab, visions of the famous girl bandit rose before his eyes."

Fortunately for the nervous clerk, lurking in the darkness across the street were three plainclothes detectives on the lookout for bobbed haired bandits. They were rookie school detectives, mobilized to aid in the hunt for the girl bandit. At last the strategy of posting hundreds of men to the streets and stores of Brooklyn was paying off.

When the detectives saw the taxi pull up to the curb they became suspicious, noticing that the driver was a bit too well dressed and "not of the usual chauffeur type."

The rookie detective said to his brother students:

"Bobbed-haired, both of them. And there is nobody but the clerks in that store. I'll bet a nickel cigar . . ."

Before he could lay his wager, Wildee threw back his coat and exposed a shield. And Graff spoke up:

"Ladies, we're detectives. We want to ask you . . ."

Just for an instant the ladies froze those earnest detectives with their eyes. One of the women had black, curly hair, topped with a natty turban. Across her shoulders was thrown a cape, Carmen style. Beneath that was an evening gown, flesh silk hosiery, and dainty pumps.

The other was a blonde, wearing a picture hat and a black velvet dress, exposing a neat ankle.

Both wore wrist watches and carried vanity bags, and had cheeks and lips rouged.

"You horrid men."

That's what one said, falsetto. The other spoke a different tongue, basso profundo:

"Come on kid—beat it. They're dicks."

The two "ladies" turned and ran, hoisting their skirts above their knees to make running easier. They made it five blocks, halting only when the detectives fired nine shots into the air.

The bullets convinced the pair that the game of chase was over, and the detectives took their prisoners back to the Gates Avenue station house, where the pair were to be "scrutinized" by detectives and victims of the Bobbed Haired Bandit. Upon questioning, they gave detectives several explanations for their choice of dress and cosmetics, finally settling on the story that they had dressed up as women for fun to attend an "'artists' ball — Greenwich Village style," at Webster Hall on Friday night. Their costumes had been so successful that they had decided to dress up again on Saturday night to get photographs taken, "hoping to get theatrical jobs." They claimed to have been on their way to a photography studio when they were arrested at the Butler chain store that night. The detectives weren't buying it. There was no photography store in the vicinity, and any reputable photo studio would have been long closed by eleven o'clock at night.

The police were able to get some facts out of the "ladies." One was named Clarence Wilson; he was nineteen years old and worked as an elevator operator. He lived in a room on Ryerson Street in Brooklyn with another young man. Wilson's companion, Fred Martini, was an eighteen-year-old senior at Boy's High School who still lived with his parents. The morning after the arrest, the boys were taken to the Gates Avenue police court for arraignment before the magistrate.

One of the rookie detectives testified that when he went to search Wilson's room on Ryerson Street after the arrest, he found Wilson's roommate in possession of a loaded revolver; also in the room were twenty-seven pawn tickets for musical instruments, jewelry, and coats. More important, the would-be detective also testified that Wilson and Martini fit the description of the "two youths, one dressed as a girl," who had held up the drugstore of Leo Weinstein. Weinstein's store, which Celia and Ed robbed on January 15th, was just a few blocks from Wilson's rooming house on Ryerson — an unfortunate coincidence for the suspects.

Wilson and Martini stood for a lineup but were not picked out by any eyewitnesses to Celia and Ed's crimes. Nevertheless, the magistrate charged the pair with the crime simply on the strength of the

Clarence Wilson and Fred Martini on the front page. "Cops, Hunting Bandits, Nab Boys Dressed as Bob-haired Girls; Find Gun, Flashlight in Home," *Brooklyn Daily Eagle*, March 3, 1924. (Library of Congress)

rookie detective's assertion that the boys answered the description of the Bobbed Haired Bandit and her tall companion. The judge sent them without bail to the Raymond Street Jail to await trial.

News of the arrest of these two bobbed haired bandits traveled swiftly. When Martini and Wilson were moved from the police court to the jail, an excited crowd began to gather. Hundreds of curious persons jammed the court, and police reserves from the Gates Avenue station had to be called to clear a path from the court to the prison van outside, which conveyed the young men, still clad in their smart frocks, to jail.

The press, predictably, had a field day with this caper. Transvestite bandits were just the twist the plot needed to keep the Bobbed Haired Bandit story alive. The *New York Telegram* wrote that this most recent capture of the latest bobbed haired bandits "reads like a romance of detective lore, with so much melodramatic humor that the terror in the mere mention of the 'girl bandit' is completely lost sight of."

What was also lost sight of was the fact that the boys never actually committed a crime; Wilson and Martini had done nothing more than get out of a cab in front of a Brooklyn grocery store. Their odd look had been enough to arouse the rookie detectives into hot pursuit.

Felony or not, the titillating novelty value of transvestite banditry made it one of the "highlights in New York's week-end carnival of crime." Much of the "melodramatic humor" of the caper was provided by the papers themselves, who lavished attention on the way the alleged bandits were dressed: as in the case of the Bobbed Haired Bandit herself, it was the accessories that made the man. Consider the following description from the *Telegram*:

> Wilson and Martini made wonderful "girls." Both used lipstick and rouge like artists. Both had their hair shaved clean at the back of the neck and had their eyebrows plucked in the most accepted style.
>
> Wilson wore what he termed to be the "vampire" costume. This consisted of a short, bobbed black curly wig, which he threw away during the chase and which has not been recovered. It was topped with a natty turban. Under his yellow cape he wore a black velvet evening gown, with canary yellow silk stockings and pumps to match. On his left arm he wore a white gold wrist watch and on the right a bracelet of diamonds.
>
> Martini affected the blonde style. He had a large picture hat and a black velvet dress and cape similar to his companion's. His stockings were of black silk, with pumps also of black. His jewelry was similar to that of Wilson. [Wilson called Martini's] the "Palais Royal" costume.

Martini and Wilson were quietly released on the morning of Thursday, March 6th, "there being no evidence against them that they were concerned in a hold-up." The *Brooklyn Eagle* article mentioning their release, however, was less concerned with the lack of evidence of banditry than with the headline news that the BOB-HAIRED BOYS were DELUGED WITH LOVE NOTES. When the police searched the room of "the slim young elevator boy," Clarence Wilson, they found "endearing" letters, telegrams, "and even pictures of one devoted admirer," who wished to do "anything I can do in my power to make up again," promising that "I shall give you anything your heart desires." Another admirer gave Martini forty dollars to buy a gown for a "forthcoming masquerade ball." According to the *Eagle* this was evidence that these boys "played havoc with the hearts of numerous admirers of the sterner sex with their feminine disguise."

Even though the transvestite arrests had been a bust, the police were still on the lookout for mannish-looking women. Their common sense — as well as their superiors — told them that a stickup woman should stand out from the average bobbed female in a fur coat by her masculine characteristics. Crime had a physiognomy that was decidedly male; real women didn't pack automatics.

This strategy produced little in the way of results other than material for another amusing vignette for the *Eagle*, whose imaginative reporter brings the reader out on patrol with a nervous officer, eyes open for the tell-tale masculine traits of the elusive female bandit:

Patrolman Stewart Donnelly was nervous. He fingered his club and studied it intently. He almost refused to glance across the aisle of the Steinway ave. trolley car in Long Island City in which he was riding. But he did glance once in a while at an expanse of flesh-colored stocking and at its neatly dressed, heavily veiled owner. . . . But what made the patrolman's jaw drop and beads of perspiration stand out on his brow was when he dared another sly glance he saw the young lady hastily retrieving her hat and veil which had rolled into the center of the aisle, and the young lady's head was decidedly scarce of hair.

Patrolman Donnelly was nervous. He fingered his club in a different manner.

"Was it or was it not?" he thought.

Thinking of bob-haired bandits and rewards and medals, the patrolman followed the object of his now intense stare out of the trolley car, and as soon as he had set both feet on the street, snatched the hat from the young lady's head. A gruff voice cried out.

"Hey, what's the idea?"

When Joseph Angelo of 33 North Washington ave., Astoria, was arraigned in the Long Island City court yesterday he admitted that he was the person who had interested the patrolman in many ways. He offered the explanation that he was on the way to a masquerade ball, when the man next to him stood up quickly and knocked his hat off.

"Until then I was making a grand success of being a woman, eh, officer?" The officer blushed as the magistrate suspended sentence.

The speculation as to the gender of the mysterious girl robber continued almost until her arrest. There was also a flip side to this debate: if women like the Bobbed Haired Bandit were turning hard and

OF course he's only a man—"but he looks like that bobbed-hair bandit to me," a detective remarked when Francis Harmon was taken to police headquarters, charged with possession of burglary tools. Harmon obliged and attired with feminine garb to appease the investigators. Detectives are convinced he is not the girl bandit but are holding him. Below is Harmon "as is."

Under pressure to make an arrest, detectives dressed up at least one male suspect as a woman to parade before witnesses and the amused eye of a news photographer, who captured the transformation for the *New York American*, April 17, 1924. (Harry Ransom Humanities Research Center) masculine, then the reverse must also be true: men were becoming soft and feminine.

At the time of the Bobbed Haired Bandit's debut back in January, the *Brooklyn Standard Union* ran a front-page headline announcing THREE 'CAKE EATERS' SOUGHT IN HOLDUP of a grocery store. The term was slang for effeminate young men. The front-page article fairly crackled with masculine anxiety and homophobia about these "slicker" youths:

> Attired in Bell-Bottomed trousers, dancing pumps and single-buttoned coats, the three youths of the type which infest dance halls and tea rooms are being sought by the police today for the holdup of John Frederick, grocer, of 55 Seventh Avenue.
>
> "We need sugar for our sweeties," is the explanation they gave the frightened Frederick as they robbed him of $285, while scores of persons were passing on the street outside.
>
> The boldness of the crime seems to indicate that the trio left on the highly-polished floors the quiet unaffected manner of their calling. There was nothing, save their attire, to stamp them as "Drug Store Cowboys," "Finale Hoppers" or "Cake-Eaters," pseudonyms heaped upon young men of the type. Tea-tippling was abandoned for the sole purpose of obtaining the necessary funds with which to purchase the beverage.

As he lifted eighty-five dollars from the grocer's pockets, one of the robbers apologized, saying, "Sorry Old Topper . . . but we just had to have some jack to carry us over Saturday and Sunday." Then, according to the *Standard Union*, "the three left. Frederick telephoned the police, but by the time they arrived the youths in all probability were safely ensconced in close proximity to a jazz orchestra." What could be scarier than an effeminate youth with an automatic? The fears of decadent youth spoiled by dance halls, movies, jazz, and the consumer luxuries of prosperity itself were played out here in this portrait of the male emasculated by modern living.

Ed Cooney, playing the gungirl's passive accomplice, was used as a frequent stand-in for the part of the neutered modern male.

When the couple was sticking up stores, the newspapers habitually reported Ed playing second fiddle. After the Fishbein robbery, for instance, the *New York Herald* put the BOBBED HAIRED GIRL front and center in the headlines and belittled Ed with a dismissive sub-head, "Male Aid in Customary Role," his credit appearing just above the touring car used in the robbery: "Waiting Automobile Whisks Pair Away." After Celia and Ed had made their escape from that crime, a witness — the obstinate Mrs. Phillips — told police that "she had ample time to study the girl and considered her pretty and intelligent." Ed, however, was labeled a fancy-pants sheik: "a slim youth of the 'cake eater' type, well dressed."

Ed got even less respect now that the press filled their columns with speculation as to the character of the couple. The same detective that pegged the Bobbed Haired Bandit as a "coke fiend" had these unflat-tering words to say about her sidekick:

> We look upon him as "weak-kneed" and "yellow." He remains at a safe distance until after she has subdued their prospective victims, and then, when there is little danger, he enters the store and takes the money while the girl covers the victims. And what is more he is the first to leave the place.

Ed wasn't the only man publicly bested by a modern she-bandit. At the end of February a young man by the name of Frank Mollide, age twenty-three, who lived at 426 Central Park West, was accosted by a bobbed gungirl. Mr. Mollide was on his way home around eleven-thirty at night when he entered the park at the Fifth Avenue and Fifty-ninth Street entrance. Walking north through the darkness on the pathway just inside the avenue stone wall, he approached the 110th Street exit:

> Quick footsteps sounded back of him and a young woman came up to his side. Without any preliminaries the girl whipped a revolver from her coat and said: "Hands up!"
>
> Mollide turned to face her and as he did so he knocked the weapon from the girl's hand. It fell to the concrete pathway. For a second the girl hesitated. Then she leaped on Mollide and began to punch him. Mollide tried to fight her off, but she buried both hands in his hair, tore some of it out, dug her nails into his face and kicked him vigorously.

The young man "was forced to flee," dashing out onto Fifth Avenue and into the arms of a patrolman from the East 104th Street station, who took the battered victim to Mt. Sinai Hospital where his wounds were treated. The officer, joined by detectives from two station houses near the park, set out into the night to search for the "gunmiss," but she had vanished.

In an editorial entitled "This Amazonian World," the *New York Telegram and Evening Mail* responded to this incident, questioning what was happening to the balance of power between the "weaker" and "sterner" sexes:

> Instances of feminine pugnacity multiply. . . . In Central Park a brave and stalwart citizen, after giving proof of his mettle by disarming a pretty highwaywoman, was set upon and unmercifully beaten by his fair attacker.
>
> Men have grown soft. There must be a revival of the noble art of self-defense by the despised and weakly male struggling to hold his own in an Amazonian world.

This particular young man was softer than even the editors of the *Telegram* had imagined. According to a follow-up *Times* item, detectives working the case grew a bit suspicious of Mollide's dramatic tale of misadventure. They applied a bit of pressure, and he cracked, telling them he had fabricated the whole story. Mollide "confessed that the scratches on his face, which he had declared had been made by the female footpad, were self-administered." It seems that he had "invented a bobbed-haired girl bandit for the purpose of winning the sympathy of his sister who was angry with him." The attempt failed miserably because now "she was angrier than ever because of all the publicity resulting from the hold-up yarn." Frank Mollide had proven himself twice over a "despised and weakly male."

The very thought of soft men trapped in an Amazonian world, of weak men ruled by the women in their life, and of feminine men who dressed as women reflected the anxious fantasies of the modern male who watched with trepidation woman's crowning glory swept away from under the chairs of a thousand barbershops and witnessed women voting, driving, smoking, petting, and rolling their stockings down. Men were no longer men, and women, well, what were they? Did the Bobbed Haired Bandit represent a new kind of woman?

For Mrs. Thomas Slack, the president of the City Federation of

Women's Clubs interviewed in the Sunday *Eagle* magazine, the Bobbed Haired Bandit represented nothing less than an entire world in revolt:

> The revolt against the corset — and the revolt against the Czar. Both are part of the same thing. The uprising of the Fascisti and the uprising of Brooklyn's girl bandit — aren't they both connected, just different phases of the universal revolt, the great unrest and dissatisfaction with all established institutions which inevitably followed the World War?

As to Celia's shorn locks: "The bobbed hair is an emblem of freedom and is unconsciously worn by many girls for this reason. It's their little flag of revolt. During the war women acquired ideas of freedom and self-assurance which they will never give up." Mrs. Slack was confident that "the pendulum will swing back," but only "to a certain extent." Now that women had tasted freedom, there was no going back to the corset.

"The Bobbed-Haired Bandit Is A Revolt," read the title to Mrs. Slack's interview, and to many it seemed she was. She was an Amazonian who bossed around men, dressed to vamp in her sealskin coat and bobbed hair. She was smart and sassy, going toe to toe with the NYPD. Was she an outlaw to be feared — or admired?

◉ **10**

> Brooklyn: Who said the age of romance is past? Robin Hood may be dead but his spirit is still with us. What is to be desired in a person more than courage and brains and who has them more than Brooklyn's bob-hair bandit? I can not help but admire any one who can make a monkey of the N.Y. police force as only a super man or woman can do this.
>
> —Bill B., letter to the *New York Daily News*

On Sunday morning, February 24th, the press announced that the Bobbed Haired Bandit had emerged. The "Daring Thief" had made another "Saturday Night Visit." Her two-week hiatus had ended. The reviews were positive:

> The performance was the same as most of the others except this time the soft-voiced young woman essayed a new Bill Hart two-gun man role. She wore the now familiar black turban and the three-quarter length sealskin coat, but she juggled two automatic revolvers in a business-like fashion.

It was shortly before eleven o'clock, closing time for this branch of the James Butler grocery chain. The store was located at the intersection of Third Avenue and Dean Street. The manager and his two clerks were waiting on the last few customers of the night.

Around the corner on Dean, where it couldn't be seen from the interior of the store, a Ford sedan was idling. No one was at the wheel. Ed stood on the corner looking up and down the street, while Celia walked into the brightly lit store. One of the clerks was cleaning up, getting ready to close. The manager was helping two customers, and the other clerk was also assisting a customer when

> the door swung wide and in strode a fine looking, well developed young woman in a three-quarter length sealskin coat and a black fur cap perched jauntily upon her bobbed locks. She might have been a customer but this illusion faded as soon as she was well within the store.
>
> In her coat were slits and very suddenly through those slits two uncompromising automatics peeped and a crisp command came in a rather coarse voice for everybody to put their hands up. Her manner was reminiscent of the gunmen of the old Western frontier days who shot through the pocket.

"Up! Everybody! Throw 'em up! Be nice and there won't be any one hurt," Celia Cooney commanded. She corralled the silent customers and clerks to the rear. "At this point the 'cake eater' partner, a slim youth, entered." Ed was wearing a brown suit, a cap, and a revolver:

> "Everything all right there Sweetie?" he called to the girl.
> Without shifting her dark eyes from the frightened men and women, she answered "Sure. Make it snappy!"

Ed went behind the counter and rifled through the cash register, finding only sixty dollars in cash. He took it. "All right, kid! Let's go!" he said and moved to the door.

With her black fur turban "tilted at a saucy angle on her pretty black bobbed hair," the girl bandit backed toward the street. She warned her victims to stay quiet and still, "keeping them covered with both guns held steady in her small hands." The Ford awaited, motor running, ready to escape west on Dean Street. Celia and Ed hopped in and "whirred away" into the night. With the couple out of sight, the grocers put in a call to the Bergen Street police station, and the cops "hurried to the scene on the jump in fast cars, but the bandits had escaped."

The robbery was covered as if it was the return of a star who had been away from the stage for a spell. The *Brooklyn Citizen* headline read GIRL BANDIT COMES BACK AFTER REST, and the teaser in the paper's subhead was "Bobbed-Hair Thief Reappears after Two Weeks as 'Two-Gun' Woman." A police detective, when asked about the girl bandit's character, replied that "the only difference between her and Jesse James is that James used a horse." The bobbed haired one was now being compared with real-life desperados like Jesse James, as well as masculine idols of the Western screen like William S. "Bill" Hart.

The addition of a second gun to her act received top billing in all the stories. "Uses Two Guns Looting Store; Aided by Man" read the front-page subhead on the *New York Telegram and Evening Mail*. The "two-gun" woman was a hard-boiled celebrity, calm and levelheaded. She held her two guns steady, keeping her victims at bay and making way for her slim "cake eater" partner. The papers were, yet again, implying that her tall companion was not quite all man because he was following her lead. The leading lady, however, was all woman. The *Eagle* cited the witnesses at the Butler robbery as their authority for concluding that "the 20th century bandit is a sure enough girl and not a man masquerading in wig or woman's clothing."

The witnesses at this latest robbery may have resolved—temporarily—the gender question, but this was the only dubious help they offered to the detectives dispatched to the scene. Enright's boys in blue were still no closer to capturing the Bobbed Haired Bandit than they had been when Celia and Ed started their spree nearly two months ago.

The weather was bad the week following the Butler stickup. There was snow on the ground, and it must have been unpleasant for the policemen lurking in the shadows, watching for the Bobbed Haired Bandit to strike again. Columnist Tom W. Jackson of the *Standard Union* rhymed a dreary weather report in topical doggerel:

> East Side, West Side,
> All around the town,
> Oh, the walking's awful
> After snow comes down.
> Autos they are dashing
> Through a sea of slop
> Giving one a shower
> Of mud from foot to top.

Jackson then slipped in a jab at the police:

Brooklyn Police Headquarters now locks its doors at 5 P.M. and does not unlock them until 9 A.M.

Don't know why this is done, but it may be that the Bobbed Hair Girl Bandit has been seen in the neighborhood of Poplar Street.

The girl bandit had not been seen on Poplar Street, but she did send a note. Jackson was alluding to the fact that the doors of the detective bureau at Brooklyn police headquarters on Poplar Street were indeed closed on Tuesday, February 26th — two days after the latest robbery — for yet another secret meeting, this one of one hundred fifty Brooklyn detectives. When Captain Daniel J. Carey was asked about the meeting, he was tight-lipped: "Only a family gathering. Nothing important at all."

The *New York Evening Post*'s confidential sources in the detective bureau told a different story. The meeting had everything to do with the bobbed bandit. The police had received a note in the mail: "It was on paper of inferior grade, printed in irregular, penciled letters of copybook size. The time of its arrival has been as completely suppressed, as the name of the official to whom it was addressed." It was that note which was read aloud to the one hundred fifty detectives assembled in the detective bureau rooms at headquarters. In it "the girl bandit apologized for taking a vacation which deprived the police of their Saturday night diversion." It was a taunting note that invited a shooting. According to the *Post*, "Miss Bandit said she understood the police had orders to 'shoot to kill'" but that did not faze her; she "cared no more for their threats than for those of a 'chain store clerk.'" When asked about the note, Captain Carey "said he knew nothing of the note and denied that it was the cause of the meeting."

Two days later the real purpose of the meeting leaked out: DETECTIVES HERE ORGANIZED 'BOBBED HAIRED BANDIT SQUAD' the headlines of the *Brooklyn Standard Union* revealed, explaining that DEPREDATIONS BY GIRL ROBBER AND MAN COMPANION ROUSE POLICE OFFICIALS TO ACTION:

> Completely bewildered by the daring manner in which the bobbed-hair girl bandit and her tall male companion have successfully perpetrated more than a dozen bold holdups in Brooklyn stores, officials in charge of the local detective bureau have organized a special squad of sleuths, which has become known as the "bobbed-hair squad."

Captain Carey might have refused to discuss the creation of the squad, but other police sources informed the *Standard Union* that the new "Bob Squad" would be composed of eight Brooklyn detectives — including Detectives William Casey, Frank Gray, Joseph McCarthy, Joseph Owens, Peter Mathers, and Charles Motjenacker — each of whom was responsible for "carrying" at least one of the gungirl's holdups. These eight detectives would be relieved of their regular duties and would not be "required to take 'squeals,' as crimes are generally called by members of the bureau." Instead of having detectives from different precincts investigating each stickup separately, there would be a coordinated effort to catch the bandit behind all the robberies.

The Bob Squad's first job was to tackle a stack of more than a hundred letters that had been arriving at police headquarters claiming to have information about the bandit girl's identity, "a pile of correspondence as deep as a screen stars mash notes," the *Tribune* noted. It was learned that Brooklyn detectives had already been as far as New Jersey, Connecticut, and Long Island following up on various leads relating to the case, "but to date, all efforts to bring about her capture have proved futile."

Police Commissioner Richard Enright standing outside of police headquarters on Centre Street. (Brooklyn Collection, Brooklyn Public Library)

"Futile" was a word increasingly used to describe the actions of the New York Police Department and its head, Commissioner Richard E. Enright. At age fifty-two, Enright was "in the prime of his life." With more than twenty-five years on the job, he had risen through the ranks to be the commissioner of the largest metropolitan police force in the nation. Now he was being ridiculed daily in the city's newspapers for being unable to capture a girl. Wounded in previous skirmishes, Commissioner Enright rarely spoke at length to reporters. One paper dubbed him the "sphinx of the New York City Police Department." Enright was at war with most of the papers; he had been since he took office in 1918, and he would be for the rest of his career. A few days after the creation of the Bobbed Haired Bandit squad, the first day of March, the commissioner granted the privilege of an exclusive interview to a friendly reporter from the *New York Evening Post*.

In the *Post* interview Enright reiterated and expanded upon a claim he had made many times before. He argued that the real force harassing him was not the criminal in the streets but the press and his political enemies. It was an insidious fifth column striking from behind the frontlines of the war on crime: "Already the 'sniping' has commenced," Enright told the reporter. "What is before us and visible we can cope with; that which shoots from the rear is more difficult to contend with. Still we must go forward."

This was politics, and there could be no armistice in New York City. There were two warring factions in these trenches, the "political outs" and the "political ins," forever engaged in a dirty war for control of the city. Violent crime, graft, corruption — and in the spring of 1924, bobbed haired banditry — were the slanderous propositions, the ammunition of the "political outs" who were gunning for Enright, his boss Mayor Hylan, and ultimately the political institution behind them: Tammany Hall.

Nevertheless, the commissioner could not plausibly claim that crime in New York was only the creation of imaginative reporters and politically motivated publishers. So he invited the reporter with him on a tour of his war room to demonstrate his modern methods of criminal apprehension. At his command post at police headquarters on Centre Street, the commissioner had a room filled with movable charts on four walls, from floor to ceiling. These sectional maps in room 101 showed the entire city; different-colored pins studded the map, showing every crime and accident since 1922. (Did the rash of bobbed haired banditry warrant its own special color?) In another room were the "nerves of the entire police system": the telegraph, telephone, and radio lines that connect headquarters to the far-flung outposts of the field of battle.

According to the commissioner, New York was the "hardest nut to crack in the world" when it came to crime prevention. The masses of foreign-born New Yorkers "do not understand our laws and institutions," and there were six million residents "moving about" and more than a million more "strangers" and commuters driving more than four hundred thousand automobiles through a congested maze of streets. In purple prose the commissioner explained:

> New York is a monster mesh of great and small "get-aways" for the criminal and is filled with perfect "hide-outs" for the wrongdoer. Arrayed on the side of the gambler, the panderer to vice, the parasite and the criminal is an unseen but nevertheless very formidable army which fattens and wallows in the reeking revenue which it is their business to wrest from their more daring but less cunning associates and dupes.

This rabbits' warren of vice needed an army of men to flush it out:

> In the greater city there are 3900 miles of streets when they are stretched end to end . . . and every yard of this distance must be patrolled by a man on foot, a man on a bicycle, a man on a horse, or a man on a motorcycle. . . . Upon this "thin blue line" covering a first line trench depend the lives and fortunes of approximately seven millions of people, and the safety of ten billion dollars of stored-up wealth and property.

Enright wanted to fatten the blue line up a bit. The commissioner was asking for fifteen hundred more cops to add to the six thousand patrolmen available for duty, mostly to combat the snarling traffic problems of motor-mad New York but also to fight crime, which "must be recognized as a disease with all the dangers of a pestilence."

Commissioner Enright's request to increase his force by more than a fifth wasn't likely to be fulfilled by the politicians or voters of New York any time soon. Still, his wish stood a better chance of being granted now that a certain vacationing New Yorker was on his way back north. After more than six months of convalescence, first in Saratoga and then Palm Beach, Mayor John Hylan was returning to his office at City Hall.

At the Hotel Astor, the "Inner Circle," an organization of political writers, poked fun at the long-absent mayor in front of a politician-packed audience that included Governor Alfred E. Smith. "But you don't know the great magician Hylan," one wag jested:

> He can crawl out of any kind of a hole just by saying he is sick. And he is a wizard at picking out fine places to be sick in. He's got his followers so well trained that whenever he coughs they look up the time tables for Palm Beach. He is the best non-resident Mayor the city ever had.

The *New York Telegram and Evening Mail* reported that the mayor would "return quietly" and that, contrary to custom, the "band will not go to station to help celebrate homecoming." The paper noted that the mayor "will find many problems confronting him when he returns to his desk." One of his problems was his police commissioner's failure to manage the news of the latest crime wave.

There was no band playing when Mayor Hylan rolled into Pennsylvania Station on the afternoon of March the 4th, but there was a welcoming party of more than one hundred well-wishers and reporters. Hylan smiled and waved at the crowd from the rear platform of his private car as it pulled up to the platform. "No more loafing from now on," he told the crowd; he was "ready to get back in the harness."

The very night that Mayor John Hylan returned from Palm Beach to his home on Bushwick Parkway, "Brooklyn's Famous Feminine Jesse James" rode again. "She of the bobbed hair is at it again in Brooklyn," reported the *New York Evening Post*. "The bobbed-haired girl appeared in another role early to-day and earned more than $1300" read the front page of the *Standard Union*, with the added development: "This time she starred as a moving target before the revolver of Louis Pfeiffer."

According to the papers the "famous feminine bandit" and her "tall man companion" attacked a Mr. Louis Pfeiffer shortly after midnight on March 5th. Pfeiffer was the manager of Silver's lunchroom on Fulton Street. He was carrying almost four hundred dollars in cash and sported a diamond stick pin with nine stones stuck in his cravat, a diamond ring on his finger, and a gold watch in his pocket. He also had an automatic pistol in the pocket of his overcoat. These were perhaps luxurious and dangerous accessories for a "lunchroom" manager but de rigueur if the lunchroom doubled as a speakeasy.

Pfeiffer had just put his automobile away in his garage across from his home on Crown Street when the she-bandit stepped in front of him and "viciously jabbed a revolver in his stomach."

> "Hold 'em up and keep quiet, or I'll shoot," came a feminine voice in the darkness. Pfeiffer "put 'em up" and looked into a pistol barrel.

While her male companion frisked the restaurateur for cash and jewelry, the fur-clad, bobbed haired girl "seized Pfeiffer by the throat . . . and struck him in the face, leaving three or four scratches." After knocking the victim on his rear, the couple leaped over a fence and ran down Crown Street to Albany Avenue where a "closed motorcar the bobbed haired one has used before" was waiting. As the girl bandit jumped over the fence she tripped and fell, calling out "Dick, pick me up!"

The couple had run about twenty feet when the frightened victim realized that the pair had — by some miracle — not found the automatic pistol he carried in his overcoat pocket. "Pfeiffer opened fire. All his shots went wide. The girl and her companion made no attempt to return the fire." After his wild shots missed the fleeing sedan, Pfeiffer blew a police whistle, but when police came they could find no trace of the bandits.

Detectives from the "Special Bobbed-Haired Bandit Squad" were summoned to question Pfeiffer. They didn't have far to travel; the detectives were staked out and diligently watching stores only a short distance away. When the detectives questioned the well-accessorized lunchroom manager later at the police station, he described a girl with a "dark complexion," a "distinctly pretty" bandit. The Bob Squad detectives (or at least the reporting newspapers) quickly came to their conclusion: "The description of the girl bandit tallies with that given by the store keepers she has terrorized."

The robbery did occur in the Crown Heights neighborhood, just blocks from some of the bandit girl's previous jobs and only eleven blocks from the home of the commissioner himself. But this holdup was not the work of Celia Cooney and her husband. Ed's name wasn't "Dick," and the crime, directed against an individual and committed with violence, wasn't their style. Still the Bobbed Haired Bandit was the story the papers had built, and the one their readers wanted, so they worked to sustain it.

The press claimed that the police attempted to suppress the story, with several papers reporting that news of the robbery came from "other sources" and that "the police made a careful attempt to keep the case secret, but failed." Whether this suppression was because the detectives doubted the veracity of Pfeiffer's account or because the police were tired of reading about their failure to apprehend the bobbed one is unknown. It's even possible that the so-called suppression was an exaggeration, if not a fabrication, on the part of the papers. The news of an attempted cover-up by the police made just as good copy as the robbery itself. There may also have been a political motive, as papers that opposed the Hylan administration sometimes accused his police department of suppressing crime reports. Louis Pfeiffer, in any case, had little faith in the police; he later offered a five-hundred-dollar reward for the return of his jewelry and asserted that the police "are asleep and don't know anything."

The very next morning, Wednesday, March 5th, the red-haired mayor was back at City Hall "at five minutes before nine." Acting Mayor Murray Hulbert "handed over the reins of City Government" and, standing in the center of a City Hall reception room banked with flowers, John Hylan declared, "I shall continue on the path of progress and righteousness."

The afternoon papers that day carried the story of Louis Pfeiffer's mugging, highlighting the presence of detectives posted — ineffectually — at stores nearby. If the police *had* tried to suppress the Pfeiffer crime, they were acting wisely: this was not press to endear them to the recently returned mayor. On his first day back in office in six months, Hylan wanted to give the impression that the reins of the city were in firm and responsive hands. Backsides needed warming. The police reaction to the negative publicity surrounding the Pfeiffer holdup was swift. Not waiting for his wished-for fifteen hundred new cops, Enright ordered more police out on the streets. The commanders of all precincts in Brooklyn were ordered to place half their reserve police force — about two hundred fifty men — in plain clothes and assign them to aid detectives every night, for an indefinite period, watching chain groceries and drugstores "on orders from Commissioner Enright to 'shoot to kill the bobbed-haired bandit on sight.'"

The Cooneys were not intimidated. The Brooklyn bandits went out that very night and gave Hylan and Enright and the entire New York Police Department a grand Bronx cheer. In Celia's words, it was "some stunt."

◉ 11

There was a while when we made them look like brass
monkeys almost every time the sun went down.
—Celia Cooney, *New York American*

Celia was "on the crest of a wave" that night. She was "all pepped up by excitement, and having a thrill." "Things were going so good that it seems we took chances just for the fun of it," she later wrote in the *American*. "I don't think I really knew what I was doing those days." After having neglected the past few robberies in her serialized memoir, Celia returned to the task with enthusiasm, providing a level of physical detail and personal insight into her stickups that second-hand newspaper accounts cannot provide.

According to Celia, around nine o'clock in the evening, on Wednesday, March 5th, the winter sun was down and the streets were dark. She and Ed were "cruising along as always in the old bus" looking for their next job: something that was "open and easy meat." The Cooneys knew that the police were on the lookout, with men posted everywhere:

Here was a lot of the "finest" hand picked and nicknamed the Bobbed Hair Bandit Squad, sent out to chase little me.

Here was 200 plainclothes men stuck around all grocery stores in that part of Brooklyn, hiding behind a fish barrel maybe, and waiting to shoot me the minute I walked in and said "Stick 'em up."

The bandits found a likely target when they motored slowly past the corner of Sumner and Jefferson; there was "the little Sam Weiss drug store all lit up like a church, with globes of green and yellow colored glass in the windows." Ed was for taking up a collection immediately — until he looked across the street. On the opposite corner was an imposing brick edifice that stretched more than halfway down the block. It was the Thirteenth Regiment armory of the New York State National Guard. The windows were open wide, and light spilled out onto the sidewalk; something was going on inside. As they cruised slowly by, they saw policemen going in under the glow of the street light. Inside "there was already a lot of them in there drilling. You could hear the tramp and the hep, hep, hep." It was the sound of one hundred fifty police reserves marching in the armory. Ruffled, Ed and Celia "slid along around the corner" into the night. But their fear — as well as their common sense — evaporated in the minutes that followed; according to Celia they turned the car around, went back, and "tried it, just because it would be such a sweet joke."

That evening the Cooneys would live up to their billing: they truly were daring bandits challenging their pursuers to catch them if they could.

Ed circled the Ford sedan he was driving back on Sumner, slowing down in front of the brightly lit store. Through the three large windows, illuminated by arc lights, it looked empty. Ed turned east onto Jefferson Avenue out of sight of the storefront windows. He parked the car just across the avenue from the armory and left the motor running.

"Nobody paid the least attention," Celia recalled. Unlike the desolate streets they had prowled for previous robberies, Sumner Avenue was jumping. Not only were one hundred fifty policemen drilling in the armory, but also several hundred militiamen were at a dance for the men of the 13th Coast Artillery, and there were scores of taxi drivers and pedestrians in the immediate neighborhood.

It was a busy night for a quiet entrance. As was their practice, Celia probably entered first, followed shortly by Ed, who was watching the street. Sam Weiss, the proprietor, was behind the counter toward the back, his wife upstairs in their apartment. Hidden from view were two girls in the telephone booths off to the side of the drugstore. Celia went up to the counter "brisk" and asked Weiss for a bottle of tooth powder. The proprietor retrieved the item and returned to the counter. Celia waited to see his hands:

> The minute he got it and both hands came out on the counter to wrap it up and tie a string around it, I pulled two guns, one out of each pocket, the little automatic in my left hand and one of the big thirty-eights in my right.

The druggist got his hands up quick. At Celia's direction he came out from behind the counter in front of her where she could cover him while she "tended to the two girls in the telephone booths."

She had her eye on the girls. Women victims were so unpredictable — men would do as she told them, but "you could never tell what a woman would do." These two Jefferson Avenue girls, Adelaide Weinstein, age twenty-two, and Margaret O'Brien, age twenty-one, would prove her point.

Sitting in the booths, busy chatting on the phones behind glass doors, the two women had no idea that they were in the midst of stickup. Celia decided it was time to force them into the store where she could cover them. With one gun trained on the druggist standing in front of her, Celia half turned toward the telephone booths:

> I tapped sharp on the glass of the first booth and the girl turned around with a look like she was sore and saw the pistol. I motioned to her to come out, and out she came, and didn't that fool jane act as if she thought she was at a movie or something.
>
> Her eyes were popping, but not from being scared. She just couldn't get 'em wide enough for she might miss part of the show. She spied Ed. She said, "Ooo, you're burglars!" Then she took another look at me and said, "Why, I believe you're the Bobbed Hair Bandit!" And she started, so help me, trying to talk to me about it.
>
> I said, "Shut up, this ain't a comedy. If you don't want to get hurt go over there and keep your mouth shut."

The second girl was not starstruck; she was terrified. Celia tapped her gun on the glass:

> The girl in there took one look and slumped down in a sort of faint, and I thought first we were going to have to drag her out or let her lay

huddled on the floor of the booth, but I kicked open the door and she crawled out shaking and crying.

Celia was ready to herd her captives to the back of the store behind the partition where the prescriptions were prepared, out of sight of the big windows. Just then two men walked in to buy something: "There was nothing to it. We couldn't stop. We made them join the procession." The Bobbed Haired Bandit took charge; she "waved two revolvers in her manicured hands," herding her flock of five toward the back at gunpoint, and lined them up against the wall. Ed stayed out front of the partition and began to search for money.

Celia was distracted by all of these interruptions; there were too many customers, and it was hard to keep them in line even with two guns:

> Before it was through I thought all of Brooklyn was going to be in that store. Ed was in front working and I was back keeping them quiet, when I heard something out front, and before I could make out what it was here comes another man around the partition with his hands stuck up over his head to join my little social party.

She kept her party quiet. "The bobbed haired one whispered soothing phrases to calm the nervousness of those under her care," the New York Tribune reported: "'Don't be afraid,' She cautioned her charges."

Ed found only thirty-five dollars in the register. Sam Weiss had been robbed two years before and kept only a small amount of money in the till. There was a safe in the back, and the bandits forced Mr. Weiss to open it. He "was on his knees before the safe whirling the combination in a nervous attempt to open it. The girl was prodding him in the back with a gun." Then Celia heard a noise. Another interruption: someone was on the stairs. Celia hadn't noticed the stairway behind her; it was an unpleasant surprise. Mrs. Weiss, the druggist's wife, was coming down from the floor up above. Halfway down the stairs she stopped. "What's going on here?" she asked.

"Nothing Lady, we're only robbing the store," said Celia. She'd had more than enough with the telephone girls' antics, and now this woman had something to say as well:

And she started to jaw at me too, and by that time I was getting sore at so much talk and I called her good and hard and made her go stand with the others, without any foolishness. I'd had enough talk from women that night.

One paper quoted Celia snapping at Mrs. Weiss, "Shut up you! Keep your trap closed or I'll blow your brains out!" The druggist's wife, "realizing that argument would be futile in the face of the two menacing weapons in the girl's hands remained silent." One newspaper account, true to type, had Ed apparently faltering when they were surprised by the druggist's wife. Pointing his revolver at Mrs. Weiss, Ed appeared "visibly nervous" from the frequent interruptions:

> The girl bandit may have noticed the uneasiness of her "partner" for she spoke for the first time and said:
> "Leave her alone, I'll take care of her, go ahead now, hurry, hurry." She spoke in a soft tone and crossed her forearms so that she had her revolvers covering all six of her victims. She stood in this position, the victims say, until her companion finished ransacking the drawers of the safe.

Inside the safe were three locked drawers containing the druggist's old Spanish-American war medals, as well as papers and trinkets, little of value for the Cooneys. There was also a four-hundred-twenty-five-dollar diamond ring belonging to Mrs. Weiss, but that would be hard to unload. This robbery was a bust; too much risk for too little return.

The "cowed group" watched as Ed left with the money and the drawers from the safe. Celia "covered his retreat with her revolvers. With a final word of warning the bobbed haired girl flashed through the door and entered an automobile which stood, with motor running, facing East on Jefferson avenue."

Celia thought her parting threat would keep their victims in the store until they had made good their getaway:

> But some of them must have had more nerve than most, for we hadn't hopped into the car and gone around the first corner before they were out in the street yelling bloody murder and police.
> I found out afterwards that in five minutes the cops had all poured out of the armory and the soldiers had joined in, and they telephoned to

headquarters and brought out the reserves with flivvers and motorcycles and chased people all the rest of the night, some of them all the way to Coney Island.

I guess they must have stopped every car in Brooklyn that night — except ours.

A call was placed to the nearby Gates Avenue police station, summoning the detectives. The reserves from across the street "were turned loose in the neighborhood," joined by patrolmen, detectives, soldiers, and even some taxi-drivers who fanned out into the streets hunting for the notorious couple. A dragnet involving taxi drivers was certainly a novelty in New York where chauffeurs had a reputation for driving getaway cars rather than chasing after them. But even with these informally deputized drivers, the Cooneys eluded the urban posse's pursuit.

At first they considered ditching their sedan at the first side street, knowing that the police would be trying to "put it on somebody in an automobile." But they figured the police would find the car and through it track them down. "So we took a chance," Celia explained, "and beat it like a streak to the garage, and I don't know how we made it but we did, and walked home safe."

On the morning after the robbery, Thursday, March 6th, the bold banner headline on the front page of the *Tribune* blared, COOLIDGE ORDERS WAR ON ALL GRAFT promising OFFICIAL LIFE TO BE PURGED OF DISHONESTY. The scandalous news of national graft and political intrigue framed the story about the Weiss drugstore robbery: "Mocking police orders to 'get her dead or alive,'" "Brooklyn's Miss X" was back.

The *Brooklyn Eagle* called the robbery the MOST DARING RAID yet by the BOLD GIRL BANDIT, writing that the "police in every corner of the city today are out to 'get' the Brooklyn bobbed-hair bandit girl who last night for the second time in two days staged one of the most daring holdups of her career." As was to be expected, the press coverage emphasized the defiant, mocking act of staging a robbery under the noses of so many policemen and detectives — "the bandit girl struck in their very midst" — and the futile efforts of the officers to catch the bold bobbed one. The *New York Telegram and Evening Mail* commented favorably on the gungirl's methods, noting that "the girl appeared in a two-gun role, using two weapons" while her "cake eater aid" only carried one. The paper even outfitted the Bobbed Haired Bandit with Rube Goldberg gadgetry: "Her guns apparently were tied to elastics, for they disappeared up the sleeves of her sealskin coat when she left the store." The *American* emphasized the nobility of "the girl bandit, who as usual, refused to pick the pockets of the patrons," before she "leisurely departed." The press expressed real admiration for the character they had helped create, even if they had to invent things to admire, like elastics up the bandit's sleeves.

When the police questioned the witnesses to the robbery, they found a new twist: the bobbed hair girl had gone blonde. Her female victims got a very close look at her while they were lined up against the wall. They described her as "about 20 years old, five feet two inches tall, weighing 125 pounds, good-looking, using powder, but no rouge." Mrs. Weiss noticed that her skin was "a little rough and she may have a few pimples." Of course she was sporting her trademark "sealskin coat of three-quarter length." But for this robbery she was topped by "blonde curls, which peeped coyly from beneath her blue tam o' shanter."

After eight robberies, and many cases of mistaken identity and rattled memories of frightened victims, the police were beginning to assemble a few accurate descriptions of the pair. Celia knew she needed to alter her appearance. She wrote about the addition of blonde curls to her get-up in her King Features Syndicate tell-all:

> I told Ed about reading in a magazine about how regular bandits used a disguise, and I said, "Ed, I want a disguise too." And I got those curls from the five-and-ten-cent store and took them home and stuck them up under my hat and looked at myself in the glass, and said: "Ed, see my disguise! You wouldn't know me yourself, would you? Ain't I the cute little blonde?"

If Celia was worried about being recognized, she had little to fear from the accuracy of most eyewitnesses. The *Brooklyn Eagle* interviewed victims of the girl bandit and, considering that all of them were actually robbed by Celia and Ed and not some pretenders, found remarkable discrepancies. Leo Hecht, the clerk on duty at their fourth robbery at Weinstein's drugstore, said she was "dark, short and chunky.

Her feet were fat feet. Her nose was a round, fat nose. She was the Italian type." There was "no doubt" in his mind whatever because he "watched her for fully five minutes." The manager of the Bohack grocery and their seventh victim, Peter Kossman, was "equally positive" about his identification: "She was thin and hungry looking, a little dark thing with thin features. She didn't weigh 100 pounds. She was dark, but she looked American born to me." He described her voice as "high pitched" and "excited."

The *Eagle* also spoke with a couple of the witnesses of their eighth and most recent stickup at Weiss's drugstore. Adelaide Weinstein, the telephone girl who had been starstruck in the presence of the bobbed haired one, described the bandit as having "bleached blonde hair": she was a "cultured girl, with well-groomed hands and a slightly Southern manner of speech. She was genial and gracious — not underfed or a chunky foreigner." Another customer, Mrs. Mary Freitag — who is not mentioned in any other account — noted that the bandit had "a charming voice and her hands showed grooming. . . . Her English was good. She called me honey and suggested that I take a seat while waiting under her revolvers."

Celia Cooney was alternately a chunky foreigner, a nervous skinny American brunette with a hungry look, and a well-groomed Southern blonde who offered her victims a chair. The *Eagle* used these stark discrepancies to ask, "Has Brooklyn a gang of bobbed haired bandits?" According to the paper it was "evident" from the differing descriptions that "more than one young woman is operating in this boro." They decided that the "2-Gun Blonde" was "Cultured" and the "Brunette" was "Nervy" and wondered if they were working in "cahoots." "Brooklyn, in fact," the *Eagle* concluded, "is experiencing a feminine crime wave greater than any it has ever undergone before," and a bobbed haired bandit gang might be the reason. It must have been an odd gang of women, however, because all the descriptions agreed that the bandit was about five feet two inches tall. Alas, the petite she-bandit gang was a newspaper fantasy, wishful thinking based on exaggeration, unreliable witnesses, and reportorial creativity. But it made for a good story and amusing speculation.

The Brooklyn papers were especially grandiose in their editorial overstatements of the girl bandit's significance. The *Brooklyn Citizen*

editorialized on the idea of a feminine crime wave under the headline
GIRL BANDIT UBIQUITOUS:

> Perhaps the most interesting, at all events most spectacular, crook of
> modern times is the girl bandit who appears here, there, and every-
> where. She circulates around Brooklyn at her own sweet will, cheer-
> fully pointing a revolver at who ever she believes is in charge of
> available loot, with a pleasant, "Hold up your hands."

The *Citizen*'s headlines, as headlines often do, overstated things
just a bit. Bobbed haired bandits were *not* ubiquitous in Brooklyn, but
it seems her trademark coif was, and beneath each bobbed head in
Brooklyn lurked a potential bandit. Bobbed haired girls who stayed
out after dark were eyed suspiciously all over Brooklyn. And in
Queens, too: F. Scott Fitzgerald claimed that his wife Zelda was detained by police on the Queensborough Bridge on suspicion of being
the Bobbed Haired Bandit.

Those who had always disapproved of shorn locks and fast girls, but
merely thought them frivolous, now had reason to fear. A light-hearted
but "Uneasy Citizen" wrote in to the *Daily News*:

BEWARE THE BOBS

> Brooklyn: The bobbed-haired situation over here has become funny, if
> not ridiculous. Every other man one encounters has a police whistle
> ready to blow at the sight of a bob and our poor flappers are now classed
> as gunwomen and highway robbers. The toughest man in Brooklyn is
> not half so feared right now as the girl with shorn locks, especially if one
> or both hands happen to be under her coat.

Another Brooklyn man was inspired by these escapades of cops and
bobbers to offer the police a way to cut short the bobbed bandit's career, in meter and verse:

> I notice by the papers that some dame is cutting capers, and doing
> some stunts in moving picture style; and no one can seem to hand it to
> this dapper bobbed-haired bandit who has kept the force a-stepping
> quite a while.
>   They've arrested bobbed-haired beauties, also two be-skirted cuties,
> who had doffed their trousers just to masquerade; though it may not last

much longer, her stuff is getting stronger, and she has a liking for the grocery trade.

How to get her is the question, and we offer the suggestion that they take a census, accurate and fair, of each maid from 5 to 50, who has made herself look nifty by the wearing of abbreviated hair.

We must hurry for time presses; so let those who clip the tresses in the hundred thousand parlors here and there, give a list of those they've shorn, in the weeks and months now gone, and we'll trap the bobbed-haired bandit in her lair.

We have no evidence that the police took up this citizen's remedy for their malady.

But Police Commissioner Enright was taking action. And with the bobbed bandit paradoxically both illusive and ubiquitous, he took aim — once again — at something that seemed to be sitting all too still: his own force. Surprisingly, the *New York Times* picked up on the story. The *Times* normally considered itself above showing more than a passing interest in Brooklyn stickups and sensational crime reporting, but this case was beginning to shake up the already embattled police department.

According to the *Times*, Enright summoned his top two men, Chief Inspector William J. Lahey, chief of all New York uniformed officers, and Inspector John D. Coughlin, chief of all the city's detectives. The commissioner sent them on a mission to Brooklyn. As the *Times* delicately put it, Enright was "reported to have expressed the belief that sufficient vigilance had not been exercised by the Brooklyn police in coping with her depredations." In other words: Brooklyn cops were lazy.

On Saturday night, March 8th, the two inspectors went to visit every police station in Brooklyn to apply direct pressure. Their visit was unannounced and must have come as a shock: "At many of the stations Inspector Coughlin found detectives comfortably at desks in their quarters. . . . they were told that they could not capture the bandit that way." Coughlin also intimated that if the Bobbed Haired Bandit got away with another holdup during the night, many detectives would find themselves walking a beat and wearing a blue uniform.

"Good Morning Judge," *Brooklyn Citizen*, April 26, 1924.

Of Commissioner Enright's top two men, it was Lahey who was responsible for the uniformed force, and he concentrated on the work of patrolmen in the hunt. Each precinct was led by a captain who was in charge of uniformed officers. But most of these captains, it turned out, were out in the streets hunting the Bobbed Haired Bandit themselves, looking for that big collar that might get them a small promotion. Lahey rattled the chain of command: he warned the desk lieutenants to ride their patrol sergeants to ensure that "every policeman remained 'on the sidewalk' for the full period of his tour and to warn them that each would be held responsible for the escape of the girl if she perpetrated a robbery on his post."

Word of the top brass's surprise visit spread like fire through the precincts of Brooklyn. Within a short time of their appearance at the first station house, there was "unusual activity on the part of the uniformed force who seemed to have received word of their presence in the borough." The *Times* reported that many of the officers whose tour of duty had ended at four o'clock in the afternoon returned — of their "own volition" — to their posts after dinner and "sallied forth in quest of the gunwoman." Detectives, patrolmen, and reserves were posted in the vicinity of chain stores and druggists in the gungirl's stomping grounds.

Lahey and Coughlin were paying particular attention to the precincts in which the girl had been active: the Atlantic, Classon, Grand, and Gates Avenue precincts, shifting men over from Manhattan and the Bronx to these station houses to help in the search. The police were looking in the right place. The Cooneys lived just a stone's throw from the Atlantic Avenue precinct, and their latest robberies continued to fill in the rough circle surrounding their neighborhood. The inspectors "rode back and forth through avenues and cross thoroughfares, observing the work of policemen on post. Squads of detectives and uniformed men also criss-crossed those districts in automobiles." The readers of the *Times* were informed that the "Whole Brooklyn Force Now on Look-out for Marauding Girl and Her Accomplices." But Celia and Ed had disappeared.

12

A WORD FOR THE YEGG

Nothing could be more unjust than the complete attention paid by the police to the operations of the
bobbed-haired bandit. She is getting all the publicity,
and sincere and hard-working yeggs, holdup men and
gunmen, who take pride in their work, are passed over
unnoticed. This is not as it should be in a democracy
where the work of men, as well as women, is entitled to
generous consideration by all. . . . None would blame the
police for suspecting that she is at the bottom of everything, since she appears to be everywhere at once.
Nevertheless, impartial justice demands that they pay a
little more attention to masculine criminals. No reasonable citizen will complain if they do.   —*Brooklyn Eagle*

With the whole Brooklyn police force on the lookout for
them, Celia and Ed knew they had to lie low. "Brooklyn began to get
too hot to hold us," Celia recalled: "Nobody was talking about anything but the Bobbed-Haired Bandit." The gungirl and her tall male
companion went underground, leaving the chain store grocers and
druggists of Brooklyn in peace for nearly a month. The machinery of
policing and press, however, was in high gear. The temporary disap-
pearance of the real Bobbed Haired Bandit merely meant that these
institutions expended their furious energy elsewhere.

District Attorney Charles J. Dodd and the judges of the Kings
County Court stepped up their involvement in the campaign to wipe
out banditry in Brooklyn. The massive police sweeps carried out to
trap the girl bandit were catching a large number of other "self-
confessed holdup men and gun toters" and the prosecutors and judges
were making fast work of them. One judge sentenced twenty-eight
men in one sitting, a record in Brooklyn, the majority of the offenders
going to Sing Sing for the maximum term of twenty years.

This mass sentencing "marked another milestone in District Attorney Dodd's campaign to rid Brooklyn of the robber gangs. With the
police, the District Attorney and judges and the Grand Jury working at

top speed, criminals were caught, indicted and allowed to plead." Another batch was due to be sentenced later that same week. The criminal justice machine in Brooklyn was operating at peak efficiency in a well-oiled process of mass incarceration, which began with a grilling at the local police station and ended with a number at Ossining State Prison. If they couldn't catch the Bobbed Haired Bandit herself, any gunman would do. Samuel Scharfman, alias "Detroit Red" — husband of bobbed suspect Jean Scharfman — was one unlucky felon on the way to Sing Sing. March was a hot month for gun-toting offenders swept up in the search for the bob-haired girl.

The machinery of justice finally got around to Helen Quigley, but only after letting the first suspected Bobbed Haired Bandit sit in jail for a month and a half. Standing before Judge Bernard J. Vause in Brooklyn County Court, the assistant district attorney moved to dismiss her charges because her alleged accomplice, "Apples," recanted and admitted she was not involved in any robberies. She was exonerated and free to go at last. But freedom was fleeting for Helen Quigley. Minutes after the charge of first-degree robbery against her was dropped, a detective stepped up and arrested her again. The manager of the Bohack grocery store on Brooklyn Avenue that Celia and Ed Cooney had robbed on January 12 declared that Helen Quigley was the gungirl who did the job. He done her wrong. Nevertheless, Miss Quigley was escorted back to jail on the detective's arm, still accused of bobbed haired banditry. (She was released quietly, and for good, soon after.)

The March of bobbed haired bandit stories continued. Any incident involving a young woman with a bob could be turned into another installment in the serial with the simple insertion of the phrase "bobbed hair" into the headline, especially if it involved a motorcar and a gun. Some reports claimed that the woman in question actually was the real bobbed bandit, while others just headlined the participation or mere presence of a bobbed haired girl in the action, knowing that it had drawing power.

Sometimes the woman hunt itself created its own drama, as when suspicious police tried to stop an automobile with two bobbed heads riding up Broadway in Manhattan. The vehicle sped away, and the police gave chase. Shots were fired. The car overturned at the corner of 103rd Street, spilling the two women and their four male companions onto the pavement. Contusions, a skull fracture, and six arrests ensued. Apparently the car was stolen, but it was the hairdos that led to this front-page headline: BULLETS FLY AFTER BOBBED HAIRED GIRLS; MOTORCAR WRECKED.

These stories were becoming routine, a narrative formula into which any facts could be inserted. The lead sentence in one *Brooklyn Eagle* item began: "News of an attractive, bobbed-haired young woman figuring in questionable happenings in Brooklyn again came to the police early today." In this case the bobbed haired girl was a passenger in a speeding Cadillac that swerved out of control, sideswiped a parked car, and crashed through the three plate-glass windows of a cigar store, lodging the vehicle deep in the shop. Two policemen helped pull the four stunned passengers from the tangled wreckage of cigars, glass, and automobile. Suffering only cuts and bruises, the perpetrators convinced the officers that they needed no further assistance than a taxicab to the hospital for the bobbed haired girl who had fainted. With the aid of the helpful two patrolmen, her male companions commandeered a taxi and carried her off toward Bellevue Hospital, on a curiously circuitous route. On their way they robbed the chauffeur at pistol point, dumping the luckless cabbie in the gutter with a fresh lump on his head before racing off once more into the night.

Two hours after the crash the policemen standing at the wrecked cigar store learned that the cab carrying the accident victims away had been robbed: "Then they remembered that the woman in the party had bobbed hair." After this news flash, "every detective in Brooklyn was called out of bed and sent out to get the trace of the bobbed haired young woman, whom police believe to be the same one who for many weeks has been a thorn in the side of the Brooklyn police." It was that bobbed head — even out cold, lolling in the backseat — that attracted the police's attention and made the headlines the next morning.

Another report had the Bobbed Haired Bandit on a jaunt out on Long Island. While motoring, she reportedly pulled over to the side of the road, ostensibly to ask a gardener, John Hancock, for directions. Stepping smartly out of her sedan, she poked the gardener in the ribs with her revolver, roughly telling him to "keep your mouth shut." Two men suddenly jumped from the machine and searched Hancock's empty pockets. He had no money, and the 'BOBBED HAIR' GIRL was

OUT OF LUCK ON LONG ISLAND, as the *Eagle* headlined. Empty-handed, the bandit instructed her victim to turn his back and not budge until the car was gone: "However, he endeavored to get the license number, but just as the car drew away from the curb a curtain, mechanically arranged, fell over the plate." The man with the memorable name described his tormentor as dressed in an expensive fur coat and the "boss" over her two male partners. If this weren't enough to seal the case, the local police were further convinced that this was Brooklyn's bandit "in view of the fact that she was unfamiliar with the roads."

The popular excitement surrounding the Bobbed Haired Bandit saga was generating its own news. A reporter from the *Brooklyn Citizen* was right on target when he wondered if another minor bobbed-hair incident would "prove to be a comedy of errors due to hysteria over the 'bobbed-haired bandit'" (a case of much hairdo about nothing).

On Thursday, March 20th, over the river in Manhattan, one such comedy was staged. That night a Mrs. Bernstein was working alone in her tailor shop on St. Nicholas Avenue and 175th Street around nine-thirty in the evening. In walked a young woman wearing a mink coat. Her hair was bobbed, and she was blonde. She wanted her costly fur relined and repaired. "Under the coat she wore an olive-blue silk beaded evening gown. On her head was a turban." The elegant blonde was followed by two young men who emerged from a Cadillac coupe moments later. Mrs. Bernstein thought they were together and asked the gentlemen to take a seat while she discussed the quality of the lining with the young woman. Suddenly one of the men "stuffed a bolt of suiting under his overcoat" (another account reported him merely knocking the bolt over). The seamstress let out a scream and the hysteria began:

> A throng of passersby, recalling the bobbed haired bandit's criminal debut in Manhattan the night before, ran in search of a policeman. They found patrolman Ringen a block away and exclaimed: "The bobbed-haired bandit is sticking up a tailor shop down the block!"
>
> As Ringen neared the store two men ran out and attempted to spring into the automobile.
>
> Mrs. Bernstein held the young woman's arms. Ringen drew his revolver and ordered the fugitives to stop. One flung his overcoat and the

cloth in the doorway. Then both fled around the corner in 175th Street and escaped. Because the street was so crowded Ringen dared not fire. With the crowd following, Ringen took the young woman and the automobile to the West 152nd Street Station. For an hour the police struggled with a mob of more than a thousand men and women, who milled in front of the station. Scores of motorists also blocked traffic.

At the station the frightened young woman denied everything and asked for an attorney. She claimed not to know the men who had escaped from Mrs. Bernstein's clutches. She asked for cigarettes, and they seemed to quiet her nerves. She said her name was Billie or Betty Santos and gave the police a false address on Riverside Drive. The lady also told the bulls that she was a model but would not say if she modeled cloaks or posed more creatively for an "artist."

When the police determined that the address was fictitious, Santos changed her story, giving up another address and admitting to being the wife of one Albert E. Guimares, who was then serving time down in the federal penitentiary in Atlanta for using the mails in a fraudulent stock scheme. Guimares was also suspected in the murder of a woman named Dot King who had been chloroformed and killed in her West Fifty-seventh Street apartment more than a year ago. Missing from King's apartment were jewels and furs — including a mink coat worth thousands of dollars. Examining Mrs. Guimares' mink the detectives found — as Mrs. Bernstein had — that there was nothing wrong with it; confronted with this, she "puffed indifferently at a cigarette." The coat was then taken from her as evidence.

Outside the crowd that had followed her from the tailor shop was growing to several thousand as news of the capture of the Bobbed Haired Bandit spread quickly through the neighborhood. The curious attempted "to climb to the window ledges to get a glimpse of her. Automobiles could not get through and it required several efforts by the reserves to keep traffic open."

After three hours of questioning, the detectives decided to hold Guimares for a lineup the next morning. She was to be taken downtown to the West 123rd Street station where a matron was on duty. Her mink was returned briefly for the cold trip to the next station house. Girded in her beaded evening gown, turban, and fine fur coat, Mrs.

Guimares emerged to face her public: "There was almost a stampede as she was escorted from the station house door." The *Brooklyn Citizen* commented that "the waiting crowd would have done credit to a screen star of the first magnitude, though it was past midnight when she was led out to the patrol wagon." But the surging crowd that was eager to see her didn't get much of a chance: she turned the collar of her mink up to cover her face as she was led through the mob. After the arrival at West 123rd, her fur was taken from her once more in exchange for a handful of cigarettes.

The lieutenant in charge sent out a general notice to all "victims of short-haired girl robbers," especially in Brooklyn, to appear the next morning in Washington Heights court for a chance to identify the bandit in a lineup. Arrangements were made to control the crowd that "is expected to gather through curiosity."

But the curious would be disappointed. The fashionable Mrs. Guimares was not identified by the victims of the short-haired girl robber; instead, the suspect went home on three-thousand-dollar bail, without her mink coat.

The press that all the bobbed bandits received was making big city banditry something of an international tourist attraction as well. On the front page, under the headline GIRLS WOULD LOVE TO SEE REAL BANDIT BUT A WOOZY WOMAN HATER IS ENOUGH, the *New York American* reported another tale of media-inspired bandit mania. Three young women visiting from New Zealand, "having read the newspapers attentively since they arrived here several days ago . . . thought that it would be 'just lovely' to see a real live bandit. So they applied at the West Thirtieth Street Police Station." Sadly, upon arriving at the station they found only "several assorted burglars, pick-pockets and gold brick artists on hand, but no bandits." Discouraged, the trio prepared to depart when

> James A. Carr, a steamfitter, was led in, waving a muzzle-loading horse pistol of the 1850 variety above his head and shouting:
> "Down with Women!"
> The three girls said: "Oo-oo-ooooo!"
> Then they departed, amply satisfied, while Carr was led to a cell to sober up.

Many of the stories about bobs and bandits were comical, and most were inaccurate. But the sheer number of newspaper stories on bobbed haired banditry, and the fact that they continued even after the couple had put down their guns, was worrying Celia: "Every day the papers were full of it," Celia remembers. All through the month of March, Celia was "nervous and cried a lot" and Ed was "all the time worried." The strain of being hunted was starting to show.

Not only were the police hunting them every night, easy targets for stickups were getting harder to find. The shopkeepers of Brooklyn were on edge. Celia noted that the "storekeepers that were cowards began closing up at sundown and hundreds of others got permits to carry guns." Even in her own neighborhood Celia encountered signs that the days of easy picking were over: "I went to our own butcher shop one night to get Ed a steak, and there lying beside the cash register was a blue-steel .45 big enough to have blown the head off a horse"—or the much smaller bobbed noggin of a girl bandit.

Celia Cooney knew that the mounting public ridicule of the police would lead to a violent end. "Nobody likes to be made fools of," she recalled. All of the notes written by bobbed haired bandits, both real and imposters, belittling the force and poking fun at the detectives out on the streets every night, were fanning the flames. Celia had certainly done her part, calling the police "dirty fish-peddling bums" and threatening to "kill you off one by one" in her two notes, but she was infuriated by the copycats who sent notes that seemed designed to provoke the police to violence: "Some fool girl wrote a note to Captain Carey, saying she was the bandit, and swearing she would shoot any policeman on sight that tried to stop her and that when the shooting began she wouldn't be the one picked up full of holes." The Cooneys knew that every cop had orders to shoot on sight, and Celia came to a disturbing conclusion: "They weren't looking to arrest us. They were looking for us to kill us, like they do out West."

It was time to get out of Dodge before the shooting started. Brooklyn was too hot for the Cooneys, but they were broke. Getaways required money, and the couple didn't have the means to escape the tightening dragnet. Their career of banditry had netted them very little cash. Their very first robbery was the most lucrative, and their last was not much more than a week's pay for an automotive welder, barely enough to keep buying the steaks that Ed was growing accustomed to, let alone to keep up the payments on all their furniture and the rent on their Pacific Street palace. Not only had the Cooneys not saved any of the loot, they had used it to go deep into installment-paying debt. Now they had to get out from under it all. On top of everything, Celia was due to give birth in less than a month.

It was getting late. The worry weighed heavily on Ed as he searched for a solution. Then one night he sat down with Celia and laid it all out for her starkly:

> We're in dutch, so dutch that we can't stay here even if we quit. It's too late to quit. And we've played a piker's game. What have we got? Pretty good the first night, but since, a hundred dollars, fifty dollars, sometimes not as much as twenty-five. And some people got thousands. We got to beat it, and we got to have money. I been thinking hard. We got to pull one more big one, careful and different, and then blow.

"All right, anything you say." Celia was game.

PART IV

Gunmiss, Roused, Shoots Man

13

She bobbed her hair
Then got a gun
And robbed a drug
Store of its mon.
There are some girls
Who always will
When they go out
Be dressed to kill.

—Tom W. Jackson, *Brooklyn Standard Union*

Ed had the job "all planned out." Not far from their home on Pacific Street was the big one: the payroll office of the National Biscuit Company warehouse. You could look out the back window of Ed's mother's house into the window of the company's office. On payday greenbacks lay stacked up on a desk, ready for worker's pay packets. Everybody in the neighborhood knew this, and Ed, until recently, had lived in his mom's house. Year after year Ed had probably looked out that back window at the payroll office with all its ready cash. Now was the time to "clean it out." Ed's plan was to hold up the payroll office and "beat it" for Jacksonville, Florida, the same day.

Ed chose Jacksonville because he had been down there in the Navy. With plenty of money, Celia could have her baby in the hospital and Ed would buy into a garage in Florida. "We'd go straight," Celia would later claim, "and forget about all that bandit stuff, and after all, if we were lucky, our kid could have all the things we had planned for it."

The preparations for the big job began. Ed asked his mother to call Schwartz's furniture store and have them pick up their furniture at their duplex and put it into storage. The elder Mrs. Cooney wanted to know why they were leaving. Ed explained that "the 'bulls' were looking for him." She asked what he had done. "Nothing Mother," he replied, "but you know when they get after you they lock you up and keep you in jail for a couple of months. You know Celia's condition is delicate now. When it's all over we'll come back and vindicate ourselves." Ed's mother understood: she was a poor woman who had raised a handful of boys; she didn't ask too many questions, and she agreed to call the furniture store.

The Cooneys then told their landlady on Pacific Street that they would be away for a week, explaining that Ed had a "short out-of-town job." They took the subway from Brooklyn to Grand Central Station and emerged from the waiting room to find a taxi, pretending to have just arrived from out of town. The taxi took the out-of-towners to a Times Square hotel, the Claman on Forty-third Street and Eighth Avenue, where Ed signed the register as "Mr. and Mrs. Parker, Boston, Mass." Nobody paid any attention to the pair of them. Celia was visibly pregnant by this time and wearing her wedding ring; they were just another young couple arriving in Manhattan.

Celia was sick, her nerves on edge; for a day after her arrival at the Claman she couldn't eat or sleep, but the next morning she was ready. She was concerned about being recognized as the bobbed bandit. Her hair had grown out just enough so that she could "fix it up with the ends turned under" tucked up under a hair net "so that it didn't look bobbed at all." With the hair net, a thick black veil, and a little pink hat Celia was prepared to venture out; "hardly anybody could recognize me," she recalled. It was the same little pink hat that she had worn to her very first robbery back on January 5th, but "nobody had noticed it." For his disguise Ed bought a new hat and coat.

The careful preparation for their heist continued. Next, they purchased two steamship tickets for Jacksonville on the Clyde Line, again in the name of Mr. and Mrs. Parker from Boston, leaving in three days' time. Back in their hotel room, they used the telephone book to find a car and chauffeur service and then called for a closed car and a driver to be sent to their hotel. A big Packard limousine arrived to fetch them. It was driven by a fellow named Arthur West, "big and heavy enough to be a prize fighter, except that he was too fat." This was a concern—the man was bigger than Ed and, as Celia remarked, "Ed is no runt." At some point West would need to be overpowered if Ed's plan was to succeed. But not that day, for this was a scouting trip; it was time to "look things over" on a brief tour of Brooklyn. The guns were left behind, locked in a suitcase at the hotel.

They told the driver that they were moving to New York from Boston and wished to look at a house on Dean Street right near

Pacific. On the way the Cooneys told West that they wanted "to go for a little ride to see the Brooklyn Bridge." This struck Celia as fine joke. "Imagine" she recalled, "us wanting to look at the Brooklyn Bridge."

The Cooneys rode through the streets of Brooklyn in the back of the Packard limousine. Ed wanted to look the Biscuit warehouse over and needed to find a secluded spot nearby to "fix up that chauffeur the next day." Celia settled back into the seat and peered out through her veil at the streets where she lived and worked:

> It was fine going through Brooklyn that way — me now riding in a limousine where I used to work in a laundry. And I felt safe. No cop was going to look for me sitting in the back of a big Packard with a chauffeur.

Ed directed the driver to enter Prospect Park, searching for that lonely place to subdue the big man before the robbery. Once they had found a "good quiet spot," the Packard proceeded to Dean Street, not far from the National Biscuit warehouse. Ed emerged from the limousine and walked one block to the warehouse on Pacific Street to give it the once-over. If he was stopped he planned to say that he was looking for a job as a truck driver, but nobody paid any attention to him at all. Celia remembered that Ed "mooched around a little" and returned to the car. He lit a cigarette, and they drove away. Celia asked him how it was, and he replied: "It's all right, I guess, but there's a lot of clerks and a lot of Janes pounding on typewriters." After their "little ride" through Brooklyn, Mr. and Mrs. Parker of Boston settled back into their hired limousine for the short trip back to Manhattan and their hotel.

The large number of clerks and Janes working at the Biscuit should not have been their only concern. Edward Cooney was a local boy, a familiar face, the kind of guy who said hello to the cop on the beat every morning. He had lived with his mother and brothers on Dean Street, one block over from the Biscuit Company on Pacific, for at least twelve years. He crossed over Pacific Street every day on his way to and from work at Horgan's garage on Atlantic Avenue. And the apartment Celia and Ed had rented with the proceeds of their very first job was located at 1099 Pacific Street; the National Biscuit building was number 1000. This job wasn't just in their backyard, it was almost on their back porch.

On the one hand, they were familiar with the neighborhood, which gave them confidence; on the other hand, they were bound to be recognized. This "careful and different" job had the air of desperation. They could not go home again. The Cooneys were shutting the door on their life in Brooklyn, whether or not they realized it consciously. They must not have believed they had any other choice; in their minds the police were closing in on the Bobbed Haired Bandit.

When the Cooneys returned to their hotel that night, they confronted the problem of the big man. They needed a plan to subdue and restrain the driver of the limousine. They "doped it out." It would be best, they thought, to tie him securely and hide him in the backseat of the limousine. After all, Celia recalled, "we didn't want to hurt him." Having never tied anyone up before, Celia needed to practice. Ed had brought some rope with him from Brooklyn. Celia described the bedroom scene:

> That night before we went to bed, he asked me to try to tie his hands with it, to see how it would work. Well, it didn't work at all. That sort of stuff is all right in the movies. It was plenty strong enough, too. But it was too thick to make a tight knot. He wiggled his hands a little and pulled one of them right out.

Ed put his clothes back on and went out into the night. He returned shortly with a spool of picture wire. He cut off a yard with his knife. It was strong, "he had to saw and twist at it." Celia tried again. Ed assumed the position:

> Believe me, it did the trick. It's thin and shiny and almost as soft as string — made with a lot of little tiny wires twisted together so that its easy to tie knots in.
>
> I wound it criss-cross twice across his wrists and he tried to twist loose, and it cut right into him and left red marks. Why, he'd of cut his hands right off if he had pulled harder.

The next morning they were "all set to go." When they left the hotel Ed was sporting his new overcoat and a pearl gray fedora; Celia wore a gray, beaded dress and her trademark fur and turban. Celia had one of the big guns, and Ed had the other and the little automatic. They had two almost empty suitcases with them with lots of room for loot and a change of clothes.

When Arthur West arrived as promised with the Packard, they drove back to Brooklyn and into Prospect Park. "There wasn't a soul in sight" near the botanical gardens, at the spot the Cooneys had chosen. Ed looked up and down the lonely road and then tapped on the glass divider motioning the driver to pull over. "Wait, I want to get out a minute," he said. Ed jumped out and "jabbed the gun in his ribs," forcing him into the backseat and onto the floor of the limousine. Celia was waiting with the picture wire. Ed climbed in and held the gun on West to keep him quiet, while Celia performed her bondage act. It wasn't easy; he was a big man for a bandit just a shade over five feet to wrangle:

> I tried first to tie his hands behind him, but he was so big and fat I couldn't. He was trying to do what we told him, but he was scared, and there wasn't much room to work. So I made him put his hands in front and fastened his wrists together, one across the other, good and tight with the wire.

Ed tied the chauffeur's feet together and they made him lie down; "he filled up the bottom of the floor, he was so big." Celia claimed that they didn't have to gag the man because fear was gag enough: "He kept quiet, all right, without that." Ed climbed into the driver's seat. It was all going smoothly. The big Packard was no challenge to Ed; he "could drive any kind of a car," his proud wife recalled fondly. Celia sat in the back with her gun trained on the bound-up chauffeur. Her job was to keep the frightened man quiet:

> He never opened his mouth but once, when we bumped over a rut in the road and his head banged on the floor, and that was to ask me could he turn over. I said, "Sure, but no funny business."
>
> I had to move my feet so he could turn, and I got to looking down at my own feet. I had on new high-heeled pumps and pretty stockings, and they looked so little with him all hunched there, that I thought how funny it would be if I put one of them on his neck, like Cleopatra I once saw in the movies.
>
> And the more I thought of it, the more I couldn't help doing it, so I put one foot easy and rested it right on his neck, and then I pressed the heel down a little, but not enough to hurt him.

And that's the way I rode through the park, piled back in a limousine, with my foot on a man's neck. We passed two or three cars, and I thought wouldn't it be a joke if they knew.

The ride didn't last long. Perhaps not long enough for Celia (or her ghostwriter: see note on p. 338). It was only a few minutes from Prospect Park to Pacific Street and the Biscuit Company. Ed stopped in front of the building. The immobilized chauffeur was face down on the floorboards of the Packard, and they threw a scare into him to keep him there. "You stay here and watch this guy," Ed bluffed loudly, "and if he opens his mouth, you know what." Then both the Cooneys exited the vehicle, slamming the door behind them and leaving the fat man on the floor.

The office was up a short flight of stairs just off a large shipping platform. Celia entered first, quietly:

Stylishly attired in a pink turban hat, a heavy black veil, and three-quarter length sealskin coat, the girl walked into the biscuit company's offices and, in a soft voice, asked to see the manager.

She was surprised. The office was bigger, and there were a lot more people in there than she had expected, more than twenty. Too many, she thought. She "began to wonder if we could get away with it."

There was a low rail at the front of the room; behind it at a desk sat William Christie, an order clerk. There were about fifteen other clerks in the room, male and female. Holding an envelope in her hand, Celia told Christie she wanted to see the cashier. The clerk went to fetch him. The cashiers who handled the payroll for the Biscuit Company worked behind a wire cage to protect them and the contents of the big safe from intruders. But behind the cage, the door of the safe was standing open.

The cashier's name was Nathan Mazo. As he emerged from the cage, Celia held out an envelope for him. The other clerk walked off as Mazo looked down to open the envelope. Inside was a blank piece of paper. The cashier was puzzled. But when he raised his head again it was all clear: he was looking right into the barrel of Celia's gun. Ed had come in behind her and was holding two guns. He stood at the back, covering the room with his "pistols crossed, cowboy style." A handkerchief tied around his neck, hitched up to conceal his face, completed the picture.

CECILIA of the haircut and the ready gun to-day will be sentenced by County Judge Martin in Brooklyn. She is twenty now. She will be getting into middle-age when the Bedford Reformatory gates swing behind her at the end of her term. The cream of her life will be gone.

"Celia with Gun," *New York American*, April 30, 1924. (Harry Ransom Humanities Research Center)

"It all came so quick. When we pulled our guns the girls all ran and the men threw up their hands." Another clerk was standing near the big safe and edging closer. "You could see he was going to take a chance and slam it shut." Celia yelled, "cut it," and pointed her gun right at him for emphasis. The clerk "jumped back with his hands up."

It was time to restore order at gunpoint. There was a smaller records room toward the back that would contain the frightened employees.

Celia stepped up to the doorway: "Ed stood way back with two guns, and I stood close by the door, and we drove them through it like sheep. They bumped into each other to see which could get through quickest." Then, in an instant, it all went terribly wrong. At the end of the line rushing into the smaller room was Nathan Mazo:

> The cashier was the last. Just as he got in front of me, so close he could touch me, he turned and made a grab for me. I don't know whether he just had a brainstorm or whether he had it figured that he would take a long chance and grab my gun and shoot it out with Ed.
>
> Anyway, he jumped right at me and got one hand on my arm, and I stumbled back and fell over a chair and went down on the floor.
>
> He must have lost his nerve as quick as it came to him for instead of following me up he made a flying jump, too, and went through the door that somebody slammed right afterward.
>
> Almost the same second Ed shot twice. The bullets hit the door low and went through, and there was that scream and then everything went still as death.

"God I must have croaked him," said Ed.

◉ **14**

> The bob haired bandit became a real desperado today—
> abducted a chauffeur and his car, staged a daylight
> holdup, shot a man who attempted to tear from her face
> the veil she wore in lieu of a mask, and escaped. . . .
> "Shoot her on sight, if necessary!" are the police orders
> now. But again they are without any clue more substan-
> tial than the evanescent odor of a faint perfume she
> leaves in her wake.   —*New York Evening Post*

The wounded cashier's screams shattered the Cooneys' façade of hard-boiled cool. They fled in a panic: "It was murder, and the electric chair may be for both of us."

Ed leaped to where Celia had fallen. He later told detectives that when he saw Celia fall,

I thought she had been struck or maybe cut, and I fired through the door at Mazzo, who fell. I knew there was $8000 right there to be picked up, but I wasn't thinkin' about that then. My girl was down and I had to rush in, picked her up and carried her out. When we got out she wasn't much hurt and came right to. It was too late then to go back for the money, so we beat it quick.

The safe door was standing open, inside was the eight thousand dollars, and they were alone in the outer office. But their only goal was escape. Empty-handed, they scrambled down the stairs. "Who could have thought of money then?" Celia recalled.

Several National Biscuit truck drivers loitering outside the warehouse heard the shots and started in. Celia and Ed could hear them coming up the stairs, out of sight behind a turn in the stairway. Ed pointed his guns down the stairs, but Celia whispered to him to put them away and try to "bluff it out." Then, according to Celia:

> We started calmly down the stairs, trying to look like people who hadn't any idea anything was wrong. If we could pass these drivers and reach the street before they discovered the bunch of clerks in the [back room], we had a chance.
>
> But my heart was going like mad as the first driver swung around the turn in the stairway and saw us.
>
> Eddie pulled a packet of cigarettes from his pocket and shook one out. He stepped in front of the man.
>
> "Got a match, buddy?" Eddie asked calmly.

The driver stopped for a second, then shook his head and thundered up past them, followed by his friends. Celia and Ed walked out.

Once out of the Biscuit office they piled into the Packard waiting outside, its motor still running. Ed drove fast down Pacific Street, made a quick turn on Classon Avenue and then again onto Atlantic Avenue. Making the connection between the couple in the car and the shots they heard, several men from elsewhere in the National Biscuit warehouse ran after the Packard but lost the limousine as it hit Atlantic and "a maze of traffic." The shocked employees that Celia and Ed had herded into the back room opened the now bullet-splintered door. Two of the men made it down the stairs fast enough to join the chase down Pacific Street; the other called the police and an ambulance for Nathan Mazo who lay bleeding on the floor.

Celia and Ed didn't have the money, but they still had two tickets to Florida and a getaway plan. Five blocks from the National Biscuit warehouse, near the Nostrand Avenue station of the Long Island Railroad, Ed ditched the limousine, hoping their pursuers would think that they had boarded a train at the station. Taking two suitcases with them, they got out of the Packard and left the chauffeur hogtied in the back. They hailed a taxi and told the driver to take them over the bridge to Manhattan. They switched cabs on the corner of Bowery and Broome Street on the Lower East Side to keep the police from tracing them to the docks on the West Side. In the cab Celia searched her pockets for the steamship tickets. Something was missing. It was then that she knew she had lost her little notebook. She thought she had dropped it in the first taxi. "What was the difference?" she reflected later. "If they hadn't caught us one way it would have been another."

There was no time to think about that now. The cab arrived at Pier 36 and dropped them off. Celia's "stomach dropped" when she spotted a cop at the foot of the gangplank. Ed kept it cool, assuring Celia that this was normal, that the cop didn't know about them or the Biscuit robbery, and that they should walk straight toward him. They did, and Ed was right. Soon they were past him and on board the Clyde Line ship, where a steward showed them to their room. Once inside, behind a locked door, Celia and Ed collapsed.

Meanwhile, back in Brooklyn, a pedestrian walking down Atlantic Avenue near the Nostrand Avenue train station heard the sound of breaking glass. The noise seemed to come from a limousine parked at the curb. Moving closer to investigate, he noticed two bound feet sticking out of the car's rear window. He called a cop. When the patrolman arrived, he found the feet were attached to Arthur West. The beat cop drove the car and driver back to the station for questioning. Untied, West had a lot to say about the past two days.

West said he was employed as a chauffeur by a Manhattan garage on West Forty-third Street. The day before he'd been hired to pick up a couple at a hotel in Times Square and take them on a drive. Then, that morning, he was paid to repeat the trip: over the bridge to Brooklyn and into Prospect Park. Suddenly the couple asked him to pull over in the park because the woman felt sick. Then the man held a gun to his head, and they tied him up and threw him on the floor in back, covering him with a robe. The man slid behind the wheel, and the woman sat in back, resting her feet on him like he was an ottoman. As the car started moving, he heard the couple talk about the best way to drive to the National Biscuit plant. They drove for a while, and then the car stopped and the couple got out. They threatened to kill him if he caused "any trouble." A few minutes later he heard two shots. The couple piled back into the car and drove at high speed for a short time and then pulled to the curb and parked the car. As they left they told the chauffeur it was best if he "take a nap." West was not in any mood to play the hero, but once he was sure that the couple had gone he figured it was safe to try to make an escape. Unable to get himself upright from the floor of the car, he did manage to get his feet up to the rear window. He slammed his feet against it, and it shattered. Next thing he knew the patrolman had arrived. The police listened to West and, after checking on some details, decided to believe him.

Conflicting reports came in as to where the Bobbed Haired Bandit and her companion had gone after abandoning West's car. Since they had left the limousine near a railroad station, the police initially checked train boardings. They were encouraged to look in this direction by "loungers in the vicinity of the station" who insisted they'd seen the couple climb the stairs to the elevated train. Police, believing the couple may have taken the train to Long Island, wired an alert to all the towns and stations on the line. Taxi drivers, presumably also lounging near the scene, offered up a different story. They told the cops that they saw the couple hail a taxi and order it to Brooklyn's Borough Hall. This was a slightly more reliable tip. The taxi driver who picked up Celia and Ed near the Long Island Railroad station was eventually located and questioned. The driver told the cops that his infamous fare didn't go to Borough Hall; instead, he had driven the couple across the East River and dropped them on the Lower East Side. There the trail ended.

West told the police that the couple had carried two suitcases with them in the limousine; the taxi driver confirmed that they still had them in the taxi. The newspapers concluded that this meant that the bandit pair craftily changed outfits after committing each holdup. If the flapper garb of sealskin coat and turban were just a disguise, then out of costume the brazen bandit would be indistinguishable from countless respectable ladies living in New York City. As it turned out, the suitcases *were* a clue, but they didn't just point to a quick change of clothes. The bags contained a couple of extra shirts for Ed and a change of underclothes, a comb and a brush for Celia; clothes for their trip out of town. And, as Celia explained later, the suitcases were "mostly to put the money in." They were expecting a big haul.

At the Biscuit warehouse the police interviewed the witnesses. The daylight robbery had given victims a better look at the bandits than any of their previous stickups, and the press and police had solid descriptions at last. In these eyewitness accounts, the tall male companion emerged from the shadows. The Bobbed Haired Bandit's comely appearance and smart dress had been played up for months, while her partner had been neglected or belittled. Ed finally achieved a measure of the celebrity that Celia had enjoyed, a little bit of respect even, albeit Pyrrhic.

During the robbery the handkerchief that Ed had tied round his face slipped to his collar, exposing his face to the women in the biscuit office. Despite their fright, they liked what they saw. "Several of the girls who were victims of the hold-up pair yesterday," reported the *Brooklyn Standard Union*, "told Capt. Carey that the hold-up man is an Adonis and very handsome and could easily pass as a model for any collar company." The biscuit ladies further described Ed in a manner befitting a cinema star or starlet: he was a "good-looking blonde," they said. These same women were not impressed with Celia: "The girl is of a very ordinary type . . . her hands showed signs of hard manual labor," and she looked "as if she had done a great deal of dishwashing," they told the reporter. Given Celia's long years as a laundress, this was quite perceptive. The newly merged *Herald-Tribune* was more generous with Celia, describing her in a manner that their middle-class readership could understand: she was "a rather refined type, the girl small and such as might apply for a stenographer's position."

A general alarm was broadcast at nine the next morning, crackling over police wires and via the wireless — the use of this relatively new technology thrilling enough to warrant its own headline: POLICE

USING RADIO IN GIRL BANDIT HUNT. Armed with accurate descriptions, the police combed the city: "Several hundred detectives have searched during the past twenty-four hours in every possible haunt the elusive bobbed-hair bandit and her man companion might frequent," visiting "many hotels and furnished room houses where the girl Jesse James and her companion might take refuge." But according to the *Brooklyn Standard Union,* "the pair were not found, and every clue has failed to materialize." Seven employees of the National Biscuit Company were taken to Manhattan for a day in the rogues' gallery at police headquarters, but no one could pick out the culprits from the several thousand mug shots arrayed before them.

At the end of the day the newspapers were once more reporting that POLICE ARE BAFFLED BY BOB-HAIRED BANDIT, and Captain Daniel Carey had to admit—at least publicly—that they "were no nearer the capture of the bobbed-haired bandit and her 'tall male companion' than before the pair's audacious attempt yesterday." Shopkeepers were warned "to be on their guard" as the Bobbed Haired Bandit, now desperate for funds, "will be forced to stage another hold up."

But Celia and Edward Cooney were no longer a danger to the shopkeepers of New York. They were steaming away from the city, heading down the Atlantic seaboard. It was not the scenic cruise the lovebirds might have hoped for. As soon as they boarded, they barricaded themselves inside their cabin, sure that the police would be only minutes behind. "I was limp as a rag," said Celia, remembering these first hours:

And Ed's face looked gray. In about a minute we heard steps running on the dock, and we'd thought they'd come to get us. I said, "Oh, Ed, what'll we do?" And he said, "What can we do? I guess it's finished."

We waited for them to knock on the door, and we went through it, but they went right by. Then came more steps hurrying, and they slowed up, and this time they did stop, and a man with a coarse voice said "I guess it's here." But it was only some passenger looking for his room.

Well that went on, it seemed to me forever. And I wouldn't go through it again for all the money in the world. It seemed like the boat would never start. But at last the whistle gave a big blow, and then another and we could feel that we were moving.

Even then we were afraid to go out on the deck. And when dinner time came we didn't dare to go out. And we turned off the lights and tried to go to sleep. But every time I sort of dozed I felt hands on me, and that same voice we'd heard outside the door saying we were arrested — for murder!

But the cashier wasn't dead, or rather newspaper reports of his death were much exaggerated. The wounded man, Nathan Mazo (or Maeze, Maizo, Mazzo, Maezo, or Mazio — every newspaper seemed to use a different spelling), was first reported to have been taken to Jewish Hospital with "little hope for . . . recovery" with "wounds that may cause his death." Shot in the abdomen and in "dangerous" condition, he was "reported to be dying." Within a day, however, newspapers started reporting that the critical wounds that they had imagined were in fact "superficial," with two shots into the "fleshy part of his hips," where the doctors had left the bullets, saying it would do more harm than good to remove them. The *Brooklyn Standard Union*, the paper that followed Mazo's story the most diligently, still held out a macabre hope: even when they had to report that the wounds were slight, they still dangled the "fear that complications may set in."

Seriously wounded, or merely shot in the derrière, Mazo was determined to have his own moment in the limelight. Talking to a reporter from the *Union*, grinning widely and surrounded by the letters and telegrams of congratulations that he had received, Mazo recast his somewhat comic bit-part in the robbery into that of a dashing hero. "There was a little mistake at first," he explained:

> They said I tried to grab the girl's veil. I didn't. I went for the gun she was carrying. I grabbed her arm and while I was fighting for the revolver she pulled the trigger and plugged a bullet into the wall. Just as I was about to get a hold of it I heard three heavy shots as if they had come from a high caliber revolver.

"Believe me," Mazo continued, dreaming of his lost chance to be a hero:

> If I'd got that gun I would have saved the police a lot of trouble. I'd have killed them both. That's what I'm going to do next time. I'm going to get the gun then and I'm going to shoot her.

Mazo may have exaggerated his heroism, and certainly engaged in some mental maneuvering to bring his tale of bravery in line with the fact that he was shot in the buttocks through a closed door. Still he was the first and last man to lay a hand on the Bobbed Haired Bandit; no one else had ever resisted. Mazo was accurate regarding at least one detail: it was Ed who had shot him. But the gungirl finally using her gun to shoot down a man made for a much sexier story. The *Daily News* classic tabloid headline GUNMISS, ROUSED, SHOOTS MAN sets the tone for this version of the tussle:

> Mazo lunged forward and grasped the veil on the woman's face. The gun-miss pushed him roughly from her into the room. Then, with an oath, she fired twice through the panel. Mazo, wounded sank to the floor.

Likewise, newspapers played up "the girl who used her toy-like automatic for the first time," painting the Bobbed Haired Bandit as a dangerous "Jessica James." The added component of violence heightened the drama of the Bobbed Haired Bandit: "The hold-up was the most spectacular and daring that the girl has yet put over." After a few days, however, when the police deemed it likely that it was Ed who had pulled the trigger, the papers let the shooting angle disappear. There was nothing newsworthy about a dangerous gun*man* in 1924. In fact, after a few more days with no new leads on the story, and with the police not providing any more details of their investigation, the New York newspapers moved on to other fare entirely.

For the Cooneys and their pursuers the story continued. For two more days and nights Celia and Ed steamed down the coast. Seasick and afraid, they kept to their bunks the entire time. They finally docked in Jacksonville on the 3rd or the 4th of April. Leaving the ship, they hailed a taxi at the wharf and asked the driver if he knew of any cheap rooming houses. The driver took them to one at 125 Ocean Avenue. There they rented "a dirty little dump of a room," as Celia described, "worse than any I'd ever lived in when I used to work in the laundry." That wasn't its only detraction. The house was only a block away from the Jacksonville police headquarters, but the wanted couple decided to stay anyway. They were safe; nobody knew them there.

Dreams of buying a new life in Florida faded fast. After the steamship tickets, the hotel rooms, and all the taxi fares they were nearly broke. They had a talk about what they were going to do: "We had less than $50 left—and my baby was coming soon, which would cost money, and we had to eat. The bandit stuff was over. We never even thought of trying that again. Ed was a good mechanic, and figured he'd get a job around a garage."

The next day Ed went out to look for work, but he never made it to a garage. "And this," Celia claimed later, "is why: The New York newspapers had beat us down here, coming on the train, and he got one and brought it home and didn't want to show it to me, but I made him —and there it all was." The papers held details of their holdup at the National Biscuit, news that Mazo was dying in a hospital, and the most accurate descriptions of the Bobbed Haired Bandit and her pal to date. In itself this was not enough to raise suspicion about the "young Northern couple" who "lived quietly," as their new Florida neighbors came to know them, but Celia also claimed the newspapers carried information far more threatening: their names, ages, aliases, and the information that Ed would likely be looking for a job in a garage and Celia was expecting a baby and might be found in a hospital. The law knew who they were.

◉ **15**

> In fiction the detective starts his work by examining cigarette ashes, analyzing blood stains, and doing other spectacular stunts. The detective in life rarely duplicates the activities of his counterpart in fiction. With us the tip of the stool-pigeon gives us a direct lead more often than not. Detecting unusual circumstances, such as a well-dressed woman eating in cheap restaurants, a shabby derelict leaving a wealthy house where he has been a guest—these apparently incongruous circumstances are the clues that really lead to the solution of crime. So it was in the case of the Bobbed-Haired Bandit.
> —William Casey, *True Detective Mysteries*

Celia was mistaken about the timing of the all-points bulletins released to the newspapers that Ed picked up in Florida. The police department wouldn't release such details for another ten days. But the Bobbed Haired Bandit Squad *was* closing in on the Cooneys and likely "suppressing" this information from newspapers. Several months after Celia and Ed's capture, Bob Squad detective William J. Casey sold his story of "How We Caught the Bobbed Haired Bandit" to *True Detective Mysteries* magazine. While the byline of the story contains the telling line "as told to," it's doubtful that the *True Detective* story was composed solely from the words of the Brooklyn detective. Casey's general description of how the police discovered the identity of the Bobbed Haired Bandit and her tall male companion does jibe — for the most part — with what was revealed later in newspaper accounts of the police investigation. It was not some spectacular stunt that led to their capture, but solid, unspectacular, and by our standards today, maybe even a bit unethical, police work.

As Casey tells it, the police got their first lead even before the National Biscuit robbery. A local Brooklyn cop had received a tip from a neighbor of the Cooneys that a young mechanic named Ed, who along with his new wife Celia, lived "a stone's throw" from the Atlantic Avenue police station, "appeared to be spending more money than usual" and considerably more than his presumed thirty-dollar-a-week salary.

"The report was one of thousands turned in," responding to a general order that went out to all beat cops telling them they should report any "suspicious circumstances, no matter how trifling" to their superiors. In this case the cop did, passing his tip up to the head of Brooklyn detectives, Captain John McCloskey. McCloskey repeated the tip to the bandit squad, including Detective Casey.

Casey thought the Cooneys were unlikely suspects. Celia Cooney had dark hair — not blonde as some victims had reported, and her locks, he thought, "hung to her shoulders," and were not cut in a tell-tale bob. Besides, Mrs. Cooney was noticeably pregnant, and who had heard of a pregnant bandit? As for Ed, he was just a neighborhood nice guy: "All of us had known Cooney for a considerable time as a hulking, good-natured youth, who daily went to his work as an automobile mechanic, passing the time of day and a joke with any of us he met." According to Casey, Edward Cooney wasn't in any gangs, and the police "looked upon him as a home man, who spent his evenings with his wife." Casey did recall that Ed had been in trouble with the law, but only "when a small boy—and in that instance the sentence imposed upon him had been suspended." Because of this the police didn't pursue the tip with any urgency. By the time they did follow up on the tip they found the Cooneys gone "and that their flight had been hasty." The rumor of cash and their rapid flight were suspicious, but not suspicious enough to distinguish the Cooney case from the countless other sightings and false clues reported to the police.

Then the National Biscuit warehouse was robbed in broad daylight in front of nearly a score of people. While the police were telling the papers that none of the witnesses identified the bandit pair from the mug shots in the rogues' gallery, they were being only partially accurate. The eyewitnesses hadn't recognized the known rogues, but at least one of the biscuit company employees recognized the Bobbed Haired Bandit's tall companion "as a man who had been employed at a nearby garage." Other witnesses also "recognized in the man and woman a newly married couple who had been living in the vicinity." This was hardly surprising considering that the Cooneys had been living just down the street.

Questioning the Cooneys' trussed-up chauffeur, the police learned the name of the hotel where he picked up his fare, the Claman; its location, Eighth Avenue and Forty-third Street; and even the couple's room number, 821. With this information police went to the hotel clerk and grilled him about the guests in room 821. While the clerk was no help identifying the couple in the rogues' gallery, he was able to give the police a few critical bits of information: the pair had checked into the hotel on the 29th of March, and the woman who had registered as Mrs. Parker was with child.

Now, as they say in detective stories, the pieces were coming together. An installment collector for Schwartz's furniture store was located as another witness to the Cooneys' out-of-character affluence. When the bill collector knocked at Celia Cooney's apartment door to claim his payment in the middle of February, "she came out of the bedroom and appeared suspicious." He told the *Brooklyn Daily Times*:

> In each hand she carried a wad of bills. She handed several to the collector. He counted them and told her only $100 was due and she had given him $150.

"Oh, did I" she asked, and took back the $50.

The collector noticed that the doors of the place all had padlocks.

Neighbors, likely interviewed by the police and then found by reporters later, revealed more about the Cooneys. Ed, it was said, "was always out in taxicabs and went out frequently at nights. He was said to have sudden rises of fortune, one day being 'broke' and the next 'rich.'" To explain his newfound wealth Ed had let it be known around the neighborhood that he had patented some invention having to do with motorcars.

But the clue that cinched the connection between a free-spending, local young man and his pregnant wife and the notorious Bobbed Haired Bandit and her confederate came from the Cooneys' landlady at 1099 Pacific. She told the police that Ed and Celia had vacated her building on March 29, four days before the Biscuit robbery and, more important, the same day that Mr. and Mrs. Parker of Boston checked into the hotel on Times Square. As the *Brooklyn Daily Times* later explained, the "sudden departure of Cooney and his bride from the home they had furnished luxuriously at 1099 Pacific Street was timed by detectives with the arrival at the Hotel Claman."

To confirm their suspicions, the police compared the writing on the envelope containing the blank paper that Celia had handed to Nathan Mazo in the Biscuit robbery, the writing in the address book Celia had dropped, and the signature at the Claman Hotel with two samples of Ed's writing, one from his Navy records and another "secured at a previous arrest." They all matched.

With this information the police could connect the two sets of characters: the Brooklyn couple named Cooney whom they had been tipped off about, and the couple who kidnapped the chauffeur and robbed the National Biscuit office. "With these last facts in our possession," Casey writes, "we at once sent descriptions of Celia and Cooney broadcast." On the morning of Tuesday, April 15th, the police department released the names of Celia and Edward Cooney as the Bobbed Haired Bandit and her male companion.

Their names and descriptions were "broadcast throughout the country" by "telephone, telegraph and letter" and "posted conspicuously in all post offices and other public buildings." These wanted bulletins were reprinted verbatim in a number of New York newspapers. Ed's was listed first:

> Make inquiries at garages, auto repair shops and filling stations for Edward Cooney, alias Parker, alias Lyons, alias Ruppert, alias Harrington, alias Roth, alias Smith, twenty-seven years old, five feet eleven and one-half inches tall, weighing 175 pounds, brown hair, ruddy complexion, rash on right side of face. When last seen, wore a light tan overcoat with belt at back. May wear blue or brown suit, pearl gray hat or light cap. May give reference as chauffeur or mechanic.

This was followed by Celia's:

> Make inquiry at doctor's offices, lying in hospitals, sanitariums or other places where confinement cases may be treated for Celia Cooney, maiden name Roth, married Edward Cooney May 13th 1923, and may use the name of Ruppert, Lyons or some fictitious name. Bobbed dark hair; is a German, but looks like an Italian or a Jew. May be wearing brown cloth coat. Last seen wearing three-quarter length seal coat, gray beaded dress, pink turban hat and gray veil.

The alarm went on to warn that "the couple may have guns in their possession" and that they were wanted in New York for assault and robbery.

MYSTERY OF THE GIRL BANDIT SOLVED announced the *New York World,* and in the days following the release of Celia and Ed's names, New York newspapers uncovered more details to flesh out the couple's portrait. One of the more titillating details, hinted at in the police circular, was that something was medically amiss with the Bobbed Haired Bandit. She was being hunted in hospitals and lying-in hospitals, and good reporters knew how to read between the lines of official reports. Mrs. Cooney was described as being in "delicate health," by the *Standard Union.* The *Daily News* was characteristically more brash: STORK HOVERS, NET TIGHTENING ABOUT GUNMISS, they headlined, reporting that "the secret of the elusive bobbed-hair gunmiss, the feminine Jesse James who has been terrorizing merchants in Brooklyn and Manhattan during the last three months came out yesterday." The Bobbed Haired Bandit was having a baby.

With this news a more sympathetically shaded picture of the Bobbed Haired Bandit and her companion began to emerge. Ed, it was discovered, was a Navy veteran who worked steadily as a mechanic, and the couple was legally married by a priest in a local Brooklyn church. Celia was still referred to as the "feminine Jesses James" and Ed as "her cake-eater companion" in the newspapers of mid-April, but alongside this picture of a wild woman and an irresponsible youth another portrait was being assembled: that of a traditional couple, forced by hard times to take extreme measures. The *New York Telegram and Evening Mail* reported that according to police headquarters it was Celia's impending motherhood that pushed her into crime "and that the proceeds of the robberies were destined to defray the expense." The *Telegram and Evening Mail* went on to remind their readers of the letter that Celia had left for the police, declaring Helen Quigley "completely innocent and insisting that the money acquired in the hold-ups was to be used 'in a good cause.'"

Other papers built on and expanded the compassionate portrait. "When Cooney married Celia, less than a year ago," the *New York American* reported, "he was a mechanic at a good salary in an Atlantic avenue garage. But he lost his job." This was not true. Ed kept regular hours over at Horgan's auto shop until they skipped town. Most papers, however, agreed that he had lost his job long before. The *New York Sun* reported that when Celia and Ed "set up housekeeping" they "furnished their home with furniture bought on the installment plan. Then, only a few weeks after the marriage, Cooney lost his job, and a few weeks later the furniture was removed." It was only after this reversal, the *Brooklyn Citizen* added, that "the couple resorted to banditry." The *Citizen* cited its source as Captain Daniel Carey, the man who two months earlier had compared Celia to a "dope-saturated gunman" and gave orders to his men to "shoot, and shoot to kill." Not one word was printed of Ed's previous criminal record, and at least one newspaper made note of the fact that the police told them that Edward Cooney did *not* have a police record. The newspapers, their readers, and at least a few detectives had fallen for the Bobbed Haired Bandit — they were ready to believe the best: that Celia and Edward Cooney were simply good people who had fallen on hard times.

They were young and foolish, and it wasn't hard for many New Yorkers to empathize with the couple. A competing narrative was emerging, contradicting the dominant hard-boiled accounts of cold-hearted daring.

It could be that the police, the press, and other respectable New Yorkers wished that there was a reasonable motive behind these crimes; they might have hoped that jazz age youth weren't so different from previous generations. The apocalyptic vision of strong-willed, pleasure-mad young women and effeminate "cake-eating" young men had filled the pages of tabloids and fueled the fires of countless religious sermons and political jeremiads since the Great War. To discover that the infamous Bobbed Haired Bandit was an expectant mother and that the crimes had been motivated out of concern for family and simple economic want must have been a great relief. This was a world that older folk, normal folk, respectable folk could understand. GIRL BANDIT BELIEVED KNOWN, the *Brooklyn Standard Union* headlined on April 15th, quickly adding the information WED AND LIVED NEAR POLICE. Yes, the Bobbed Haired Bandit was still the brash and daring gunmiss — taunting fate by living near the police, yet now she was also "wed" and thus, somehow, traditional. This is how Celia would increasingly become known in the weeks to follow.

In the *American*, Celia's new portrait was juxtaposed with her old image, now superimposed on a different young woman. Right next to an article on the hard-luck Cooney family was a piece on a nineteen-year-old girl named Irene Johnson, "whom the Spring hunger for lovely clothes led into banditry" — and the paddy wagon when she was pinched for a robbery in which a policeman's bullet killed a passerby. The article on this new girl bandit begins by asking a series of rhetorical questions, decrying the materialism of the age and especially that of working-class youth:

> Has Easter come to mean glittering gowns and silken hosiery instead of the rebirth of the spirit?
>
> Has civilization turned from a glorious progression of progress into a pageant of blatant luxury?

Irene Johnson then tells her tale of the circumstances that led to her first crime:

I had to do something—just had to. I had been without a job for weeks except a little factory job at $12 that I had for a short time. Twelve dollars is just enough to get into debt on. I had to pay $5 a week for my room and $1.50 for street car fare. Lunch money had to be taken out of that. Say, how can a girl look Fifth avenue on that?

Johnson explained that she needed to "look Fifth avenue" in order to secure a job, but the conclusion is still clear: Johnson robbed for consumer luxuries. Illustrating the article is a crude courtroom artist's sketch of Johnson—with lithe figure, lipstick, eye shadow, and her hair cut in a discernable bob.

There were other papers, however, that held out against the wave of sympathy for the expectant bandit. These papers resisted her moral makeover, continuing to play her up as a pleasure-seeking, materialistic youth like Miss Johnson. "That Mrs. Cooney had a taste for comfort in retirement," commented the *New York World* under the subhead "She Wanted the Best," "was evidenced by the fact that she and her husband rented the basement and first floor of an old frame two-story house in a poor neighborhood and made a duplex for themselves . . . and purchased $1000 worth of furniture, rugs and tapestries."

How much the couple enjoyed their expensively appointed Brooklyn duplex was also a matter of speculation. "She liked the nightlife. She loved cabarets and shows," claimed the *Brooklyn Eagle*, continuing:

Tenants in the [Pacific Street] house say they were rarely home at all. Never at night. Four or five nights a week they would go out the early part of the evening dressed in the latest fashion. On those occasions it was always the small hours of the morning when they returned.

Another landlady of Celia's had even less positive things to say about her tenant. The *Eagle* located Mrs. Catherine Gallagher, the owner of the Franklin Avenue flat where the couple had first lived, who accused her former tenant of stealing twenty dollars and, more fantastically, a framed wedding picture of the landlady herself as a bride. Celia, Mrs. Gallagher also claimed, lay in "a filthy bed in a filthy room until noon every day," reading "bad novels and magazines." (When the reporter pressed Mrs. Gallagher to name the novels in question, she maintained that *all* novels "are not fit to read.") To make matters worse, Celia was a boxing fan: "She was always talking about fights. . . . She'd say 'I wuz glad he got him' and 'he socked him one in the eye' and 'wallop' and all kinds of slang." "What kind of a woman could any woman be who went to prize fights?" Mrs. Gallagher asked the *Eagle* reporter. "They were a bad lot," the Franklin Avenue landlady concluded, "bad, bad, bad! . . . She wasn't a woman at all, at all — she was a she devil."

A *New York Times* reporter canvassing the Cooneys' old neighborhoods "pierced the mask" of the couple's respectability. One neighbor, who insisted on anonymity, claimed he knew all along that Celia was a crook:

> I got to know the girl by her using the [public] telephone often. In the evening she would be all dolled up and she wore a three quarter length fur coat, I remember, but when she would come to telephone in the early morning she had a very hard look on her face. She would talk to men on the telephone who had Italian names, and I had a suspicion then that she was talking to members of the underworld. That's the way she struck me.

All aspects of Celia's life were fair game for examination and judgment, but it was the ready money and reported good life the couple was living that the papers kept returning to. From a police source the *Eagle* learned of the witness who had initially tipped off the police to the Cooneys. The witness had visited their flat the month before, and while there "Mrs. Cooney displayed a large roll of bills with great joy," saying: "That's the stuff that gets you the things you need in life."

For some of the newspapers, especially those with middle-class aspirations and readership, the desire of working girls for the good life was something to be condemned. For papers with a more working-class readership, meanings were more ambiguous. The *Daily News* tagged Celia as a person "whose love of luxuries led her to turn to a life of crime." But the *News* was not being censorious. It was offering its own brand of economic reasoning behind Celia's crimes. To the tabloid's working-class readership, a burning desire for luxuries that couldn't be afforded was completely understandable.

On April 16th the newspapers splashed a photo of Edward Cooney

The public's first look at Edward Cooney from his driver's license photo, *New York Daily News*, April 16, 1924.

obtained from the department of motor vehicles across their front pages. Under a light fedora turned down at the brim, wearing a dark jacket and tie, Ed stares out, neither smiling nor scowling, wearing the common expressionless look of a driver's license photograph.

The public now had a picture of Ed — was he truly an Adonis as the Biscuit girls claimed? Celia's looks could still only be judged second-hand. One paper reported her as "unusually attractive"; another heard from a neighbor of the Cooneys that she was very quiet and "not good enough looking for anybody to look at — twice." There was also specu-lation that her hair, now definitively described as black, may have been dyed different colors at different times. An enterprising reporter for the World tracked down Celia's pre-marriage address at the Brook-lyn Marriage License Bureau. From another of Celia's former land-ladies, Mrs. Rose Vitelle, the reporter learned that Celia had used sample hair dyes left on her doorstep and that her hair was sometimes red and other times black. Another, anonymous, source offered up the observation that Celia had blond roots peeking out below her black locks.

While ex-neighbors provided good copy, a reporter from the World had trouble getting information out of Ed's relatives. Locating Ed's mother's house on Dean Street, only a few blocks away from Celia and Ed's last home on Pacific Street, the reporter "rapped on a window pane." A man, probably one of Ed's brother's, responded. "That Cooney don't live here, Jack," he said. The reply to the Brooklyn Eagle reporter who followed later was even blunter: "You ain't looking for Cooney here," a "big burly fellow in his 20s" said, blocking the door: "Beat it! You'll get hurt."

The press who had made Celia into the notorious Bobbed Haired Bandit was feeling their importance in her hunt and capture. The newspapers, by spreading the couple's description, had "turned the town into a detective agency in the quest for the elusive matron with a gun," bragged Brooklyn's largest daily, the Eagle: "It was the old tried and true remedy, 'When everything else fails, give it to the newspa-pers. That will bring results.'" A week later the World boasted on its front page that the chief of New York detectives, Inspector John Coughlin, credited a tip dug up by their paper as the tip that linked the Cooneys to the Biscuit robbery and led to the "sudden capture" of the

Bobbed Haired Bandit. It was a dubious claim, likely revealing more about the self-importance of the *World* and Coughlin's efforts to curry favor with the Pulitzer family newspaper than any real detective work, but these reports do demonstrate the self-conscious role the New York papers were playing in the Bobbed Haired Bandit saga.

By April 18th, the story and the trail had grown cold — again. The couple still made news but now in the back pages. The papers used the "new development" of an old description of Ed by the clerk at the Claman Hotel to jump-start interest. In a story buried on page twenty-eight, the *World* reported: "As Luther Boddy, slayer of two detectives, was identified and captured owing to a long scar on the side of his face, the police hope Edward Cooney . . . may be located by the red rash in his right cheek." After this tidbit, the *World*'s story, like the others, merely rehashed old details and reported routine utterances from the police department: tips on the Cooneys' whereabouts were coming in from around the country, and "all such reports are being investigated." For the umpteenth time, the police brass "warned the detectives to be prepared for a gun battle."

The story was a motorcar running on fumes. By April 20th the *Brooklyn Daily Times* was reporting the BOBBED BANDIT ABOARD RUM SHIP, weaving together a story of a disgruntled ex-employee of a Long Island bootlegging boat who tipped off the police that just before dusk a man and two women — one young, the other older — boarded the rum runner from a small launch:

> The younger woman carried a pistol nonchalantly. The man carried two guns. The trio was greeted enthusiastically by the commander of the ship. The man became sort of a second mate and was given little to do. The women went to the galley as cooks.

According to the reporter, Captain Daniel Carey showed the "tipster" pictures of the Cooneys (pictures that had evidently not yet been released to the press), and they were positively identified as two of the three who boarded the ship. Carey then speculated that the older woman might be a domestic nurse. This tip was "more than usually trustworthy," said the captain, who should have known better than to buy a watery story from a bootlegger.

Commissioner Enright's police force had finally identified the

Bobbed Haired Bandit, and the newspapers could put names, histories, and a face to the formerly phantom-like bandit and her partner in crime, but that was all. Confidently, the police asserted the couple "will be caught within a month," and newspapers headlined BOBBED BANDIT AND MATE NEAR CAPTURE. Whereabouts unknown.

⊚ 16

> I suppose I could write a lot of bunk . . . to get sympathy, but I was too miserable then and I'm miserable now when I think about it, to put down anything but the plain truth. I just laid there like a person doped when they showed it to me and I thought, "You poor little kid, we've made a nice mess of things for you."
> —Celia Cooney, *New York American*

In the weeks following the National Biscuit robbery the police became convinced the Cooneys had fled New York City. They discovered that Ed's mother had the couple's credit-bought furniture collected at 1099 Pacific and put into storage; this suggested that they weren't planning on coming back any time soon. Furthermore, the detectives thought that Ed and Celia knew they had been recognized at the Biscuit offices and this had put them on the lam and would keep them far away. Now they had to find them.

The police initially looked for the Bobbed Haired Bandit in the wrong direction. Ed and Celia's ruse of signing their name as Mr. and Mrs. Parker *of Boston* in the hotel register, then leaving the same name and city with the limousine company, worked to send the police north instead of south. In his account in *True Detective*, Bob Squad Detective William Casey explains that the police traced the Cooneys to Fall River, Massachusetts, and later to Boston, where he claims they found rooming houses and hotels where a couple had registered under the name of Parker. It was likely a case of seek and ye shall find. The number of young couples spending the night in cheap hotels as Mr. and Mrs. Parker probably falls just a bit below the number registering as Mr. and Mrs. Jones or Smith. After this little wild goose chase, the

New York detectives were back where they began: without a solid clue as to Celia and Ed's location.

With the whereabouts of Celia and Ed unknown, and no new facts forthcoming from the police department, further speculation on the character of the Bobbed Haired Bandit filled up the columns of the New York newspapers. These opinion and "analysis" pieces, like those that came before and after, were more about a women's place and threats to male power than they were about any bobbed haired bandits. Now, however, there was a new theory about the bandit girl.

After the personal details about Celia and Ed were revealed by the police, a reporter from the *Brooklyn Eagle* visited the New York Police Department's Training School of Detectives — the same institution that had supplied the one hundred fifty rookie detectives for the bobbed bandit hunt — and consulted a police psychiatrist for his opinions regarding the Bobbed Haired Bandit's "crime impulse." The doctor took a broad view of the problem. His real concern was not merely the "crime impulse" but explaining something far more disturbing: Celia's power over men. "She seemed to be hypnotic in her powers," the reporter relayed:

> It was remarkable that she could so easily terrorize not one, nor two, but often five or six men. In the case of the robbery at Roulston's, in January, she backed half a dozen into the rear room at the point of her pistol, and all the time swearing like a Billingsgate fishwife. She is little, but the fact that she is a slip of a woman seemed to have no effect on her victims. To all intents and purposes, she was a giantess in mental force.

This "giantess" held sway not only over her victims but her partner as well: "The man was usually in the background, and his function was to smash the cash registers and gather in the loot," while Celia took center stage. "There was something abnormal, and not womanly about her actions," the police psychiatrist explained to the reporter. "She was acting under an impulse that was apparently unnatural. And in every case she dominated the man who was with her. She was the director and he was simply a tool." This analysis was based on the good doctor's reading of the daily papers' portrait of the patient.

What could explain this "not womanly" and "abnormal" behavior?

The psychiatrist laid the blame on "a condition of temporary psychosis, brought on by the physiological changes that precede motherhood." The bold and brazen, masculine, and modern behavior of the Bobbed Haired Bandit could be explained by the most traditional and feminine of explanations: Celia Cooney was pregnant.

Late-nineteenth-century medicine had ascribed great powers to the reproductive biology of woman. Abnormal symptoms from hysteria to criminality could be attributed to the power of the womb to draw energy away from the critical, rational faculties of the brain. A woman criminal was deemed abnormal because criminality was seen as a masculine trait. Celia Cooney's crimes were a symptom of a mental abnormality brought on by the demands of pregnancy on her limited physiology and mental powers. The root of feminine crime was not social; it was not poverty but biology that determined character.

Hunkered down in Jacksonville, Celia was in her last stages of pregnancy. Ed was still afraid to look for a job, so he and Celia spent the days and nights of the fine Florida spring hiding inside their shabby room on Ocean Avenue, "afraid to even go out to the corner delicatessen for a can of beans." It was a "plain hell I wouldn't wish on a dog," Celia claimed.

Their dream of owning a garage had disappeared. So did the fantasy of setting up a "nice" home for the baby that drove them to crime in the first place. "I wanted to have nice things," Celia wrote about her time in Jacksonville. "And now I was afraid to have my poor little baby born anywhere—and we were flat broke and in a worse dump than I'd ever lived in."

What little money they had didn't last long—and they needed even more. Celia's baby was due early in May, and it would take money to pay for the delivery:

> We were down and out. We were a thousand times worse off than we were before we ever started stealing money. It got us nothing and worse than nothing.

With Ed scared to show his face looking for legitimate work and Celia eight months pregnant, it would have made sense to go back to being bandits. They still had the guns, and even if Celia was too far pregnant to be of much use Ed could do a job or two solo. But Celia had soured on robbery. It seems that Celia's tale of fall and redemption that she later penned for the *American* while awaiting sentencing was not just a fairy tale dreamed up for the judge and the paper's readers. The "bandit stuff," as Celia called it, was in the past, and they were trying to start a new life. Or perhaps they were just afraid of being shot.

On Thursday night, April 10th, two days after her twentieth birthday, Celia got "awful sick." She was going into labor, and much earlier than they had expected. She "had the most terrific pain," and it scared her. But Celia was also fearful of things you "oughtn't have to worry about . . . when you are in that fix." She was afraid to have Ed take her to a hospital and even frightened of having him go out and bring back a doctor: "I thought the minute they saw what was the matter with me I'd be arrested, and then the baby would be born in jail. Even a dump would have been better than that. I'd rather have died."

Ed was afraid that Celia really was dying and decided to go fetch a doctor no matter what the consequences. "Celia," he said, "I don't care what happens to either of us, you can't suffer like that." He asked a woman who lived in their rooming house to come stay with Celia and left, returning an hour later with Dr. Sisson, a local Jacksonville doctor. Sisson examined Celia and insisted that she must be taken to a hospital quickly. Delirious by this time, Celia didn't put up a fight, and an ambulance took her to a local lying-in hospital, Humphrey's Sanitarium, where she lay on a hospital bed expecting the baby . . . and the police, "wanting to scream every time the door opened, thinking the cops had come to take me away." The cops never came. The New York police bulletin wouldn't be released for another five days, and the Jacksonville authorities had no reason to watch hospitals for bandits bearing babies.

What did arrive, after a difficult labor, was a baby girl. Celia was exhausted. But without money to pay the bills she couldn't stay at the hospital, and the staff told her that she and her newborn baby had to leave. Now completely broke, the couple couldn't pay the rent a week in advance that the landlady of their Ocean Avenue digs demanded. Ed looked all over town to find a place that didn't ask for cash up front. He finally found a place on the second floor of a rooming house on the poor side of East Jacksonville where a woman believed Ed's story that money was on its way. Their new home on East Monroe Street was safer than their old place, which had been a block away from the Jacksonville police headquarters, but it was even more decrepit. "It was dirty," Celia remembered, "and I had no proper things for the baby, not even a can of talcum powder."

The baby "was little and pitiful and sickly from the start," and its health did not improve. Later Celia blamed herself for its condition: "I was weak myself, and I guess my milk was not good. Worry is bad for mother's milk." "You could see it was sick all the time," she explained, "and I didn't know what to do for it. I wanted my baby to have a chance." The baby didn't have much of a chance. Less than two days later, on Saturday morning, April 12th, in a dingy room in a broken-down rooming house in a strange city, Celia and Ed's baby daughter died.

They had named their baby girl Katherine, after Ed's mother. Both Catholic, they had worried about her baptism, but Katherine died before they could arrange one. "I guess God won't hold that against my poor baby," Celia later reasoned. They were determined, however, to give Katherine a proper burial. They got the name of a local undertaker, probably from their old landlady on Ocean Avenue. With no money, "we had to get the undertaker to trust us for its little coffin." At the baby's burial the only people present were Celia, Ed, and the undertaker.

Fate was doubly cruel that day. It was the undertaker who buried their child who led the police to the bandit couple.

According to Detective Casey, the Jacksonville police had put out a notice to all area hospitals and medical facilities in response to the general alarm broadcast on the 15th that the bandit was on the run and nearing childbirth. Alerted by an undertaker that a couple matching the bandit and her partner's description had buried a newborn baby a few days earlier, the Jacksonville police forwarded a description of the pair to New York along with the name they were using: "Parker." Bingo. "Certain at last that our quarry was in a trap," Casey recounts, "we wired the Jacksonville authorities not to permit the suspects to leave the city, and Detective Gray and myself took the first train South." After an embarrassingly slow start, the police had wrapped the case up tight. "It was a guessing contest," Captain John McCloskey told the *New York Sun*, "and we finally outguessed them." It was a neat piece of police work.

It *was* neat — until you look a bit closer. Then you find too many holes in William Casey's *True Detective*'s account of the Bobbed Haired Bandit's capture to take it as the whole truth. While the general arc of his story is sound, there are a few important things that simply don't hold water. Celia and Ed were not foolish enough to keep the same alias in Florida. They left the name Parker in New York and to their Jacksonville neighbors, and probably to Dr. Sisson and the undertaker as well, they were Mr. and Mrs. Sheehan, a name not included on the list of aliases sent down in the police bulletin from New York. While it is possible that the Jacksonville police could have made the connection between a pregnant northerner and the description on the circular even without a matching alias, it's unlikely that the New York police would have followed up on the tip. The number of sightings of the Bobbed Haired Bandit in New York City alone were astronomical, so it's hard to believe that the New York police department would have sent two of their best detectives from the Bob Squad all the way to Florida on a Jacksonville cop's say-so. In addition, the undertaker, according to most reports — including the local *Florida Times-Union* — did not volunteer information about the Cooneys to the Jacksonville police but was tracked down and questioned only after Detectives Casey and Gray arrived in Florida.

Casey also remembered earlier that Cooney was a surprising suspect because he was a good kid who had only been in trouble with the cops as a boy. This is partially true. Ed had been in trouble before when he was a fifteen-year-old, just as Casey claimed. He was pinched once on a petty burglary charge for stealing scrap metal and another time for the equally petty crime of shooting craps; for the former he was given a suspended sentence, and for the latter the charges were dismissed. But he had also been arrested more recently as an adult. On November 20, 1923, only a couple months before the Bobbed Haired Bandit's crime spree began, Edward Cooney was picked up on a burglary charge. He got off after a magistrate's hearing, but it was a serious enough charge that one of his buddies was convicted and given an eight- to fifteen-year sentence in prison. Who was one of the arresting officers in this case? Casey's partner in the Bob Squad: Detective Frank Gray. How did Casey forget that his own partner arrested Cooney only six months prior? He probably didn't. But it made the police seem a lot less like bunglers if the tip about Ed and Celia living beyond their means was not initially pursued because they were such unlikely suspects. "The detective in life rarely duplicates the activities of his counterpart in fiction," wrote Detective Casey in *True Detective*. Indeed.

A slightly truer "true" story of the capture of the Bobbed Haired Bandit may have gone something like this: After the death of their baby the ex-bandits were flat broke. As Celia remembers, "our money gave out and we hardly had enough to eat." Medical expenses cleaned them out of what little cash they might have had, they still owed more to the doctor and the undertaker, and they needed money to survive and maybe even attempt a getaway to another city. (Several newspapers reported that the Cooneys had reserved passage on a steamship for New York, or in one intriguing report, New Orleans, and were scheduled to sail several days after they were caught.)

Desperate for money, Ed wrote his mother back in Brooklyn telling her that Celia had given birth and they had lost the child and asking her to send them a hundred dollars. He instructed her to send the money in care of Sheehan at their old Ocean Avenue address, where they likely had an arrangement with the landlady to hold their mail. The couple never got a reply, but this is no surprise because Ed's mother never received their request.

Enright's police, now acting on their strong suspicion that Celia and Ed Cooney were the Bobbed Haired Bandit and her companion, were intercepting all of Mrs. Cooney's mail. In the more official language of the police commissioner's *Annual Report* of 1924, "tracers were placed on mail of all relatives and friends and their wires were tapped." On April 19th, "the watchful authorities," as the *Eagle* referred to them, seized Ed's note with its Jacksonville return address. Steaming open an old woman's mail and finding your quarry's location written out by the prey himself was solid police work, but it was hardly the sort of deductive reasoning, interdepartmental cooperation, and police heroics that make up a selling story in *True Detective*, so it's understandable why Detective Casey — or more likely, his ghostwriting coauthor—neglected to mention this *little* detail. But heroic or not, it was effective.

Immediately, Casey and Gray, both of whom knew Ed by sight, took the fast train to Florida, alerting the Jacksonville police they were coming. They arrived in Jacksonville on Sunday the 20th and went directly to the local police headquarters. The New York cops warned their Florida counterparts "that the pair we were after were dangerous [and] probably would shoot to kill," then went to work. Cooperating with local detectives A. A. Wethington, S. H. Hurlbert, and L. B. Harvey, Casey and Gray began to trace the Cooneys.

At the nearby Ocean Avenue rooming house they discovered that the "Sheehans" had already moved out. The police had missed them again. "Here the detectives' only hope of locating the couple was lost," reported the Jacksonville paper, the *Florida Times-Union*, "but an hour later, through the clever work of Jacksonville detectives, the New York sleuths said they uncovered their most important clue." "They learned," the story continued, "that the baby had died Saturday morning. The undertaker who handled the baby was located. Then, running down a dozen other clues, the detectives located them at the East Monroe Street address."

The Jacksonville reporter was being a bit dramatic, and definitely favored the home team, but he got most of his facts right. The landlady at 125 Ocean Avenue confirmed that "Mrs. Sheehan" had been treated by a local doctor and been taken to a Jacksonville lying-in hospital. She also told the Brooklyn detectives that the baby had died and been buried by an undertaker. Throughout the day Casey, Gray, and the Jacksonville detectives visited Humphrey's Sanitarium and tracked down Dr. Sisson and the unnamed undertaker. They went through the records of the hospital and questioned the two men. From at least one of these sources—the majority opinion lies with the undertaker—they obtained Celia and Ed's new address on East Monroe Street. It was night by the time the detectives confirmed the location. Enright's men had the gungirl in their sights.

⦿ 17

The spectacular career of the most-advertised woman desperado and her tall male companion was ended— they are through. . . .

There was, however, in the shifting eyes of Celia Cooney, the self-conscious smile on her face and the swagger in her walk, as she stepped from the train and realized that she was the single interest of hundreds of people gathered in Pennsylvania station, a suggestion that this, the hour of ignominious defeat, was at the same the hour of her greatest triumph.

—*New York Daily News*

In the hour after midnight on the warm Florida morning of Sunday, April 20th, the police brought their caravan of cars to a halt on East Monroe Street in the poor neighborhood of East Jacksonville. On foot they stole down the quiet street to a cheap rooming house and surrounded the place. A dog barked. Two men went up to the roof, and two more covered the back fire escape, guns drawn. The Black Maria police van was parked out of sight down the street.

Detectives Casey and Gray walked up the front steps of the ramshackle two-story building. They pushed their way through the front door and mounted the interior stairs. On the top floor, Lieutenant H. C. Brown from the Jacksonville police pointed to a door. Bill Casey stepped up and pounded on it: "Open up in the name of the law."

A man's voice called out: "All right, but wait till my wife gets her clothes on." The detectives could hear noises; someone was moving behind the door.

Celia and Ed were half asleep in their bed, but the raid was not a surprise. They had been cowering behind that door for days, waiting for the cops to bust in. "We just sat, sort of dumb, and waited," Celia remembered. The waiting was over. Celia had heard the dog barking, and they knew the police were out there; they could hear "a whole crowd of them, talking low and shuffling their feet." When Casey pounded on the door Ed jumped up and switched on the light, Celia got up, and they both threw on their clothes. Ed had the guns out, two

AS THE DETECTIVES BATTERED IN THE DOOR OF THEIR APARTMENT IN JACKSONVILLE-FLORIDA- THE BOBBED HAIR BANDIT TOLD HER HUSBAND NOT TO SHOOT BUT TO SURRENDER.—

The capture, *New York Evening Journal*, April 23, 1924.

on the bureau and one stuffed in his trouser pocket. The detective hammered on the door again. Celia turned to her husband and whispered, "Ed, what are you going to do?"

"Well you know the best thing I could do," Ed replied, "would be to end it for us before they break in."

Celia and Ed had discussed suicide before. The week since their baby Katherine had died had been bleak. Celia summed it up:

Baby gone, money gone, the cops wise, pictures of us in the papers — even the radio sending our description to every little hick town.

We knew pretty well we were through.

"Ed told me he wanted to kill himself," Celia told reporters after the arrest. "He wanted to kill me too and said he had made up his mind that the police would not get either of us alive."

Celia didn't want to die: "No, let's wait," she told her husband and "begged him not to shoot at me or the dicks unless they shot first." Some accounts had Celia still pleading with Ed not to shoot even as the police were crossing the threshold.

The detectives heard them whispering through the door. It was time to bust in. They hit the door with their shoulders. The door rocked two or three times on its hinges as the detectives hit it again and again. In the instant before the door burst in, Celia's mind was racing:

> I remembered about that "kill us on sight" order that was sent out in Brooklyn, and I was afraid if we'd give them half of an excuse they'd do it. A minute before, I didn't care what happened. Now all of a sudden like, I knew I didn't want to be killed, and I knew I didn't want Ed to be killed.

The detectives threw all their weight against the door, and "it went down with a bang." In the *Post*'s dramatic account:

> The door gave way. Facing the men of the law were Cooney with two pistols and his wife holding an automatic. The blue steel of the bob-haired bandit's gun glittered unsteadily. Then she cried out not to shoot. They would surrender.

There were plenty of cops who would not have minded if Celia was shot dead and buried, putting her out of their misery. The shake-ups, the demotions and reassignments, the long cold nights of lying in wait for the girl bandit, and all the jokes and sarcastic editorials would finally end then and there on a warm Florida night.

According to Celia, as the door was rocking on its hinges she had jumped to the bureau and grabbed the two guns sitting there, holding them by the barrels with the "ends pointing toward me and their handles sticking out away from me." She got in front of Ed shielding him from the police as the door crashed in. It just wasn't true that she was pointing the guns at the detectives, despite what some of the papers said. Since there weren't any reporters in the room, Celia thought that the detectives might have lied to "make them sound braver."

Ed hadn't resisted either, Celia protested. Ed didn't have his hand on the gun in his pocket when the door flew open. "That was a lie," said Celia:

> Ed stood there dumb-like with both his arms hanging down and his chin ducked. I don't believe he even remembered he had the gun in his pocket. Any man could of looked at him and seen he was through.

When the cops burst in, the *New York World* had Ed emerging from the back room, "his right hand on a .38 revolver half drawn from his side trouser pocket." But he stopped with the gun still in his pocket. "I quit, Bill," he said, recognizing Detective Casey from the neighborhood. Pushing the gun deeper into his pocket, Ed surrendered; he raised his hands high in the air. Standing there with his hands up he looked more like a stickup victim than a notorious holdup man. "I'm through, no more," he muttered. Edward Cooney was a punctured tire; all the fight had gone out of him.

According to Detective Casey's account for *True Detective*:

> This man, a daring crook whose escapades have startled the entire country, who stood upon the threshold of a twenty-year prison sentence, turned to me and with tears streaming from his eyes, said: "Bill, I suppose you know the baby died."

The *Brooklyn Eagle* summed it up, casting the pair, as the papers had done for the three months of their crime spree, as actors in a dramatic production:

> The light of high drama played about the arrest as a fitting climax to the thrilling incidents which have accompanied everything done by the country's most talked of woman bandit and her pal. The denouement was stirring in the extreme.

As the leading lady of this high drama, Celia was determined to play out the last act with her signature charming bravado. While Gray disarmed her husband, Celia held her automatic down at her side and handed it over to Casey with a smile. "Her poise never deserted her" as she donned her fur coat and grabbed a beaded bag. Then the officers led the fugitives out to the motorcars parked down the street: Ed in cuffs with his head hanging low, and Celia on the arm of a detective, jauntily making her exit from the cheap lodging house.

Local reporters had been tipped off to the arrest and were eagerly waiting outside. A writer for the *Florida Times-Union* described how Celia laughed and talked with Lieutenant Brown as she was escorted out to the police truck:

> "You're an awful little woman to shoot a pistol," the Lieutenant said.
>
> "Yes," she answered, "I'm small and I can use a pistol too, you just ask that detective that broke through our room door."
>
> "But you didn't shoot."
>
> "Not that time, but if he had shot at me I would not have hesitated."

In a later account, an obviously ghostwritten Celia remembered playing the part that she felt was demanded of her:

> I felt that strange vanity stirring in me like yeast now as the reporters crowded around us, big-eyed. Shooting questions at us as if we were important people. I felt my grief and my desperation slough off me like dead skin. They expected me to be hard and gay and reckless. And like a cloak I felt cynicism and gaiety settle jauntily on my shoulders. The newspapers had built me up as the iron-nerved bandit — and I found myself taking my cue, living up to it.

When they arrived at the Jacksonville police station, Celia and Ed were taken to a little office for interrogation by the two detectives from Brooklyn. They were initially charged with "suspicion," but the detectives were really trying to pin seventeen holdups and one assault-with-intent-to-kill charge on the Cooneys. When Casey and Gray had them alone in the little room the questioning began.

Celia was ready to talk. "What was the use to stall?" she remembered later. "Sure we're the ones. You know it. What's the use of telling you?"

Casey wanted more. He pulled a paper from his pocket, a list. He began to ask a lot of questions about the jobs they had pulled back in Brooklyn, about the Bohack robbery, Fishbein's drugstore, the A&P store, and on and on. He told them it would go easier on them if they told him everything then and there, concealing nothing. Celia was tired and ill. She listened distractedly. Not wanting to hear any more, she said: "Sure, all right, we did it all."

And Casey said: "That's fine; you both confess, eh?"

Ed jumped in. He had been quiet, but this wasn't his first run-in with the cops. He'd been grilled before and didn't want to talk about their crimes. He was fed up with all these questions: "What the — what is there to confess — you've got us, haven't you, and you know who we are. Why can't you lay off her? She's sick."

They were tired from being on the run for weeks and traumatized by the death of their child. Celia was still recovering from childbirth and the rigors of pregnancy on the lam. But the detectives weren't quite ready to quit.

Detective Gray took over. He played good cop and offered them a bone. In a soft voice he responded to Ed's outburst: "Sure thing, Cooney. We'll lay off you right now but there's one question I'd like to ask. Which of you shot the cashier?" This was the most serious charge against the couple. The Cooneys feared that the cashier was critically wounded and they could face the electric chair. Gray reassured them that Mazo was still alive, so they weren't facing a serious murder charge. Celia took the bait: "I shot him," she confessed.

"You know that's a lie," Ed said and took the blame himself.

In the *Daily News* account you can almost hear the sad violins playing softly in the background of that little office in Jacksonville. "Her Baby Dead," the *News* subhead read:

> The baby that the police had been informed was about to be born to the girl had come and gone. The little one arrived last Thursday, weak and undersized. Saturday it died. Cooney and his wife were heartbroken over the infant's death.

"New York's feminine gun terror, diminutive, dimpled Cecelia Roth Cooney, the celebrated bobbed-haired gunwoman" and her husband were not "the hardened, steel-nerved desperadoes" that the police and their victims described. The "youthful pair" were "amateurs" on the "verge of collapse" who "surrendered without the slightest resistance and immediately began a series of confessions."

With the stage dramatically set for a confession he did not actually witness, the *News* reporter imagined these lines for his tragic heroine: "Yes, I'm the bobbed haired gun woman you're looking for," she exclaimed. "But I was the only one responsible. It was through me that dear Eddie went wrong. I shot Nathan Mazo. My husband had nothing to do with that."

Dear Eddie contradicted her: "'That job at the National Biscuit was mine and so were the others' he declared, 'I'll take all the blame.'" This touching display of loyalty even softened up the reporter at the *News*, who wrote that the Cooneys' "anxiety to protect each other as both tried to take all the blame for each robbery would have brought the blush of shame to the grizzled cheek of a genuine footpad."

A *New York World* reporter later asked the Cooneys why they had chosen each other as partners in crime: "Mrs. Cooney answered that they were sure of each other. Cooney added that he knew his wife would stick it out." Ed shot the cashier that day on Pacific Street to protect his wife, and she confessed to try to save him. There was love and honor between these two thieves as each tried to take the fall for the other.

The Brooklyn detectives were pleased with themselves: they had their confessions. They laid off the "youthful pair" and locked them up in the Jacksonville jail for the night. As they led Celia to her cell, they patted her on the shoulder and said: "Sleep well, kid." Perhaps they, too, were moved by the Cooneys' commitment to each other; probably they were giddy with the satisfaction of capturing the Bobbed Haired Bandit.

"It's the biggest arrest we have ever figured in," said Detective Casey. "The smiles on the faces of Detectives F. S. Gray and W. J. Casey . . . will never wear off" said the caption, as the detectives posed beaming in triumph for a photographer from the *Florida Times-Union*.

Casey and Gray immediately sent a telegram to their boss, Captain Carey. They had captured the Bobbed Haired Bandit, and the right one this time. The Bob Squad could disband, and the largest manhunt in New York police history could be called off. The good news traveled quickly: "Police headquarters was jubilant at the news of the confession," and the *Brooklyn Citizen* headlined BROOKLYN POLICE NOW

BELIEVE IT IS THEIR TURN TO SNICKER OVER BOB-HAIR BANDIT
EPISODE.

The New York newspapers got the news nearly as fast as the New
York police. At least one reporter flew down to interview the couple,
and the capture of the Bobbed Haired Bandit was front-page news.
Sensational—and often conflicting—accounts of "the arrest that had
all the spectacular thrills of fiction" got top billing in all the New York
papers. Even that staid, old gray lady, the *New York Times*, found their
capture "news fit to print" on the very first page. And the news wasn't
limited to the city where the tabloids had been building the story for
months. From Washington, Philadelphia, and Chicago all the way to
Los Angeles and San Francisco, the capture of the Bobbed Haired
Bandit captured page one.

Alone in her Florida cell, exhausted, Celia was just glad the adventures of the famous gunmiss were done. A week later Celia would
write: "Anything was a relief after what we'd been through." She slept
solid—for the first time in nights—until they woke her up at seven the
next morning. "I'd have slept longer if they'd let me," she recalled.
Celia Cooney was nothing if not resilient: she was "brightened up,"
and "almost cheerful," after a just a few short hours of sleep. That may
"sound funny," she explained, but

> I'll tell you flat, I knew my little baby was better off where it had gone.
> And I knew that whatever they did couldn't send Ed to the electric
> chair now. And they couldn't shoot us, not on sight, or any other way.
> I'd worried so much that I guess I was just worried out for a while. I had
> ham and eggs and two cups of coffee, and felt fine.

After her morning coffee, Celia and her husband were ready to return
to New York. The papers claimed that they were "glad the chase was
over" and were even "so anxious to return to New York and plead
guilty to the crimes they have admitted that they waived extradition."

The Brooklyn bulls were anxious to return to New York as well.
They handcuffed Celia's right wrist to Ed's left wrist, but Celia's wrists
were so small that they had to clamp the cuff down almost as far as it
would go. Concerned, Detective Casey asked Celia if the cuffs
pinched her. "No," said Celia, doing her best to be agreeable (though

later Celia would ask him to loosen them for her). From the jail, the four made it to the Jacksonville station to catch the 12:01 "Florida Special" express to New York City. When they arrived at the station, there was already a throng gathered to gawk at the famous woman bandit.

If Celia was "almost cheerful" after breakfast, by the time she reached the station she was positively radiant. Celia flashed a demure smile to the crowd of reporters and onlookers at the Jacksonville station as she was led on board. CAPTURED, BOBBED-HAIR BANDIT STILL SMILES was the headline in the *Washington Post*. According to the *New York Times*, Mrs. Cooney was "calm, indifferent and vivacious. She smiled and waved good-bye as the train pulled out." Ed stayed in his funk, still "glum and nervous."

It was a long trip up from Jacksonville — more than twenty-four hours — with the weather gloomy all the way. Before boarding the train Celia wanted to buy a detective story magazine, but in Jacksonville "there were none at the news stands and she was much disappointed." She settled for "one full of beauty hints." The four of them sat down in the Pullman state room, the detectives locking the door so "as not to be bothered by reporters and people."

As the train rolled along into the evening, the trip "got sort of tiresome. Ed said hardly anything. Casey read a newspaper and Gray just yawned and twiddled his thumbs." Celia's cuffed arm was hurting: "It's no fun being chained by the arm all day long." She wanted to sit next to the window and look out, but she was cuffed on the wrong side and so Casey obligingly adjusted the cuffs for her. Still bored, Celia suggested a game of cards. The detectives asked the porter for a deck of pinochle cards, but he had only a standard deck. They played hearts instead. The detectives were nice to Celia: "By that time I had it figured out that they'd let me do about anything I pleased as long as I didn't try to get away," Celia recalled. They took her side of the handcuffs off and used it to chain both of Ed's hands together.

After a hearty dinner of chicken and steak and lots of coffee in the stateroom, Celia had the detectives call for the porter whom she instructed to make up her bed. Mindful of her appearance, Celia did up her hair in papers to "insure curls" for her arrival in New York the next day. This small act of vanity merited a headline in the *Post*: BANDIT COOL; CURLS HAIR ON TRAIN. Still fully dressed, she climbed into the upper berth — Casey called it the "caboose," Celia called it the "shelf" — and pulled a blanket over herself. She slept soundly through the night, eight solid hours. The two detectives sat up, sleepless, keeping an eye on a manacled Cooney sitting across from them.

It was a long night, and even taciturn Ed could not keep silent. Though still nervous he perked up a bit and stayed awake talking with the detectives. Perhaps he opened up because, according to Detective Casey, they were not strangers to each other. The detectives had known him for some time, and he hadn't always been sullen and withdrawn. Back in Brooklyn Ed had been friendly with the police. Sitting up that long night, Ed "fought shy of his bandit operation in the conversation," avoiding discussion of the robberies. "The talk ranged from baseball to police methods," a reporter noted, adding wryly, "in the latter Cooney showed particular interest."

News of Ed's dark mood preceded him to New York City. The talk of suicide and Ed's morose silence led the *Brooklyn Citizen* to speculate that upon his arrival in the city "Cooney's belt and necktie will be taken from him, and he will not be allowed to use a knife or fork in eating but will be placed on a diet of sandwiches." A SPECIAL GUARD would prevent the GIRL BANDIT'S HUSBAND FROM TAKING HIS LIFE read the *Citizen*'s headline.

As the train sped northward, the crowds in the passing stations grew. News of the capture of the Bobbed Haired Bandit had burned up the wires. The reporters were on them from the start, some riding from Jacksonville and more boarding in Washington and Philadelphia. The press corps was on the move. The reporters tried to gain entrance to the locked stateroom, knocking again and again, but Casey and Gray had orders not to let their prisoners talk to anyone. This was fine with Celia — at first: "I ain't gonna say nothing to nobody." She explained to a reporter: "I wouldn't see anybody because I'm not like an animal at the circus. I'm not on exhibition and won't have people looking at me. I won't be stared at."

But the Bobbed Haired Bandit *was* on exhibition. She was a traveling show. The Florida Special "was awaited by throngs" as it rattled the rails to New York. Everyone wanted to catch a glimpse of the famous girl bandit. Celia was prickly at first about all the attention, unsure how to handle all the adulation. The curtains were drawn in compartment H at Baltimore and Wilmington, but Celia kept lifting the curtain, offering a "free glimpse" of the bobbed bandit to the many who scanned the train for her. As the train left Washington, a reporter from the *New York American* discovered Celia and her police escort standing in the corridor outside her stateroom; Celia was looking out the window at the low-lying clouds. He asked her if she was afraid.

"Afraid? I should say not!" she shot back. "I don't fear anything, and I am feeling fine. But I don't want to see nobody about nothing — stall!" Turning on her heel she went back into her lair, the stateroom door locking behind her.

But Celia would not stay shut in. Later, the train "slowed up at a small town, and hundreds of natives had turned out for just a look at the girl." They were not disappointed; Celia was again standing in the corridor, one hand cuffed to the detective, "peering through the window panes, she smiled at the morbidly curious and waved a free hand at them." As they rushed north the crowds grew larger; thousands showed up at the station in Philadelphia as Celia and Ed passed through.

At Philadelphia some "Big Ikes" with wives in tow got on the train and bribed the steward to get the detectives to bring the Bobbed Haired Bandit to the dining car so they could eyeball her. Celia guessed "they thought they'd get a grand thrill seeing a girl dragged handcuffed through the train." The waiter claimed that he couldn't deliver lunch to the stateroom, but "Gray was wise to it. . . . He flashed his badge and said 'You go back and tell that Steward to send what we ordered and send it damn quick.'"

The reporters kept up their assault on the stateroom door and were ultimately rewarded for their persistence. Neither the detectives nor Celia Cooney could withstand the temptation of so much fawning attention, and reporter after reporter managed to gain an audience with the bandit couple. Sitting beside Celia, dressed in an army overcoat and a rough brown cap over a brightly striped silk shirt, Ed was characteristically curt when asked a question by a reporter from the *Daily News*: "I don't want to talk to no newspaper reporters and I won't talk to them," he growled. "His personality is sullen, pugnacious," the reporter went on to comment. But it wasn't Ed that the press or the public was really interested in hearing from. The story was Celia.

Celia rose to the occasion, playing the part of captured criminal celebrity for her public. By midday Tuesday the train was outside of Philadelphia and rolling on to New York. Celia could no longer contain herself; stalked by reporters, "the feminine desperado rebelled for hours against submitting to an interview but finally consented to talk" — after promising Ed that she would not discuss any of their stickups.

Celia met first and longest with a female reporter, Mary Mallon of the *New York Evening Post*, who cajoled her way into the stateroom by claiming to be even shorter than Celia. When Detective Gray told Celia there was a woman outside smaller than herself, Celia retorted, "Aw, there is not!" Her curiosity aroused, she sighed and said: "Well, let's see for our selves." The door opened, and the first reporter "slipped in." If the press seemed to have had little trouble recounting what went on in the stateroom before they were even admitted, once they breached the stateroom door the description grew richer.

This is what Mallon saw:

> A Pullman compartment with five persons in it — two detectives, one conductor, one husband, and one other — the bobbed haired bandit.
>
> A card table, over which the little bandit leaned.
>
> A window sill on which rested a big box of powder and a little box of rouge and half of a wide tooth white comb.
>
> Two packs of cards, one neatly in its box and the other scattered over the table.
>
> A pair of handcuffs, on which the eyes of the bandit fastened themselves — and from which she slowly lifted them to gaze at the reporter.
>
> She looked long out of rather bold black eyes, laughed and said, "You win — I bet I've got four inches on you."

Mallon and the other reporters, male and female, were fascinated by Celia. The mystery surrounding the identity of the Bobbed Haired Bandit had built to such a fever pitch that any detail about her character — who she was, what she thought, and especially what she looked like — was seized upon and printed:

> She's five feet four inches tall, is this bandit, and weighs 106 pounds. She's got coal black hair, straight and bobbed, and she's got black eyes. . . .

A thin gold wedding ring was on her hand and close by it a little gold ring with a small red stone in it. That was her engagement ring.

Until her capture the Bobbed Haired Bandit had been glimpsed for only a few panic-stricken minutes by her victims as they cowered before the business end of her automatic pistol. Now detectives, reporters, and the public could get a good look at the notorious bandit whose sartorial style had piqued so much curiosity. Beginning with her ride to the Jacksonville jail, the *New York World* described Celia as if commenting on the fashions at Palm Beach this season, drawing attention to her "mouse grey crepe de chine dress, a small helmet hat of cerise silk, white silk stockings and black patent leather ankle strap shoes." Since Celia and Ed refused to discuss their crimes, reporters filled the demand for news of the bandit with details of her appearance and manner. One *Daily News* reporter who talked to Celia a little later in the trip had little to report about her other than "her cheeks were rouged. Her famous bob was tucked up, caught with hairpins at her neck and confined in a net." "It's about down to my shoulders," Celia explained; "I've let it grow ever since it was first cut."

Not surprisingly, the bobbed bandit's hair was the subject of the most intense scrutiny. There was a lot invested in the bandit's locks, and the "bob question" filled many column inches in the daily papers. Declaring that the bandit's hair was no longer bobbed, the *World* voiced a very middle-class sigh of relief, reassuring its readers that this notorious criminal was nothing like their own bobbed haired daughters, those fun-loving flask-toting flappers: "She is not the flapper type and never was. She is the laundry worker she was before she sewed a pocket in the sealskin coat and packed an automatic in it." The *New York Sun*, with its working-class readership, arrived at much the opposite conclusion. An "odd factor was the fact that the bob haired bandit had her hair up when arrested," but to the great relief of the *Sun* reporter, "she admitted . . . that it really was bobbed." What she looked like was of such importance because her looks told the public who she was and what she represented in this new age of appearances. And that went a long way toward determining who was to blame for her very existence.

The other great sign of her pretension was the Hudson sealskin coat. After a lengthy discussion of Celia's hair, the reporter from the *World* got around to the almost-as-legendary fur coat. The mere "mention of her seal coat brought a grin" to Celia: "She looked up at it on a hook with its bright green lining showing."

In the public's eyes, however, Celia Cooney was now accused of a charge far more serious than vanity or perhaps even banditry. She was cited for being an uncaring mother, a woman whose actions had resulted in the death of her child and, far worse, a woman not sufficiently grief-stricken about the death of that baby. Other than the robberies, the subject the press most wanted to talk to Celia about was the fate of baby Katherine. Celia posed a problem for the press. Was she a hardened criminal or a bereaved parent? Could one be hard-boiled and a mother? Motherhood and banditry were not reconcilable in the American psyche, so once again two very different character portraits of the Bobbed Haired Bandit were assembled.

In the *Sun*'s interview with mother Cooney she was portrayed as cheerful, but "only once did the smile fade from Mrs. Cooney's face. That's when she told of the death of the baby." The baby represented hope in a hard life. "She was our first and we both loved her," Mrs. Cooney said. "Everything hard and bitter seemed to melt for a while and—" she broke off. "For a moment" the notorious bandit "seemed on the point of tears. Then she smiled again, but it was rather a weary smile." The press and its public wanted tears for the lost child. How close was she to crying?

In the *Post*, Mallon's interview with the Bobbed Haired Bandit turned to the subject of the lost child:

> "Baby just lived eight days," she said slowly, "then she died. Eddie and me we went to the funeral, we picked the coffin. It was hard to lose the baby."— She bit her lip and stopped talking.
>
> Her dark eyes looked out of the window as she spoke about her baby, but she didn't cry when she said the baby died.

Some newspapers seized on this lack of visible tears as a sign of Celia's true, hard-hearted nature. Where the *Sun* empathetically had Celia on the verge of tears, the more bourgeois *Herald-Tribune* noted that when Mallon asked about the baby, the question "brought no tears" from Celia Cooney. This was "a woman's question to a woman and mother bereft of her babe" that was "designed to touch the heart of even a girl bandit." But it hadn't: "If it touched her heart it touched a hard one, for Celia answered without a quiver of an eyelash." "Wasn't that a shame?" she was reported to have said, and "that was all, and Celia proceeded to powder her nose." A clear indication of vanity over maternity. "No Tears for Her Baby" scolded the *Herald-Tribune* in a subhead.

Celia's conversation with Mary Mallon was petering out; she was tired and depressed after talking about her baby. Just then the conductor was leaving the car. Celia called out to him, "We'll see you in about six months," and laughed a little. Celia turned to the reporter; she knew better. She looked outside the speeding train, "a glaring signboard flashed past the windows that announced the grandest circus ever." To Mallon she said: "This ain't no age of miracles. I guess it's more than six months for us and here's the circus in town." Ed perked up and finally smiled. "Say Celia," her husband said, "if you're out in time to see the circus, I'll give you money to go. You'd be lucky wouldn't you." It was a bit of gallows humor, and they both had a big laugh.

But laughter was not appropriate for a grief-stricken mother. The headline on Mallon's article in the *Post* read MISSING THE CIRCUS FRETS BANDIT CELIA. The hard-boiled bandit was not concerned with her fate, or the loss of her child, but only her own amusement. This version of Celia fit the legend of the devil-may-care girl bandit better than a grieving mother in shock. The telegraphic shorthand of the *Herald-Tribune* summed it up:

BOBBED-HAIR BANDIT, HOME, UNREPENTANT

"AIN'T SCARED OF NOTHIN,'"

SHOWS NO GRIEF FOR HER BABY,

HOPES TO SEE CIRCUS
BEFORE IT CLOSES.

Mallon herself was more understanding, even if the headline writers for the *Post* and the *Herald-Tribune* weren't; she remarked that, after all, the Cooneys were young and "the circus means an awful lot to them."

Mallon gamely tried to turn the conversation from circuses to robberies. Sitting at the card table in the stateroom, Celia was toying with the handcuffs the detectives had taken off of her. When asked about "her nerve and skill" with a pistol, Celia balked. This wasn't a subject for laughter or discussion. "I guess I won't talk about that," she said coolly to Mallon. Then, just as suddenly, her cheer came back, and she held the handcuffs out to the reporter. "They can make these fit any size wrist," she said: "Let's see if yours is as little as mine." "She clicked the sharp little teeth of the cuffs" until she found the size of Mallon's wrists. "'Almost the same as mine,' she said, and then dropped them for a powder puff."

As the train pulled toward Pennsylvania Station, Celia lost interest in the attention of the reporters and prepared for her grand entrance. The train was nearing Manhattan Transfer, the last junction before the city. Casey "signaled that the interview must close because Celia had to 'doll up' some more before facing the curious throng of New Yorkers at the station." Her powder, rouge, and Detective Casey's comb were laid out before her:

> "Look at my make-up stuff," she said. "Wait till you get out of here and I am going to use that stuff. We'll soon be in New York, and when you see me get off that train I'll look a lot better than I do now."

Celia thought about her gray crepe dress. She had worn it to their fateful last robbery at the National Biscuit Company when the cashier was shot, she was wearing it when she was arrested in that dingy room in East Jacksonville, and she would be wearing it when she stepped off the train in Manhattan. "This dress is not so good," she confided to Detective Casey, "but it's the best I got."

Celia looked into a glass set into the wall of the Pullman compartment and set to work. "Sprightly as a chorus girl before a big night," Celia put on some powder and lipstick and pulled the detective's little white pocket comb through her hair. "My nose — gee, it is shiny," she said. The detectives watched her and laughed.

The Florida Special pulled into the station. President Calvin Coolidge himself was leaving for Washington from the Pennsylvania Station on a train just ten minutes before their arrival; in fact, the two trains passed each other in the tunnel. But the crowd "practically ignored the departure of President Coolidge to rush to the lower train level to get a glimpse of Mrs. Edward Cooney": "Neither Presidents nor Jack Dempsey had attracted such a throng to Pennsylvania station as Celia Cooney, Brooklyn's Bobbed Haired Bandit and her husband, Edward did when they reached this city at 3:30" read the lead sentence in the *World*'s article announcing the Cooneys' arrival on April 22nd. "I guess it's true what they said," Celia later wrote, "that no President of the United States ever had a bigger mob to meet him."

PART V

Child of Misfortune

> And then suddenly, there was Celia Cooney . . .
> diminutive, seeming actually less than five feet as she
> stood before the fire of cameras and the eagerness of
> thousands of eyes. She wore the same seal skin coat,
> the sight of which terrorized Brooklyn storekeepers as
> the sight of Robin Hood's green doublet terrorized fat
> abbots.   —Mitzi Kolisch, *Brooklyn Citizen*

"The arrival of the couple from Florida bordered on the spectacular," the *New York Times* reported; the crowd that arrived to "cheer" the president stayed to "jeer" the bandit. As much as it must have insulted the sensibilities of the *Times*' editors, it was not the president, however, whom most people came to see. The Bobbed Haired Bandit was expected: the morning papers had published the hour of her arrival, and the crowds assembled to see her. The *Brooklyn Eagle* estimated that there were ten thousand people there to see that bandit and fewer than five hundred "to view the departing chief executive of the nation." After all, Celia Cooney was a home-grown celebrity, and Silent Cal did not pack a baby automatic or a sharp tongue. GIRL BANDIT CHEERED ON ARRIVAL, the *Evening Journal* headlined on page one. The public's priorities were clear.

Women outnumbered men in the EXCITED MOB that gathered just to see her: "They hung from every stairway and rail landing leading from the train level." Ring Lardner commented that Penn Station was "so crowded with photographers and hero worshippers that the detectives can't hardly get the couple out. Everywhere the little gal is greeted with smiles and murmurs of approval and the only wonder is that some of her admirers did not rush up and kiss her." The police attempted to keep the platform clear, but then they made the mistake of opening a special gate for all of the newspaper men and photographers, and the "unruly throng" surged through and "jammed the platform":

> The crowd left the presidential party flat and rushed to catch a glimpse of her. Stairways were thronged. Hundreds of faces pressed against the

grilled fences. Camera men who a moment before had been snapping the nation's Chief Executive rushed to points of vantage to photograph the nation's most talked about bandit.

"The sound of an approaching train was heard." The press was all elbows. The cameramen set their machines. A hush fell over the crowd. "I haven't had a thrill like this in the game before," a photographer was overheard saying. "Chasing the 'Wolf of Wall Street' across three States is nothing compared to this." The train had almost come to a standstill now. "They'll bring her out on a stretcher," someone called.

The *Daily News* reported:

> An army of photographers shoved and upbraided each other, seeking a vantage point from which to photograph her. In their turn the photographers were jostled and eclipsed by surging waves of humanity, in which each individual was regardless of everything but his chance to see the bobbed-hair bandit.

It took ten minutes for the police to clear the way to open the door of the car in which Celia and Ed were riding. Standing in the crowd on the platform was a full complement of police brass. The men who led the Bobbed Haired Bandit hunt for Police Commissioner Richard Enright were impatient to get their hands on Celia Cooney. The chief of detectives himself, Inspector John S. Coughlin, and Detective Captain Daniel Carey, who ran the day-to-day investigation in Brooklyn, were both part of the platform party.

Detectives Casey and Gray were unprepared for the crush that faced them. Captain McCloskey, who had been assigned the task of getting the couple to police headquarters downtown, didn't have enough officers to manage the mob. At first they drafted the railroad detectives to aid them, but even they were not enough.

After all of the other passengers had exited the train, the detectives decided it was time to move the prisoners. Edward Cooney was handcuffed to a tired, unshaven Detective Carey. With the collar of his brown overcoat turned up and his brown cap "pulled low over his face," he was quietly taken out the other side of the car and rushed up a back stairway. But the "police and station guards were almost power-

Top: "Detectives vainly fought to keep back the hundreds who jammed into the Pennsylvania station to catch a glimpse of the bobbed hair bandit and her husband and companion in crime." *Bottom left:* Celia Cooney as she was later escorted from court by Detective Casey. *Bottom right:* "President and Mrs. Coolidge waved goodbye at Pennsylvania station yesterday after a brief visit." *New York Daily News,* April 23, 1924.

less when the moment came for the girl to alight." Celia had a guard of four strong men surrounding her, and as they got out of the train, "immediately a battery of flashlights was let go that sounded like a cannonade."

"Grinning behind the magazine she held to hide her face from the cameras," the gungirl stepped onto the platform. As the "flashlights exploded and motion picture cameras ground," Celia recalled, "there was a wham, bang, flash that made me think the whole place had been hit by lightning." She blinked her eyes, threw a hand up in front of her face and ran the gauntlet of reporters and cameramen. Then the "crowd rushed in" under "a whole barrage of flashlights" and "amid the wildest excitement."

The detectives propelled Mrs. Cooney toward the stairs: "Most of the crowd from the train went one way and we went another, up some iron steps. As we neared the top some man gave a yell, 'Here she comes,' and then there was such a yelling you would think it was a ballgame."

They were heading for the street toward the Thirty-first Street exit where two police cars awaited, engines running. The Cooneys were to escape their pursuers in a motorcar once more. The windows of the buildings facing the exit were crowded with curious men and women who were literally climbing the lampposts for a good view. But the detectives and their prisoners could not reach the exit where the cars were standing; the crush of the mob was too intense. When they reached the concourse, Celia recalled:

> I never saw such a sight. Do you know how big that Pennsylvania Station is? Well, it was filled, jammed with people crowding, yelling, pushing. "Hi! Yes, that's her! The Bobbed Haired Bandit."

Finding their way blocked by the surging crowds, they bullied their way to the nearby headquarters of the Pennsylvania Railroad police. Sitting down to get their breath, the detectives placed a telephone call to police headquarters asking for reserves to clear a path that would allow the beleaguered party to make its escape. The reserves, including a squad of mounted men, arrived and quickly set to work cutting a swath through the mob: "From the temporary refuge the police sallied out at ten minutes to four o'clock."

"The cops had their clubs out—and even then we nearly got pushed off our feet," Celia remembered. The detectives were determined to make the final push: "A rush was made by the party for a waiting automobile in the station's driveway. The girl was swallowed up by the swirl of humanity. Only the little lavender pink hat she wore marked her passage through the crowd." The wedge of officers struggled against the press of bodies: "Again the barrage of flashlights came as the slight girlish figure was half led and half carried through by detectives with uniformed policemen and special officers of the Pennsylvania [Railroad] bending every effort to clear a passageway."

But then there was more trouble. From out of nowhere a "little fellow pushes in waving a piece of paper all excited." It was a writ of habeas corpus. The detectives were none too pleased: "Who the ——— are you?" Casey and Gray demanded.

The excited little fellow waving his arms about was Sam Leibowitz, a thirty-year-old criminal defense attorney from Brooklyn. The young lawyer was making a name for himself among Brooklyn judges, lawyers, and "the professional criminal fraternity" as an exceedingly capable and ambitious criminal attorney. But outside this small world he was unknown. A case like the Bobbed Haired Bandit could change this.

Leibowitz would soon be very well known. Within a year he would successfully defend Al Capone on a shooting rap, and from then on there was rarely a high-profile case in New York in which Leibowitz was not somehow involved. At the time of his retirement from criminal defense his record was near perfect. Out of one hundred thirty-nine capital murder cases Leibowitz took on, he won one hundred thirty-two straight acquittals and bargained six lesser sentences. Only one of his clients went to the chair, and that man, Leibowitz claimed, had withheld critical information. Other lawyers of the time, such as the great Clarence Darrow, are better remembered, but as a criminal defense attorney Sam Leibowitz was one of the best.

In the spring of 1924, however, Samuel S. Leibowitz was a near nobody. The newspapers consistently misspelled his name, transposing the "ei" in his last name, and sometimes giving him an erroneous middle initial "I." And to Detectives Casey and Gray he was simply a pain in the ass.

As Celia remembers, Casey and Gray were "awful sore" about the arrival of the lawyer. The detectives thought they had the Cooneys all sewn up. All the way up on the fast train they had "pumped" the Cooneys "full of hop about getting off lighter" if they "pleaded guilty and wouldn't have a lawyer." Celia didn't "know whether we were simps or not," but "we believed them."

Inspector Coughlin expected that his minions would rush the suspects directly to police headquarters downtown for questioning. From there they would be taken to District Attorney Dodd's office in Brooklyn for more questioning. They were to be arraigned in a police court that very afternoon and then indicted by a Kings County grand jury "without delay." When Sam Leibowitz stuck his mug in, frantically waving those writs of habeas corpus and yelling "it's the law, it's the law. Don't you know it's the law!" in the detective's faces, all hope of a speedy resolution vanished.

The writs of habeas corpus ordered Captain McCloskey to produce his captives "forthwith." Leibowitz had argued before a State Supreme Court judge that since the Cooneys had been arrested without a warrant they were actually being detained illegally and their seizure was unconstitutional. One judge was unconvinced and turned him down, but the lawyer found another who reluctantly agreed.

The lawyer wanted Celia and Ed out of police custody, and quick. He told the papers that he wanted to keep them from "being put through the 'third degree' by the police and to insure them every protection guaranteed by the law." His plan was to get the Cooneys taken before a magistrate and then straight to jail in the custody of the department of corrections. Jail was a far safer place for them than the quiet office of Brooklyn District Attorney Charles Dodd where the DA could sweat them.

The writ and the little lawyer infuriated the haggard cops, but they had a more immediate concern: to get the celebrated criminals out of Penn Station and away from the increasingly pushy mob of onlookers. They piled into their cars, and Leibowitz jumped in with them. With the mounted police and the reserves clearing a path through the thousands, they drove south from Thirty-first Street down Seventh Avenue, bypassing police headquarters where a crowd was awaiting the arrival of the girl bandit, heading toward the Supreme Court on Chambers

Street in Lower Manhattan where yet another crowd was gathering to witness the Bobbed Haired Bandit and her confederate dragged before a judge in handcuffs.

At four-fifteen in the afternoon they were ushered into the courtroom of Justice Leonard Giegerich. Leibowitz couldn't expect much sympathy from this judge. The day before it was Giegerich who had denied him his writ in the first place. According to Celia, Leibowitz "was just getting good started in a speech when somebody got up and said: 'Your honor, who is this man? I don't believe he's their lawyer at all.'" Assistant District Attorney Walsh from Brooklyn and Manhattan's Acting District Attorney Driscoll wanted Samuel Leibowitz out of the courtroom. Before the dispute got out of control Justice Giegerich stepped in and took command.

"Put them on the stand," Justice Giegerich demanded of the Cooneys. Ed was first in the witness chair.

"Do you approve the employment of counsel?" Sam Leibowitz asked him.

"No sir," Ed replied.

Leibowitz pulled out a letter written by Ed's brother Tom and showed it to him. "Did he have authority to hire a lawyer for you?" the lawyer asked.

"No."

Leibowitz tried another avenue: "Do you object to his hiring a lawyer for you?"

"Yes, sir."

What kind of a defense was this? Leibowitz couldn't even get his own client to admit to being his client. Frustrated, Leibowitz asked Ed to read the letter he had handed him:

> Brother Ed: We have retained Counselor Leibowitz to represent you and Celia. Do whatever he tells you. Don't worry. We will do all we can to help you. Brother Tom.

After he read it, he didn't know quite what to think. Ed "appeared confused" and changed his answer to a more ambiguous "undecided."

One reporter noted that Ed had "wilted." He "faltered, stumbled for his words, almost cried." At the table together, Celia was Ed's lifeline: "When her husband appeared confused in the courtroom, she bent forward and listened to him. He leaned forward like a child seeking comfort, and when he looked up again his face was composed." When Celia took the stand the same reporter painted a very different picture:

> There is something strange about this twenty-year old girl—something fascinatingly unusual in her manner. She is not pert, not aggressive. If she were of a different social order, one would say that she is dignified and had absolute poise and balance. As she sat on the witness stand beside Justice Giegerich in Manhattan Supreme Court, her voice was even, clear, cool. It was not defiance. It was again—poise. . . . the girl was calm, certain of every word and action. Where does she get her strength? It is more than a physical matter. It is something which comes from her mind, untrained as it is.

Celia's answer was decisive. The judge asked, "Do you desire counsel?" "No," she replied. "Everybody seemed glad," Celia remembered, "but Leibowitz." Another report had the lawyer "stunned," and not surprisingly. Celia and Ed were throwing away their right to a first-rate lawyer, and Leibowitz's first chance to make front-page news as a criminal defense attorney was rapidly disappearing. After Celia's curt response, there wasn't much else to argue. Justice Giegerich dismissed both writs, and Celia and Ed were officially surrendered to the police. "Edward Cooney had to be supported as he left the courtroom for District Attorney Dodd's office," but "she walked out with a firm step," remarked the reporter from the *Brooklyn Citizen*. The detectives hustled them out of the courtroom toward a waiting automobile.

It took some doing to get them into the car. The press had followed them downtown, and "a battery of cameras greeted their appearance in the corridors." As they hit the street, they were met by yet another crowd of two thousand persons. Anywhere the Bobbed Haired Bandit appeared, a mob of press and onlookers swelled up. Fortunately for the police, the entrance to the Brooklyn Bridge is just blocks away from the tall granite columns of the State Supreme Court, and in minutes the vehicle holding the Cooneys had left the crowds and cameras of Manhattan behind and was headed over the bridge to Brooklyn. Having cleared the legal hurdles, the detectives were eager to get the couple to District Attorney Dodd's office for some serious "sweating."

When Celia and Ed reached the Court Street offices of the Brook-

Celia Cooney, carrying her magazine, escorted by Detectives Casey and Gray. (Library of Congress)

lyn DA, they were met by an even larger crowd of the curious than the one they had just escaped. Court Street was "filled." The hometown mob was a little less adoring than the ones across the river. "This time," Celia remembered, "they booed and yelled at me something disgusting. And one woman yelled out, 'I hope they hang her.'"

The detectives herded their prisoners through the crowds and into the Brooklyn courthouse. Safely inside, with all outside doors locked behind them, the couple took an elevator to an office on an upper floor where Assistant District Attorney Thomas C. Hughes was seated behind a large desk, smiling, openly pleased with himself now that the criminal couple was caught. In the room with him were two other Brooklyn ADAs, Police Captains Carey and McCloskey, and the couple's chaperones: Detectives Casey and Gray. For Celia's benefit, three policewomen were also present. Celia didn't like them: they were "dressed like anybody else — you'd have thought they were manicures or stenographers, and they eyed me up and down to look at my clothes and hat and shoes and whispered about me not being bobbed haired at all."

Hughes began the questioning. After trying to "lay a lot of stuff on us that we hadn't done — holding up a milk wagon, and robbing a truck and shooting at a cop," Celia, "calm and straightforward in her statements," took the lead and made a complete confession. Speaking clearly and looking over to Ed periodically for support and affirmation, Celia admitted to all ten jobs they had done in Brooklyn, beginning with the first Roulston robbery on January 6 and ending with the botched National Biscuit job on April 1 that led to their capture. The district attorney's office prepared ten separate charges of assault and robbery against the pair based on this confession. "Her attitude, Mr. Hughes said," and the *Herald-Tribune* reported, "was that of a girl who had 'come to the end of her rope' and was willing to tell everything and take her punishment."

Whether Celia was "willing to tell everything" is debatable. She admitted to the ten robberies, but she also made sure that *her* version of the Bobbed Haired Bandit story was heard by the attending cops and prosecutors, as well as the journalists who were sure to interview the lawmen later on. One delicate topic was the taunting and threatening notes to the police that were attributed to the girl bandit. In her confession to Hughes, Celia admitted to writing two of these notes to the police but denied writing the note that called the detectives a bunch of fish peddlers. Later, in her newspaper memoirs, she claimed just the one note that cleared Helen Quigley (which, incidentally, calls the police "dirty fish peddling bums") and denied writing any others. Celia also took pains to point out the moral code that she and Ed had followed in conducting their crimes. As the ADA reported to the press: "They were careful never to take money from the persons of their victims, confining their search to cash registers and stamp drawers."

At one point Hughes claimed he asked her: "Why did you really go into this business?" "Only to provide a good home for the baby when it arrived," Celia replied. She elaborated: "Eddie remarked to me one night how easy it was to get away with hold-ups. I agreed, and we began to think of doing it. We kept coming back to having a baby on $30 a week." Maybe remembering the newspaper reports of her and Ed's free-spending ways, Celia wanted to set the record straight:

> When I went into that that first store and said "Stick 'em up," I wasn't seeing diamond earrings and gin and jazz and a good time — I was thinking of pretty little pink shoes, pink leather baby shoes like the ones I saw on Atlantic avenue, and I was thinking, if I can get away with a big wad once and quit, maybe this baby that's coming won't have the rough time I had.

She told the ADA that she had hoped their final robbery would raise enough money so that they could get a new, clean start in Florida and, in a *Herald-Tribune* reporter's words, "the baby would be born in a real home with flowers about the door and green grass and trees." ROBBED TO GET HOME FOR BABY GIRL was the normally unsympathetic *Herald-Tribune*'s headline on this day. Celia's assembly of her own story seemed to be working.

Ed described the shooting of Nathan Mazo at the National Biscuit office as a gesture of chivalry as much as an act of violence. "I was afraid she would be hurt," Ed told Hughes, explaining that the cashier had thrown Celia to the floor in an attempt to grab her gun: "I shot through the door more to impress the man he couldn't hurt my wife than to hurt him." Ed also claimed that "we had decided to make the biscuit company haul our last job holdup. I knew that drivers brought a lot of money into the office." He echoed Celia, claiming the stickup was just to get enough money to get down to Florida where "he would have gotten work from a man he knew and 'gone straight.'"

Hughes was pleased that he had obtained a full confession from the lips of the Bobbed Haired Bandit, and he seemed charmed by the couple. "They are much in love with each other and each desires to shoulder most of the blame," the ADA reported, and, including a plug for Ed's much maligned masculinity, added that "certainly her husband acts in a most manly way toward her and she in turn would save him if she could."

Following Celia's lead, and knowing a good story when they heard one, the *Herald-Tribune*, one of the two papers to report in any depth on this first meeting at the DA's office, led their day's article on the Bobbed Haired Bandit with this:

> Celia Cooney, Brooklyn's bobbed-hair bandit, dreamed of the tiny stranger that was to come to her, and she resented the fate that ordained that her baby would be born in a cheap furnished room. Her husband was a mechanic for $30 a week. It was difficult for two to get along. But with three, and with all the incumbent expense —

With this pregnant pause the paragraph ends, leading into details of the robberies committed in the name of the then-unborn babe.

Others were not buying — or selling — Celia's morality tale. The *New York Times* reported essentially the same story, but from a different angle. With a condescending air befitting its stature and audience, the *Times* reported that "notwithstanding the fact that there are facilities in New York which permit the birth of children at little or no expense, Celia Cooney stuck to her original story that it was because of the expected baby that she and her husband . . . turned to a career of crime." The *Times* then sniffed that Celia felt "the world owed them a living." More perceptively, the *Times* reporter went on to comment that Celia "seems to consider herself the heroine of a melodrama."

◉ 19

Celia was playing the heroine as she left the district attorney's office on April 22nd, waving a hand at the assembled photographers and "motion picture men" while the police hustled her and Ed through the halls, down the elevator, and out the doors where "police reserves had to be called to keep the crowd back and the traffic open." According to the *New York World*, Celia Cooney "had confessed and felt better." The Cooneys were off for the night to a holding cell at the Brooklyn police headquarters on Poplar Street.

The Poplar Street station was an unadorned and unimpressive three-story shoebox with barred windows, constructed out of light brick turned gray by soot and located within sight and sound of traffic rumbling by overhead on the Brooklyn Bridge. It was a five-minute drive to the station from the DA's office, but it was still late, after midnight, by the time Celia and Ed got there. Ed's mother was allowed to see her son for a moment at police headquarters: "He embraced her, as did his wife." When they arrived Celia was "tired but smiling," and as she went to her cell she called out: "Well — so long Eddie." Edward was led off to the men's cells.

The sleeping accommodations at the station house were jail standard: a hard mattress on a narrow wood bench in a small cell. It didn't seem to matter to Celia. At one in the morning, spent, she took off her turban and the famous sealskin coat and was sound asleep in a few minutes. She slept through the entire night, checked on the half hour by a "six-foot giantess," cell matron Christina McPeth. Ed wasn't so fortunate. He took off his hat, coat, and shoes and lay down but still couldn't sleep. He was up a half-dozen times at night, smoking cigarettes and pacing his five-by-eight cell. No doubt nerves were partly to blame, but the "continual howls and outcries" of drunken fellow inmates didn't help much either.

"How's Ed?" Celia asked the giantess as she was awoken at six o'-clock. She then requested a comb and set to work styling her "short but unbobbed" hair, as several papers saw fit to comment. "How's the kid?" Ed asked from his cell across the station house. Neither Celia nor Ed could eat the breakfast they were offered; they stuck to coffee, Ed gulping down several cups "as if nerving himself for the ordeal he knew was before him." Celia seemed unconcerned and asked for her lipstick and mirror, which the matron first refused, but then they were "gallantly surrendered by that Southern Beau Brummel of the Brooklyn Force, Lt. Reuben Conner of Georgia." Meanwhile, groups of young girls, likely from the public school around the corner, gathered around Brooklyn police headquarters hoping to catch a glimpse of their new heroine.

Celia was still inside, waiting, as the police readied the "guest room" for the lineup. When they were ready, Ed, looking disheveled, and Celia, unwashed but pulled together in her pink turban and trademark sealskin coat, walked out, single file, taking their positions in the lineup that took place every morning at Brooklyn police headquarters. Facing them were fifty anonymous detectives wearing black masks. As the Cooneys were led into the room, Celia recognized Detectives Casey and Gray, even under their masks. She smiled and gave them a "hello." The detectives returned Celia's greeting, and "then the business of the day began."

It certainly wasn't business as usual. As the *Brooklyn Eagle* reported with a certain amount of affection:

> Celia at bay was just as impudent as Celia at large. Her dirty, impudent, little gamin's face crinkled with smiles, and many were the sallies which flew about. The black masked detectives grinned frequently, and Capt. Carey, who presided, smiled too.

After the lineup, the couple was led upstairs to a large trial room where their victims and witnesses against them were brought in one at a time. In front of the people they had held at gunpoint, Celia played the part of the sassy gungirl once more. Abraham Fishbein, the proprietor of the grocery store the couple robbed on January 22nd, was the first up. "She came and asked me if I had any whitefish," Fishbein told the assembled lawmen, then looked over Celia: "Yes, this is the girl all right. That's the young lady. Why she nearly scared me to death with her gun. I had $85 in my till. She took every cent."

"Bobbed-Hair Girl and Husband Pose for Camera," *New York World*, April 24, 1924.
(Library of Congress)

"'You poor fish,' said Celia, almost under her breath. And then, 'Are you sure you had that much?' She grinned at the storekeeper. 'We counted it, very carefully — it was only $17.'" The room erupted in laughter.

That was the *Brooklyn Eagle*'s version. The *Daily News* got it the other way around, with Fishbein claiming that they had stolen seventeen dollars and "Cooney, his usually scowling face wreathed in smiles, winked at his wife, then said: 'Say, you were so scared you didn't know what we took. We lifted $85 from you.'" But in every newspaper report, the Cooneys teased and taunted their victims, disputing the amount they had stolen. Next up were Mr. and Mrs. Weiss, the couple whose drugstore the Bobbed Haired Bandit robbed while squads of police were drilling in the armory across the street. Mr. Weiss stepped forward and spit out his accusation: "You took $35 from me." "'Taint so," Ed shot back, "we only got $7 from you — don't care what you say." Peter Kossman, manager of the second Bohack's robbed by the Cooneys, followed: "You robbed me of $150 on February 2. Haven't forgot that, have you?" Celia "feigned great surprise," replying with "you know we only got $60." Ed jumped in, making a pointed distinction regarding property and labor: "And we only got that $60 out of the cash register too — not your pants pocket."

When there wasn't joking, there was high drama. Helen Foggerty, an employee of the National Biscuit Company, was brought face to face with Celia in the lineup. "Yes — yes — that's the girl," Helen managed to gasp out before her knees gave out and a detective had to catch her. As the girl was carried out of the room in a dead faint, "Celia Cooney's smile broadened." "It was a disdainful smile," claimed the *Herald-Tribune*.

Celia and Ed kept up the circus as thirteen of the fourteen witnesses positively identified them as the Bobbed Haired Bandit and her tall male companion. Only at one moment did they seem repentant. Nathan Mazo, the wounded National Biscuit cashier, walked up to the couple and looked them over carefully, first Ed, and then Celia.

"That's the bobbed-haired bandit, Cap," said Mazo.

Celia turned to him. "Mazo, I'm sorry you were shot," she said. "It's all a mistake."

Her sincerity was questioned. The newspapers were not quite sure how repentant the Bobbed Haired Bandit really was. As she issued her apology to Mazo, "there was trace of a smile on her lips," the *Herald-Tribune* noted, editorializing that "it left room to wonder just how much was meant."

The papers were running two competing versions of the Bobbed Haired Bandit story. Was she the brazen gunmiss who enjoyed her notoriety with a smirk upon her lips? Or was she a bereaved and remorseful mother, a devoted wife who stole for her baby and was now eager to take the blame and accept her punishment? The press flipped and flopped between these two narratives. The *Herald-Tribune*, which only a day before had led with a heart-wrenching story of Celia's pregnancy and the Cooneys' poverty, had this to say the very next day when describing Celia in her lineup:

> Basking in the limelight? — Yes.
> Repentant? — How did they get that way?
> Hard-boiled? — Mind yer business!
> At times of repose Celia's small eyes became even smaller. The lines around her mouth hardened into a cold, stony expression. It was if she would say, "Well what of it? We showed 'em while it lasted, didn't we?"

The *Daily News* couldn't even make up its mind how to package Celia within the same story, leading the day's article about the bandit couple's lineup with the headline TAMED GUNGIRL PLEADS GUILTY, then continuing the report a few pages later with the headline BOBBED GUNWOMAN JEERS VICTIM. Was Celia still jeering at the law, or was she tamed? Was she sorry or — in the words of the *World* — still "SAUCY"?

After the lineup, Ed and Celia were taken off to be fingerprinted. Celia didn't like it one bit. They "took my hand," she remembers, "first one and then the other, like it was a horse's hoof or something not human, and smeared it with black and pressed it down on a piece of paper." These weren't the detectives getting their names in the paper for the capture of the Bobbed Haired Bandit; they were the ones who did overtime staking out the cold streets trying to catch her. They tried to make Celia "feel like dirt." But Celia had her ways of boosting her self-esteem. Turning her attention to the ranking officer, Captain Carey, she pleaded with him for the return of her rouge and lipstick.

Seeing no harm, the captain relented, and Celia "went at once to a mirror in the fingerprint room and with a slowly blossoming smile applied cosmetics." "She brightened appreciably in the process," the *Sun* reported.

Meanwhile, over at the Kings County courthouse, Assistant District Attorney Harry Sullivan assembled a grand jury, calling before it witnesses from the recent lineup so the DA's office could get immediate indictments on robbery and assault charges. After hearing evidence, three indictments were returned almost immediately for the couple, while Ed picked up a fourth. For the Bohack robbery on February 2nd and the Butler robbery on the 23rd, Celia and Ed were charged with robbery in the first degree, grand larceny in the second, and assault, second degree. For the National Biscuit heist, both Ed and Celia were charged with attempted robbery in the first degree, and for shooting the cashier Ed received an additional charge of assault in the first degree. As soon as the indictments came in, District Attorney Dodd was notified. Of all of these indictments, he chose to press only the robbery and assault charges stemming from the Bohack job against the couple because of the comparatively large sum of money that was alleged to have been stolen: two hundred fifty dollars (Celia and Ed claimed they grabbed only sixty). Warrants for the other indictments, Dodd explained, would be lodged with the respective prison authorities, holding out the possibility — or threat — that the Cooneys would face these indictments after serving their first sentence.

It was still before eleven o'clock in the morning when the Cooneys were brought over to the Brooklyn court building. A crowd had formed outside police headquarters awaiting Celia's departure.

"Is that her?"

"I don't know. What do you think?"

"The attention was amazing," the *Telegram and Evening Mail* reported:

Windows in the house opposite headquarters were at a premium. Several perched on the fire escape. Girls in gingham "boudoir" caps leaned out over the sills. One woman who lived across the street was so afraid she would miss sight of the "bobbed-haired bandit" that she combed her own hair at the window where she would be sure to miss nothing.

All this excitement to see one little girl.

Celia and Ed escaped the excited crowd at Poplar Street only to arrive at the courthouse a few minutes later to find another mob, one that would grow to thousands as word spread that the famous gungirl was inside. Ed and Celia were first brought up to Dodd's office for a private meeting, then back down to the courtroom where they were to be arraigned.

Waiting for the DA and the Cooneys in the courtroom were Samuel Leibowitz and his law partner, Jacob Shientag. "Sam Bobs up Again, " the *Eagle* commented wryly. Sam's partner stepped up beside the prisoners, in front of the judge, and said, "Your Honor, we represent these two. They desire to enter a plea of not guilty."

The judge sitting before the Cooneys was Justice George W. Martin. Judge Martin, like Sam Leibowitz, was relatively unknown outside the Brooklyn court community in 1924, having sat on the bench only a few years. Like Leibowitz, he would later make headlines and gain fame. But in Martin's case it would be infamy: a little more than a decade later the judge was accused by the New York State attorney general of using the bench to gain money and influence.

Leibowitz had faced Judge Martin before. Just the year before, he had won his forty-sixth acquittal in a row — reversing the conviction of chicken-store thief Frank di Martine — in front of Martin. And years later, Leibowitz would himself stand before Judge Martin charged with "fixing" a witness in the famous Acuna police scandal trial until Martin dismissed the case. But today, April 23, 1924, the judge who would later be vilified for his rank favoritism was not showing Sam Leibowitz or his partner any leniency.

"Are you sure you know what you are doing?" Judge Martin asked after the lawyers entered the plea of not guilty for the couple. Then, turning to the Cooneys, he said:

Well, let me tell both of you that if you expect any consideration; that is, if you deserve any consideration, the time to lay the basis for it is now. If you have been guilty of these robberies you can expect no mercy if you compel the county to accept the expense of a trial and add perjury.

"I might advise the Court," District Attorney Dodd spoke up, "that only this morning in my office both these defendants told me that they did not have a lawyer and did not desire any."

Seeing his case slipping away — for the second time — Leibowitz piped in: "Let me say that while the man may be guilty of these robberies, the girl has a perfectly meritorious defense, even if she did commit the robberies alleged against her."

The lawyer never had a chance to expound upon this "meritorious defense"; the impatient judge was not going to listen to an argument if he didn't have to. He cut in, declaring, "we will settle this matter of attorney's right now," and asked Celia and Ed if they wanted legal representation.

Celia fingered a button on her sealskin coat and then whispered to Ed. Then she spoke, softly: "We have no lawyers — don't want any Judge."

Addressing Samuel Leibowitz and Jacob Shientag, Judge Martin said: "Gentlemen, you are not in this case, kindly retire."

The judge then turned to the prisoners and asked them how they wish to plead. Ed hesitated and then half mumbled the word "guilty."

"They plead guilty your Honor," the clerk reiterated.

"Very well, I remand you to Raymond Street Jail until Tuesday for sentencing." With that, Celia and Ed were marched out of the courtroom.

When the pair had left the room, Judge Martin, no doubt pleased with himself now that he had extracted a guilty plea from the pair, was magnanimous enough to share the credit. Addressing the reporters he launched into a speech praising the detectives and prosecutors for the "excellent example of perfect work" and cooperation in "running down and arresting these bandits who had spread terror for several months in Brooklyn." He then congratulated them all for the rapidity with which they had dispatched this case. Speed and economy were at a premium in this Brooklyn court. Martin was proud of his efficiency. With a guilty plea the courts could clear another case off a schedule

Top left: "After being positively identified by thirteen persons who had been held up by them, the feminine Jesse James and her husband (arrows) were taken from Brooklyn police headquarters, thence to court." *Top right:* "Celia Cooney through it all never lost her smile, the smile she wore since her capture, nor did her husband lose his sullen air as the two appeared in County court, Brooklyn, to take their medicine." *Bottom:* "Mounted police had to force lane through mob for auto as the Cooneys were taken from County court, Brooklyn, to jail." "Girl Bandit Faces 20 Years," *New York Daily News,* April 24, 1924.

already overburdened with cases stacked up from Prohibition and its attendant lawlessness.

"Not in the history of Brooklyn," Brooklyn's *Eagle* opined, "has the round up of any crook caused so much celebration between the local forces of law and order." The paper continued on, perceptively speculating as to the reason behind this jubilant celebration:

> Celia, as a matter of fact, has "got the goat" of all cops, the detectives and the District Attorney. With this slip of a girl at large it was impossible for these public servants to maintain any sort of dignity, flouted as they were by the bob-haired flapper who had made a laughingstock of the law for so long a time.

While the judges, DAs, and detectives were patting themselves on the back, Celia and Ed were being hustled out the back door of the courthouse. Some twenty-five hundred gawkers had gathered in the street, blocking every exit. The police captain in charge again had to call out the reserves and bring in mounted police to clear a path so that the automobiles holding Celia and Ed could make it through the crowd.

It was two o'clock when the Cooneys arrived at the Raymond Street Jail. Brooklyn's main lock-up was an imposing gray stone jail with high corner turrets. "Brooklyn's Bastille" was built before the middle of the last century. By 1924 the jail was known to be a dilapidated and overcrowded firetrap, tagged a "medieval dungeon" by reformers. But at least the dungeon master of 1924 was a humane and progressive man. Warden Harry C. Honeck was public in his opposition to what he called the "legal murder" of the electric chair and apparently known for his compassion for his prisoners. His jail was to be Celia and Ed's home for the next couple of weeks.

With a "Good-bye Eddie" and "So long kid," Celia and Ed were separated into the women's and men's divisions of the jail. As Celia was being booked, the clerk asked her occupation. Celia replied: "Oh, laundry worker, I guess." Then, with a mischievous smile, she amended that to "bandit." "But I'm not a bandit now," she thought, looking over the clerk's shoulder and guiding him: "That's right—ex-laundry worker."

A prison matron then led Celia to her cell. Flopping down on the bunk, Celia began to cry. The reality of jail was beginning to hit her. "When I was a kid," she recalled, "I used to go out to the Zoo of a Sunday afternoon — not the Bronx Zoo, the one in Prospect Park — and I used to look at the animals in the cage behind the iron bars and wonder how they felt. Well, I know now, and it's an awful feeling."

But almost as quickly as the tears started they stopped, and Celia's mood swung in the opposite direction. She sat up and, wiping her eyes with the back of her hand, said to the matron watching over her: "Gee, no use doing that — and there's a long, long trail ahead." She rose from the bunk, smiled at the matron, and did a short dance. Then she stared down at her stockinged foot and, raising it high, examined it. "Granny," she said to the matron, "that heel's run down. Better get a new pair before next Tuesday."

The papers reported closely on Celia's mercurial moods. The warden informed them that she "wept covertly" at times and was "gay and talkative" a moment later. On January 25th, the cover of the *Daily News* featured GUNGIRL'S HAPPY JAIL LIFE while the *Sun* reported that the BOBBED BANDIT WEEPS IN CELL, her BRAVADO SLIPPING AS GLAMOUR FADES INTO GRIMNESS. The hard-boiled bandit was reduced to a girl in trouble crying in her cell: the "glitter of the crowd's curiosity having worn off, the girl is losing her bravado and her braggadocio and is in much the same temper just now as any other girl in deep trouble might be."

Over in the men's division Ed was pacing his cell. Without Celia around to keep up his spirits, he slipped back into the funk that had gripped him during his trip up from Florida. He was "morose and uncommunicative," wrote the *Sun*; "keepers said that he sits for a long time with his head in his hands." A special guard was later placed outside Ed's cell to watch him in case he decided to kill himself.

After all the excitement and crowds, it was a rough, sleepless night for Celia. All night long she was kept awake by the drunken tirade of a woman in the cell next door. The old drunk berated Celia for holding up stores when she was expecting a baby, asking Celia if she was ashamed of herself. "Shut yer mouth," Celia would periodically yell back at the inebriated moralist, but the woman had stamina, babbling through the entire night. Ed, it was reported, slept soundly. What little sleep Celia enjoyed ended early that morning when the prisoners were roused and fed the usual prison fare of oatmeal and milk, bread and coffee.

Ed had his suicide guard to watch his every move, and his wife was under close surveillance as well. Some of those with an eye on Celia, however, were not interested in the danger of her taking her life but in the prospect of her sharing it. The press were all over Celia, even behind bars. They accompanied her through her booking and passed notes into her cell, given surprising access to the female felon by the easygoing Warden Honeck. At first, as she

New York American advertisement for the "Bobbed Haired Bandit's Own Story." (Harry Ransom Humanities Research Center)

had on the train, Celia played hard to get: "Nothing doing—I don't care to talk—leave me alone," Celia told reporters as she was being booked. Later her tune changed: "Say—if you want to talk to me let me see the color of your money."

The color was green. Photographers and movie camera operators tried to get Celia to pose for them in jail. "What's in it for me?" Celia asked. A cameraman offered her twenty-five dollars. "Piker," Celia laughed, "that's only cigarette money." She could afford to be cocky, the bold headline on the cover of that morning's *Daily News* had proclaimed her GIRL BANDIT PRISON IDOL. William Randolph Hearst's King Features Syndicate ponied up considerably more than cigarette money, offering to pay Celia one thousand dollars—a sum higher than what she and Ed claimed to have made on all of their robberies combined—for the exclusive rights to the "true story" of the Bobbed Haired Bandit, written by the infamous gungirl herself. Celia quickly agreed.

Billed in advance publicity as "the Strangest, Weirdest, Most Dramatic, Most Tragic, Human-Interest Stories Ever Written," Celia's tale stretched over twelve "chapters" for two weeks in Hearst's *New York American*, beginning on April 28th and continuing to May 10th, running every day except Sunday. Each new installment titillated readers with headlines like WHY AND HOW I STUCK 'EM UP and were accompanied by staged photographs: Celia in a turban and sealskin coat, Celia in handcuffs, Celia sitting demurely in her cell, a montage of four shots of Celia's face from profile to face front. Incredibly, the ex–Bobbed Haired Bandit poses with an automatic in three pictures, pointing the barrel of the gun straight at the reader in one of them under the tagline "A Nervous Trigger Finger."

Celia's story reads like a tale out of one of the confessional *True Story* and *True Detective* magazines that Celia—and much of the American public at the time—voraciously consumed. Her tale conforms to genre formula: vicarious thrills as the reader is brought along step by step on a trip through the underworld; tragedy as the National Biscuit robbery goes horribly wrong, their baby dies, and the couple is

"This is exactly what six grocery clerks faced when Cecilia Cooney, the 'Bobbed-Hair Bandit,' used the command, 'Stick 'em up!' on the victims of her first Brooklyn robbery. This picture was exclusively posed to accompany her story to-day of just how she did it." "A Nervous Trigger Finger," *New York American*, May 1, 1924. (Harry Ransom Humanities Research Center)

A photomontage captures the many moods of the bobbed bandit. "Intimate Close-ups of the Bobbed-Hair Bandit," *New York American*, May 5, 1924. (Harry Ransom Humanities Research Center)

caught; and then a final repentance for their sins as Celia and Ed are forced to pay for their crimes.

Although it was not publicized at the time, the words typed out for the *American* were written by a writer named William Buehler Seabrook. In his autobiography Seabrook remembers getting the assignment. His boss called him into his office, locked the door, and said:

"All we want on Cecelia Cooney is her own full confession, her own exclusive full-length signed story, to start the day after tomorrow and run for ten or twelve installments in the daily news columns of the *American*."

I said, "All a baby wants is the moon. How you goin' to get it—blow up the jail and kidnap her?"

He smiled at me like a benevolent hyena and said, "No, *you're* going to get it for us. The *Graphic* strong-arm guys and the Pulitzer wrecking crew are after it, but you're going to get it for us."

I said, "That's nice. How?"

He said, "We've greased some wheels and we'll give you a couple of names, and we're also giving you this, but the rest is up to you."

He pushed a piece of paper across the desk, a thick wad of hundred dollar bills, and two certified checks made out to Cecelia Cooney.

The wad of bills would open locked doors and the extra check that Seabrook carried was a higher offer in case the bandit girl held them

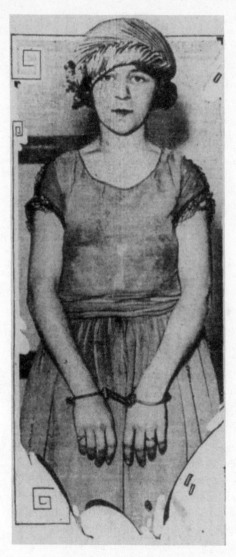

"Jailed after a series of daring exploits which terrorized the city, Cecilia Cooney looks toward the world with a wistful expression on her youthful face. She is shown here in this exclusive picture with irons on her wrists after the barred doors clanged shut against her." "In Shackles but Still Pert and Smiling," *New York American*, April 29, 1924. (Harry Ransom Humanities Research Center)

The photos of Celia writing were published to prove the authenticity of her ghostwritten life story: "Here is the bobbed-hair bandit's own story—one of the most amazing documents ever penned." "Gun Girl Reveals Tragedy of Career That Amazed Nation," *New York American*, April 28, 1924. (Harry Ransom Humanities Research Center)

up for more money. With the wheels greased and money in hand, Seabrook and a Hearst photographer set up a photo shoot in the Raymond Street Jail, bringing with them a suitcase full of clothes and props. As Seabrook recalls:

> With flashlight bulbs popping in Cecelia's cell corridor, myself as master of ceremonies, the jail matron as wardrobe mistress and the poor girl's iron cell with door ajar as dressing-room we staged a one-model fashion show which had the other female prisoners pop-eyed.
>
> We photographed Celia in imitation sealskin with her automatic leveled, and in a Spanish shawl, eyes downcast, with glycerin tears as a repentant Magdalene. We photographed her half the morning. Finally I photographed her in one of [Seabrook's wife] Katie's turbans and [his Greenwich Village mistress] Deborah Luris' handcuffs!

Even at a time when newspapermen were known as colorful characters, Seabrook stood out. Starting his writing career as a cub reporter in Atlanta, he was promoted to city editor when, on a slow news day, he jumped out of a balloon with a parachute and then wrote about it. By the time he met up with Celia in the Raymond Street Jail, Seabrook had tried his hand at advertising, studied philosophy in Geneva, fought with the French Army and been gassed at Verdun, then hoboed around Europe for a couple years.

Seabrook came to New York to be a reporter at the city desk of the *New York Times*. He found the work boring: "The work was routine, factual reporting, which must always be deadly accurate, and was mostly deadly dull." By the end of the month he was gone. His new job was writing feature stories for the news service of Hearst's King Features Syndicate. "They wanted good, clear, exciting, vivid writing and were willing to pay for it." Entertainment was much more lucrative than reporting the facts. The big stars at King Features were famous

"Before they separated Cecilia wrote the note shown below, beginning 'I still love Ed' —That is all that holds them together now. Bandit-husband and bandit-wife . . ."
New York American, May 10, 1924. (Harry Ransom Humanities Research Center)

Celia Cooney's authorized signature was reproduced at the head of each installment of her story in the *American*. Even her signature was edited, the "ed" was
masked, transforming her from a "Bobbed Haired" to a Bobbed Hair Bandit. (Harry
Ransom Humanities Research Center)

cartoonists like George "Jiggs" McManus and George Herriman, the
creator of Krazy Kat.

Feature writing allowed for creativity — within limits. As Seabrook
described it: "It had to fit always in the one frame, follow always the
one formula — it was always Hearst feature page syndicate writing."
There were three formulas to follow: pseudo-science, society, and
crime-and-horror. According to Seabrook, a crime-and-horror story
"must be presented in all its red juicy thrills, but always with suitable
moral reflections — Madame Tussaud flavored with Mary Baker Eddy
— the Marquis de Sade mixed with John Haynes Holmes."

Given the Hearst formula, and William Seabrook's penchant for
drama, how much of Celia's "own story" was truly hers, and how much
was the creation of her ghostwriter? It's impossible to determine. According to Seabrook, "she was going to tell me the story and I was

going to write it, in the first person — not as 'told to.'" And while feature writing for Hearst allowed for creative license, it didn't condone outright falsification. Seabrook explained, "I gradually learned that while a certain amount of twisting and distorting was permissible, outright concoction, faking, lying, were taboo." Certainly the *American* was at pains to prove that it was Celia's own story. Between the mock holdup poses, Celia is shown at a desk with a pencil in hand, and a facsimile of her writing is displayed above the printed story. Celia practiced her signature with the matron's fountain pen, "biting her lips and screwing her eyes as she tried over and over again until she got it to please us, like an interested school kid with a new Spencerian copybook." Thirty-six hours later that signature was published "at the top of a two-column lead on the front page of the *American*."

The story certainly *could* have been composed of her words, even if not in her own hand. While Celia had a fitful education, first going to school at age nine and attending public and parochial schools off and on until she was fourteen, she certainly was literate, as both prison records and her avid appetite for magazines and newspapers attest. Tom Vitale, the fifteen-year-old son of one of Celia's former landladies, told a *Brooklyn Eagle* reporter that when she was living with them:

> Every day she'd send one of us out to buy the *New York World*. She used to read the *World* every day, but sometimes she'd get the *American* and the *Journal*, too. There was a big stack of these papers in her room when she left, together with a few of the comic supplements of *The Eagle* and a batch of *Police Gazettes* and *Argosy-All Story* magazines.

As a reader of "True Stories," "All Stories," and the more sensational newspapers, Celia understood what a gripping story demanded, and she saw her own life and crimes through this lens. She knew that her life was "like out of a detective story magazine," as she described it. It is not unimaginable that she was the primary voice of the "Bobbed-Hair Bandit's Own Story."

There was also independent reporting that Celia was writing in her cell and that she seemed to be thoroughly enjoying her new role as author. The *Brooklyn Eagle* reported:

Celia last night sent out for a pencil and a pad to be used to jot down her reminiscence. For several moments she was observed concentrating and scribbling. Then irked at a loss for inspiration she exchanged experiences with some of the girl prisoners. "Gee, that's a good job. I'm going to put it in my book," one of the attendants heard Celia tell a girl who had given her a hair-raising story.

Celia wished to not only entertain her audience but also shape their perception of the Bobbed Haired Bandit. She stressed that she and her husband robbed for the sake of their baby and not for earrings, gin, and jazz. She refined the story she had begun with reporters and detectives on the train up from Florida. It was a sympathetic portrait of a woman driven to banditry, narrated by Celia Cooney and shaped by William Seabrook. Ghostwriter Seabrook was pleased that Celia had not actually killed or shot anyone: that would have broken the moral code at King Features, which could offer no sympathy for killers or real hard-boiled criminals. According to Seabrook, the job of ghostwriting was "going to be easy":

> She assured me — and I believed her — that she had never shot anybody, and that as "star performer" in the long series of robberies she had simply obeyed the orders of her young husband. Her defense was going to take the line that she had played Trilby to a gunman Svengali, which was apparently more or less true, so I was going to be free and the *American*'s skirts would be clean in presenting her romantically and arousing as much sympathy for her as we could.

Celia knew what to provide Seabrook. The couple that Celia described were Catholics who attended mass regularly and were married in a church by a priest. "Outside of this bandit business, I'm a good girl," Celia wrote, elaborating to make sure her meaning was clear, "and I mean good girl, and I dare the world to say I'm not":

> Say, I used to dance in Coney Island, and play around in chop suey joints in Brooklyn where you put a nickel in the piano, but in my set ladies don't drink. And they don't smoke, neither. So help me, I've never had a drink or smoked a cigarette. I leave that stuff to the swell dames that can get away with it and still be ladies.

As far as the speculations about her drug use, well, they were bunk, too:

> All the hop I ever had either before or after sticking up those poor, scared boobs, who said "Oh, lady, please don't shoot," was tea at a chop suey place, free in little cups without handles, along with a big dish of chow mein for thirty cents that was big enough for Ed and me both.

In addition to distancing herself from upper-class flappers and drug-addled hopheads, there was also a certain matter of ethnicity and patriotism Celia wanted to clear up. The All Points Bulletin the police had issued a few weeks before mentioned that while Celia might look Italian or Jewish, she was, in fact, German. In the years following the Great War and the attendant anti-German xenophobia, these were fighting words. Even Ed's mother condemned Celia's lineage. "I was not pleased because she was a German girl," the elder Mrs. Cooney told a reporter, recalling the first time she met her son's bride-to-be. "I would have liked him to marry one of his own kind, because he is an Irish-American boy." In the first installment of her memoir Celia counterattacked. "I'm American, get me, 100 percent American," she claimed, adding the even more important fact: "I'm a New Yorker, born in New York. How many can say that?"

> My grandfather was a German, but papa was born in the United States, and so was mama. They were American citizens, and I'm an American citizen. Everybody's got some relatives that came somewhere on the other side. . . . If I was any more American I'd have to be a red Indian I guess.

The Hearst organization, however, was not paying Celia a thousand dollars so she could spin her story for public and judicial sympathy while awaiting sentencing. A sympathetic character was only valuable for them insofar as she also had a thrilling tale to tell. The Bobbed Haired Bandit did, and over twelve installments she gave a blow-by-blow account of their robberies, escape, and capture.

Over in the men's divison of the Raymond Street Jail, Ed was still sulking. He was reported to be a bad mixer ("he is not popular with his cell mates" the *Daily News* claimed), but Celia was the life of the party. JAILBIRDS ENVY BOBBED BANDIT was the *News* headline, followed by this glowing review: "Celia was still a star yesterday, playing to a diminished but esoteric audience." "Gee, kid you're a wonder. Tell us all about it. Where didja get the nerve?" the thirty prisoners in the women's ward asked as they peppered Celia with questions. The stories Celia told in response "were greeted with delight by her fellow prisoners." Even the old drunk who had kept her up the night before quieted her "noisy demonstration" to listen. If the other women prisoners were envious of the special food that Celia had been able to buy with her King Features Syndicate money, they weren't showing it. "They crowded around her at every opportunity," the *Daily News* observed; "Celia was the big act."

⊚ 20

It is just and necessary that crime should be punished and Celia Cooney should pay the full price of her swash-buckling career of police defiance and predatory proclivities. But the fact that Dick Turpin was hanged in York in 1739, for the crime of murder, does not make him less of a romantic character in 1924. . . . Mrs. Cooney . . . has been described as a demi-mondaine of careless habits, but she is more than a naughty scamp. The pride of self-expression is written large in her confessions. Yes, she is an artist, even if her only gallery show is to be prison in a cell block.   —Editorial, *Brooklyn Eagle*

Celia and Ed were reunited on Saturday, April 25th, after five days of incarceration: "At sight of each other the couple rushed into each other's arms and remained in a long affectionate embrace. . . . Mrs. Cooney later told one of the matrons that they had never been parted before in their brief married life." As they let go of each other, the warden moved off by the window to give them a moment together. Celia and Ed spoke in whispers, holding hands for the half hour they were allowed to meet. Immediately after their meeting Celia sent word to Samuel Leibowitz by telephone and special messenger that she wanted to meet him. Although twice bit, Sam wasn't shy. He quickly made his way over to the Raymond Street Jail and met with Celia for an hour and a half later that afternoon. While Leibowitz would not disclose the content of their conversation, he did say that she had asked him to defend her and that her request was urgent.

This was good news, dramatic news, news that sells papers: the BOB-HAIRED BANDIT DECIDES TO FIGHT read the *New York Times* headline. A feisty bandit fighting for her freedom made a much better story than a fallen women resigned to her fate. Leibowitz, it was rumored, was planning on using a temporary insanity defense.

Since the stories about suicide watch for Ed on the trip up from Florida, the press had been raising questions about Ed's mental well-being. These were fueled when it leaked that his mother and brother, at the urging of Sam Leibowitz, revealed to Judge Martin that Ed's father had died fifteen years previously in an insane asylum, and they had concerns about Ed's mental stability as "he has shown evidence of deranged mind on previous occasions." This evaluation was shared by many other papers, one of which noted of Ed that "his lips are thick, his eyes dull, his utterances slow," all sure signs to the *New York Times* that "if not mentally defective, Cooney at least has a mind of poor quality."

Celia's mental quality and emotional state was also up for debate in the newspapers. Some saw her as good humored, wise-cracking, and quick witted, with the *Daily News* going as far as printing pictures of a smiling Celia next to a sullen Ed, posting a title above that read A STUDY OF CONTRASTS. The *Washington Post*, however, was not convinced that the two were all that different. Regarding Celia's mental state, they reported that "psychologists have unofficially declared her to be a 'moron bordering on feeble mindedness,'" and solicited the opinion of County Judge W. Bernard Vause — a man who seems to have no official connection to the case — that Celia "is a woman of low type, if not feeble minded" whose "craving for detective stories . . . contributed to her criminal career." Still other newspapers reiterated the theory that Celia was *normally* stable and sane, but currently under psychological strain from her pregnancy and the death of her baby.

It is important to note that not everyone took the idea of prenatal insanity seriously. Ring Lardner penned a sardonic column in the tortured syntax of a crank letter to the editor touching on this maternity defense:

One of the reasons they give for robbing people was on acct. of expecting a family and a certain well known physician in N.Y. made the statement that people in this situation was hardly responsible for what they done, which if true it looks to me like instead of it being vs. the law to sell books on birth control it ought to be vs. the law not to.

The less prospective parents running around shooting up the town, why so much the better.

In 1924 many criminologists and psychologists believed that criminal behavior was most often a result of mental defect, and they used the intelligence tests of incarcerated felons as proof that the average criminal was a moron, an imbecile, or some other category of mental defective. Some states even sterilized the feeble-minded as a eugenic solution to the crime problem. The correctional system offered psychologists a captive sample of subjects for testing. Women incarcerated at the Bedford Hills correctional facility were studied and tested as a means to establish the abnormal psychology of the female criminal. The expectation was that a normal woman could not possibly be a violent criminal; femininity did not allow for banditry, no matter how well-coiffed or fashionably dressed.

The next day, on April 26th, after having met with Celia and Ed in jail for two hours, Leibowitz explained to the press that Celia had told him that she "was rushed off her feet and did not know what [she] was doing" and now, given the time to think about her case (and, it was suggested in other reports, advice from her new-found criminal girlfriends), she realized that "we ought not to have pleaded guilty." With one of the defendants finally agreeing to be defended, Sam outlined his plan of attack. "There are two main angles of defense in Mrs. Cooney's case," the lawyer explained to the *Sun*. "First there is high medical authority that she was mentally irresponsible throughout the period during which acts charged against her were committed. The truth of this will be demonstrated by calling prominent physicians to the stand."

Leibowitz could have called Dr. Sisson, the physician from Florida who had attended Celia during childbirth. He had already gone public with his belief that her pregnancy rendered her not responsible for her actions. The fact that Dr. Sisson had treated Celia while she was still an outlaw would no doubt give his testimony added credibility. But Leibowitz had another card up his sleeve: "Another and even more important phase of the defense I am unable to discuss at present," he teased, hinting that "it is, perhaps, not too much to say that we have a witness whose testimony should weigh heavily in Mrs. Cooney's defense." Who was this other witness? Was the lawyer bluffing to get Judge Martin to allow Celia to withdraw her guilty plea? Why wasn't Ed included in Leibowitz's insanity defense strategy?

Later that day the *Herald-Tribune* had the answers: Ed was the surprise witness in his wife's defense. Although Leibowitz would not confirm it, "another source" stated that Ed would plead guilty and take the witness stand in order to clear Celia. The same source told the *Herald-Tribune*'s reporter that Celia agreed to this plan only after an hour's pleading on the part of Ed, "whose arguments she met with tearful negatives." Celia also demanded that her husband try to change his plea to not guilty. Ed refused, insisting that he alone take the blame for their string of robberies. Having been characterized by the press for months as something less than a *real* man, Edward Cooney was stepping up and taking responsibility for leading his woman astray. In this version, she was not the real criminal; she was only following her husband's lead. For one of the first times since the couple made news, Ed got star billing in a headline: COONEY OPENS FIGHT TO SAVE BANDIT WIFE.

Judge Martin, getting wind of Celia's new temporary insanity defense, acted quickly to head it off. The evening papers carried news that he had named his "lunacy board" and that it consisted of four alienists: two to study Ed, and two to examine Celia. While the judge would later stand accused of appointing well-connected and free-spending incompetents to his commissions, this lunacy board seemed to be on the up and up. Celia's sanity was to be determined by Dr. Cecil McCoy, a psychiatrist with the Kings County Hospital who had served on a number of high-profile cases already, and by Dr. Anna M. Ralston, described as the wife of "political leader" Harry Ralston but a

"Is the bobbed-hair bandit insane?" According to Rollin Kirby, cartoonist for the newspaper, the bobbed-bandit's sanity or insanity was getting too much coverage, overshadowing more serious issues. "Comparative Values," *New York World*, April 30, 1924.

doctor with several famous cases under her belt as well. Ed was left in the hands of Dr. Siegfried Block, of Ward's Island and Bellevue hospitals, and Dr. John Meager, another frequent "expert witness" and future author of the monograph A *Study of Masturbation and the Psychosexual Life*. Because of the appointment of this board, the couple's sentencing, which was supposed to have taken place on Tuesday, April 29th, was put off until the alienists could make their report.

Celia and Ed were dragged over to the county court on Monday morning for a hearing—a hearing to schedule yet another hearing—but they didn't mind the trip. The Cooneys were delighted to see each other again, even if there was not much privacy in the back of a police van with two other manacled prisoners. And the public was delighted to see Celia as well. "One would imagine the County Judges were expecting a visit from Royalty," the *Brooklyn Eagle* reported. "The police were kept busy pushing back the crowds, but despite their efforts the backyard fences in the rear of the court were alive with men and boys, each eager to catch a fleeting glimpse of the girl." Escorted into the courthouse, Celia gaily waved a handkerchief to her fans.

Once inside the court, they waited for half an hour for the hearing to be scheduled. As they were about to leave the court for the department of corrections van outside, the couple was called back and led up to Judge Martin's chambers for a private conference. What went on in that conference remained private. Leibowitz wasn't there, nor were keen-eared and chatty guards or matrons, and the Cooneys and Judge Martin were not talking. Whatever was discussed was important. The three stayed in conference until the early afternoon, at which time Celia and Ed were loaded back into the van and brought back to the Raymond Street Jail. Celia then announced that she no longer planned to mount a defense and wished to accept her original plea of guilty. Martin had convinced them to give up the fight.

Poor Sam Leibowitz. "Disheartening" was the gentle word he used when talking to the press about this latest turn. For the third time now he had mounted a defense only to be dismissed by his clients. And this time he had been outmaneuvered. Calling a "private conference" with his clients when the two were ostensibly called to the courthouse for a mere formality was a clever play by Judge Martin.

The on-again-off-again dance between the Cooneys and their lawyer even prompted a joke by Tom W. Jackson in his "Periscope" column:

> Van Brunt—I see that the bobbed-hair girl bandit and her husband have decided to take no more chances.
> Hamilton—How so?
> Van Brunt—They have refused to accept the services of a lawyer.

It probably wasn't very funny to Samuel Leibowitz, either; the case he hoped might make him a public figure was making him into a public laughingstock. Satirist Ring Lardner was particularly merciless when it came to the lawyers defending the celebrity bandit. Lardner's column was written in the style and grammar of a letter to the editor from a cranky reader:

> In fact it was a cinch that 1/2 the lawyers in Brooklyn tried to come to her defense without no invitation knowing they couldn't loose and it meant a lot of publicity and maybe she would be generous enough to give them 10 percent of the million dollar picture contract which was bound to follow acquittal.

Lardner also had some advice for Leibowitz on how to get Celia acquitted. He was of the opinion that there was no way that Celia Cooney would be convicted by a jury of her peers — that is, people who shared her hairstyle:

> All the lawyers had to do to get her off free was to first see that she really got her hair bobbed which it turns out it was no such a thing and then choose a jury made up of single men mixed with bobbed haired women, either that or left her hair unbobbed like it was and insisted on a jury of married men and the minute that they seen her hair was long they would of said she must be O.K. after all and voted not guilty without listening to the testimony.

Like Leibowitz, Judge Martin was also concerned with how his performance played in the press. A county judge, he was an elected official who needed to consider how he would be seen by the voters. As a supporting actor in the Bobbed Haired Bandit show he now had the public's attention, and it was an opportunity that he was not going to pass up.

According to the press, the city was in the grip of a crime wave. Two or three crime waves had swept across the city since the Great War. It was difficult for an impartial observer to tell when one crime wave had crested and broken before another swelled on the horizon. The crime wave was a standing wave. One New York paper or another always seemed to be attempting to publicize the lawlessness of the city; the rising tide of holdups, gunmen, automatics, and getaway cars threatened to wash away public safety and order. The papers that opposed Mayor Hylan's administration were especially vocal in attacking the police commissioner's inability to hold back the tide of gun crime. The Brooklyn district attorney and Judge Martin responded to these criticisms by championing swift, harsh justice for the malefactors. The prosecutor and the magistrate intended to make the court system an efficient machine for meting out quick sentences for gun crime. When the Bobbed Haired Bandit and her accomplice had pled guilty in his courtroom, the judge had made a speech, reported dutifully by the press, that drew attention to the fact that the couple's guilty plea had sped up the process of the law, claiming that the "criminal calendar" (that is, the schedule of cases awaiting trial) was "lower than it has ever been before in the history of Kings county." Martin was promising assembly line justice for the new industrial age.

The pressure on Judge Martin to sentence the Cooneys to hard time was substantial. LET THE LAW EXACT A POUND OF FLESH SAY SHOPKEEPERS trumpeted the headline of an April 27th *Daily News* article:

Thumbs down!
    The century-old cry that rang through the gladiatorial arena is repeated by the victims of Brooklyn's notorious bobbed-haired bandit and her mate.

Those shopkeepers "whose gaze crept steadily along the barrel of her automatic, leveled steadily at them" could see no "extenuating circumstances" in Celia Cooney's predicament. "She's no heroine," said Peter Kossman, the manager of the Bohack store that the Cooneys robbed on February 2nd. "The fact that she was an expectant mother does not excuse her. Why didn't her husband stop her instead of joining in her robberies? They deserve severe punishment." Louis Hecht, the young clerk from the job at Weinstein's drugstore on January 15th, admitted that he pitied her, but he needed to be "protected from another such experience" so "she and her husband should be drastically punished." Abraham Fishbein, the grocer from Albany Avenue, was blunt: "No mercy for them." He called for twenty years for these "dangerous bandits." "They were pretty rough when they held up my store," he remembered. Samuel Weiss, the druggist from Sumner Avenue, told the reporter he was "glad she's captured. She ought to get a stiff sentence. She certainly is an artist with a gun." He was "wasting no tears" over the girl and her mate. He concluded that "a life sentence for her would make the community safer."

Judge George Martin listened to the vox populi. The day after Celia rescinded her plea of not guilty, Martin made the front pages for dismissing the grand jury that had handed down Celia and Ed's indictments. This was hardly a newsworthy event, but Martin made it into one by using it as a platform to act tough on crime and hard on criminals. He told the assembled group they would long be remembered as "the Grand Jury which returned the indictment against the famous bob-haired bandit and her husband" and praised them for this decision. Now that the grand jury had done its job, the judge promised them — and the newspaper-reading public — that he would do his, with "the imposition of a proper and well-deserved sentence." Judge Martin then shifted into high rhetorical gear:

> This disposition will be made of their case despite the maudlin sentimentality of certain individuals whose views and opinions on the matter of crime, were they allowed to serve as a guide, would soon render any community a paradise for robbers, thieves and other criminals and a place of terror for law abiding citizens.

Martin's message was clear. He would not be easy on Celia and Ed. The first time he had the bandit couple in his courtroom, he had warned them that they could expect no mercy if they pled not guilty and demanded a trial; it seemed that pleading guilty wasn't getting them any mercy, either.

Back at the Raymond Street Jail, mercy is exactly what Celia was reported to be hoping for, giving the one-word answer "Yes" in response to a reporter who asked if she hoped for the judge's leniency in his sentencing.

There was one more chance for Celia and Ed. Before sentencing, the lunacy board had to make its investigations and report. Ed had instructed Celia to act nutty before the lunacy board, but Celia had a hard time. "They skinned back my eyelids and tapped on first one of my knees and then the other with a rubber hammer," Celia remembered of her examination by "enemy alienists," commenting that

"that's a funny way to find out if anybody's crazy or not." She continued: "Then they asked me a lot of questions, and I got sick of answering them, and said, 'Here, you know perfectly well I'm not crazy, so what's the use of all this bunk?'" "Ed and I were both fools to do what we did," Celia reflected. "Anybody is a fool to do such things. But that's not being crazy." Evidently the lunacy panel agreed; less than a week later they came back with their report.

After subjecting Celia to four mental examinations and interviewing a number of her relations, landladies, and past employers, Doctors McCoy and Ralston were "unable to find anything which would indicate a suspicion of disorder in Celia's mind at any time." Celia, the cursory report went on, was "at all times quick, clear, coherent and responsive" during her examination and "revealed nothing . . . that indicated an abnormal mind."

The official report on Ed by Doctors Meagher and Block was more extensive but came to much the same conclusion. While noting that Ed's father had been in the Brooklyn State Hospital for "Alcoholic Psychosis, paranoid form," and that his son displayed "a few psychopathic traits, e.g. reticent, moody and impulsive at times, certain discontents, lack of enthusiasm, superficiality, etc.," the doctors reported that Ed "emotionally feels regret for his acts and affirms that he deserves punishment" and that he "shows no mental defect." They concluded that there was "no evidence whatever of insanity." Both Celia and Edward Cooney were declared legally sane and fully responsible for their actions.

It would be almost a week before Celia and Ed would come up for their final sentencing hearing, after spending their days and nights locked away in separate cells. Warden Honeck, who was evidently quite taken by the couple, allowed them to meet periodically, being "quite impressed by the genuine affection existing between the couple." He also commented favorably on Celia's performance as a prisoner, telling the newspapers that she doesn't smoke or swear and "her morals are of the best." Celia spent her time reading magazines, which Warden Honeck described as "magazines of the better class and not 'trash.'" The report on Ed was not as positive; morose, he did little reading and "apparently finds some difficulty in finding anything to do to pass his time in his cell."

Befitting her star status, Celia received fan mail while in jail. Most of the letters were from sympathizers, including one from a woman who had recently lost a baby of her own. But not all the writers approved of Celia's performances. One man penned that he wished he could be on the jury that tried and sentenced the Cooneys so that he could vote to send them "away for life."

It would not be a jury that would sentence the Cooneys but, as he had made very clear in his public statements, Judge Martin himself. A few days before sentencing Celia wrote a direct appeal to the judge, asking him not to split her and Ed apart. "She determined upon a desperate move to spend the remainder of her youthful years with the man she loves," reported the *American* in a tone of, well, maudlin sentimentality. The note "was couched in simple language that bespoke the agony in her heart. She begged the judge to sentence them both to the same prison."

Early on the morning of Tuesday, May 6th, Celia and Ed Cooney were taken from their cells and loaded onto a paddy wagon to be brought back to the Kings County Court to receive their sentence. They arrived at nine-forty in the morning. Celia was wearing a new outfit, and her appearance was carefully reported upon by the press: "In a new blue-tailored suit, carefully pressed, tan silk stockings, patent leather pumps and a gray lavender tocque, trimmed with rosebuds, Celia presented a picture mighty easy to look at." And looked at she was. Crowds packed the street outside the courthouse and fought to get in: "The back tenement windows were crowded with women and children." The *Herald-Tribune* described how "men and even girls hung over the tall brick walls about the courtyard. Youths lined an adjoining roof and craned their necks."

Celia stepped lightly from the side door of the police van, shielding her face from the cameramen as she moved quickly into the courthouse. Then the back door of the van opened, and Ed came out with his cap pulled low over his face, chained to three lesser felons. Once inside, Celia and Ed were kept for almost an hour and a half in holding cells underneath the courtroom. Meanwhile, the courtroom was filling up with relatives, victims, and, of course, newspaper reporters, occupying every inch, perching on radiators, and sitting on the steps leading up to the bench. The room was hot and the air stale as the assembled crowd waited until eleven o'clock, when a clerk called for order and Judge Martin entered the court. A moment later Ed was brought into the courtroom, wearing a dark suit with a soft-collared shirt and a blue tie. Pushed gently into the room by a guard, he looked around for his wife, grinning over his shoulder as he turned to try and spot her.

Celia was still being held outside the room, scribbling a note in pencil on a scrap of paper to be sent up to Judge Martin in a last-ditch attempt to mitigate their pending sentence. It read:

> To those girls who think they would like to see their names in the paper as mine has been, or think they would like to do what I have done, let me say: "Don't try to do it: you don't know what you suffer. While I smile, my heart is breaking in me.
>
> CECILIA COONEY

As the conclusion to one of those good-girl-gone-wrong "True Stories" it was perfect. But its literary virtues were evidently lost on the judge. Whether Martin even had the time to read Celia's note is not known, but he certainly wasn't exhibiting any signs of maudlin sentimentality. "Where is the wife?" the judge growled as he demanded that Celia be brought into the courtroom.

For her part, Celia seemed more smiles than heartbreak, using her last few minutes "feverishly primping for her farewell performance before her Brooklyn public." She entered the courtroom, "pausing in the opening for a brief instant, after the manner of a stage star who expects an outburst of hand clapping." With a deputy leading and her chin in the air, Celia sashayed theatrically across the courtroom, glancing at the spectators and smiling slightly, taking her place beside her husband, standing before the judge's bench.

The court clerk called out: "Edward and Cecelia Cooney, have you anything to say why judgment should not be passed on you?" Ed silently shook his head. Celia just stood there. Prodded by the clerk to say something, she released her upper lip from between her teeth long enough to utter "no — nothing."

From behind his bench Judge Martin asked the court for silence. Addressing himself to the couple, he boomed out in a deep voice:

DAILY ✦ NEWS

HOME EDITION

NEW YORK'S ✦ PICTURE NEWSPAPER

Vol. 5. No. 272.   16 Pages   New York, Wednesday, May 7, 1924.   2 Cents

10 YEARS FOR BOBBED BANDIT

Page 3

The Cooneys, in patrol wagon, were taken from court in Brooklyn while great crowd saw them off on first leg of their journey to long imprisonment.

PAYMENT—Celia Cooney, the now famous bandit, and her husband were yesterday sentenced to from ten to twenty years in prison by Brooklyn Judge.—Story on page 3.

Flanked by court attendants, Celia Cooney, as jaunty as ever, and her husband, Edward, as nervous as ever, stood side by side while Judge Martin pronounced sentence on them, their payment for the sensation they had afforded New York city with their acts of outlawry. Each drew from ten to twenty years in prison.

Mrs. Nielson and baby (above) were away at time of attack.

HAMMER ATTACK—Police last night scoured Newark for J. Vollmer, a nerve sufferer, who boarded with Dr. Nielson, in hope of clearing up hammer attack.—Story on page 3.

Dr. George A. Nielson (above), chiropractor, was near death last night, his skull crushed in from blows from hammer delivered by man while Nielson was alone in home.

TUT'S MUMMY—This is believed to be first and exclusive photograph of the interior of sarcophagus found in the tomb of King Tut-ankh-Amen in the Valley of the Kings in Egypt, showing mummy mask (inset); this mask is believed to be the mummy of the Pharaoh who held sway over the Nile country 3,000 years ago. Story on page 8.

I have talked to you before, both of you, about this crime which you have confessed and other crimes — many of them — which you have committed. I have given you every opportunity to tell the police and to tell me in my chambers about those crimes. I have had you examined as to your sanity, and you have been found sane. I am going to give you a lesson that you cannot carry on as you have been doing around here.

Judge Martin paused dramatically — Celia's and Ed's hearts must have stopped as the whole courtroom went silent:

"You are sentenced, both of you, from ten to twenty years."

Top: "The Cooneys, in patrol wagon, were taken from court, while great crowd saw them off on first leg of their journey to long imprisonment." *Left:* "Flanked by court attendants, Celia Cooney, as jaunty as ever, and her husband, Edward, as morose as ever, stood side by side while Judge Martin pronounced sentence on them, their payment for the sensation they had afforded New York city with their acts of outlawry." Notice that the bobbed bandit story is already being pushed off the front page by a skull-crushing murder of a Newark chiropractor and the opening of King Tut-ankh-Amen's sarcophagus. "Ten Years for Bobbed Bandit," *New York Daily News*, May 7, 1924.

21

A silence as the mass of people waited breathlessly.
Would she break down? Would she bow her head? Celia
Cooney's lips were tight together, but the eyes were hard
and cold. Break down? Not her! Cry? What was there to
cry about? Wasn't she Brooklyn's bobbed bandit, and
hadn't she been in tighter places than this? Huh, she'd
played the game, hadn't she? They didn't need to
wonder. What did they know about it anyway?
—*New York Herald-Tribune*

Ten to twenty years was the maximum. And they were sentenced to separate prisons: Celia to Auburn, Edward to Sing Sing. Celia went out as a bandit queen, captured but not conquered — that was the way the reporters told it. Of course, the Cooneys may just have been stunned. Ten to twenty years, Auburn, Sing Sing.

The *New York Sun* reported that Celia "exhibited the same amazing composure and perkiness that has characterized her every moment since her arrest. . . . She turned after hearing sentence before a courtroom crowded to its last inch of space and walked out with her head held high." A regal bandit: "She walked like a pompous queen on a state occasion." The verdict was unanimous: the Bobbed Haired Bandit had guts. "Celia won the crowd," taking her punishment "like a plucky child swallowing quinine without a whimper."

Not everyone admired her pluck, however; there were many in her "audience" who wished to see the hard-boiled girl break down in tears but, as the *New York American* reported, "the hundreds who packed the courtroom and the other hundreds who lined Schermerhorn street to see Brooklyn's terror in petticoats shed her first tear went away unsatisfied." The bandit's dry eyes forced the reporters to read all sorts of complex emotions into her every tic and twitch: "Her underlip projected slightly as if she had put all of her pluck into her mouth," wrote one suggestively. If Celia had a mouthful of pluck, Ed's jaw was sagging: "Cooney stared ahead stolidly. His mouth was open." With his eyes mostly on Celia, Ed ranged all the way from "expressionless" to "sullen" and back. By contrast, Celia's "gaze was not vacant," wrote the *New York Evening Post,* "Plainly Celia was the brains of the bandit firm of Cooney & Cooney."

The *Herald-Tribune* reported that after their sentence was read Celia turned slowly to face the people lined up on benches in the courtroom: "For a moment she glanced at the spectators — an impersonal, curious glance with just a trace of gratified vanity in it." Then she walked briskly though the courtroom. Ed's eyes followed her, and then he trailed behind her in a haze, "as if he did not realize anyone was watching."

The *New York Telegram and Evening Mail* provided this flinty description of the Bobbed Haired Bandit's curtain call:

> Game to the last, however, the young woman whose crimes stand almost without parallel for coolness and impudence heard the sentence without the flicker of an eyelash. Judge Martin had predicted that she would "take her sentence as she would take a swallow of milk," and the Judge was right.
>
> Coolly, almost contemptuously she turned away as he left the bench. She tossed her head, looked up toward the ceiling, filled her lungs and exhaled slowly puffing out her lips as one who would say with relief: —
> "Well, that's that!"
>
> If it was mere outward bravado Celia ought to have been an actress. Not once from the time she entered the room did she give the slightest indication that her pulse had increased by so much as a single beat or that her nerves were less steady than when her hand held a revolver.

It was a grand exit, but the play was not over. Watching the proceedings from the front row was a pair of cadavers, male and female. They were Michael and Anna Roth, Celia's parents — the parents that Celia had insisted to both press and police were dead:

> But actually they sat in the courtroom, the mother a drab, hard-looking woman, stolidly chewing gum. She had a bruise under her eye which looked as though she had been in a brawl. Her father, an undersized, shriveled-looking man, sat with his eyes nervously fixed on the door.

The shriveled man and the woman with the blackened eye hadn't "moved a hair" when the sentence against their daughter and her husband was handed down; they were "apathetic, wasting no tears." They were, in the words of a *Brooklyn Daily Times* reporter, "miserable dejected-looking persons."

The reporters were watching carefully to see if Celia would react to the presence of the walking dead. Celia did not give them the satisfaction. According to the *Telegram*:

> Within arms reach of her were her parents. . . . Not once did she allow her glance to rest upon them. On the contrary, her eyes passed over them as if they did not exist or were mere parts of the courtroom furniture, and many wondered whether she had recognized them at all.

It soon became clear why Celia did not.

In the weeks before sentencing, Judge Martin had ordered a court investigation of Celia Cooney. A probation officer, Miss Marie Mahon, was given the case. Miss Mahon found Celia's sister, Mary Roth, who in turn led her to the tenements of the Lower East Side of Manhattan where Celia was born. There the probation officer located Celia Cooney's parents, "buried away in the darkness and squalor of a cellar hole of an east side tenement, a stone's throw from Avenue A."

The parents had not seen their youngest daughter for four years, ever since she ran away from home. Celia had left home — according to her mother — because she wanted to stay out later than they would allow: "So after a scolding she flared up one day and left." Celia's parents had learned of their daughter's troubles only through the newspapers. According to the *Daily News*, the old couple was "fearful of the notoriety," so they had "kept their silence and hid their sorrow in the one little room in the cellar that they call their home." When the court investigator, Celia's sister, and the reporter from the *News* "groped their way into the gloom of the cellar cubicle" they had to convince Michael and Anna Roth that their daughter Celia really was the infamous girl bandit. Mrs. Roth wept and told them:

> It's so hard for me to believe that my little Celia did all of those things. But I guess she must have.
>
> That fellow she married couldn't have been much good or he never would have let her go with him to hold up people.

Then she was going to have a baby, too. I think that had a lot to do with it. I remember that just before my babies were born I used to want things that we couldn't afford.

I used to feel that nothing was too good for the baby that was coming. Maybe I would have taken things too, if I had married the kind of man Celia did.

After reading all the news stories about Celia, Mrs. Roth had been "unable to restrain the yearnings of a mother's heart any longer." She gathered her courage and went to Brooklyn to find her daughter. But "after visiting Judge Martin she came back without seeing Celia." Mrs. Roth tearfully explained to the *News* reporter:

I wanted to take her in my arms as I used to when she was a little girl. But when I went over to Brooklyn — I had an awful hard time getting there — they didn't seem to think I ought to see her now.

They told me that if I went near the jail it would get into the newspapers and that that would make it harder for Celia. So I just came home and cried.

"Mrs. Roth wept again," the reporter concluded, "as she described her fruitless mission to see the girl whom she feels needs a mother's comfort now more than she ever did before."

Celia Cooney didn't want her mother's comfort — and for good reason. After the Cooneys were sentenced, the court released the probation officer's official report on Celia's childhood and upbringing. Anna Roth's moving tale of wanting to comfort her daughter who had been a "good girl" until she left home didn't match up with the wretched tales Marie Mahon uncovered. The account of Celia's life was tragic and sensational: all the city papers carried excerpts, and the *New York Times* and the *New York World* ran it in full. The *Post* compared the report to a "realistic novel of the Russian school." It was an appropriate comparison. The report read:

The defendant was born at 38 East Fourth Street, New York City, 20 years ago in a basement. The parents had eight children and Celia was the youngest. Her father's name is Michael Roth and her mother's name is Annie Roth. The parents were born in New York City. The mother can neither write nor read and never went to school. The father had very little education and has been an habitual drunkard all his life. He has never worked steadily and never supported his family. What little support came into the family came through the mother. The children were sadly neglected; were sent out to beg; they had been known as little children to sleep all night on the coal in the cellar and in the early morning sent out on the street. Half the time the children were scantily clad and had very little to eat.

The father's record is as follows: Oct. 28, 1899, summoned to the Third District Court, Manhattan and ordered to keep sober and send the children to school. None of the children had been attending school, but had been sent begging. Lived in one furnished room, 169 Allen Street, Manhattan. The house was visited by disreputable people. When neighbors took pity on the children and gave them clothing it disappeared and was used by the father for drink. They were finally put out of this room, the children and the parents, and they moved to 171 Essex Street.

On Nov. 21, 1899, the Charities Department recommended that the children be committed to an institution.

On Jan. 16, 1900, the father was sent to the penitentiary for three months. He pleaded guilty to violation of Section 288 of the Penal Code. It has been alleged that the father has been arrested several times for illegal voting and fighting in the saloons. It is said that he had also been beaten up on several occasions and taken to the hospital.

On Jan. 22, 1900, three of the children — Mary, Maggie and Annie Roth — were committed to St. Agatha's Home because of improper guardianship. They had been found deserted by their parents. These three girls remained in the home until they were 14 years of age, when they were taken away by an aunt, a Miss Margaret Roth, and Mrs. Shorlein, another aunt of the children, residing at 304 Grove Street. These two aunts have stated that the children were sadly and painfully neglected. The children never had a home; the parents had absolutely no love or affection for them, and the aunts were not surprised at the actions of Celia, their brother was a habitual drunkard and had never worked.

The mother had an illegitimate child before she was married to Roth. This child, when he was 13 years of age, was adopted into a family in the country, through Pastor Leonhart of the Oliver Chapel, Twentieth Street.

The mother was always heartless and most unnatural to the children; seldom visiting or seeing the children while they were with the aunts, and not even seeing them for years at a stretch. Although at times she worked and made a little money, her attention was turned always towards her husband, and the children were totally abandoned and uncared for by her. She has worked at different times in different hotels, the last place being the Ritz-Carlton, where she worked from June, 1923, to Feb. 22, 1924, as a scrub woman. She left this place on a telephone call from her husband and never returned. She is apparently temperate. She had a record as a good worker.

The defendant, Celia Cooney, about June 25, 1908, then about 4 years of age, was in the charge of the Children's Society of New York. On Dec. 17, 1908, Celia was given to her mother through the Children's Bureau of the Department of Public Charity. Shortly after Celia was found by her neighbors deserted and had been deserted for three days in a furnished room. Miss Roth, the aunt, took Celia to live with her in Brooklyn. She sent Celia to the Catholic parochial school. From the time Celia was first taken by the aunt until she was 14 years old the mother came on several occasions, had Celia all dressed up by her aunt and took her to New York with her. She kept her in a furnished room and later deserted her after she had taken the child's clothes from her.

When Celia would be found by neighbors, she would be dirty and ragged and would be returned to her aunt. This happened on several occasions. Meanwhile two of the older sisters had grown up and gone into business and had established a home here in Brooklyn, asking the mother to take care of the home and little Celia. The mother came there with Celia, but it was not long before she brought the father in, too, meeting and feeding him during the day at the home and at the expense of the two girls, neglecting Celia and failing to properly provide dinner for the girls when they returned in the evening, and finally leaving them altogether, going away with the husband.

At the age of 14 years Celia left her home here in Brooklyn, going to live with her mother. There she remained for a very short period and came back to Brooklyn to live with a married sister at 97 Prospect Place.

She remained there about one year. During that time she worked steadily in a brush factory. This sister states that Celia left her home because she disapproved of her remaining out at night and associating with and bringing sailors into the home. Although Celia was ambitious and always worked, the sister states that she would steal little things. Celia left her sister's home and went to live with her mother in a furnished room in New York. Celia was then 16 years of age and the sisters heard nothing more of her until the present case came up.

The report went on to detail Celia's employment history after she went out on her own at the age of sixteen. Her career as a laundress began in February of 1919 at New York Hospital. She stayed until June. They had "nothing against her." From there she went to the laundry at St. Luke's Hospital, where she worked off and on until December 27th, 1920: "Authorities say she was very noisy, troublesome and very impertinent." She was fired. In the spring of 1921 she found a job at Lincoln Hospital, where she was said to be a "good worker, steady, jolly disposition, no trouble at all." After April of 1921 the seventeen-year-old laundress toiled at Woman's Hospital off and on until she was discharged. There "she was considered a ringleader, upsetting the place. She was very bold; she would take the good girls from the place, taking them to out-of-town places, and when questioned about their movements she would lie." The last job detailed in the report was for a Brooklyn laundry, Sheldon Foster, on Dekalb Avenue, where "she was considered a good worker, steady and no fault could be found with her; in fact they would give her a recommendation."

After trailing the mercurial laundress through her employment history, Marie Mahon turned to another fertile source of character information: the landladies. And as was the case with her employers, the references offered up by Celia's landladies were conflicted.

About March of 1922 Celia rented a furnished room at 439 Franklin Avenue for thirty dollars a month. But she was not alone. She rented the room "for me and my husband." She lived there until April 18, 1923, with a "Mr. Cherison." According to Miss Mahon, "this man is positively not Cooney. She left the place dirty, but she never took anything in the house and the house was always left open."

A

A: "Buried away in an east side tenement, THE NEWS yesterday found Michael and Anna Roth, parents of Celia Cooney." B: "There is nothing in this photograph of Celia Cooney at the age of two which would indicate her future—" C: "Nor in this picture of the girl at the age of twelve. What she later became newspaper readers know." *New York Daily News*, May 6, 1924.

B   C

When Celia left the mysterious Mr. Cherison she moved a couple of blocks further up the avenue to a furnished room at 461 Franklin. It appears that she left for another man, Edward Cooney. According to the report, Edward and Celia were married in May of 1923 and paid eight dollars a week rent to a Mrs. Gallagher until September: "Mrs. Gallagher states that she stole $20 out of her pocketbook and a picture worth $40. Mrs. Gallagher states she used vile language, fought with all the roomers, and they were all afraid of her, that she left the place filthy and dirty." Mrs. Gallagher finally threw her out.

From Mrs. Gallagher's house, Miss Mahon followed the trail to 52 Madison Street, just down the block from the church where Edward and Celia were married. At number 52, the Cooneys rented a furnished room from Mrs. Ford, "who says the girl was a good tenant and she was sorry the girl left."

Marie Mahon had retraced Celia's life from birth all the way to the fall of 1923. Her conclusion to the report was short but emphatic:

> The investigator located two aunts, two sisters, an uncle in New York and the parents of Celia Cooney. The sisters, the aunts and the uncle have all stated that the environment of the house while these children were small was the worst that could possibly exist.
>
> It is alleged that Celia Cooney, her brothers and sisters feel so bitter toward the parents that they have denied their existence.

The court report on what the *Times* called, with characteristic reserve, Celia's "unfavorable heredity and early environment" seemed to have little influence on Judge Martin's harsh sentencing. But it was a bombshell in another court: the court of public opinion. The probation officer's report helped make Celia Cooney's case, already sensational, into a platform for discussing issues of crime and society. Now that the world knew who the Bobbed Haired Bandit was, the question became: Who was *really* responsible for her crimes?

22

For her crimes are on our heads too. No record could be clearer or more eloquent. None could leave less room for doubt that Cecilia Cooney is a product of this city, of its neglect and its carelessness, of its indifference and its undercurrents of misery. We recommend her story to the pulpits of New York, to the school men of New York, to the law makers of New York, to the social workers of New York, to those who are tempted to boast of its wealth, its magnificence and its power.
—Walter Lippmann, *New York World*

The myth of the Bobbed Haired Bandit collapsed under the weight of Celia's real life story. In the days following sentencing and publication of the probation officer's report, her story was written many times anew. The experts and the editors, the newspaper writers and their readers, all pounded out their own verdict, their own moral to the story.

In Celia's upbringing many found evidence of her downfall. The *New York Times*'s account of the probation officer's report carried the pithy subhead, "Sad Record of Bad Heredity, Parental Neglect and Low Environment," and the *New York Telegram and Evening Mail* almost complimented Celia for withstanding her wretched childhood in the manner she did:

> It was a journey which, for the girl at least, began twenty years ago. The robberies she admitted were but a more or less obvious culmination of a life begun in squalor, amid poverty, destitution and violence. That she became a highwayman, instead of something else was probably due to her magnificent physical courage and coolness.

Judge Martin himself declared that environment — hereditary as well as literary — was "largely responsible for the troubles" of the Cooneys. In the days after his sentencing he told an audience of Brooklyn Rotarians assembled at the Hotel Bossert:

> They lived in furnished rooms all their lives and they were anxious that their own child should not be born and brought up in a furnished

room. The lure of easy money from hold-ups described in the newspapers and shown in the moving pictures was too much under these circumstances. They sought by force what they could not gain by toil.

Celia and Ed had their own explanations for their life of crime. Ed blamed himself. In the words of a *Times* reporter: "Cooney still insisted he was to blame for all that had happened, that it was his idea to hold up stores and that he had induced his wife to help him." Celia denied it: "Eddie was a good boy and I made him go crooked." The editorial pages were not satisfied with this romantic shouldering of the blame. The *Brooklyn Daily Times* correctly predicted at their arrest that "we shall have all sorts of scientific explanations of this strange excursion into crime of two young folks on a honeymoon."

The Bobbed Haired Bandit was now a subject for "scientific" study. Celia's subjection to psychological and sociological scrutiny was most inevitable in an era when the experts in these fields were gaining new public prominence, and the study of individuals within their environment was seen as providing the key to social progress. At the Raymond Street Jail, a written questionnaire was submitted to Celia asking about her childhood. She began by "first denying indignantly that she ever had used liquor or tobacco or been immoral." This was followed up by other questions:

Q. Did you ever play when a little girl?
A. I played on the streets, we never had a playground.
Q. Did you ever have a doll?
A. Yes, not with my father and mother.
Q. Did you ever belong to a girl's club?
A. No, I didn't know about any.
Q. Did you ever go to Sunday school?
A. Yes, every Sunday.
Q. Do you think your childhood and early environment had any
   influence in shaping your life?
A. Yes.

On Wednesday, May 8th, the day after the probation officer's tragic report was published verbatim, the *New York World* published a powerful editorial. The author was Walter Lippmann, young at age thirty-four but already a well-known newspaperman, famous for his liberal political and social criticism and having the ear of Presidents Teddy Roosevelt and Woodrow Wilson. *Public Opinion*, his important 1922 book, had secured Lippmann's reputation as an agenda-setting intellectual, and by the spring of 1924 he was the lead editorial writer for Pulitzer's *World*.

The news columns of the *World* were considered second rate, but its editorial pages were recognized as some of the best and most influential of the city's newspapers. In 1924 the *World*'s editorial policy was contemptuous of crime reporting. The doings of a Brooklyn stickup artist were covered by reporters, but not worthy of editorial comment; local political corruption, scandals in Washington, and foreign affairs were of *real* significance. However, all the attention garnered by the Bobbed Haired Bandit could not be ignored, and the court report of the harsh, unromantic reality of Celia Cooney's childhood was an ideal platform for Lippmann to launch a blistering critique of society at large. His editorial began:

CECILIA COONEY

For some months now we have been vastly entertained by the bobbed-haired bandit. Knowing nothing about her, we created a perfect story standardized according to the rules laid down by the movies and the short story magazines. The story had, as the press agents say, everything. It had a flapper and a bandit who baffled the police; it had sex and money, crime and mystery. And then yesterday we read in the probation officer's report the story of Cecilia Cooney's life. It was not the least bit entertaining. For there in the place of the dashing bandit was a pitiable girl; instead of an amusing tale, a dark and mean tragedy; instead of a lovely adventure, a terrible accusation.

What was this "terrible accusation"? Whom did it accuse? Not the "pitiable girl" Cecilia Cooney or her bandit husband but, instead, the "twentieth-century civilization" that had failed to prevent the emergence of the Bobbed Haired Bandit from the slums of New York.

According to Lippmann, bad heredity and parental neglect were important factors, and Celia's parents Michael and Annie Roth had much to answer for, but so did society for letting such people "reproduce their kind." Lippmann continued:

> Five years before she was born her father was summoned to court for drunkenness and neglect; the Charities Department recommended that her older brothers and sisters be committed to an institution. That did not prevent her parents from bringing, with the full consent of the law, three or four more children in the world.

Like many other elite liberals of the day, Walter Lippmann was a believer in birth control for the poor and degenerate. They believed it would improve the living standards of poor families, solve problems like crime, and scientifically improve the race. It was not unusual for social reformers of the day to cite "bad heredity" as a primary cause of social problems and to call for the government to step in and regulate the fertility of the poor. In some states sterilization was carried out on feeble-minded felons who were considered unfit to breed. The eugenic implications of Lippmann's argument were clear: if Celia's degenerate father and illiterate mother had not been allowed to reproduce, Celia would never have been a problem for the storekeepers of Brooklyn.

But her parents were not the only ones to blame for Celia. Society and its institutions should be held accountable for her fate. To support his argument, Lippmann launched into a two-paragraph summation of Celia's nasty, brutish, and short life in the city. She had been a child laborer, and she had associated "at night with sailors picked up on the waterfront." How could a girl like Celia Cooney grow up in this modern day of 1924? Why hadn't somebody done something?

Walter Lippmann pointed out that "in the twenty years she has lived in this city she has come at one time or another within the reach of all the agencies of righteousness." The courts, the Department of Public Charity, the Children's Society, parochial schools, the factories and hospitals where she worked all had roles in the "dark and mean tragedy" of her life. Lippmann continued:

> This is what twentieth-century civilization in New York achieved in the case of Cecilia Cooney. . . . Fully warned when she was an infant, society allowed her to drift out of its hand into a life of dirt, neglect, dark

basements, begging, stealing, ignorance, poor little tawdry excitements and twisted romance. The courts had their chance and they missed it. Charity had its chance and missed it. Schools had their chance and missed it. The church had its chance and missed it. The absent-minded routine of all that is well-meaning and respectable did not deflect by an inch her inexorable progress from the basement where she was born to the jail where she will expiate her crimes and ours.

Lippmann's polemic elicited strong reactions from the *World*'s readers. While no one took issue with his eugenic reasoning, his condemnation of the social services of the city generated a heavy response. The very next day the paper printed replies from officials from the Woman's Court, Children's Court, and the Charity Organization Society. According to the *World*, these officials "agreed that public and private agencies alike were guilty of culpable neglect in failing to provide an approach to a normal environment for the girl who came repeatedly within their jurisdiction." All, however, countered that such a situation could not occur today. Bernard J. Fagan, the chief probation officer of Manhattan, said: "I do not think it possible that such a child today could be so neglected, with the increased social consciousness existing in the various public and private agencies." The general consensus was that the "righteous agencies" of the modern city were much better organized, sensitive, and cooperative than in the bad old days at the turn of the century. The system was working. The *Times* agreed, headlining that CELIA COONEYS OF TODAY HAVE A BETTER CHANCE.

But still more could be done. "The time to put on fire escapes is not when a building is burning down," wrote the superintendent of the Charity Organization Society, Joanna C. Colcord, in a letter to the *New York Telegram and Evening Mail*. Calling for preventive medicine, Colcord argued that more money was necessary to fund social work "patient and skilled enough to get to the core of things — to analyze in a scientific way the make-up of the disrupted home so as to decide intelligently whether there are enough elements of promise in the home to build on." Democratic Governor George S. Silzer of New Jersey concurred, citing Brooklyn's girl bandit as "an example of unwholesome family influences" in an address calling for a "comprehensive State institutional program" to prevent New Jersey institutions from failing future "unfortunates." Celia was a poster child for those seeking to solve society's ills with the welfare state.

In the conclusion to his editorial, Walter Lippmann had called on the moral and political elite of New York City to consider the story of the bandit girl's upbringing: "We recommend her story to the pulpits of New York, to the school men of New York, to the law makers of New York, to the social workers of New York." The social workers and politicians had responded, and there is evidence that at least one minister heeded the call.

A sermon about the life of Celia Cooney was preached at the Sunday evening service of a church in "the newly developed Kings Highway section of Flatbush, where almost everybody is paying for his own house with a lawn around it, and everybody owns an automobile." A reporter from the *World* happened to be in attendance with his notebook. Undoubtedly there were other sermons preached on the same theme, but not everyone had thought to summon a reporter to record it for posterity. "In a measured voice and with all the dignity of his grey hair, the Rev. David B. Cheney, pastor of the Kings Highway Baptist Church addressed his congregation":

> "Can the terrific problem of the city's waifs ever be solved?" the pastor asked, taking the sordid life history of the "Bobbed-Hair Bandit" as his theme. Then he answered his own question:
>
> "Some things will help mightily," he said. "Vagabonds, drunkards and criminals like Cecilia Cooney's father should be prohibited by law from propagating their kind. If this cannot be attained in any other way, these people should be physically incapacitated from breeding offspring."
>
> "Why cannot humanity exercise the same sort of care and effort in the breeding and training of our future citizens that we do in rearing dogs, hogs, and cattle?
>
> "I am not moved by any maudlin sympathy or any emotional sentimentalism. I appeal only for justice for the unfortunate waifs and the misguided youths."

Later, at the pastor's residence, the reporter asked the preacher for "more particulars about the proposed sterilization of the unfit." The Rev. Cheney said that there would have to be laws passed: "The proper authorities ought to be enabled to take a ne'er-do-well like the Cooney girl's father and say, 'Here, you, straighten up or we'll put you out of business.' " The reporter pressed the pastor further, asking:

> If a man might possibly change his habits through conversion, and if, before permanent sterilization was decided for any man, should he be instructed in the practice of birth control?
>
> Unhesitatingly, the pastor said, "No, I have no sympathy with birth control."

The dismal facts of Celia's childhood were interpreted from different political perspectives. The story could be pushed and pulled to make almost any point, and in the days that followed the release of the report on Celia, interested parties explained the tragedy of her life according to their own particular agenda.

In the spring of 1924 the political battle over the enforcement of Prohibition was raging. From the dry perspective, the enforcement of the Volstead Act in New York State was a travesty. The newspapers poked fun at the straitlaced drys and exposed the farce and corruption of the enforcement of the liquor laws with a nod, a wink, and a bad joke. The governor of New York, Al Smith, was openly derisive of Prohibition; John Hylan's city government was no better. Even the president of Columbia University, Nicholas Murray Butler, had recently publicly declared that Prohibition was unenforceable. In 1924 the wets were on the offensive and the drys were digging in for a bitter fight over a glass of beer and a broken home.

The Anti-Saloon League, the national organization at the forefront of the fight to enforce Prohibition, saw in Celia Cooney's life story an opportunity to strike a blow against the liquor interests. It was the "wet environment" that had "made her an outcast." Celia had grown up in a nation where the sale of alcohol was still legal and her father could walk freely up to the bar. Her story was a rallying call for the forces of dry righteousness. The league released a statement to the press:

> Celia Cooney never had a chance. Liquor robbed her of a chance which was given to other children more fortunate than she.
>
> When she was sentenced with her young husband to not less than ten or more than twenty years in prison, the judge who imposed sentence

had before him the probation officer's report. This report should be filed in the archives of the Association Against the Prohibition Amendment. It should be given to Dr. Nicholas Butler, of Columbia University, to Gov. Al Smith, to all who give aid and comfort to the liquor traffic in its attempt to come back. It is an arraignment of the saloon, and exposition of the effect of alcohol on the human race.

The statement recounted the now familiar tale of drunkenness and degradation contained in Marie Mahon's report to the court. Based on these sordid facts, the Anti-Saloon League fired its final salvo at the wets:

The home was the product of the saloon, and Celia was the product of her environment — she was probably subnormal, she was underfed, abused and neglected. It is the old story — and this child (for she is little more than a child) pays the price to-day, as the child has always paid the price of the sins of the parent.

We cannot help Celia Cooney now. The law will have to take its course with her. But we can prevent the perpetuation of the institution which created Celia's environment and made her an outcast. We can and have redeemed the poor from the blight of drunken fathers and brothers. We can fight with the last ounce of our strength for the enforcement of the prohibition laws, which are giving the children of the nation the right to be properly born and bred and brought up. We can remind the nullifiers of the Eighteenth Amendment and the selfish personal liberty advocates of the way in which this girl's father exercised his "personal liberty" and now his daughter in consequence will serve out in shame and ignominy her ten or twenty years in prison.

Mrs. Carrie Chapman Catt, a longtime advocate for women's rights and a prohibitionist, drew a similar lesson from the Bobbed Haired Bandit's story. Speaking before a crowd of almost five hundred women of the League of Women Voters assembled for a luncheon at the Briarcliff Lodge in Westchester, she said: "The story of the Cooney girl's life has been published. She was badly born of a drunken father and an illiterate mother. The League of Women Voters stands for prohibition and literacy." And that was enough for Carrie Chapman Catt: good schools and dry laws would prevent the next generation of bobbed haired delinquents from taking to the streets.

But Celia Cooney was also a poor working girl who had sweated away at the mangle, day after steamy day, far from the country clubs of Westchester County. Working-class New Yorkers understood the strain of laboring hard hours for low pay, and this sparked both sympathy and resentment for the bandit-laundress. When the *Brooklyn Eagle* wrote an editorial portraying Celia Cooney as "distinctively a jungle product," one reader, A. A., thought the editor's tone "somewhat superior." She felt the editor and the businessmen of Brooklyn needed to be chided for their condescension toward the working girl:

> You, Mr. Editor, were all content that she should be of the jungle children because they make convenient "kitchen wenches and horse boys" but you punish her to the very limit of the law's allowance, for such inconvenience as she puts on you.
>
> Indeed, it is not well for the more fortunate to sneer at the jungle folk, for if you read your own paper you will know that girls born to every advantage may fall, and while those in charge of cash registers may be secure now, the rest of us must clutch our pocketbooks in fear of some well connected thief who could not possibly get a prison sentence.

There were readers who felt that the story of Celia Cooney's life should be read as more than an indictment of the public and private agencies responsible for child welfare in New York City. They accused the economic system itself. A reader of the *World*, who signed his letter "Fair Play," argued:

> The roots of conditions that conspire to produce the Cecilia Cooneys lie in an inadequate wage scale that keeps the average toiler on the edge of oppressive want all his life, that forces children out to work at an early age with an incomplete education dooming them to a life of drudgery.

Extending this line of reasoning, Julius Lichtenfeld wrote in with a polite suggestion for the editor of the *World*:

Permit me to ask you your personal opinion of a system of society under which such dramas are possible. Do you think that such tragedies would be possible under a system of society based on production for use and not for profit? Your editorial suggests the study of Socialism.

Other readers turned writers came to quite the opposite economic conclusion. Such was the case with R. H. Towner, a gentleman whose analysis of the case involved the division of humanity into "higher nervous organizations" and "lower nervous organizations." Towner felt that the *World* had fallen for a popular misconception of society: "The truth is that the mortal units which compose 'society' are not fungible; and the lower nervous organizations among them are more prolific than the higher." Fortunately for civilization, the higher nervous organizations prosper under the system of laissez-faire, "which leaves each and all to their own independent struggle for existence and survivorship." The competitive conditions of laissez-faire lead to increasing numbers of higher nervous organizations because their "superior spiritual and moral stature" gives them a competitive edge over the more prolific lower nervous organizations. "At the beginning of the eighteenth century" according to Towner, "the number of prolific, low nervous organizations like Cecilia Cooney and her mother was very large in proportion to the less prolific higher nervous organizations." Luckily, because of laissez-faire and the struggle for independent existence, two centuries later the more civilized higher nervous organizations were regaining control. But there was a problem: "If the higher nervous organizations devote themselves by legislation, regulation, 'welfare work' and other supposedly reformatory devices to the preservation of the lower nervous organizations" as the *World* editorial had argued for, then "the latter, who multiply rapidly, will soon outnumber the higher nervous organizations and degrade the social structure by their numerical superiority."

The sympathetic attempt to explain Celia Cooney as a victim of circumstance provoked readers, like the odd fellow above, to respond in rebuttal. But it wasn't just crackpots like R. H. Towner who thought Celia deserved little sympathy; not everyone agreed that society should be held responsible for the rearing of girl bandits.

Celia Cooney had to take responsibility for her own actions as an individual; she was a sinner standing at judgment day. Dr. John A. Cutter wrote a letter to the *World* stating that all of this editorial " 'sob-sister rhetoric' does no good" and adding, "How about other members of her family — did they go wrong?" Dr. Cutter's point was simple: "There is such a thing as sin for which the individual is responsible — not society." Another newspaper reader agreed; E. S. wrote to the editor of the *Telegram* explaining that if the authorities used their "common sense we would have fewer bandits." He continued, spelling out his notion of common sense:

> When we have been taught reverence and love of God, "honesty is the best policy," "golden rule" and that "I am the master of my fate and the captain of my soul," it will do much to make this world better.

An angry working girl wrote in to the *New York Daily News* letters section, the "Voice of the People," to complain about the way the bandit girl had been portrayed as a "child of misfortune." It was Celia's fault, she wrote resentfully, not her environment: "Why blame Celia Cooney for what she did?" she asked rhetorically:

> I have a drunken mother usually sprawling on the floor and a step father who takes all my earnings. Still I don't go out and stick up people even if my mother does encourage me to paint and powder.

She closed on a maudlin personal note: "Yet, with it all, she is my mother and nobody can possibly know the heartaches I suffer every night and day."

The city's newspaper editorial pages were also split in their verdict on the Bobbed Haired Bandit. While some editors sided with Lippmann, citing mitigating circumstances and calling out for social welfare, others made the case for personal responsibility and stern justice. "The court's investigation showed that she had been reared in squalid and miserable surroundings," the *Brooklyn Standard Union* acknowledged on their editorial page, *but* "so were thousands of others in her neighborhood, and of those thousands precious few turned to banditry or any form of lawlessness for relief." "The city is well rid of her," the editors concluded.

However tragic her past might have been, Celia needed to be used as an example to others of "her kind." "There is sympathy for the girl, whose heredity was bad, and whose environmental influences never were very good," wrote the editors of the *Standard Union*'s competitor, the *Brooklyn Daily Times*:

It is necessary, however, that during the present unsettled conditions severe penalties be inflicted in order to dissuade other young women of

"Answering the Challenge," *New York Daily News*, February 17, 1924.

THE PUBLIC'S VERDICT

"The Public's Verdict," *New York American*, May 13, 1924.

her kind from activities which might have a far more serious effect, both for themselves and society.

An editorial in the *Telegram* argued that the Cooneys were lucky to get only ten to twenty years instead of the "quick dispatch which the electric chair provides" for capital offenses. The editors thought Judge Martin made a "good example" of the Cooneys, praising the jurist for being "unswayed by any of the mawkish and silly sentimentality which has been invoked by the idle folks of loose habits of thought regarding their case."

Celia's own biographers, the *New York American*, also turned their back on her, asking their readers to think instead of the poor unfortunates on the other side of the Bobbed Haired Bandit's automatic:

> Shall we have sympathy for the wrongdoer or his victims? Shall we shed our tears for the bobbed-haired bandit or for the number of those hard-working people who were deprived of their gains by her misdemeanors? She has broken the law and she must suffer, as greater than she and lesser than she have suffered.

But were those greater than she suffering the same consequences for their misdeeds? The Cooneys' fast conviction and harsh sentencing was used by progressives to point out the inequities of justice. Not surprisingly, it was Lippmann's *World* that led the charge in another editorial on the Bobbed Haired Bandit, posted two days after the first:

> Cecilia Cooney and her bandit husband were sentenced from ten to twenty years in prison. Whatever reformatory effect such a sentence may have, it is no doubt necessary to the safety of society.

But:

> James C. Rabiner, stock-broker, applied the securities of a customer to his own use and was sent to jail. He was released in three months by the New York Municipal Parole Board. . . .
>
> It is not a new observation that, if one must be a criminal, it is much better to be a criminal Class A — which is restricted to men of keen brain who could easily earn their living, and whose depredations far exceed the modest sums that may be filched from shopmen's tills.

The *Nation* magazine, paraphrasing Anatole France in their own editorial on the Bobbed Haired Bandit, satirically reminded their readers that "the law, with majestic equality, forbids rich and poor alike to steal."

Doctors, ministers, politicians, editors, social workers, intellectuals, working girls, cranks — seemingly everyone had something to say about the crimes and punishment of Celia and Ed Cooney. Even fellow bandits got their chance. One "Billy Nickel," a self-described crook since ten (who also claimed to know Ed), was solicited for his opinion by the *World*. "Rank amateurs," he dubbed the Bobbed Haired Bandit and her partner, explaining:

> Us fellows don't go like a mad bull at a gate. They had the sensational idea. Robbing a store ain't a sensation, it's a job, and it has to be done cute and slick.
>
> That couple of fools were racing. It never pays. The girl messed it up. She had no right to be in it. Cooney ought to be stood up against a wall before dawn and riddled with lead to slow music, and the girl should be sent to Alaska. They are a disgrace to the profession. . . .
>
> What makes me sick with the Cooneys is that they got so little out of their hold-ups and showed themselves sick quitters when the cops got them down in the swells' State.
>
> Their kidding won't hold when they get on to the wood and taste bread without the jam. It's all stage stuff at present. Prison takes that out of you. Mrs. Cooney will be No. what-not at Auburn, and in a month she will work, eat, sleep and think like a machine. That ain't a woman's place. Her place is with the baby at home.

A *New York Evening Post* editorial supported the harsh sentences as "lessons for other youngsters with a touch of the lawless in their make-up," but the same editor added wistfully that there "was a touch of the romantic in the adventures of a gun-moll in a great city defying the whole police force and continuing her career with scores of detectives after her." Alas, he concluded, "the romance is at an end."

Others were not so sorry. Jane Dixon, a columnist for the *Telegram*, was glad that the media spotlight was going to dim on the impudent girl from Brooklyn:

The Bobbed-Hair Bandit is gone.

A long-suffering public with a respect for law-and-order and decency and a wholesome regard for the fine fibre of the feminine equation will be spared the sight of such saccharine narration as has to do with Brooklyn's notorious gungirl.

Today the young woman who handled loaded hardware so recklessly is not a figure to thrill the readers of cheap novels.

She is merely a prisoner.

She is a disease which society has seen fit to segregate for the good of the majority.

She lives by the clock drably.

There are no flesh colored silk stockings where the Bobbed-Hair Bandit now grinds out the weary waste of ten to twenty years of days.

There are no bright lights, no lipsticks, no gaudy cabarets, no curious crowds milling about to feast curious eyes on the heroine (?) of so many shocking events.

There is only the watchful eye of the prison guard.

The debate over Celia Cooney was both contentious and voluminous — and for some New Yorkers, a bit absurd. After all, Celia was just another Brooklyn stickup artist robbing the corner store, a petty criminal at best. A week after the torrent of editorials and letters began, a columnist in the *American* poked fun of the whole hullabaloo, teasing pundits like Lippmann, as well as his own paper's editorial writers, by reducing the whole Bobbed Haired Bandit controversy to a minor squabble over the spelling of Celia's moniker:

The newspapers should agree whether they should refer to the unfortunate Mrs. Cooney as the bobbed bandit, the bob hair bandit, the bob haired bandit, the bobbed hair bandit or the bobbed haired bandit. . . .

Sympathy for the girl who never had a chance has been at times obscured by the rising tide of hectic debate as to where the "ed" should go, if in fact it should go anywhere.

And not only laymen have been devastated. College presidents have cast their dignity to the winds in heated discussions with other college presidents; no less than eighty-five of the investigating committees at Washington are now wrangling about it and for a while it threatened to

"Orders from Moscow," *New York World*, April 26, 1924.

disturb the relations existing between President Coolidge and Secretary Slemp.

For the common good we should come together and reach a decision in the matter.

Celia's sentencing unleashed editorial excess. One critic later lambasted both the bandits and the newspapers themselves for publicizing these crimes. William L. Barnhart, a "crime analyst" for the National Surety Company, raised the specter of communism as he attacked the press for the "glorifying of crime as in the case of the bobbed-hair bandit, whose 'autobiography' was purchased and published for a thousand dollars. These bandits are all anarchists and bolshevists," he concluded. While Barnhart was serious, not everyone took the threat of bolshevist bandits quite so seriously.

The facts about Celia's life and crimes had always been numerous and divergent, but now that newspapers were venturing into the terrain of explanation and analysis, the stories multiplied. Whatever recognizable shape she had taken previously softened into a pliable form out of which editorial writers and columnists could mold their own constructions. She was hard to pin down: reported as both sassy and contrite, spoiled by love for finery and horribly neglected by her parents, a grieving mother and a gay-hearted flapper. These contradictions meant that her case could be used to defend or attack nearly any cause. The reality of Celia Cooney as a woman who lived and loved and robbed diminished directly in proportion to the volume and vituperation of the political and moral polemics constructed from the reporting of her life story.

PART VI

End of a Thriller

◉ 23

Cooney, Inc. Celia president and general manager; Ed, treasurer and general roughneck, late specialists in chain store banditry in the Brooklyn field, dissolved partnership and suspended operations for from ten to twenty years yesterday.

Law and Order, relentless, uncompromising creditors in Kings County, foreclosed with a swift vengeance on the moral bankrupts. When the available assets of the defunct firm were inventoried in Raymond Street Jail last night, Celia and Ed found themselves rich in the wisdom that comes from sorrowful experience. The liabilities——?

—*New York Daily News*

Celia had enough of staring crowds and an attentive press, hiding her face as she was led out of the Kings County courthouse after their sentencing. Waiting outside was a bright red wagon with "Department of Corrections, No. 8" emblazoned in gilt lettering on the side. "So long Cecelia" someone yelled out from the crowd as she stepped aboard the van. Dropping the newspaper that hid her face, she pressed up to the wire window, looked "out upon her last hometown audience," and yelled back: "So long!" On her face "was that characteristic smile, half-amused, half-jeering," noted the *Herald-Tribune*; "it was the same defiant bit of feminine banditry, playing the same devil may care role." She was "Brooklyn's bobbed-haired bandit, still as hard-boiled as a ten-minute egg."

Just before leaving, Celia spotted her sister in the crowd. Remembering that the police still possessed a piece of "evidence" that was hers, she called out to her, "May, don't forget my sealskin coat."

Among the well-wishers offering up advice and goodbyes — "keep your lip up," "'at-a-girl" — a reporter yelled out from the crowd, asking Celia if she had seen her parents. When she said she hadn't, the reporter followed up, asking her if she wanted to. "I won't answer that," Celia snapped, cutting off the line of questioning. A different reporter tried a different tack: "Was it worth while, Cecelia?" "That's my business," Celia shot back in a taunting voice. "Hey, Sweets, don't say anything more," advised Ed, who was locked in a separate compartment next to her. Celia gave her husband an ambiguous "maybe," but she kept quiet and smiled and waved as the van rumbled away, rolling back toward the Raymond Street Jail.

Back in her jail cell Celia finally broke down, "lost her nerve," weeping as she lay on her bunk, head in arms. She talked with one of the ladies in the jail yard who had done time upstate: "She told me a lot of . . . stuff about Auburn that made me see for the first time what I was up against." Prison wasn't looking pretty: "Ugly clothes, uglier than I'd ever had to wear when I was poorest, cotton stockings, heavy shoes — up at half past six o'clock in the Summer and Winter. And work, work, work till your arms and legs ached." Celia asked her what kind of work she would have to do in prison. "Well, dearie," the woman inquired, "what did you do before you started to stick 'em up?" Celia replied that she'd worked in a laundry. "Well, if they know that they'll put you in the laundry."

This was simply too ironic for Celia:

> I threw back my head and laughed and laughed until she thought I was crazy, [even] if the doctors didn't. And a matron came running and said "Cecelia, whatever is the matter?" And I couldn't stop laughing, and then I started to cry like a fool.
>
> Say, ain't that a joke? Back to what I hated most, back to aching feet and wet steam and the mangle.

But Celia wasn't one to stay down for long. Within a day, jail authorities were telling reporters that the once-and-future laundress "eats well and retires early" and "spends much of her time reading detective stories."

Judge Martin gave Celia and Ed the maximum sentence to be spent at separate prisons, but neither of the two seemed to bear him a grudge. Quite the opposite: "He was a nice Judge," Celia explained. "I expected the limit and I got it. I was not disappointed. I thought the Judge would give me a lecture, but he didn't. I deserved what I got." Ed, too, seemed relieved that this part of their ordeal was done and they hadn't had to sit through some sanctimonious tirade. "I'm glad it's over," Ed told a reporter. "I liked the way the Judge spoke. I'm glad he didn't bawl us out. We were treated all right all the way though." Already looking forward to the future, Ed finished off what was likely his longest statement to the press to date, promising that "both of us are going to start all over again when we get out." "We're going to get on and be happy. And I'm going to work — to start an auto welding shop and be respectable."

The day after their sentencing Celia wrote a note to Warden Honeck asking if she could visit Ed to give him "just one more smile" before they parted ways. The warden told reporters that he was reluctant to grant Celia's request because she was "cracking under the pressure," her "sardonic quips and stoic indifference" giving way to tears. He worried that seeing her husband might cause an "imminent collapse." But Honeck must have noticed the change in Celia's condition because he soon relented, allowing her visitors. Her sister May and May's husband came to Raymond Street, stopping by to bid their farewells; Celia was happy to see them. Her next visitor was not nearly so welcome. As Celia sat in her cell, the barred door swung open and in walked "a little old woman, unkempt, her eyes bloodshot" — her mother.

Anna Roth had told the *New York Daily News* reporter that she had gone over to Brooklyn to visit her locked-up daughter the previous week, but someone had told her that it was not a good idea and she left. It may have been her own daughter; Celia had left instructions with her jail keepers that she didn't want to see her parents. But on Celia's last day in Brooklyn her mother made another trip to the Raymond Street Jail, and Warden Honeck brought her up to her daughter's cell.

With her chin up and eyes defiant, Celia sat awaiting her mother. But as the old woman toddled in, she started to cry. They each reached out and wrapped their arms around each other. When the warden returned to tell them that their time was up, he found them both in tears. The *Brooklyn Citizen* described the scene as the bandit's downfall:

> Celia admitted defeat in her attempt to resist an urge to see her mother yesterday and at the last moment crept into the arms of the dull-faced, illiterate woman who took her to live in the filthy East Side cellar twenty years ago. They clung to each other, each begging the other not to cry and both crying profusely for a while. It was the final surrender of the bad little girl who played bandit.

Celia was still wiping her face when the warden informed her that the keeper of Auburn Prison and his wife, a prison matron, were ready to collect her for the first stage of her journey up the river. Honeck had one more surprise in store. While the prison officers waited, the warden brought Ed in to say his last good-byes. Celia tried to pull herself together, shaking out her hair and dabbing her eyes with a handkerchief, putting on the smile she had promised for Ed. But when she saw him, the smile was "washed away . . . in a gush of tears."

Celia wasn't the only one crying. "It'll be a long, long time," Ed sobbed, "a long time before I see you. But we've got to make the best of it." Celia tried to smile again but couldn't and just cried. "Yes, we got to," she managed to get out. "But the time ain't going to be so long, Ed. We'll soon be together." As they kissed for the final time, Honeck turned away. "Couldn't stand it," the soft-hearted warden told reporters when asked to describe the couple's final parting. As Celia walked out, she looked back at her still weeping husband, set her face, and "sent Ed away with a smile."

Celia was transferred to Jefferson Market Jail in Manhattan in preparation for the train trip to Auburn. Settling into a cell in the red brick Victorian Gothic building with its distinctive pyramidal turret, Celia lay down to a restless sleep. In the morning she went to the window and looked through the bars, across the rainy city and over the elevated train that rattled by on Sixth Avenue through Greenwich Village. "It won't be like this in Auburn, will it?" she turned to ask her keeper. "No chance." "Gee, I like the city," Celia said wistfully. She read the papers — there wasn't much about the Bobbed Haired Bandit — and ate a hearty breakfast. Dressing carefully in the new blue suit she had worn at her sentencing, she accompanied the keeper and his matron-wife downstairs to catch a taxi to the Empire State Express and her new country home.

No crowd was waiting as she stepped out of jail at a little after eight o'clock in the morning, only two soggy photographers. She posed for a picture, and one of them called out, "Where are you going little girl?" "I'm going away for a long time, for a long vacation," she laughed. But the weather soon dampened her spirits. "By gosh, the last time I finished a big journey from Florida it was raining and here it is again. Even the weather is against me."

Celia Cooney leaving Jefferson Market Jail for Auburn Women's Prison with her newspaper in hand, May 9, 1924. (Library of Congress)

Celia arrived at Grand Central Station to a handful of curious on-lookers, but bad weather and "waning interest" had eroded their numbers. In the station she threaded her way — "timorously and unheeded" — through the normal rush hour crowd. Celia was leaving New York City on May 9th in a style quite different from when she had arrived less than a month ago. GONE THE DEFIANCE OF BANDITRY WHEN NONE GIVES CECELIA A GLANCE IN STATION, the *New York World* quietly headlined over a quarter column buried on page eleven. There was a brief flurry of excitement when news spread that Celia was aboard the express, and passengers left the train to crowd around outside the infamous Bobbed Haired Bandit's Pullman window. Celia sat, unconcerned, reading the newspaper, and without much effort the passengers were convinced to return to their seats and the train pulled out of the station, heading north. To the papers and the public, and perhaps to Celia herself, the Bobbed Haired Bandit was no longer big news.

If Celia's departure attracted little attention, Ed's went unnoticed. At one o'clock that afternoon, five hours after Celia had left for Auburn, Ed walked out of the Raymond Street Jail with a goodbye to Warden Honeck and a last thank you for all his consideration. Handcuffed to a deputy, Ed rode over the bridge to his own departure at Grand Central Station. No one took note of Edward Cooney.

Ed's train rolled up the Hudson River in the rain. At the Ossining station the rain had stopped. Flanked by two deputy sheriffs, Ed walked under a leaden sky to the gates of Sing Sing. On the receiving blotter he was entered as Edward Cooney, "Husband of Celia Cooney 'The Bobbed Haired Bandit.'" His wife's fame still preceded him. Dressed in his suit of prison gray, Edward gave up his name for the next anonymous number in the book: 75,907.

Located in the Finger Lakes region of New York, Auburn Prison is a long way from the city. It was late in the day when Celia arrived at the Syracuse train station. Several eager reporters were there to greet her. It was Celia's last chance to be a star for a long time, and the ex-bandit didn't disappoint. Celia was asked if she had anything to say that might keep other girls from "going wrong." She replied:

> What I have to say is to mothers . . . To mothers I would say, take care of
> your daughters. If mothers watched their daughters as they should there
> wouldn't be many of them that go wrong. Let them keep their daugh-
> ters out of dance halls, and know where they are nights. That is all there
> is to keeping a girl straight and decent and out of trouble.

Maybe it was just a line. Celia knew what to say, she had read
enough magazines to know that her story needed a moral, something
maudlin and penitent like a young anti-heroine weeping on the steps
of the big house in *True Detective* magazine. Or was she sincere? The
pathos of her own mother's tear-filled visit was still fresh; Celia had
just given birth and lost a daughter of her own; Mother's Day was only
a few days off. Perhaps her advice to mothers was more than a pulp
fiction cliché; it could have been sincere. Probably it was a little bit of
both.

At Auburn, Celia was registered, probed, and prodded. She was
measured according to the Bertillon system (head length: 18.0; head
width: 14.7+), as was the custom in those days when a person's physiognomy was thought to be a clue to their criminality. She was then
asked what kind of labor she could perform. "I might be used as a
guard," she quipped. "They say I know how to handle a gun."

She had her clothes taken away from her and received her prison
garb of heavy knitted underwear a couple of sizes too big and a blue
and white striped dress. Celia was then led to to her new home, a six-
by-nine-foot cell. The next morning at seven o'clock her door was un-
locked and she was told to go to the bathroom and get ready for
breakfast. In the corridor she met her fellow prisoners, and, as Celia
recalled:

> I found they all knew who I was and how long I was in for; and they
> treated me with respect, although they all seemed surprised that I was
> so young and so small. I didn't feel quite so lonely then.

Celia learned the routine of prison life at Auburn: coffee, oatmeal,
and watery powdered milk for breakfast while sitting at one of the
benches at the long tables in the ward dining room. Work from eight
to twelve, then back to the dining room for another meal, this one usually a thick hot soup with pieces of meat, followed by tapioca or stewed

Celia Cooney dressed in blue and white stripes after her arrival at Auburn Prison. Her hair, no longer bobbed, is pinned up. (New York State Archives)

prunes. Work again from one to four and then a quick wash-up before a cold supper at four-thirty, often tea and bread and more prunes ("I ate all the prunes I ever want to eat at prison," Celia remembered). After supper the inmates could go outdoors until six. The routine didn't seem to dampen Celia's spirits, however. She was heard singing and whistling snatches of popular songs in her cell. Soon she'd have a very good reason to sing.

On June 22, a little over a month after the lovebirds were sentenced to their separate prisons, Ed made the newspapers. It was only a quarter column, buried on page twenty-two of the *Brooklyn Eagle*. Ed was being moved out of Sing Sing — "handcuffed and leg-ironed" — to the men's wing at Auburn Prison. The official reason given was that Ed and another inmate, Marquis Curtis, needed to be transferred because they were too "hard" for Sing Sing.

Marquis Curtis seemed plenty hard. He had just arrived at Sing Sing on a thirty-year robbery charge, and it wasn't his first arrival — or departure. Eight years earlier he had led an escape of seven convicts from Sing Sing, getting himself shot on John D. Rockefeller's nearby estate by a prison keeper. He was, by all accounts, "an exceptionally vicious and dangerous crook." Edward Cooney was not in the same league; he may have looked a little like Jack Dempsey, but he was certainly not too hard for Sing Sing. He was here on his first offense and would later be described as a "model prisoner."

So why was Edward Cooney transferred to Celia's prison so soon after Judge Martin's very harsh and very public sentencing? It could have been the work of a soft-hearted prison official. There was a recent amendment by the State Board of Prisons mandating that couples in prison could meet once a month, and since sentencing, Celia, Ed, and Ed's family had all been petitioning the prison board to have Ed transferred to Auburn; they may have found a sympathetic ear. Regardless, the story fed to the press about the "hard" Cooney who needed to leave Sing Sing for closer supervision provided the political cover necessary for a humane transfer coming so soon after Judge Martin's severe sentence.

Celia had heard nothing about Ed's pending transfer. "Then one day," she recalled:

I was told to go to the visitors' room. I couldn't imagine who it would be, though I hoped it would be someone who would talk to me about Eddie.

Imagine my joy when I saw Eddie waiting there for me. They let us hug and kiss and talk to each other for half an hour. He had just arrived and was to stay at Auburn. I was so excited I could hardly talk. I had to keep wiping the tears away.

Celia thought now that Ed was at Auburn they would see each other every day. She was disappointed. They were allowed a half hour visit only once every month and spent the intervening time writing letters to one another, though "it seemed funny to be writing letters when we were right there together in the same building." It was less than ideal, but it was better than Ed miles away at Sing Sing. For, as Celia recalled, at least once every thirty days "we could hold hands and kiss and look at each other — and give each other courage."

Their good fortune ended sharply. Two months after Ed's arrival, on August 18th, the license plate machine that Ed was working on in the

Auburn Prison shop jammed. One of the plates that Ed was stamping out had gotten caught in the press. As he reached in to free it, the twenty-ton pressure press slammed down, catching his left hand and crushing it so badly that three of Ed's fingers had to be immediately amputated in the prison hospital. The operation didn't go well. The wound got infected and refused to heal. In an effort to halt the infection, the prison doctors tried cutting away half of Ed's hand. When that didn't work, they moved farther up and cut off his entire hand at the wrist. His wound still wouldn't heal. After nearly a year and a half of unsuccessful operations Ed was taken down to New York City to see specialists. It was discovered that he had developed osteomyelitis, an infectious inflammatory bone disease that kills off and then peels away surrounding tissue. To stop the infection the doctors sliced away even more of his arm, amputating it below the elbow. The last operation was a success.

Ed's arm eventually healed, but his health problems were just beginning. Weakened by his injury, Ed contracted tuberculosis in the prison hospital. Now severely sick, he was transferred out of Auburn and taken to the TB hospital at Clinton Prison in Dannemora, up on the Canadian border where the high altitude was thought to be helpful to tubercular patients. Ed would spend the next five years confined to a prison hospital and hundreds of miles away from his wife. Heartbroken, the couple consoled themselves by writing to each other every week.

With her husband gone, Celia built a life for herself at Auburn. Her jailmate back in Brooklyn was right about the job Celia was assigned. Notwithstanding her plea to be made a guard, Celia's first three years were spent working in the prison laundry. Then Celia learned to type and take shorthand, and soon she had a trusted position in the offices of Frank L. Heacox, the warden of the Women's Prison at Auburn. By the end of her stint, Celia had mastered her new trade so completely that she was spending seven-hour days teaching typing and stenography to the other inmates in the prison school.

As Celia's life in prison became monotonous, her identity outside of Auburn's walls took on a life of its own. Soon after Celia headed off for prison and anonymity, the Bobbed Haired Bandit detached herself from a flesh-and-blood woman and passed into the vernacular. She was at first an image invoked in the mass media and popular culture as a warning, a cautionary tale for young girls, and then quickly reduced to a figure of fun and ridicule.

According to the *Washington Post*, a gun-waving bobbed bandit menaced Calvin Coolidge himself in a daring raid on high society. The gun-girl struck during the Gridiron Club's annual spring dinner at the Willard Hotel. The "famous dinner club, composed of Washington newspaper correspondents," offered a "hodge-podge of song and satire" to entertain the assembled elite. The club's guests that evening "included the President, the cabinet, justices of the Supreme Court of the United States, senators, representatives, party managers and other national figures of politics and business." This crowd of savvy newspapermen and politicos laughed at the portrayal of the girl bandit from Brooklyn eluding her pursuers once more. In the skit, the unexpected entrance of the Bobbed Haired Bandit early on in the Gridiron dinner caused a "great furor." The president of the Gridiron Club called for a policeman to arrest the impudent girl. Fortunately, there was a policeman from Philadelphia among the swells. Brigadier General Smedley D. Butler of the U.S. Marines was summoned from his seat, but he was too late. The Bobbed Haired Bandit had vanished, much to the amusement of the crowd. It seems that General Butler, the scourge of Philadelphia's bandits and bootleggers, was no match for the Brooklyn bandit.

Closer to home, a similar scene was played out. Enjoying his success in the wake of the Bobbed Haired Bandit's capture, Police Commissioner Richard Enright was photographed with a big smile on his face, hands in the air, as he and three colleagues at a fancy dress dinner were held up at gunpoint by a girl bandit with mask, fur coat, and bobbed hair. The bandit had passed from public enemy to the subject of good-natured political ribbing.

In the weeks and months that followed Celia's incarceration, the character became the subject matter of the following:

Weak Jokes:
   He: Aren't you going to bob your hair?
   She: Well, you know, I can't decide whether to bob it or bandit.

Hands up! Police Commissioner Richard Enright (*second from left*) seems pleased to see this bobbed bandit at the New York Press Club dinner. (Paul Thompson, Museum of the City of New York)

Public Lectures: G. Arthur Gayer, Ph.D., gave a talk at the Astor Hotel on "Sleep and Dreams" (promising music, "audible meditation," and free admission) prefaced by musings on "The Bobbed-Hair Bandit and Society."

Theater: The "Gossip of Vaudeville" section of the *Times* announced that "Alice Lake will appear in 'The Bobbed Bandit' with Robert Williams for a tour of the Middle West and then a return to New York."

Burlesque: Chester "Rube" Nelson's "The Bobbed Hair Bandits" opened at the Mutual, "Washington's new home of burlesque," and was praised as "one of the most tuneful, snappy and funny shows" on the circuit.

Song: The great blues singer Ethel Waters recorded "Throw Dirt in Your Face," in which she sang:

> I ain't no bobbed-haired bandit,
> I'm just a good gal from the South,
> And if she fools with my man,
> She might as well stick her head in the lion's mouth.

Bobbed Haired Bandit also became a hollowed-out journalistic tag. Reporters found bobbed bandits in Buffalo and Chicago, among grade school girls in Connecticut, and even as far afield as China, where the *American* reported that "China's Bobbed Hair Bandits Steal Wealthy Young Men and Marry 'Em." Unlike previous stories, these accounts had no conceivable connection to Celia or her crimes, nor did the reporters attempt to draw any. Bobbed Haired Bandit was just an attention-grabbing phrase to refer to any female criminal. She was the female counterpart to the bootlegger as a sign of the times, "bobbed bandits" and "bootleggers" being handy labels, another cliché for the decadence of the younger generation.

The Bobbed Haired Bandit became an image, an epithet which others picked up, used, transformed, and then eventually cast off and forgot when the term no longer evoked any social meaning. A year after Celia was sent upstate, the only "Bobbed Bandit" making the news regularly was a racehorse picking up a seven-hundred-dollar purse one race and finishing out of the money the next.

In 1930 the *Daily News* reconnected Celia to her moniker, running a special update on the Bobbed Haired Bandit in prison. The *News* reported that Celia was devoted to her "two ruling passions in jail — literature and baseball." Once a week prisoners at Auburn were allowed a "library day" — a visit to the prison library. Celia later recalled that "it was the first library I had ever made regular use of." Auburn prisoners were allowed to take out three books and two magazines every two weeks, and Celia borrowed them all. The *News* divulged that after work, Celia retired to the cell she describes as "'an old fashioned hotel room' except, of course, for the bars," "and buries herself in her books." "I had never had a chance to study as much as I wanted," she remembered, "and I began now, reading a lot and taking my correspondence courses."

Celia used her time to educate herself in matters domestic as well, learning "practical nursing" in the hospital and attending cooking classes. As she explained, "I had found when we took the apartment that I wasn't a very good cook — so I thought now was a good time to learn. When Eddie and I got out I would be a better housekeeper." But Celia's prison life wasn't all work and school: "The flapper bandit," the *News* revealed, "plays third base on the women's prison team."

METROPOLITAN MOVIES

Another bobbed hair bandit raids Fifth Avenue shop.

"Metropolitan Movies," *New York World*, May 13, 1924. The legend below the cartoon states: "Another bobbed hair bandit raids Fifth Avenue shop."

At the time of Celia's sentencing, the *Daily News* had run a pessimistic piece on the reform of incarcerated criminals, asking WILL PRISON REFORM GIRL BANDIT? and answering their own question with the next line: "Law of Averages Gives Little Hope in Celia Cooney's Case." Celia, however, seemed determined to prove them wrong. According to officials, she was a model prisoner who followed prison routine and discipline to the letter. There were also reports that Celia had found God in jail. She was now "imbued with a deep religious spirit" and "never will make a move hereafter without first getting a priest's advice." She had even given up her namesake coif. Celia "no longer has bobbed hair, and she is through with banditry," the *New York American* declared, as if linking the two were the most natural thing in the world. "She is letting her hair grow and says she will never bob it again." "I've laid away my guns for good," Celia insisted.

It's hard to know how much of this story was shaped by the desire of the newspapers — and Celia herself — to create a satisfying narrative of redemption for the working-girl-gone-bad. But what is certain is Celia knew that with good behavior she and Ed could get out on parole as early as 1931. Celia had plans for when they were released: "I have a wonderful dream," she told the female *News* reporter who interviewed her in 1930; "the dream is a little home with the one I love and perhaps" — here Celia paused as she "gazed wistfully at the potted plant on the window," then continued — "you know, what every real woman longs for when she loves a man."

It was a macabre twist of fate that brought Celia closer to her dream. In 1930 the New York State Legislature passed a bill that allowed convicts injured while incarcerated to sue for damages. On April 3, 1931, New York City newspapers announced that Edward Cooney was bringing a one-hundred-thousand-dollar suit against the state for the loss of his arm and subsequent contraction of tuberculosis. His lawyers? The irrepressible Samuel S. Leibowitz and his partner on civil cases, Jacob Shientag. Later that month Ed's case was heard in the State Court of Claims in Syracuse, New York. Shientag argued that the embossing press that flattened Ed's hand was not properly guarded and thus the state was negligent. In fact, three other men had lost their hands, crushed in the very same machine. To make his case, Shientag called on nine prisoners to describe the unsafe working con-

Celia and Ed hold hands during their brief reunion in Claims Court, April 1931.
Jacob Sheintag stands behind them—masked and cropped out of the picture.
(Harry Ransom Humanities Research Center)

ditions in the prison shop at Auburn. Also called to testify was the ex–
Bobbed Haired Bandit herself, attesting to the health of her tall male
companion before his accident.

The meeting was bittersweet. They kissed and cried and embraced
in court and later posed for a picture outside the courtroom holding
hands. Celia looked radiant in a fur scarf and a dark suit, her now-
shoulder-length hair tucked up under a cap. But Ed, despite the
smiles he directed toward Celia, looked terrible. Dressed in his woolen
prison grays, Ed was hunched over and gaunt, having lost eighty-five
pounds during his sickness. Where his left hand should be there was
nothing, only his sleeve neatly pinned up.

Seven months later a decision was handed down by the court. Leibowitz and Shientag, finally allowed to represent the Cooneys in
court, demonstrated just what they could do. On December 24, 1931,
the state was found negligent in Ed's accident, and the Cooneys were
awarded a cash settlement. It couldn't have come at a better time.
After seven years in prison, Celia and Ed would soon be free.

◉ 24

Don't tell me there isn't any Santa Claus.
—Celia Cooney, *New York American*, on Christmas Day

Celia had been an ideal prisoner, and Ed was so ill. The
furor had subsided; now they were both good candidates for early parole. On a ten to twenty charge, that meant seven years. However, they
could not be released without the promise of employment on the outside. "I don't suppose that any one is going to hire Celia Cooney while
he's conscious," Celia joked to a reporter; "he'd be afraid I'd walk off
with the safe." Finding a job wouldn't be easy. When the felons went
upriver it was the Roaring Twenties, and now it was the Great Depression. But with the state's help, Celia and Ed found work. Ed's health
had put an end to the old fantasy of opening an auto welding shop, but
Celia's new skills landed her a job as a secretary-typist in a law office.

Ed, now a one-armed bandit, was offered a position as an office assistant and process server in the same office as his wife.

Celia's parole hearings took place on October 15th and 16th of 1931. Three other women came up for parole the same day as Celia, but Celia's case was distinct. She may have been a role model as a prisoner, but before she came to Auburn she was the notorious Bobbed Haired Bandit. The parole board was more than willing to let Celia Cooney walk out of prison, but they wanted to make sure the Bobbed Haired Bandit stayed locked up. A little line at the bottom of the surviving record of the minutes of the Auburn parole meetings for October 1931 tells the story; it reads: "Notice: The data in the case of Celia Cooney is to be confidential."

Sealing the parole records on the former gungirl was not enough. Even in her reformed state, Celia was a walking, talking advertisement for the excitement, drama, and tragedy of the bandit life. And Celia, as she had demonstrated countless times, liked to be seen and heard, enjoying the part she played on the public stage. No doubt with this in mind, the parole board took the unique step of making the ex-bandit's anonymity part of the condition of her parole. Celia was never to act in a movie or write her life story, nor was she to give any formal interviews. She was, to the best of her ability, to avoid publicity. Any violation would return Celia to prison. As added insurance, the additional robbery indictments against Celia that were sent up to Auburn when she started her sentence were kept open—until 1945. (Ed's, by way of comparison, were dismissed in 1932.) This was not a standard practice.

The Bobbed Haired Bandit had been gagged. Celia had told the press that she wanted the quiet life, to go where no one knew them and didn't know anything about their past. The law was making certain this would happen.

In the dark early hours of November 6, 1931, Celia Cooney left the New York State Prison for Women. There was a gaggle of press shivering on the street outside. Celia was "smuggled out," bundled in thick robes and driven in Warden Heacox's sedan through blinding snow to Syracuse. There at eight forty-five she boarded the New York Central. It was her first time out of prison in seven years, and she immediately sensed the changes:

I was wearing the clothes I had been sentenced in: the blue serge suit with white collar and cuffs, the lavender turban with cloth violets. They still fitted me, but they were rather the worse for seven and a half years in the Auburn storage. And how different the styles were. I looked eagerly at every woman in the car. So much had happened between 1924 and 1931.

Ed had been released a week earlier; there had been no press waiting for him at the gate. He was now waiting to meet Celia at the 125th Street station in Harlem in an effort to avoid the press and public who might be waiting for his wife's return. But Celia was so excited on her first day of freedom that she missed the stop and sailed by him on her way down to Grand Central. Ed needn't have worried; it was a small homecoming this time. Waiting in the station were a handful of reporters and photographers but no crowd of thousands. CROWDS UNAWARE AS CELIA COONEY ARRIVES IN CITY, reported the Herald-Tribune, describing how the once infamous gungirl "arrived inconspicuously at Grand Central Station in mid-afternoon, to be swallowed up in the hurrying crowds of the city."

It had been seven long years, and New Yorkers had forgotten about the Bobbed Haired Bandit. Since 1924 there had been thousands upon thousands of new stories and new faces to talk about; there was the stock market crash and the Depression. "Just look at that!" exclaimed Celia, as she left Grand Central and looked up at the new Empire State Building rising out of the cityscape a few blocks south. "Why the whole town seems to be different." Looking over her changed city, Celia must have been awestruck: new skyscrapers, new fashions, new breadlines.

After marveling at the new city rising around her, Celia dutifully took a taxi directly to the Parole Board offices to check in. It was late, and the offices were closed, so Celia directed the cabdriver over the East River to Ed's mother's house at 887 Dean Street. Celia probably had mixed feelings about returning to the old neighborhood. It may have been good to be back in familiar surroundings, but a block away from the elder Mrs. Cooney's house was the National Biscuit warehouse with its sharp memory of their final botched robbery. Everyone knew who she was in this neighborhood.

The Cooney family's warm welcome must have assuaged Celia's anxiety. Ed's mother had been preparing the house for their home-coming for months. Her three-story frame house was freshly painted and stuccoed, new curtains hung in the windows, and the second story of the house had been remodeled to be the couple's new home. As a cab pulled up and Celia got out, skin pale against her green prison coat, Ed's mom and three brothers rushed out to greet her. But no Ed. Where was Ed? He was still making his way back from Harlem and his missed rendezvous. An hour later he rushed in, breathless. Complete, the Cooney family closed the door to reporters and celebrated the couple's return.

And the door remained closed. The day after Ed and Celia's arrival, Ed's brothers told the press that Ed and Celia had gone upstate to live on a farm with Celia's aunt. "This, at least, was the story given out," the *Eagle* reported, with well-deserved skepticism. For a day or two, reporters and newsreel photographers camped out in the neighborhood, waiting for the good copy and pictures that the sassy gungirl had provided seven years before, but there was no longer any story here and eventually they drifted off.

Christmas delivered a welcome present to Dean Street. On Christmas Eve Ed received a telegram from Samuel Leibowitz and Jacob Shientag. It contained the message that the state was awarding him a cash settlement of twelve thousand dollars for the loss of his arm. It wasn't the hundred grand he had originally sued for, but combined with whatever little money may have been left over from the thousand dollars that the Bobbed Haired Bandit's story had netted years earlier, it was more than enough money to finance Celia's fantasies of middle-class life.

"It means the fulfillment of a dream I had all those years in Auburn," Celia explained, briefly breaking her public silence on Christmas Eve to her old friends at the *New York American*: "It means a cottage with a farm and chickens . . . It means fresh air and sunshine. A chance to forget." "Oh, I'm so happy it makes it difficult to tell all that I'm going to do," Celia continued, climbing onto a stepladder to arrange ornaments on the Christmas tree: "Don't tell me there isn't any Santa Claus."

After this Christmas interview it would be nearly five years before newspaper readers were treated to another interview with the Bobbed Haired Bandit. But on September 5th, 1936, readers of the *New York World-Telegram* were treated to a nostalgic surprise. There, in a large three-picture montage, was Celia Cooney. Celia was captured in classic suburban repose: outdoors on an early autumn day, garden hose in hand, watering her lawn. She looked older now, no longer the grinning flapper. Her brown hair brushed her shoulders, and she wore a simple dark dress under a domestic white apron. Above her was a picture of a neat brick cottage, surrounded by leafy trees and low shrubs, her house in Copiague, Long Island. And to her left was a picture of two cute young boys, playing on the cottage lawn with a toy car. They were her sons: Patrick, four years old, and Ed Jr., just six months. Celia had finally gotten what she said she always wanted: a nice place to live in comfort and raise a family — the American Dream.

It almost seemed as if crime did pay. Celia and Ed, had they remained working stiffs back in Brooklyn, could never have saved up the four thousand dollars Celia reported it cost to buy their five-room, red-brick dream home — especially not now that the Depression was on. It was crime and getting caught that got them where they were. Even Celia saw the absurdity in this. "It doesn't make much sense does it?" she said to the reporter who interviewed her in her suburban home. "We got what we wanted. I guess if you want things hard enough you get them some way in the end."

Celia and her sons and the brick house made a nice family portrait, but there was one thing missing: Ed. Happiness doesn't make newspaper stories, tragedy does. The *World-Telegram*, like other newspapers, had rediscovered the Bobbed Haired Bandit when it was learned that Ed had died from tuberculosis and Celia was about to lose her dream home.

Ed never recovered from the TB he contracted in prison. The couple flirted with the idea of going out West, to a better climate for Ed's lungs and away from all the publicity. They were going to buy a farm or ranch in Texas. But the city couple knew nothing about cattle or crops, and their family and friends — and, just as important, the conditions of their parole — tied them to New York. The jobs the pair were supposed to get at the law firm never materialized, and soon Celia was pregnant with Patrick.

To illustrate that the "bob-haired bandit days" were "long gone for Mrs. Celia Cooney," the *World-Telegram* published a domestic montage of her "quiet life" in Copiague, Long Island. (Library of Congress)

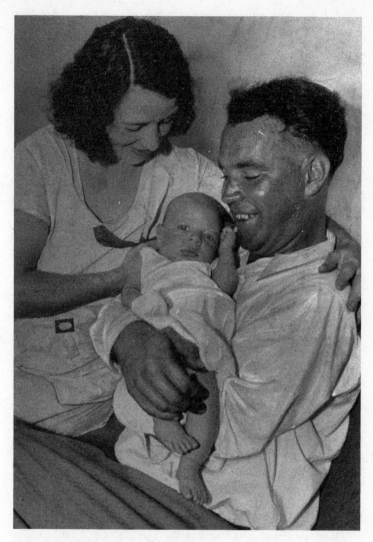

"Young Patrick Michael Cooney probably won't be deprived of his parents, Celia Cooney (the original bobbed-hair bandit) and Ed Cooney. Released from prison last Christmas, they've gone straight, living in Copiague, L.I. with their new baby, Patrick, one month old and weighing 11 lbs. today." "Celia and Ed with Baby Patrick," *New York Daily News*, September 9, 1932.

After they had spent their settlement — only six thousand dollars after Leibowitz and Shientag took their cut — Ed went to work as a timekeeper for the Works Project Administration, and when his lungs wouldn't allow even this light employment the family went on relief. By the time Celia gave birth to Ed Jr., Ed Sr.'s health was far gone. A month after his second son was born, Ed was taken to the Holtsville Sanitarium, a Long Island TB hospital. He lasted only two more months. On May 26, 1936, Edward Cooney, thirty-seven years old, died. The newspapers reported that the HUSBAND OF 'BOBBED HAIR BANDIT' was to be brought back to Brooklyn to be buried in the Holy Cross Cemetery. Even in death Ed got second billing.

Broke, alone, and with two kids to support, Celia said she was going back to Brooklyn as well. "They had four years of the kind of happiness they dreamed about in a Brooklyn rooming house when they were very young," the *World-Telegram* staff writer waxed romantically. "But now it's all over," a sober Celia acknowledged. Newspaper reporters gently teased Celia, asking her if the Bobbed Haired Bandit was going to come out of retirement now that she was broke. "I know better than that," Celia insisted; she had gone straight for good and had no intention of taking up her gun-wielding "former occupation." The reformed gungirl was already planning her next move: "I've got to take care of the two kids. I can't get a job out here in the country." She explained: "I've got to sell the house so I can move into town and get a job. . . . I can get a job as a scrub woman at night. I ought to be able to earn $11 a week scrubbing. . . . Then I'll brush up on my stenography so I can get a day job too." "It's funny isn't it?" she mused out loud, "I'll end up in a Brooklyn rooming house again so I can take care of the kids." But even faced with the death of her beloved Ed, the imminent loss of her house, and the full circle back to manual labor in Brooklyn, Celia's seemingly endless reserve of optimism didn't tap out. "I'm not bitter," Celia assured the reporter. "Ed and I had four years of happiness. Given half a chance, I'll start all over and come out on top."

Three years later Celia hadn't gotten there yet — nor did she make it back to Brooklyn. On April 22, 1939, several of the city's papers ran a small news item about a terrible fire in Jamaica, Queens, that destroyed a dry goods store and the apartment above it. The apartment's tenant, a widow, narrowly escaped, fleeing to safety with her two sons, aged three and six, with only the clothes on their backs. The woman gave her name as Mrs. Roth, but detectives investigating the fire recognized her as Celia Cooney, the Bobbed Haired Bandit. The *New York Mirror*'s header, EX-'GIRL BANDIT,' GOING STRAIGHT, LOSES ALL IN FIRE, said it all. Celia was thirty-four years old, a single mother with two young kids, living on relief checks of fifty-five dollars a month, without a home or possessions. Crime, in the long run, may not have paid, but neither, in the short run, had going straight. This was the last New York newspaper article printed about Celia Cooney. With this final, depressing epilogue, the story of the Bobbed Haired Bandit seemed to be over.

But it wasn't. Beginning in March of 1940, and continuing over four installments, a pulp magazine called *Modern Romances* published "What the World Didn't Know: The True Story of the Bobbed Haired Bandit." Celia told her story one more time. Or at least we think she did, for as usual, we can't be exactly sure how many words are really hers. In the years since her release Celia had stretched her parole restriction on not discussing her life and crimes with scattered newspaper interviews; by "writing" her own story she definitively broke it. But now that it was nine years since she'd been in prison, and with the country in a depression and a world at war, she probably, correctly, figured that no one would notice. And as a single mother with two young children, a burned-out home, and no money it was worth a gamble.

The *Modern Romances* series, though not the cover story, was impressive. Illustrated by old newspaper photos of Celia and Ed from their wedding—the Bobbed Haired Bandit in fur coat and turban, the couple posing cockily after their capture, then Celia in a jail cell—and bracketed by a montage of newspaper clippings, the series ran for four months with close to forty pages of tight text. Celia offers a few new and interesting details of her life of crime, in particular about her life in prison and afterward when the newspapers had lost interest. But most of the story conforms to what a careful reader of the press would already have known. In fact, Celia (or rather, her ghostwriter) lifts sections nearly verbatim from earlier newspaper accounts to fill out dialogue and description. The real function of "What the World Didn't Know" was not revelation but the recasting of Celia's story as a romantic drama.

Modern Romances was a "confession" monthly published by George T. Delacortes's Dell Magazines, whose stories reflected the struggles and hardships, as well as the fantasies and desires, of its female audience. The heroines of *Modern Romances* were mostly working girls with a shameful secret who paid the price but persevered, if not triumphed, by adhering to the core values of American womanhood: love and family. The moral universe of pulp romance was displayed in titles like "Notorious Girl" and "Fallen Woman: My Sinful Secret" or "Wandering Waitress: The Astounding Truth about the Tips."

The story that Celia tells in *Modern Romances* conforms to stock tropes of the genre: a tragic childhood with a drunken father, true love at the first sight of Ed, the desire for the good life that tempted her and her husband into a spate of stickups. Baby Katherine's death was the terrible price for these crimes. Over all, it is the redemptive love story of a devoted wife and dutiful mother. A life of fur coats and fast ways leads only to trouble; home and marriage is where happiness lies. As Celia remembers her first night in Raymond Street Jail:

> In the silence of that night, in that hard, cold jail with pickpockets and harlots and petty thieves all around me, I came to realize how much Eddie meant to me. How important love is — and how *unimportant* is every other thing in this big world.

The formula of the pulp romance not only dictated the general contours of Celia's story but shaped the way it was told: its language and imagery. The heroine of *Modern Romances* couldn't just say yes, she had to give her "breathless assent." Here is Celia showing off a new dress to her landlady, about to go out on her first date with Ed:

> "Do I look alright? I turned around. "Is it too tight? Do you like the color?" I had got a red silk.
> "You look lovely, Celia."
> "Do I really? I'm going out tonight."
> "Well it's time you did. You're always at home working," she said. "When I was your age —" She was cut off by a ring of the doorbell.
> My heart jumped, and I looked at her.
> "That's him now, maybe."

"You don't have to look so scared," she teased me. "Your eyes are as big as saucers." Then she went to the door, and I held my breath till I heard Eddie's voice asking for me.

The final story of the Bobbed Haired Bandit allowed Celia to have the last word, even if it was ghostwritten. This was a settling of accounts. Celia's grudge wasn't against the police or courts, and she didn't blame her family or society; instead, she reserved her anger for the press. She wanted to bury her hatchet firmly in the forehead of a reporter. It is the nosy newspaper reporter covering the 1939 apartment fire that tears her out of "quiet obscurity," revealing the sinful secret of her dark past to the city, her neighbors, and — in an account at odds with theirs — her sons. As she tells it:

> Pat came bursting in. His cheeks were white and his blue eyes flashing indignantly.
>
> "Mom! The kids are saying you're the Bobbed-haired Bandit!" His mouth tightened in an attempt to hide the trembling of his lips. "They say you and Dad used to hold up stores and steal their money! They say it's in the paper. It's a lie, isn't it?" He looked so *sure* it wasn't so! He was so confident that I would deny it!
>
> But I couldn't deny it. It was true.

But Celia, the reluctant celebrity, is angry at the press for another reason: they got her story wrong. Sandwiched alongside the gushing demonstrations of love, and tearful acknowledgments of sorrow and regret, is Celia's fury at the press for what she sees as their misrepresentation of *her* story. Recalling her railroad trip up from Florida she writes:

> I asked for a newspaper and I was given one with the write-up of the reporter who had flown down from New York. He had twisted everything I had said. He had distorted everything I had done. It was then I wished I hadn't talked to him. There was nothing romantic about what he said. It was sordid and cheap.

Celia takes the reporters to task over small details:

> The newspapers claimed to know all about me and said I was born on East 98th Street. I never even lived on 98th Street at any time — so that shows how incorrect 'most everything they wrote about me was.

It's not incorrect names, dates, and places, however, that really upset Celia; it's the way in which the press constructed her character and represented her motives:

> They also said the reason I became a bandit was because I had read so much "crime trash" that my head was full of it. That was a lie, for I didn't have time to read *anything*, either good or bad. I read my first detective magazine *after* our capture, when I was in the Raymond Street jail. And a reporter gave me that.

Celia then sets the record straight:

> I didn't become a bandit because my head was full of "crime trash" but because I found I was going to have a baby, and I didn't want my baby to grow up in the kind of pigsty that I was born in.

It's a rich explanation. While Celia denies the influence of detective magazines on her decision to become a bandit, castigates the newspapers for printing stories that reported this, and lays the blame on a reporter for introducing her to "crime trash" in the first place, her counterexplanation, that she did it for her baby, appears in a romance magazine and conforms to the pulp romance formula of selfless love and devotion.

As Celia understood, the "true story" of the Bobbed Haired Bandit was elusive. It depended on who was doing the telling and the audience they were trying to reach, as much as it did on any set of definitive facts. From the first robbery reported in January of 1924 to the final *Modern Romances* story in 1940, the bare facts of the robberies and the details of Celia's life — whatever they may have been — were blown up into larger cultural conflicts of crime and sex, of youth and class, of the influence of the mass media, and ultimately of the obligation of society to the welfare of the poor. This story was pushed and pulled to fit literary genres and political and personal agendas. The Bobbed Haired Bandit was a screen onto which the press projected the hopes and fears of their reading public.

Reading these stories, however, not only tells us how certain individuals and specific events were understood at the time but also reveals how the past is remembered and reminds us how history is made. Facts are never simply recorded; they are recorded by people for a purpose. Individuals with moral and political values and agendas shape the contours of what is imagined, remembered, and then printed. Beyond the individual are institutional constraints. "The record" of the past is documented mostly by the commercial mass media, which subject the events to a filtering of fact and fancy based on standards of popularity and profitability. For what mattered most to the newspapers of New York City in 1924 is the same thing that concerned *Modern Romances* magazine in 1940, and, for that matter, book publishers of today: telling, and selling, a good story.

"I guess when the newspapers don't know anything they just make things up," Celia herself observed. Even as Celia is tearing down previous versions of her own life story in *Modern Romances*, she is busy building up another. Celia wanted the final installment of the Bobbed Haired Bandit to be hers, and this story wasn't going to be "sordid and cheap"; this one would be "romantic." It would be the story of her love for her husband, for her children, and of the bitter price she paid for her notoriety:

> I was more ignorant than most of you — and I had a worse home life. I am not trying to excuse myself for what I did, either. I know what I did was wrong. But I think I have a right to have those things forgotten now. I was sentenced to what was supposed to be my punishment. I suffered then — and I shall continue to suffer. But I am human.

◉ **25**

> I was an entirely different Celia Cooney from the girl-bandit who had terrorized Brooklyn in 1924. Nearly eight years in prison; then four happy years with Eddie on the chicken farm; and facing life with two little boys whom I wanted to have grow up honest and straightforward . . .
> —Celia Cooney, *Modern Romances*

There's one last version of the story of the Bobbed Haired Bandit. It's the story told by her two grown sons. In 2005, Edward and Celia Cooney's sons were retired and living in the same city in New

Mexico; Patrick Cooney was seventy-three and Edward Cooney Jr. was sixty-nine. Although neither went to college, both were professional men. Ed had a career in the federal government, retiring as a manager for the General Services Administration, and Pat had been a computer programmer and systems manager, getting his start in the infancy of the digital revolution. Pat and his wife gave Celia two grandchildren, both girls, while Ed never married.

Over the phone we described our research to the two brothers, and after talking it over among themselves they agreed to help us — at first hesitantly but soon enthusiastically. They agreed to tell us *their* story of the Bobbed Haired Bandit.

Only for Pat and Ed, there was no Bobbed Haired Bandit.

Growing up, Pat and Ed knew nothing of their mother's infamous past. About their father the two boys remembered even less, only an image gleaned from a photograph of Ed Sr. with one empty sleeve pinned up, grinning into the camera from a city street. Pat's earliest vivid remembrances are of the terrible fire that destroyed their Jamaica, Queens, apartment in 1939. He remembers his mother arguing with a fireman for a shiny flashlight that the man picked up from their apartment. Celia had just lost everything and she was damned if a fireman was going to walk off with that, too.

Ed remembers moving around a lot in those early years. Right after selling the house in Copiague, Long Island, the Cooney family — now going by Celia's maiden name of Roth — moved to Fifteenth Street in Manhattan, then to the house that burned down in Jamaica, to another house nearby in South Jamaica, on to a flat in Queens Village, then finally settling down into a light and airy one-bedroom apartment on the third floor of a building at 92-07 195th Place in Hollis, Queens, where the family spent the early 1940s to the mid-1950s.

They were always poor, but during World War II, as the country climbed out of the Depression, things got a little bit better. With both her boys now old enough for school, Celia got a job as a salesgirl in a woman's clothing store and later worked behind the counter at a diner. Then, like women all across the country, Celia went to work at a war plant: Sperry Gyroscope. The hours were long, but the pay was good. Pat was old enough to look after Ed, so for a time Celia went to work on the night shift. Pat recalled that she had to lie to get the job at

Celia Cooney holding Pat and Ed Jr. in September 1936 just after the death of their father Edward Cooney. (World Telegram and Sun Collection, Library of Congress)

Sperry. Certainly she stretched the truth about her experience, or lack thereof, in manufacturing; probably she lied about her prison record as well. "The truth was totally unimportant if it didn't serve the goals that she had," her son remembers; "when it was her family she would lie to anybody."

Celia's family was her boys, and Celia did her best to do right by them. "I remember her having to patch pants and things to keep us looking neat," says Pat, "but unfortunately when you patch a pair of brown corduroys with blue denim it really shows." Still, "it was all clean, and all pressed, so she did right." Maybe the horrible experience of her own childhood, the memories of her mom taking away and selling her new clothes for gin, made Celia determined to be a different sort of mother. Whatever the reason, according to her sons, Celia was selfless in her devotion. Ed recalled that she used her rationing stamps during the war to buy shoes for his brother and himself, even when doing so meant that she had to go without new clothes for herself.

In 1939, when they were desperately poor, Ed remembers his mom getting the money together to take them to the World's Fair in Flushing, Queens. She also brought her sons to the movies, the Bronx zoo, and the circus at the old Madison Square Garden that she and her husband had once joked to a reporter about attending. The boys had an assortment of pets at home: tropical fish, painted turtles, canaries, cats, and, in the late Thirties, a dog named Duchess. She knit and crocheted and made quilts for her boys to sleep under. Always an avid reader, she read bedtime stories to her sons. "In general," Ed Jr. remembers, Celia "did all the good things that a mother would do, including teaching her children the difference between right and wrong and what's appropriate language and what's not."

Back in the Twenties certain pundits and some reporters had scoffed at Celia's claim that she had only robbed for her future daughter and a chance at domestic happiness. To them she was a working-class flapper out to grab a piece of the luxurious good life for herself. The Celia Cooney her sons remember seemed determined to prove those critics wrong.

Pat and Ed's mother never wore a flashy sealskin coat. Whether Celia's sister was ever able to get the famous Hudson seal coat back from the police is a mystery, but what's clear is that the fur coat isn't a part of the boys' early memories. They do remember Celia with one fancy coat — but the item's lineage was impeccable. As Ed remembered it, she worked at a clothing store opposite the public library on Fifth Avenue in Manhattan for a time after the war. She had her eye on a particularly nice coat in the store. But Celia was still poor, and her sons' needs came first. Come Christmas, however, the store surprised her with a gift of the very coat she coveted. It's tempting to think that the management and her fellow employees knew her past and gave her a gift that recalled her bandit days, but it's just as likely that Celia was recognized as simply a hard worker and was rewarded for her service. This was one of Celia's very few luxuries. "She wasn't one for clothes, or fancy jewelry, or any of that, she just wasn't," Ed remembers. What she was interested in was food: "To have the right food, balanced meals, that she was adamant about. [And at] mealtime, all the milk you want to drink." Celia loved to cook, annotating recipes in the cookbooks she bought, noting whether they were good or not and if the inclusion or exclusion of a certain ingredient would make them better. Her hungry childhood and seven years of prison food — bread without the jam — had made a deep impression on Celia.

That wasn't the only impression that prison had left. Outside of a lie or strategic omission here and there to help the family, and the time when she and a friend chopped down and carted away a fir tree from the landscaped island of Hollis Court Boulevard so their house could have a Christmas tree, Celia was honest, scrupulously so. Even on her income taxes Celia toed the legal line. Ironically, it was when someone tried to steal something away from her that Celia had her one brush with the law. In 1943 Celia remarried, to a Queens bus driver named Harold La Grange. It seems that another woman had her eye on Harold, but Celia wasn't one to sit by while this woman tried to woo her husband away from her. As Pat remembers, little Celia Cooney, just a shade over five feet tall and now in her middle age, "went and tore that lady apart in the middle of the street. I mean they had a real drag-down, knock-out fight." Celia was arrested again, but whatever the charges were they didn't stick — neither did her second husband. Harold allegedly drank and philandered, and they separated after only a few years, though Celia — perhaps for reasons of anonymity rather than real affection — carried the name La Grange the rest of her life.

"Always protect your family," Pat remembers his mother pounding into him; "there's nobody going to stand by you in this world except the members of your family." Celia's faith in family grew more from hope than experience. After Ed Sr. died, the Cooney family drifted out of the picture. They had their own problems: two of Ed's brothers had been arrested on robbery charges. His older brother Owen got himself shot while trying to snatch three diamond rings from a jewelry store. William, his younger brother, got pinched for a street stickup. The arresting officers in William's case were old friends of the family: Detectives Casey and Gray. Whatever the reason, the Cooneys had little time for Celia, and Pat and Ed. Jr. never knew their father's mother or their uncles. If anything, it was worse on Celia's side of the family. Celia's parents had always been criminally negligent, but even her own sisters cut their ex-con sister out of the family; "ostracized" is the word Pat uses to describe what happened. But Celia's words weren't wasted on her boys.

Ed Jr., without other commitments of his own, looked after his mother. As a grown man with a good job and decent salary, he moved Celia and himself to a series of homes throughout the 1960s and 1970s. First there was an apartment building in Astoria, Queens; then out to a house in Long Island; then to Manhattan for a brief time in the 1970s; and finally to Union City, New Jersey, where he bought Celia a co-op near his on the twentieth floor of a high-rise building. It was a world away from the Lower East Side coal cellar where she was born. Celia loved it there. But it was the 1980s, and Ronald Reagan was in office trying to downsize the federal government. Ed was offered early retirement at good terms, and he took it. Following a well-worn path from the northeast to points south, Ed made plans to retire in Florida. Happy as she was in her high-rise apartment, Celia didn't want to be away from what little family she had. She decided to follow her son to Florida, back to the state where she and her husband were hunted down and captured.

Florida was no more fortunate for Celia the second time around. Even as he helped her pack for the move down, Ed noticed something wrong with his mother: Celia's characteristic sharp mind and quick tongue were faltering; she was forgetful and easily confused. When they got down to Florida, her mental state declined fast. Celia was diagnosed with Alzheimer's disease.

She was too sick to live on her own, and her sons found a good nursing home in Florida to take her in. Celia charmed the residents and staff of the nursing home, just as she had charmed the police and press a half century earlier. Even losing her mind, Celia didn't lose her personality. Ed tells the story of receiving a call from the nursing home one day, the staff member telling him that there had been a "problem" at the home. It seems that Celia was walking down the hall, on the correct side, holding on to the grab rail, when a big woman came along walking the opposite direction, her hand running along the same rail that Celia was holding. Coming right up to Celia, the big bully told her she had to move out of her way. "I will not," the tiny, infirm Celia insisted: "You move." Celia refused to back down, and soon the staff had a fistfight to break up. It wasn't the first time that Celia had stood up as an old woman. Two young men looking for an easy mark tried to mug her when she was still living in New Jersey. Celia fought back, refusing to let go of her purse. The muggers had to beat her to the ground and severely injured Celia's arm before she would let go. "She was a good woman to people she cared about," Pat sums up; "other than that she was a tough old broad."

To her sons that's *all* their mother was: a hard-working, fiercely loyal, thoroughly charming, tough old broad. But thinking back now, Pat and Ed can recall hints that their mother was something more. Other than to tell her sons how much she had loved and now missed him, Celia didn't talk much about Ed Sr. But one day, when Pat was still a young boy, a teacher asked him how his father had died. Pat went home and put the question to his mother, who told him the — abbreviated — truth: that his father died after getting his hand caught in a machine that made license plates. Pat went back and reported this to his teacher. "Even at that young age," Pat remembers, "I could feel the absolute frost come off that lady." What the teacher knew and Pat did not was that the only place where license plates are made is in prison.

There was also a big, husky, cigar-smoking man by the name of Hoffman who stopped by wherever the Cooneys were living. Now Pat has his suspicions that the man he remembers who looked like a cop probably was one, or a parole officer, making a periodic check-up. Later in life, Ed remembers reading something in the newspaper about the famous Judge Samuel Leibowitz and mentioning it to his mother. "Oh yeah, I know him," his mother replied. "You know Leibowitz? How in the world do you know Leibowitz?" "Oh, I just met him one time," his mother blithely remarked and then dropped the subject. The visiting strangers and improbable acquaintances were odd, but given that their mother was just a simple — if feisty — woman from Brooklyn, these occurrences and others remained just that, odd, and were soon forgotten.

It was when Celia began to lose her memory that her past began to be remembered. One of the symptoms of Celia's Alzheimer's was wandering. Living now in Florida she constantly wanted to walk. "She simply couldn't stay put. She started walking toward New York. Every time she would get out of the house she would start on that long trip. And, of course, she'd be picked up by the police." One time when she was picked up by the police, she turned to her son and said: "Don't let them take me away, they'll find out who I am." "What do you mean, who you are?" a befuddled Ed asked. And then, after fifty years of keeping her secret, it all came out: Celia revealed to her son that she was the infamous Bobbed Haired Bandit.

Of course her son couldn't care less. "The who?" he asked. Having never heard of the Bobbed Haired Bandit, he chalked up her admission to the ramblings of Alzheimer's dementia. Besides, he had more pressing issues to deal with: getting his mother back home and into a facility where she could be properly cared for and could die in peace.

Within three years she was gone. On July 13, 1992, at the age of eighty-eight, Celia Cooney died. Under a headstone reading Celia Cooney, 1904–1992, Beloved Wife and Mother, Celia was laid to rest in the swampy Florida earth that covered her baby daughter a lifetime before.

The year Celia died, her sons began to unearth her secrets. Curious about their mother's last confessions, they began to do some research. "I didn't know if it was dementia or not," Ed told us, and "lo and behold it was not." In the Tampa Public Library, he looked up the Bobbed Haired Bandit in the microfilm records of the New York Times for the 1920s. He photocopied and transcribed whatever he could find

Celia "Bobbed Haired Bandit" Cooney. *New York Daily News.*

and began to read: about the stickups, about his parents fleeing to Florida, about his unknown sister and her early death, about his mother's awful childhood. "It was a terrible, terrible shock," Ed explained:

> I mean I just never *dreamed* that any of this had taken place. Then, of course, it took me a while to emotionally recover before I could sit here and talk to you right now without bawling. . . . She was a very private person, and boy she was able to keep a secret.

"You know," Celia's son told us, "one of her watchwords was, 'If you want to keep something secret, don't tell anybody.'"

Epilogue

What Ever Happened To . . .

On May 11, 1924, just two days after Celia and Edward Cooney went up the river, there was a meeting of the Executive Committee of Tammany Hall at their Wigwam on Fourteenth Street in Manhattan. The Tammany chiefs were assembled to discuss the serious question of the 1925 mayoral race. A resolution was made to support John Hylan for a third term. This was "greeted with laughter." It was open season on the mayor. Hylan had been elected twice with the support of Tammany and the Hearst newspapers, but the Wigwam was tired of Hearst's and Hylan's calls for municipal ownership of the utilities. Hylan's most grievous offense, however, was not backing Tammany's chosen candidate for governor, Al Smith. Forced to choose between Smith and Hylan, the Tammany faction quickly dumped Hylan. Tammany's new candidate for mayor of New York City was the dapper, debonair (and corrupt) James "Jimmy" Walker. This led directly to Hylan's defeat in the Democratic primary and the end of his political career.

Hylan threatened to run for mayor again in 1929 but was dissuaded by a lack of support. In 1930 he was appointed as a justice of the Children's Court where, for the next six years, John Hylan ruled on the cases of the next generation of young Celia Cooneys. In 1934 he ran as an independent for governor "and received a small number of votes." Two years later, in 1936, John Hylan died of a heart attack riding in a railway car on his way home, a fitting end for the ex-motorman who had spent his political career obsessively defending the five-cent train fare.

When Hylan lost the primary election in 1925, Richard Enright knew his term as police commissioner was over. His dismissal was equally humiliating. Mayor Walker's new police commissioner, George V. McLaughlin, made all sorts of tawdry accusations of corruption and political machination about his predecessor, including the existence of "secret crime lists" kept in Enright's home for political purposes. McLaughlin also recalled all the "diamond-studded shields" that Enright had issued to his "honoraries," the elite cronies who drove around the city with "P.D. signs on their automobiles." With a "semi-serious smile," McLaughlin went so far as to accuse Enright's cronies of bootlegging in the *Times*: "You know, some former 'honorary' might flash his diamond-studded badge and save a boatload of booze, or a carload of it, for that matter." (Enright would himself challenge Walker unsuccessfully for the mayoralty in 1929 as the candidate for the "Square Deal" party.)

However, before his exit Enright did enjoy one apparent victory over his critics in the press. Police Commissioner Richard Enright, the man who had once said "Crime wave? There is none. It's a reportorial phrase without other base than reportorial imagination," was, in this one instance at least, proved right. Statistics, albeit police ones, suggested that the "gungirl crime wave" of 1924 was bunk. In 1923, forty women had been arrested for robbery; in 1924 the number dropped to twenty-eight.

Putting his words to better use than defending himself against reporters, the ex-commissioner tapped into his own imagination and took up writing, penning two novels, a number of plays and screenplays, and a short-lived pulp magazine called *Police Stories*. "The police chief's picturesque experience," the *New York Times* reported, "gave him a fund to draw upon in his scenarios that insured a place for him as a master-writer of 'crook stuff.'" His first novel, *Vultures of the Dark*, published the year Celia was sent to prison, possessed a heroine of the flapper type: "delightfully pretty, undisciplined, capricious, enticing, irresponsible." But, alas, she was a millionaire's daughter from Manhattan, not a poor gungirl from Brooklyn. Some experiences, it seems, were not picturesque enough for Enright's brand of crook fiction.

Things initially looked good for the two other members of the police brass who oversaw the Bobbed Haired Bandit hunt. Chief Inspector William Lahey and his good friend and head of New York detectives, Inspector John Coughlin, also basked briefly in the glory of the gungirl's capture. Lahey was even considered, though ultimately rejected, as Enright's replacement for police commissioner. But in 1928 a "'bag man' of the underworld" named Arnold Rothstein was shot dead in the Park Central Hotel. The failure to solve the murder evolved into a scandal in which the police were accused of "laxity and indifference," and in yet another departmental "shake-up," the new police commissioner forced both Lahey and Coughlin into retirement.

Detective Captain Daniel Carey and Detectives William Casey and Frank Gray all received commendations for their part in the Bobbed Haired Bandit's capture, as did Captain John McCloskey. Charles Dodd, the Brooklyn district attorney who prosecuted the Cooneys, moved on from the DA's office in 1929 when he was elected a justice of the State Supreme Court, a position he held, with respect, until his retirement.

Judge George W. Martin graduated into anything but respect. Late in his life he was accused by the New York State attorney general of acts of corruption spanning nearly two decades. He was charged with lending his name and titled position to companies that issued fraudulent stock, throwing "dinners" for attorneys where admission was charged, appointing unqualified professionals to lunacy commissions for cash or free services, and dismissing an indictment against three abortionists for the reputed sum of one thousand dollars. Martin also developed a personal friendship with Leo P. Byk, the "slot-machine king of Brooklyn," and arranged for a governor's pardon and freedom for Byk in 1926. Byk later put Martin's son-in-law on his payroll. Judge George W. Martin was, in a word, crooked. Or not. In 1939 he was exonerated of all the charges leveled against him. But his reputation was ruined, and he retired from the bench two years later and died seven years after that.

The warden of Raymond Street Jail, Harry Honeck, was also to see his share of scandal, though his was the result of far nobler acts. In 1933 Warden Honeck — or one of his guards — arranged for an act of kindness similar to those he had bestowed upon Celia and Ed nine years before. The wife of a certain Andrew "Red Wild-Eye" Mc-Cormick was allowed to meet her bank robber husband for a night visit in the Raymond Street Jail. Somehow she smuggled in a gun. Unlike the prop that Celia posed with during her stay at the jail, this one was loaded, and McCormick used it to kill a guard and, after failing to escape, to kill himself. In the aftermath, Harry Honeck was charged with "dereliction of duty" and transferred out to serve as warden of Riker's Island.

William B. Seabrook, Celia's invisible literary accomplice on the "Bobbed-Hair Bandit's Own Story," left for Arabia in 1924 and continued traveling and writing for the rest of his life. He wrote a popular book about voodoo worshipers and witchcraft in the mountains of Haiti and, in 1930, received further renown by publishing a vivid account of his eight-month-long adventures with the Guere "cannibal" tribe of the Ivory Coast, describing — and partaking in — their supposed diet of human flesh. Living out the stereotype of the hard-drinking, romantic journalist/adventurer to the end, Seabrook committed suicide in 1945 after a lifetime losing bout with the bottle.

Of all the major actors in the story of the Bobbed Haired Bandit, it was the person least known at the time who eventually became the most famous: Samuel S. Leibowitz. After he successfully defended Al Capone in 1925, the high-profile cases rolled in. There was Harry Hoffman, a Staten Island motion picture projectionist, who had already been tried three times for the brutal murder of a young woman; Joseph Steinmetz, accused of surprising his seventeen-year-old bride with a bullet when he found her in a compromising position with a priest in a Knights of Columbus Hotel room; Vera Stretz, who shot her married lover, a well-to-do doctor, when he tried to force her to commit unspecified "ungentlemanly" acts; Vincent "Mad Dog" Coll, triggerman in the infamous "baby massacre" in which five children were shot, one fatally, in a drive-by gangland execution on an East Harlem street. And then there was the Lindbergh baby kidnapper and murderer, Bruno Hauptmann, whom Leibowitz visited in jail in an effort to cajole a full confession and spare him the death penalty (Hauptmann declined and was executed).

But the case that brought Leibowitz international fame was his defense of the Scottsboro Boys, the nine African American young men and boys (the youngest was thirteen) who were arrested and accused of the gang rape of two white women while riding a freight train through Alabama in 1931. On questionable evidence, all nine were convicted by an all-white jury and sentenced to death. The case became a symbol of American racism and was taken up as a political cause by the International Labor Defense, a Communist Party group. When the U.S.

Supreme Court granted a new trial in 1933 on grounds of inadequate counsel, Leibowitz came down from New York to take charge. It was a dramatic trial, covered by newspapers around the world. One of the victims recanted her testimony, and Leibowitz tore apart the prosecution's case. But the all-white Southern jury was none too sympathetic to nine black defendants supported by the Communist Party and defended by a Jewish lawyer from New York: their innocence was not declared. However, it is testimony to Leibowitz's considerable skill that four of the men eventually had their charges dismissed, while the five who were convicted were spared the death sentence.

Leibowitz did not just defend celebrity criminals but became a celebrity himself. During the Scottsboro case, four thousand people turned out in Harlem to hail him as a "new Moses." He broadcast a radio show in New York during the Depression and was a big enough public figure to be nominated for mayor of New York City in the early 1950s (he declined). When Samuel Leibowitz eventually retired from his law practice, he became an almost equally famous judge, trying important cases and building a reputation as a "hanging judge" for his willingness to sentence gangsters straight to Sing Sing and the electric chair.

New newspapers carried these new stories. Spurred by the success of Joseph Patterson's *Daily News*, William Randolph Hearst came out with his own New York tabloid, the *Mirror*, in 1924. That same year Bernarr Macfadden launched out from his odd but very profitable magazine base of *Physical Culture, Health and Beauty, True Story*, and *True Detective Mysteries* to publish the *Daily Graphic*. With this, the famed "tabloid wars" began, as each of the three raced to the bottom in search for the most lurid, thrilling, and lascivious story they could find. The march of newspaper mergers and closures continued as well. Walter Lippmann's *World* was sold by Pulitzer and merged with the *Telegram* the year Celia and Ed left prison, and across the river the feisty Brooklyn newspapers died off one by one in the years to follow: first the *Daily Times* in 1932, then the *Standard Union* in 1935, the *Eagle* in 1941, and finally the *Citizen* in 1947.

After the *World* closed, Lippmann was courted by Hearst for the *American* and by Ochs for the *Times*, but he decided to move his editorializing to the more conservative *Herald-Tribune*, where his ever less liberal columns were eventually syndicated to over two hundred dailies. By 1931 Hearst had given up New York politics, now spending his days in his California castle, San Simeon, with his mistress Marion Davies. The Depression hit Hearst's business hard, and his once profitable media empire dissolved into 126 million dollars of debt, resulting in his loss of direct ownership in 1937, a year after his *American* — the paper that once told the "Bobbed-Hair Bandit's Own Story" — stopped publishing.

DOSSIER

The Bobbed Haired Bandit

STEPHEN DUNCOMBE
AND ANDREW MATTSON

MORTALIS

In Her Own Words

After months of others writing about her in the newspapers, the Bobbed Haired Bandit finally got the chance to write her own story. In late April of 1924 a reporter from the *New York American* approached Celia in the Raymond Street Jail and offered her a thousand dollars for her "confessions." Eager for both the money (more than she and Ed had made in all of their robberies) and a chance to tell her side of the story, Celia took the Hearst newspaper up on their offer. Billed as "the Strangest, Weirdest, Most Dramatic, Human-Interest Stories Ever Written," it reads like what it is: a dramatic re-telling of the story of the Bobbed Haired Bandit, borrowing literary tropes from the *True Story* and *True Detective* magazines popular with both Celia and much of the American public at the time. It also effectively conveys the language and style employed by the crime-beat reporters who pounded out copy on deadline for the daily papers in the 1920s.

As with the rest of the "true story" of the Bobbed Haired Bandit, the tale told here plays with the truth, and certain facts don't jibe with other reports on the case. The articles were published as the couple awaited sentencing, so Celia was understandably interested in spinning a sympathetic story. "The Bobbed-Hair Bandit's Own Story" was also not entirely of her own making. Although Celia was pictured with pencil in hand, and the *American* insisted that "the only changes this paper has made have been occasional ones in punctuation and spelling," a flamboyant ghostwriter named William Seabrook was hired to put Celia's words to print. Seabrook's voice certainly overlays the Bobbed Haired Bandit's: The detailed description of Celia binding up Ed in their hotel room and her excitement at driving around Brooklyn with the heel of her shoe pressing upon the prostrate chauffeur's neck are as much an expression of Seabrook's peculiar predilections as they are Celia's actual remembrances. Nevertheless, there is a great deal of Celia Cooney in the words that follow. Seabrook wrote in a later autobiography that "concoction . . . was taboo" in his job, but what is more convincing is the testimony of the Bobbed Haired Bandit's sons. After reading her story in the *American* they told us that it sounded like the Celia Cooney they knew.

The entire series ran for two weeks over twelve installments. We've included a selection from the first chapter and the entirety of chapters nine and ten.

CHAPTER I

"Why and How I Stuck 'Em Up," As She Wrote It

Gun Girl Reveals Tragedy of Career That Amazed Nation

Here is the bobbed-hair bandit's own story—one of the most amazing documents ever penned.

This pretty girl of twenty years, who, at the pistol point, robbed many a storekeeper, describes in detail her daring exploits in the world's greatest city.

Her career will be given in full in her story, of which this is the first installment. Cecilia Cooney wrote it in the Raymond Street Jail, Brooklyn, last week. The only changes this paper has made have been occasional ones in punctuation and spelling.

No better sermon on the baneful effect of crime could be preached. The New York American *presents it here to show, as Cecilia Cooney herself admits—"crime doesn't pay."*

Yes, I'm the Bobbed-Hair Bandit, all right. I'm the girl that scared the life out of Brooklyn and made monkeys out of the New York cops for four months. I'm the kid that robbed the stores. I'm the little gun girl, and you should have seen those boobs behind the counters jump and tremble when I pulled that gun.

The grand joke is that half the time it wasn't even loaded, and when it was loaded I was afraid ever to click the safety catch for fear it might go off. And listen, people, while I tell you another secret: I've never shot off a pistol in my life. Some joke on little old New York.

In an Iron Cage

Anyway, a couple of months ago, I thought it was a grand joke. But I guess it's not so funny now—not for me.

Here I am locked up in an iron cage. My little baby's dead. All the shiny furniture, all the pretty baby clothes gone. My husband gone. He shot a man. He's locked up in another cage where I can't see him, and the lawyers are trying to prove he's crazy so they can send him to Matteawan instead of Sing Sing. As if it made any difference. I don't know if he's crazy or not, the way the doctors mean, but I think we must have both been crazy to think we could get away with what we tried.

What did it get us? What did it get the baby? What did it get me? I ask you.

It got me in this cage, for one thing, where I sit now. Iron bars and a door that locks by a machine way down the hall. No bolt or key. The only way you know you're locked in is when you hear something heavy rattle and drop. It's queer, being in a place you know you can't get out of.

When I was a kid I used to go out to the Zoo of a Sunday afternoon—not the Bronx Zoo, the one in Prospect Park—and I used to look at the animals in the cage behind the iron bars and wonder how they felt. Well, I know now, and it's an awful feeling. People come and look at me through the bars—not so many, for the matron's good about that—but some come to look at me just like we used to look at the bear.

And they talk about me and wonder how it feels, just the same as I used to wonder about the animals. And when'll I get out? Years of it, maybe in another cage like this, or worse. Say, people oughtn't be kept in cages—not girls anyway. I guess that's foolish for me to say. They have to do something with girls just the same as men, don't they, when we break the law? I guess it's thinking I'm like an animal now that makes me feel so sick.

Ashamed and Sorry

It was different a little while ago, with all the excitement. Gee! A private stateroom on the train, and strawberries and everything I wanted to eat, and people yelling and cheering at every station where we stopped long enough, and as big a crowd, they said, at the Pennsylvania station when we got to New York as ever had met a president of the United States

Cameras and reporters and limousines and people begging would I say one word so they could put it like out of a detective story magazine. It was a great ride, and a great welcome.

Maybe it went to my head a little. Maybe I was proud to be the Bobbed-Haired Bandit.

Say, why stall about it? Sure, I was proud! But every little while I thought about where it was going to get me to and I knew I was a fool. I thought, in a week they'll be yelling for somebody else—still out there in the street—and where'll I be?

Just the same I smiled and kidded. And some of those sob-sisters said I was hard boiled. What did they want me to do? Bust out crying on their shoulders, maybe, and tell them the sad story of my life so they could write it down. Just the same, I got some pride, and that's why I smiled and kidded still when the excitement wore off.

Folks, the truth is I'm ashamed and sorry for what I've done.

Here's a funny thing not funny to make you laugh, but funny to think about. I've got plenty of time now to think, when it's too late. But here's what I'm trying to get at. I said I was ashamed and sorry. All right, that goes. But I'm only ashamed of what I DID.

I am not ashamed and never will be of WHY I did it.

My little baby's gone now, and I guess it's good she's gone.

It's too late now to make any difference whether people believe me or not, but when I went into that first store and said, "Stick 'em up," I wasn't seeing diamond ear rings and gin and jazz and a good time— I was thinking of pretty little pink shoes, pink leather baby shoes like I saw once in a window on Atlantic avenue, and I was thinking, if I can get away with a big wad once and quit, maybe this baby that's coming won't have the rough time I had. . . .

CHAPTER IX

INTENDED TO QUIT GAME WITH LAST BIG HOLD-UP

Her Practice on Ed Made It Easy to Bind Chauffeur, Then She Couldn't Resist Putting Her Heel on His Neck to Show Power

Cecilia Cooney, the Bobbed-Haired Bandit, who accepted philosophically yesterday her sentence of ten to twenty years in prison, describes today in her exclusive story for the New York American *the preliminaries leading to the last robbery she and her husband perpetrated—the hold-up of the office of the National Biscuit Company.*

She tells of being nervous and worried, for the police were hunting her and Ed with orders to kill. She describes her practice of binding her husband with picture wire, and how she tied up the chauffeur of the limousine hired for the robbery.

Her foot was on the chauffeur's neck, she says, as they drove to the Biscuit Company for the robbery that was to prove their undoing.

Along toward the first of April, Brooklyn began to get too hot to hold us. Nobody was talking about anything but the Bobbed-Haired Bandit. Storekeepers that were cowards began closing up at sundown and hundreds of others got permits to carry guns.

I went into our own butcher shop one night to get Ed a steak, and there lying beside the cash register was a blue-steel .45 big enough to have blown the head off a horse.

Every day the papers were full of it, and the worst thing of all was that they began to get my description right. My little baby was due to be born about the first of May, and when they noticed about that and published it, I was almost afraid to go out on the street any more.

I was nervous and cried a lot, and Ed was all the time worried. Some fool girl wrote a note to Captain Carey, saying she was the bandit, and swearing she would shoot any policeman on sight that tried to stop her and that when the shooting began she wouldn't be the one picked up full of holes.

Plan One Last Raid

And every cop had orders to shoot on sight. They weren't looking for us to arrest us. They were looking for us to kill us, like they do out West.

Ed got to talking with me one night and said: "We're in dutch, so dutch that we can't stay here even if we quit. It's too late to quit. And we've played a piker's game. What have we got? Pretty good that first night, but since, a hundred dollars, fifty dollars, sometimes not as much as twenty-five. And some people got thousands. We got to beat it, and we got to have money. I been thinking hard. We got to pull one more big one, careful and different, and then blow."

I said, "All right, Ed, anything you say; but what'll we do and where'll we go?"

He had it all planned out. Just a block from us on Pacific avenue was a big National Biscuit Company office. We'd go there and clean it out, and beat it the same day for Jacksonville. Ed said he knew Jacksonville was a good place, because he'd been there while he was in the navy, and we could go there, and if we had plenty of money I could have my baby in a hospital and we'd settle down, and he'd buy a part interest in a garage or something, and we'd go straight and forget all about the bandit stuff, and after all, if we was lucky, our kid could have all the things we had planned for it.

We told our landlady that Ed had a short out-of-town job and we'd be back in a week. We took nothing but a suitcase and some clothes and the three guns, and went over to Manhattan in the subway, and got out in Grand Central station, and came up through the waiting room like we was coming up from a train, and took a taxi, and went to the Cloman Hotel, at Forty-Third street and Eighth avenue.

Notebook Their Undoing

I had my wedding ring, and anybody could see by then that I was going to have a baby, and Ed wrote it down on the hotel register, "Mr. and Mrs. Parker, Boston, Mass.," and nobody thought a thing.

But that got us into trouble afterward, for when the detectives found the notebook we dropped at the biscuit company and compared it with the handwriting on the hotel register they knew for sure we were the same.

For a day I was sick and couldn't seem to eat or sleep, but the next morning I was all right, and we went out. I got some hair nets and a thick veil in a store on Eighth avenue. I'd been letting my hair grow a little, and now could fix it up with the ends turned under and the net around it, so that it didn't look bobbed at all. And with the veil hardly anybody could recognize me.

And I wore the little pink hat—the same I had on when they brought me back to New York. The papers said then it was the same I had worn in all the robberies, but they made that up. I wore it the first night we robbed a store, but nobody noticed it, and most of the time afterward when we were doing the hold-ups, I wore a tam.

Looking Over Prospect

Well, Ed bought a new cap and left the overcoat in the hotel room so that he looked sort of different, too, and we went to the Clyde Line office and bought boat tickets to Jacksonville, still saying we were Mr. and Mrs. Parker from Boston. They were for three days later.

There was a telephone book and a telephone in our room at the hotel, and Ed looked through the red book and picked out a Packard renting service by the name of Wilmarth, and told him to send a closed car with a driver.

When the car came it was a big limousine, with a fellow driving it that was big and heavy enough to be a prize-fighter, except that he was too fat. He was a lot bigger than Ed, and Ed is no runt.

That day we were just going to look things over and we left the guns behind, locked in the suitcase. We told this driver, his name was Arthur West, that we wanted to go for a little ride to see Brooklyn Bridge—imagine us wanting to look at Brooklyn Bridge—and then to look at a house on Dean street—that's right near Pacific avenue.

It was fine, going through Brooklyn that way—me now riding in a limousine where I used to work in a laundry. And I felt safe. No cop was going to look for me sitting back in the cushions of a big Packard with a chauffeur, and besides I had the veil on my face.

Plan to Tie Chauffeur

One thing we wanted to do was to pick out a good quiet spot in Prospect Park, close to the biscuit company, where we could fix up that chauffeur next day. And Ed wanted a look at the place, too.

We stopped near the warehouse, and he got out, and went over, planning if anybody stopped him to say he was looking for a job as a truck driver.

But nobody did. Nobody paid any attention to him at all. And he mootched around a little and came back, and lit a cigarette, and we drove on. I asked him how it was and he said: "It's all right, I guess, but there's a lot of people in that office—a lot of clerks and a lot of Janes pounding on typewriters."

Next day we were all set to go. I took one of the big guns, and Ed took the other big one and the little automatic. We'd been figuring the night before what we'd do with that big chauffeur. We didn't want to hurt him, and we doped it out that it would be best to tie him up and put him in the back of the car.

Practice on Ed

Ed had some rope, and that night before we went to bed, he asked me to try to tie his hands with it, to see how it would work. Well, it didn't work at all. That sort of stuff is all right for the movies. It was plenty strong enough, too. But it was too thick to make a tight knot. He wiggled his hands a little and pulled one of them right out.

Ed slipped his clothes back on and went out and was gone about fifteen minutes, and came back with a spool of picture wire and cut off a strip of it about a yard long with his knife. He had to saw and twist at it.

Believe me, it did the trick. It's thin and shiny and almost as soft as a string—made with a lot of tiny little wires twisted together so that it's easy to tie knots in.

I wound it criss-cross twice across his wrists and he tried to twist loose, and it cut right into him and left red marks. Why, he'd of cut his hands right off if he had pulled harder.

Well, next morning the car came and we went over to Prospect Park to the spot we'd picked and there wasn't a soul in sight, and Ed took a good look up and down the road and tapped on the glass and motioned the fellow to stop, and said, "Wait, I want to get out a minute."

Ed jabbed the gun in his ribs and made him get out of the seat and climb in the back where I was, and then got in, too, and held the gun on him while I tied him.

Her Heel On His Neck

I tried first to tie his hands behind him, but he was so big and fat I couldn't. He was trying to do what we told him, but he was scared, and there wasn't much room to work. So I made him put his hands in front and fastened his wrists together, one across the other, good and tight with the wire. And then Ed made him lie down on the floor and tied his feet. They said we put a gag in his mouth, but we didn't. He kept quiet, all right, without that. But he filled up all the bottom of the floor, he was so big.

Ed got out in front and drove—he could drive any kind of a car—while I sat in the back with my gun to keep this other fellow quiet. He never opened his mouth but once, when we bumped over a rut in the road and his head banged on the floor, and that was to ask me could he turn over. I said, "Sure, but no funny business."

I had to move my feet so he could turn, and I got to looking down at my own feet. I had on high-heeled pumps and pretty stockings, and they looked so little with him all hunched there, that I thought how funny it would be if I put one of them on his neck, like Cleopatra I once saw in the movies.

And the more I thought of it, the more I couldn't help doing it, so I put one foot easy and rested it right on his neck, and then I pressed the heel down a little, but not enough to hurt him.

And that's the way I rode through the park, piled in a limousine, with my foot on a man's neck. We passed two or three cars, and I thought wouldn't it be a joke if they knew.

It was only a minute or two till we got out of the park and Ed stopped the car in front of the biscuit company, but of course this fellow on the floor couldn't know where we stopped. And I got out too, but before we slammed the door Ed said, "You stay here and watch this guy, and if he opens his mouth, you know what." That was a bluff, for we just left him alone.

Mazio Faces Pistol

I went in, with Ed a little behind me. It was a big office with a lot of people in it, bigger than I thought and more people than I thought. There must have been about twenty. And I began to wonder if we could get away with it.

A clerk came up to me, and I said, "I want to see the cashier"—the cashier was Mazio, the man Ed shot afterwards.

Mazio came out of the wire cage where he worked, and I handed him an envelope, and he opened it to see what was in it, while the other man walked off, and it was only a blank piece of paper, and when he looked up I had my gun on him.

Cecilia Cooney to-morrow will continue the story of the National Biscuit Company Robbery, of the shooting of Mazio, and of their flight to Jacksonville.

FIRST SHOT OF CAREER SENDS PAIR IN PANIC FLIGHT

Notebook Dropped by Girl During Struggle with Mazio Reveals Identity of Brooklyn Terrors, and They Felt Their Capture Inevitable.

Cecilia Cooney, the Bobbed-Hair Bandit, who, with her husband, is waiting in Raymond street jail to be taken to prisons to serve the ten to twenty-year sentence given each, continues to-day her exclusive story. Yesterday's chapter ended with her gun pointed at Mazio, the cashier of the biscuit company. Today she tells of Ed's shooting the man and their frightened flight from the place, believing they had committed murder.

In Jacksonville, Fla., as on the boat going there, they were afraid to appear in public; Ed did not dare seek work; their money was gone. Then the baby came—the baby she wanted to have born in a pretty place—and more than ever she realized what an awful mess she had made of things and that crime does not pay.

To-morrow she will tell how, as they were talking over suicide, the detective broke into their room.

CHAPTER X

It's too late for anything I tell to do me any harm now. When Ed and I ran out of the biscuit company office, we thought it was murder, and the electric chair maybe for both of us.

We thought it all the way to Jacksonville on the slow boat, and nothing they can ever do to me will be as awful as those days and nights.

You see, this cashier Mazio was behind a door. We didn't see how he was hit. We only heard him scream when the bullets ripped through. Ed said, "God, I must have croaked him."

That's why we didn't wait to look for money. We might have grabbed a lot of it. There was the safe door wide open. But who could of thought of money then?

It all came so quick. When we pulled our guns the girls all ran and the men threw up their hands. One fellow, I think his name was Taggert, edged toward the big safe. You could see he was going to take a chance and slam it shut. I yelled, "Cut it," and pointed my gun at him, and he jumped back with his hands up.

Attacked by Mazio

There was a small door that opened into a smaller room. Ed stood way back with two guns, and I stood close by the door, and we drove them through it like sheep. They bumped into each other to see which could get through quickest.

Mazio, the cashier, was the last. Just as he got in front of me, so close he could touch me, he turned and made a grab for me. I don't know whether he just had a brainstorm or whether he had it figured that he would take a long chance and grab my gun and shoot it out with Ed.

Anyway, he jumped right at me and got one hand on my arm, and I stumbled back and fell over a chair and went down on the floor.

He must have lost his nerve as quick as it came to him, for instead of following me up he made a flying jump, too, and went through the door that somebody slammed right afterward.

Almost that same second Ed shot twice. The bullets hit the door low and went through, and there was that scream and then everything as still as death.

Flight Across Bridge

Ed ran over and picked me up. He thought I was hurt bad, but I was just scared. He started to carry me but I said, "No, I can walk." And we ran out and jumped in the car, him in front on the driver's seat and me in the back.

There was the chauffeur on the floor with his hands and feet tied, but I'd forgotten all about him. Ed drove to Atlantic avenue and we left the Packard there on the curb with the man still in it and grabbed a yellow taxi. All we had was one little old suitcase with hardly anything in it but a comb and brush and two of Ed's shirts and a change of underclothes for me. We'd brought it mostly to put the money in. You see we thought we'd have so much it would take that to hold it.

We went in the yellow taxi over the Williamsburg Bridge to the corner of Broome street and the Bowery. We thought they were after us, so we jumped out and paid the man and picked up another taxi that took us to Pier 36 and the Clyde Line Boat.

When I looked in my coat pockets for the tickets I first found out I'd lost the little note book that was dropped on the floor of the biscuit company and that the police found with our addresses in it. I thought I dropped it in the taxi. What was the difference? If they hadn't caught us one way it would have been another.

Well, we got on the boat and they showed us to our room, and we went in it and locked the door and stayed there and hid.

I was limp as a rag, and Ed's face looked gray. In about a minute we heard steps running on the dock, and we thought they'd come to get us. I said, "Oh, Ed, what'll we do?" And he said, "What can we do? I guess it's finished."

We waited for them to knock on the deck, and we thought through it, but they went right by. Then came more steps hurrying, and they slowed up, and this time they did stop, and a man with a coarse voice said, "I guess it's here." But it was only some passenger looking for his room.

Well, that went on, it seemed to me forever. And I wouldn't go through it again for all the money in the world. It seemed like the boat would never start. But at last the whistle gave a big blow, and then another, and we could feel that we were moving.

Even then we were afraid to go out on the deck. And when dinner time came we didn't dare to go out. And we turned off the lights and tried to go to sleep. But every time I sort of dozed, I felt hands on me, and that same voice saying we were arrested—for murder! So finally I just laid there staring in the dark, and I guess that afterward I must have gone to sleep.

Afraid to Seek Work

It was that way for two more days and nights. We both got sick, and I laid in the bunk all the time and thought I'd go crazy. And at last we got to Jacksonville.

I was so all-in that I don't remember much about the first of it. But we took a taxi at the wharf and Ed asked the driver about a rooming house, and he took us to a place on Ocean avenue; it was No. 125, I think, and there we were in a dirty little dump of a room, worse than any I'd ever lived in when I used to work in the laundry.

Of course, we had to talk a little bit about what we were going to do. We had less than $50 left—and my baby was coming soon, which would cost money, and we had to eat. The bandit stuff was over. We never even thought of trying that again. Ed was a good mechanic, and figured he'd get a job around a garage.

Next day he went out to try. But he never went to any garage. He didn't dare. And this is why: The New York newspapers had beat us down there, coming on the train, and he got one and brought it home and didn't want to show it to me, but I made him—and there it all was.

Hardly Enough to Eat

They had our names and descriptions and everything, even that I was going to have a baby, and it said the police in every city outside of New

York had been wired to look for me in a hospital and Ed around a garage or a welding shop. It said that Mazio wasn't dead yet, but that he'd been hit in the stomach, and they expected him to die.

The paper said I was the one that shot him. It was that gave me the idea of claiming I did it when the detectives got us later, which is the only lie I've told, except about my parents being dead. I wanted to save them the disgrace, and I didn't care a rap what they did to me after. My baby was dead, and I thought it might help Ed if I said I was the one who shot. But that was all later.

We went through a lot of other plain hell that I wouldn't wish on a dog before we came to that. We were down and out. We were a thousand times worse off than before we ever started to stealing money. It got us nothing and worse than nothing. Anybody who tries it is a fool.

I wanted my baby to be born in a pretty place. I wanted to have nice things. And now I was afraid to have my baby born anywhere—and we were flat broke, and in worse dump than any I'd ever lived in.

Ed was afraid to try for the kind of jobs he could work at. We were afraid to show our noses in the street. Our money gave out and we hardly had enough to eat. The baby wasn't due until after the first of May. Ed wrote a letter to his mother in Brooklyn, begging her to send him a hundred dollars to pay a doctor. The detectives got that letter. They got everything from then on. We didn't have a chance.

The night of April 10, I got awful sick and had the most terrific pains. You oughtn't to have to worry about things when you are in that fix. I was afraid to have Ed take me to a hospital, afraid even to let him bring in a doctor.

I thought the minute they saw what was the matter with me, I'd be arrested, and then the baby would be born in jail. Even a dump would have been better than that. I'd rather have died.

Ed got scared and thought I was going to die, and called a woman that was in the house to come in and stay with me, and went out and was gone about an hour, and came back with that Dr. Sisson.

Before he went away he said, "Celia, I don't care what happens to either of us, you can't suffer like that."

I didn't want to go, but they made me. I hardly knew what I was doing. They took me in a place called Humphrey's Sanitarium, and I laid there for two days, wanting to scream every time the door opened, thinking the cops had come to take me away.

At last, the baby came—I suppose I could write a lot of bunk about that to get sympathy, but I was to miserable then and I'm too miserable now when I think about it, to put down anything but the plain truth. I just laid there like a person doped when they showed it to me, and I thought, "you poor kid, we've made a nice mess of things for you." And it was pitiful and sickly from the start.

Two days later, they let me out. They knew we were broke. You can't blame them for that. Ed was afraid for us to go back to the place on Ocean avenue, and he took me to a rooming house on Monroe street that was even worse. It was dirty, and I had no proper things for the baby, not even a can of talcum powder. And you could see that it was sick all the time, and I didn't know what do for it. I wanted my baby to have a chance. And look at the chance it had.

I named it Katherine, after Ed's mother in Brooklyn. She's a good woman. She didn't deserve the disgrace we've put on her. We couldn't have a real baptism or anything. I guess the priest would have done it for nothing, but we waited because we thought the money would come from Ed's mother. I guess God won't hold that against my poor baby.

Two days later it died. I wish I'd died too. We had to get the undertaker to trust us for its little coffin. There was nobody at the funeral but Ed and me, and the undertaker that buried my baby is the man that gave us away to the police.

Cecilia Cooney to-morrow will tell how the detectives broke down the door of their room and arrested them just as she and her husband were making up their minds whether to commit suicide or surrender.

Notes

NOTES TO PREFACE

ix *New York Herald-Tribune:* "The End of a Thriller," Editorial, *New York Herald-Tribune*, 4/23/24, n.p. (That is: "no page." Because we used a number of newspaper morgues as our source for stories from long defunct papers, page numbers — not often included on the clippings themselves — were sometimes impossible to come by.)

ix all the rest: "Bob Hair Bandit's Husband to Face Lunacy Board Test," *Brooklyn Eagle*, 4/24/24, p. 1.

x laugh about it: Mary Mallon, "Missing the Circus Frets Bandit Celia," *New York Evening Post*, 4/23/24, p. 9.

x looked a sight: "Bobbed-Hair Bandit's Own Story," XI, *New York American*, 5/9/24, p. 4.

x New York City: "'Doesn't Pay,' Says Gun Girl," *New York American*, 4/23/24, p. 1.

xi "guns" exploded: "Riotous Throngs Block Path of Bobbed Bandit," *New York Evening Post*, 4/22/24, p. 1.

xi they are through: "Mob Surges to Bobbed Bandit," *New York Daily News*, 4/23/24, pp. 3, 12.

xiii class of readers: "Proud Girl Bandit Describes 10 Crimes," *New York Times*, 4/23/24, p. 4; "Police Arrest Girl Robber in South," *New York Sun*, 4/21/04, n.p.

xiv Bobbed Haired Bandit: "Bobbed-Hair Bandit's Own Story." Twelve installments running in the *New York American* from 4/28/24 through 5/10/24; and then another version later in *Modern Romances*, 3/40–6/40.

NOTES TO INTRODUCTION

xvii *New York Tribune:* "The Challenge of 1924," Editorial, *New York Tribune*, 1/1/24, p. 16.

xvii district of Broadway: "3 White Light Cafes Yield No Trace of Rum," *New York Tribune*, 1/1/24, p. 3.

xvii BABY NEW YEAR: "Father Time Reels Out on a Jag," *New York Daily News*, 1/1/24, pp. 3, 20.

xviii hooch mills: "Pre-Volstead Revels Usher in 1924," *New York American*, 1/1/24, p. 1.

xviii on his hip: "1924 Born with Corkscrew in Mouth throughout U.S.," *New York Daily News*, 1/2/24, p. 3.

xviii New Year's raids: "200 Aim to Dry Tonights Revels along White Way," *New York Evening Post*, 12/31/24, p. 1.

xviii **nearly double:** Stephen Brier et al., *Who Built America*, Volume 2 (New York: Pantheon, 1992), pp. 271–275.

xix **flow of business:** "Mellon and Hoover Predict Prosperity for the New Year," *New York Times*, 1/1/24, p. 1.

xix **BANK ROLLS BULGING:** Frederick B. Edwards, "Prosperous Broadway Pours out Its Riches to Greet 1924 with Pre-Volsteadian Revels," *New York Tribune*, 1/1/24, pp. 1, 3.

xix **Paul Whiteman Orchestra:** Cholly Knickerbocker, "Society Greets 1924 at Balls and Parties," *New York American*, 1/1/24, n.p. William Randolph Hearst was Knickerbocker's employer. Walter Lippmann, newspaperman and newspaper critic, wrote at the time that "Mr. Hearst's unflagging interest in high society caters to people who never hope to be in high society, and yet manage to derive some enhancement out of a vague feeling that they are part of the life they read about." Walter Lippmann, *Public Opinion* (New York: Free Press, 1922/1997), p. 210.

xix **peninsula, Florida:** "Society Wends Its Way to Palm Beach," *New York Evening Post*, 1/5/24, p. 9.

xix **almost full:** "New Year's Eve at Palm Beach," *New York Evening Post*, 12/29/23, p. 11.

xx **less than sixteen:** "Many Women Receive under $10 a Week," *New York Evening Post*, 11/12/23, p. 4.

xx **before the decade ended:** Brier et al., *Who Built America*, pp. 271–275.

xx **inhabit the stratosphere:** Stuart Ewen, *Captains of Consciousness* (New York: McGraw-Hill, 1976); Lizabeth Cohen, *Making a New Deal* (Cambridge: Cambridge University Press, 1990).

xx **largest consumer items:** Advertisement, *New York Daily News*, 11/25/23, p. 8.

xx **during the decade:** Brier et al., *Who Built America*, p. 275.

xxi **"sin of extravagance":** John K. Mumford, "Has Our Great Country Gone Installment Mad?" *New York Herald Books-Magazine*, 2/3/24, p. 3.

xxi **two hundred ninety-five dollars:** Advertisement, *New York Times*, 1/1/24, pp. 9, 18.

xxi **"Why Wait?":** Advertisement, *New York Daily News*, 11/21/23, p.. 21.

xxi **photoplay star herself:** Maybelline advertisement, circa 1923.

xxii **only one dollar:** Youthglow advertisement, circa 1923.

xxii **Chesterfield cigarette:** Chesterfield Cigarettes billboard, circa 1923.

xxii **exercise routine:** "Valentino Has Exquisite Back," *New York Daily Mirror*, 7/1/28, n.p.

xxiii **where they were:** "Me in Hollywood," *New York Daily News*, 10/14/23, p. 20; "What Stars Really Make," *New York Daily News*, 10/25/23, p. 5.

xxiii **bells in the streets:** "New Year Finds Brooklyn Eager to Make Its Resolutions Good," *Brooklyn Standard Union*, 1/2/24, p. 2.

xxiii **Brooklyn Citizen:** "Gun Shots and Fists Fly on New Year's Eve," *Brooklyn Citizen*, 1/2/24, p. 2.

xxiii **wine or lead:** Ibid.

xxiii **the fair sex:** Edwards, "Prosperous Broadway Pours out Its Riches," pp. 1, 3.

xxiv **give them drinks:** "Suggests One Cocktail Limit for Women," *New York Herald*, 1/1/24, p. 1.

xxiv **twelve percent:** Brier et al., *Who Built America*, pp. 271–275.

xxiv **her new roles:** "Women on Juries," *Brooklyn Citizen*, 1/13/24, p. 6; " Modern Business Women Held All Right — Except for Husbands," *New York Herald-Tribune*, 4/5/24, p. 8; " NY Law to Stop Night Work by Women Upheld," *New York Tribune*, 3/11/25, p. 5; "Methodist Women in Pulpits," *Brooklyn Eagle*, 5/11/24, n.p.; "First Woman Sheriff Plans to Pack Man-Sized Pistol," *New York Daily News*, 11/15/23, p. 4; "The Inquiring Photographer," *New York Daily News*, 6/4/24, p. 15; "A Lady in the Smoking Car," *New York Daily News*, 10/1/23, p. 11; "Wives Win Fight to Use Own Names at Library," *New York Herald*, 2/20/24, p. 3.

xxv **Should Be Murdered:** Fay King, "Pretty Girls Dream of Vamping World's Rulers, Declares Fay King," *New York Mirror*, 7/26/24, p. 6; "A Car, Woman's Emancipator," *New York Daily News*, 1/6/1924, p. 33; "Coolidge Tells Women Congress Lends Ready Ear," *New York Daily News*, 11/18/23, n.p.; Anne Dunlap, "Women in Politics Lose Charm?" *New York American*, 2/12/24, p. 15; Arthur Stringer, "Are Our Modern Women Becoming More Barbaric?" *New York American*, 5/11/24, n.p.; "What's the Matter with the Women?" *Brooklyn Eagle*, 3/23/24 and 3/9/24, respectively, n.p.

xxv **shameless flirt:** F. Scott Fitzgerald, "My Lost City," in *The Crack Up*, Edmund Wilson, ed. (New York: New Directions, 1993), p. 29; "South Sea Flapper Wears Only Jewelry, But She Is Called Modest, at That," *Brooklyn Citizen*, 1/6/24, p. 3; "Fanny, the Flapper Troutess, Drives Al Crazy at Sports Show," *New York World*, 5/30/24, p. 13.

xxv **breaking up marriages:** "She Bobs, He Nags," *New York Daily News*, 5/25/24, p. 3.

xxv **strong female will:** "Only Weak Minds under Hair Bobs? No! Roars Doctor, "*New York Daily News*, 2/13/24, p. 22; "Bobbed Hair," *Woman Citizen*, 4/19/02, p. 19; "Flapper Phone Girls Blamed for Bad Service," *Brooklyn Eagle*, 3/20/24, p. 3; "Bobbed-Haired Teachers Inefficient," *New York American*, 4/18/24, p. 1; "Dorothy Dix's Letter Box," *New York Post*, 10/25/24, p. 6.

xxvi **decline of civilization:** Janet Lee, *"Wild Women": The Romance of a Flapper* (New York: Nicholas Brown, 1922); Arthur Stringer, "Are Our Modern Women Becoming More Barbaric?" *New York American*, 5/11/24, n.p.

xxvi **respectable females:** "Flapper Near to Extinction?" *New York Daily News*, 10/21/23, n.p.; Kathleen Norris, "Flappers Are Actually Going out of Style," *New York American*, 4/27/24, sec II, p. 5; "Coolidge and Bobbed Hair Boosted by N.Y.U. Seniors," *Brooklyn Eagle*, 5/12/24, n.p.; "No Wonder Wavers Are Wild; 2,000 Women Bob Hair Daily," *New York Herald-Tribune*, 3/8/24, p. 7;

Mrs. Anthony Wayne Cook, "Why I Have Faith in Modern Youth," *Washington Post*, 5/25/24, p. 5.

xxvi **GREAT NATIONAL QUESTION OF 1924:** "The Great National Question," *Brooklyn Eagle*, 4/9/24, p. 6; see also: Dorothy Parker, "The Bobbed Hair Problem," *Life*, 8/28/24, pp. 8–9.

xxvi **"Catchem & Cleanem Bucket Shop":** Winsor McCay, "The Wildcatter," *New York American*, 5/7/24, editorial page.

xxvi **oil stock to soldiers:** "Asks Wider Inquiry into Wood Affairs," *New York Times*, 1/1/24, p. 1.

xxvi **Life summed it up:** "Life Lines," *Life*, 4/24/24, p. 3. (In the 1920s *Life* was a humor magazine; it was reborn with a photo format in 1936.) For the best discussion of the oil scandal and Twenties politics, see Mark Sullivan, *The Twenties, Our Times*, vol. 6 (London: Charles Scribner's Sons, 1935).

xxviii **New Year's in history:** *New York Tribune*, 1/1/24, pp. 1, 3.

xxviii **"good of the service":** "Enright's Minor Shake-Up," *New York Times*, 1/1/24, p. 3.

xxix **out of soft jobs:** *New York Daily News*, 1/1/24, editorial page.

xxix **among other felonies:** "Chronology of Events in Brooklyn," *Brooklyn Standard Union*, 12/31/24, p. 9; "Pirates Bind Guards, Seize 100,000 Opium," *Brooklyn Standard Union*, 1/2/24, p. 1.

xxix **hold up shooting:** "Chronology of Events in Brooklyn," p. 9.

xxxi **bold murders:** "1923 Gunman's Year Passes with Killing," *New York Daily News*, 1/1/24, p. 2.

NOTES TO CHAPTER 1

3 *Brooklyn Eagle:* "Woman with Gun Holds up Six Men as Pal Robs Store," *Brooklyn Eagle*, 1/6/24, p. 1.

3 **Bedford-Stuyvesant and Prospect Heights:** Statistics on the 11th Assembly District, Borough of Brooklyn, *Fourteenth Census of the United States 1920*, Vol. 3, *Population* (Washington, D.C.: Government Printing Office, 1922). Of a total population of 78,062 persons recorded in 1920, some 15,142 were foreign born, while 28,377 had one or more parent of immigrant stock. A total of 31,843 were white with "native" parents; 3,611 were black; and 48 were Indian, Chinese, Japanese, or "other." Of the foreign born, those of Irish ancestry led the pack with 4,020, followed by Italians, 2,271; Germans, 2,035; and English, 1,549.

5 **Celia remembered:** "Bobbed-Hair Bandit's Own Story," III, *New York American*, 4/30/24, n.p. This account of Celia and Ed's first meeting is at odds with the version later recalled by Celia in *Modern Romances* in 1940. In the later version, Celia meets Ed when he offers her a ride to work. He then asks her to marry him on their first date. "What the World Didn't Know," *Modern Romances*, March 1940, pp. 84–85.

5 **furnished room:** "Bobbed-Hair Bandit's Own Story," III, 4/30/24.

5 **as fast as we made it:** "What the World Didn't Know," p. 85.

6 **pride in me:** Ibid.

6 **a *decent* home:** Ibid., p. 86.

7 **to pick up Celia:** Ibid., p. 87.

7 **Ed came home:** "Bobbed-Hair Bandit's Own Story," III, n.p.

7 **read in a magazine:** Ibid.

7 **I thought I'd ever do:** Ibid.

8 **Wasn't it silly?:** "Bobbed-Hair Bandit's Own Story," IV, *New York American*, 5/1/24, n.p.

8 **Ed wasn't there:** Ibid.

8 **anything with you:** Ibid.

8 **ready for anything:** Ibid.

9 **in the Twenties:** The number of grocery chains had grown dramatically in the preceding half century and had accelerated in the decade, leading up to Celia and Ed's crimes. According to the historical statistics of the U.S. Census Bureau, there was one grocery chain in 1872, twenty-one in 1900, one hundred and three in 1914, and two hundred seventy by 1924. This was paralleled by the growth of drug chains, the first appearing in 1887 with one hundred fifty chains by 1924. U.S. Bureau of the Census, *Historical Statistics of the United States, Colonial Times to 1957* (Washington, D.C.: Government Printing Office, 1960), p. 523.

9 **everything I had:** "Bobbed-Hair Bandit's Own Story," IV, n.p.

9 **on the counters:** Ibid.

9 **steady in a dream:** Ibid.

9 **Then I remembered:** Ibid.

10 **for my baby:** Ibid.

10 **want to laugh:** Ibid.

10 **and me so little:** Ibid.

10 **fives, tens, and twenties:** Ibid.

11 **never guessed a thing:** Ibid.

11 **and walked home:** Ibid.

11 **bulging pockets:** "Bobbed-Hair Bandit's Own Story," V, *New York American*, 5/2/24, p. 10.

12 **strips of paper:** Ibid.

12 **wish book:** Ibid.

12 **shot to pieces:** Ibid.

13 **think I was crazy:** Ibid.

13 **behind the woman:** "Woman with Gun Holds up Six Men as Pal Robs Store," *Brooklyn Eagle*, 1/6/24, p. 1.

13 **theme of the story:** "Woman Bandit and Man Rob Store of $680," *Brooklyn Citizen*, 1/6/24, p. 1.

14 **funeral to go to:** "Woman with Gun Holds Up Six Men as Pal Robs Store," p. 1.

14 **an arms race even:** "Bobbed-Hair Bandit's Own Story," IV, n.p.

15 cramped and bare: "Bobbed-Hair Bandit's Own Story," V, p. 10.
15 top floor: "Bobbed Bandit and Mate Near Capture," *Brooklyn Eagle*, 4/17/24, p. 10.
15 for his bride: "Bobbed Hair Bandit's Mate Located by Police," *Brooklyn Daily Times*, 4/17/24, p. 13.
15 said Celia: "Think Mrs. Cooney Is Both Brunette and Blonde," *New York World*, 4/17/24, pp. 1, 3.
15 think of them all: "Bobbed-Hair Bandit's Own Story," V, p. 10.
16 when the time came: Ibid.
16 fifty dollars a month: Ibid.; "Think Mrs. Cooney Is Both Brunette and Blonde," pp. 1, 3.
16 fifty cents: "Bobbed-Hair Bandit's Own Story," V, p. 10.
16 play in the street: Ibid.

17 *Evening Mail*: "Bob-Hair Bandit Robs 2 More Shops," *New York Telegram and Evening Mail*, 1/13/24, p. 1.
17 whatever you say: "Bobbed-Hair Bandit's Own Story," V, *New York American*, 5/2/24, p. 10.
17 Saturday to come: "What the World Didn't Know," *Modern Romances*, April 1940, p. 34.
18 snappy," he said: "Bobbed-Hair Bandit's Own Story," VI, *New York American*, 5/3/24, p. 6.
18 white as a sheet: Ibid.
19 where was the police: Ibid.
19 a store at all: Ibid.
19 silently behind: "Bob-Haired Bandit Gets $450 More Loot," *New York Telegram and Evening Mail*, 1/13/24, p. 2.
19 idling at the corner: "Brooklyn's Girl Robber Holds up Five in Tea Store," *New York Daily News*, 1/13/24, p. 2.
19 much danger: "Bobbed-Hair Bandit's Own Story," VI, p. 6.
20 where's the excitement?: Ibid.
20 laugh at that: Celia is mistaken. There were no speculations as to her being the leader of an underworld gang or on dope at this point in their career. Later, however, similar speculations were made in the press.
21 over the papers: "Bobbed-Hair Bandit's Own Story," VI, p. 6.
21 "Brooklyn's Girl Robber": "Brooklyn's Girl Robber Holds up Five in Tea Store," p. 2.
21 "Bob-Hair Bandit": "Bob-Hair Bandit Robs 2 More Shops," p. 1.
21 complete the ensemble: "Brooklyn's Girl Robber Holds up Five in Tea Store," p. 2.
21 getaway car: "2 Stores Held up by Armed Woman and Confederate," *Brooklyn Eagle*, 1/13/24, p. 1; "Bob-Hair Bandit Robs 2 More Shops," p. 1.
21 slightest move: "2 Stores Held up by Armed Woman and Confederate," p. 1.

21 **gathered speed:** Ibid.

22 **rib him about it:** "Bobbed-Hair Bandit's Own Story," VI, p. 6.

22 **the right, all right:** Ibid.

NOTES TO CHAPTER 3

22 **William Randolph Hearst:** J. K. Winkler, *William Randolph Hearst*, 1928, p. 32, cited in Alfred Lee, *The Daily Newspaper in America* (New York: Octagon Books, 1973), p. 217; emphasis in the original.

23 **at the *Eagle*):** As a writer at the *New York Sun* in 1835, Locke wrote a sensational series of stories claiming to have discovered life on the moon. The popularity of the hoax helped make the *Sun* the best-selling paper in New York.

23 **the city has three:** The eleven New York City dailies publishing at the time of the Bobbed Haired Bandit's reign were the *American, Daily News, Evening Journal, Evening Post, Herald, Tribune, Sun, Telegram and Evening Mail, Times, Tribune,* and *World.* By the middle of 1924 the *Herald* and *Tribune* had merged. In addition, there were four major Brooklyn dailies: the *Eagle, Citizen, Standard Union,* and *Daily Times.* Today there are no major Brooklyn dailies and only three New York City dailies: the *Daily News, Post,* and *Times.* The *Wall Street Journal* and the recently resurrected *New York Sun* also publish on a daily schedule in the city, but the former is considered a trade paper and the latter, by and large, a vanity press. *Newsday* has a Queens edition, but it is essentially a Long Island paper. In a new experiment, two free dailies have appeared on the streets as well: *AM New York* in 2003 and *Metro* in 2004. "New York City Newspapers of General Circulation 1900–1967," *New York Times*, 5/6/67, p. 15; see also: Michael Emery, Edwin Emery, and Nancy L. Roberts, *The Press and America*, 9th ed. (Needham Heights, MA: Allyn and Bacon, 2000), p. 288.

24 **Herald-Tribune:** Frank Luther Mott, *American Journalism* (New York: Macmillan, 1942), p. 640; Emery et al., *The Press and America*, p. 290.

24 **banks or manufactures:** "Reid Buys Herald from Munsey; Will Merge with Tribune," *New York Times*, 3/18/24, pp. 1, 6,

24 **"Grand High Executioner":** Mott, *American Journalism*, p. 640.

24 **rest in trust:** Cited in George H. Douglas, *The Golden Age of the Newspaper* (Westport, CT: Greenwood Press, 1999), p. 156.

24 **continuous noise:** J. K. Winkler, *William Randolph Hearst*, 1928, p. 32, cited in Alfred Lee, *The Daily Newspaper in America* (New York: Octagon Books, 1973), p. 217.

25 **Jazz Age:** "Jazz Journalism" is what newspaper historian Simon Michael Bessie called tabloids in his 1938 book of the same name (New York: E. P. Dutton, 1938).

25 **Brooklyn's gungirl:** Mott, *American Journalism*, p. 669.

25 **Mayor Hylan in 1919:** For the best general history of the New York City Police

Department, see James Lardner and Thomas Reppeto, *NYPD: A City and Its Police* (New York: Holt, 2000).

26 **political pressure:** "R. E. Enright Dies; Headed City Police," *New York Times*, 9/5/52, p. 15.

26 **unsurprising conclusion:** George Creel, "No 'Crime Wave' in New York City" (New York: Bureau of Printing Police Department New York City, 1921). Originally published in the *New York Times*, 1/23/21.

28 **even for sailors:** "Admiral Plunkett Should Be More Explicit," *Brooklyn Eagle*, 1/3/24, p. 6.

28 **will be flashed:** "Butler Makes Quaker City One Big Bandit Trap," *New York Tribune*, 1/13/24, n.p.

29 **Philadelphia police force:** "Butler's Men Fail to Find a Suspect," *Brooklyn Standard Union*, 1/13/24, p. 1.

29 **make New York spotless:** Ibid.

29 **a shade whiter:** "Philadelphia Pointed the Way," *New York Tribune*, 1/14/24, n.p.; from DA's scrapbook, New York Municipal Archives.

30 **City of Brotherly Love:** "Enright Charges 13 Inspectors with Neglect of Duty," *Brooklyn Citizen*, 1/13/24, p. 1.

30 **WEEKLY STORE HOLDUP:** Front page, *Brooklyn Citizen*, 1/13/24.

NOTES TO CHAPTER 4

33 *New York Herald:* "Bobbed Haired Girl Captured as Store Bandit," *New York Herald*, 1/15/24, p. 1.

33 *Brooklyn Standard Union:* "Ex-Chorus Girl Arrested as Chain Store Bandit," *Brooklyn Standard Union*, 1/15/24, p. 1.

33 *New York American:* Jean Henry, "Squeal Traps Girl in Thefts," *New York American*, 1/16/24, n.p.

33 **five feet tall:** "Brooklyn Police Take Will o'Wisp Girl as Daring Thief," *New York Daily News*, 1/15/24, p. 4.

33 **out so late:** "Girl Denies She Is Chain Store Bandit," *Brooklyn Citizen*, 1/15/24, p. 1; "Bobbed Haired Girl Captured as Store Bandit," p. 1.

33 **bobbed haired accomplice:** "Brooklyn Police Take Will o'Wisp Girl as Daring Thief," p. 4.

33 **'squealed':** "Ex-Chorus Girl Arrested as Chain Store Bandit," p. 1.

34 **his housekeeper:** Ibid.; "Identify Chorus Girl as Bandit," *New York Telegram and Evening Mail*, 1/15/24, p. 1.

34 **break her down:** "Girl Denies She Is Chain Store Bandit," p. 1.

34 **a year earlier:** "Ex-Capt. D. J. Carey, Policeman 41 Years," *New York Times*, 4/26/50, p. 29.

35 **standing him up:** "Identify Chorus Girl as Bandit," *New York Evening Telegram*, 1/15/24, p. 3.

35 **she smiled:** "Ex-Chorus Girl Arrested as Chain Store Bandit," p. 1.

35 he nodded: "Bob-Haired Helen Ridicules Accusers," *New York Evening Post*, 1/17/24, p. 3.

36 "bobbed haired and pretty": "Brooklyn Police Take Will o'Wisp Girl as Daring Thief," p. 4.

36 than a minute: "That Is the Girl Who Held Us Up," *New York American*, 1/16/24, n.p.

37 of the flapper: "Ex-Chorus Girl Arrested as Chain Store Bandit," p. 1.

37 bright blue eyes: Jean Henry, "Squeal Traps Girl in Thefts," *New York American*, 1/16/24, n.p.

37 Me steal! Never.: Ibid.

37 [like Apples] along: "Bobbed Haired Girl Captured as Store Bandit," *New York Herald*, 1/15/24, p. 1.

37 when I am eating: "Ex-Chorus Girl Arrested as Chain Store Bandit," p. 1.

37 Brooklyn speak-easy: "Bob-Haired Bandit Denies Thefts; Spite Victim, She Says," *New York Evening Post*, 1/16/24, p. 1.

37 and closed it: "Bandit's Lawyer Berates Court," *Brooklyn Eagle*, 1/15/24, p. 2.

38 not been committed: Ibid.

38 examination for Helen: "Bob-Haired Helen Ridicules Accusers," *New York Evening Post*, 1/17/24, p. 3.

38 influences of others: "Salesgirl Is Held as New Girl Bandit with Two Youths," *Brooklyn Citizen*, 1/18/24, p. 1.

38 the same year: "Charles Dodd, 74, Ex-Justice, Is Dead," *New York Times*, 7/25/47, p. 17.

38 I don't get it.: "Bob-Haired Helen Ridicules Accusers," p. 3.

39 by the police: "Bandit's Lawyer Berates Court," p. 1.

39 burlesque show: "Bobbed-Hair Bandit's Own Story," VII. *New York American*, 5/5/24, p. 7.

39 to my face: Ibid.

39 make much difference: Ibid.

40 think it's so: Ibid.

41 "fool them": Ibid.

41 length of the block: Ibid.

41 "Rhubarb Vaselino": "Rhubarb Vaselino" was a derogatory name used at the time for the silver screen sheik, Rudolph Valentino.

41 maybe buy something: "Bobbed-Hair Bandit's Own Story," VII, p. 7.

42 trap closed, too: Ibid.

42 to the police: Ibid.

42 and Her Companion: Ibid.

44 while in the store: "Bob-Haired Helen Ridicules Accusers," p. 3. The Roulston grocery is not a part of the Bohack chain; the *Post* was confused about where Celia claimed she broke her automatic.

44 the *Eagle* headlined: "New Gunwoman Defies Police to Catch Her," *Brooklyn Eagle*, 1/16/24, p. 1.

44 Operating in Brooklyn: "Bob-Haired Bandit Denies Thefts; Spite Victim, She Says," p. 1.

44 detective bureau: "New Gunwoman Defies Police to Catch Her," p. 1.

45 "forcible language": Ibid.; "Girl Bandit Leaves Note Saying Police Made False Arrest," *Brooklyn Citizen*, 1/16/24, p. 1; "Girl Thief Strikes Again," *Brooklyn Standard Union*, 1/16/24, p. 1.

45 difficult of solution: "Girl Thief Strikes Again," p. 1.

45 on the loose: "New Gunwoman Defies Police to Catch Her," p. 1.

46 exculpatory evidence: "Salesgirl Is Held as New Girl Bandit with Two Youths," p. 1.

46 set poor Helen free: " New Gunwoman Defies Police to Catch Her," p. 1.

NOTES TO CHAPTER 5

46 *Brooklyn Standard Union:* Tom W. Jackson, "The Periscope," *Brooklyn Standard Union*, 1/18/24, n.p.

46 Union Street: "Bobbed Haired Girl and Her Pal Again Hold up Drug Store," *Brooklyn Citizen*, 1/21/24, pp. 1, 3.

46 and go home: "Bobbed-Hair Bandit's Own Story," VII, *New York American*, 5/5/24, p. 7.

46 'Get 'em up!': "Bobbed Haired Girl and Her Pal Again Hold up Drug Store," p. 1.

46 commanded Celia: "$20,000 Bail Set for Quigley Girl Held as Bandit," *Brooklyn Eagle*, 1/21/24, p. 1.

46 said Ed: "Bobbed-Hair Bandit's Own Story," VII, p. 7.

47 and go—please!: Ibid.

47 "Where's your tin?": "Bobbed Haired Bandit Again Holds up Store," *New York Herald*, 1/21/24, p. 1.

47 stop gassin' forever: "Bobbed Haired Girl and Her Pal Again Hold up Drug Store," p. 1; "Girl Bandit on Rampage Again," *Brooklyn Standard Union*, 1/21/24, p. 1.

47 reached the door: "Bobbed Haired Girl and Her Pal Again Hold up Drug Store," p. 1.

48 her Tall Companion: Ibid., pp. 1, 3.

48 the girl bandit: "Girl Bandit on Rampage Again," p. 1.

48 such a thing happening: "$20,000 Bail Set for Quigley Girl Held as Bandit," *Brooklyn Eagle*, 1/21/24, pp. 1–2.

48 AND ESCAPES: "Girl Bandit Taunts Police and Escapes," *New York Evening Post*, 1/21/24, p. 5.

48 talking about us: "What the World Didn't Know," *Modern Romances*, April 1940, p. 90.

49 against Helen Quigley: "Police Try to Trap Saucy Bandit," *New York Evening Post*, 1/22/24, p. 3.

49 **and escaped:** "Girl Bandit Adds Another to Long List of Hold-Ups," *Brooklyn Standard Union*, 1/23/24, p. 1.

49 **red hot stove:** Tom W. Jackson "The Periscope," *Brooklyn Standard Union*, 1/22/24, n.p.

49 **couldn't make me out:** "Bobbed-Hair Bandit's Own Story," VII, *New York American*, 5/5/24, p. 3

49 **quick getaway:** "Girl Bandit and Aide Hold up Another Store," *Brooklyn Citizen*, 1/23/24, p. 2

50 **to show me:** "Bobbed-Hair Bandit's Own Story," VII, p. 3.

50 **a dozen times:** Ibid.

50 **tone of the coverage:** "Brooklyn's Fair Gunmiss Merrily Pursues Career," *New York Daily News*, 1/23/24, p. 3.

51 **the girl ordered:** "Girl Bandit and Aide Strike Again . . ." *Brooklyn Citizen*, 1/23/24, pp. 1–2.

51 **couple of bullets:** Ibid.

51 **on for to-night:** Ibid.

NOTES TO CHAPTER 6

51 *New York Herald:* Betty Ross, "Mayor Hylan on Girl Bandit, the Interests, Women and Politics," *New York Herald*, 3/20/24, p. 3.

51 ROBS GROCERY: "Bobbed-Haired Gunwoman Derides Police as She Robs Grocery," *Brooklyn Citizen*, 1/23/24, p. 1.

52 **for the police:** "Girl Bandit Adds Another to Long List of Hold-Ups," *Brooklyn Standard Union*, 1/23/24, p. 1.

52 **pure and simple:** Ibid.

52 **he to is asleep:** "'Bobbed Haired Bandit' Announces Her 'Getaway' for Neighboring State," *Brooklyn Standard Union*, 1/22/24, p. 1.

53 **places robbed:** "Girl Bandit Adds Another to Long List of Hold-Ups," p. 1.

54 **New York City was 'lawless':** "Enright Orders Charges against 13 Inspectors and Other High Officials," *Brooklyn Eagle*, 1/13/24. p. 1; "Inspectors Meet Lahey Secretly; Jobs Are Safe," *Brooklyn Eagle*, 1/15/24, p. 1. "Drastic Order Hits Captains and Deputies," *New York Tribune*, 1/13/24, p. 1.

54 **Florida sunshine:** "Hylan Goes South Today," *New York Times*, 1/27/24, p. 21.

55 **is here maintained:** "Hylan Praises Enright; Insists City Is Clean," *New York Tribune*, 1/23/24, n.p.; in Mayor Hylan's scrapbook, New York Municipal Archives

55 **five-month period:** *Annual Report of the Police Department*, 1924, New York City, pp. 3, 20–31.

55 **"thieves' carnival":** *Annual Report of the Police Department*, 1922, New York City, p. 28.

56 **carnival of crime:** "Enright Takes a Vacation," *Brooklyn Citizen*, 11/18/23, p. 6.

56 **they are exploiting:** "Editors Hear Hylan Denounce Press," *New York Times*, 7/24/23, p. 2.

56 **seven thousand dollars:** W. A. Swanberg, *Citizen Hearst* (New York: Charles Scribner's Sons, 1961), pp. 305, 310.

58 **two weeks' time:** "N.Y. Police Shake-up Directed by Hylan," *New York Evening Journal*, 1/14/24, pp. 1, 3.

58 **made one once:** Lincoln Steffens, *The Autobiography of Lincoln Steffens* (New York: Harcourt, Brace and World, 1931), pp. 285–291.

59 **knock off their competition:** Enright had employed the same tactic himself, proffering statistics of a declining crime rate to refute his critics, but without Roosevelt's success.

59 **satisfaction of all:** Steffens, *The Autobiography of Lincoln Steffens*.

59 **law and order itself:** "Hylan Praises Enright; Insists City Is Clean," n.p.

59 **infested with them:** Ross, "Mayor Hylan on Girl Bandit," p. 3.

59 **eventually be theirs:** "Girl Bandit Adds Another to Long List of Hold-Ups," p. 1.

60 **TWITS CHAUFFEUR:** "Bobbed Haired Girl Fights Detectives on Bus," *New York Herald*, 1/25/24, p. 1; "New Bobbed-Hair Bandit Mauls Man," *New York Evening Post*, 1/25/24, p. 1; "New Girl Bandit, a Blonde, Helps Kidnap Truck-load of Sugar; Twits Chauffeur," *Brooklyn Eagle*, 1/25/24, p. 1.

60 **permanent crime wave:** Tom W. Jackson, "The Periscope," Brooklyn *Standard Union*, 2/5/24, p. 10A.

NOTES TO CHAPTER 7

60 *New York American:* "Bobbed Hair in Trouble," *New York American*, 2/7/24, p. 3.

60 **still pursued her:** " 'Bobbed Hair' Girl Bandit Is Again on Job," *New York Telegram and Evening Mail*, 2/3/24, p. 10.

60 **sauntered in:** "Girl Bandit and Her Aide Back at Work," *Brooklyn Citizen*, 2/3/24, p. 1.

60 **head butcher, stood:** "Three More Hold-ups Reported; Bobbed-Haired Girl Figures in One," *Brooklyn Standard Union*, 2/3/24, p. 1.

61 **'Nice chicken. Certainly.':** "Girl Bandit and Her Aide Back at Work," p. 1.

61 **she said:** "Three More Hold-ups Reported, p. 1.

61 **very convincing pistol:** "'Bobbed Hair' Girl Bandit Is Again on Job," p. 10.

61 **rear of the store:** "Girl Bandit and Her Aide Back at Work," p. 1.

61 **in his pockets:** " 'Bobbed Hair" Girl Bandit Is Again on Job," p. 10.

61 **stepped on the gas:** "Girl Bandit and Her Aide Back at Work," p. 1.

61 **in the "flivver":** "Three More Hold-ups Reported, p. 1.

61 **left no trace:** "Girl Bandit and Her Aide Back at Work," p. 1.

61 **for two minutes:** "Burial of Wilson Halts Activities of Whole Country," *New York Evening Post*, 2/6/24, p. 1.

62 **girl bandit case:** "Gunmen's Nest Bares Crimes," *New York Daily News*, 2/7/24, p. 3; see also: "Bobbed-Haired Girl Held as Boro Bandit in Crime Roundup," *Brooklyn Eagle*, 2/6/24, p. 1.

62 **one and the same:** "Bobbed-Haired Girl Held as Boro Bandit in Crime

Roundup," p. 1; see also: "Police Arrest Two Bobbed Hair Girls on Holdup Charges," *Brooklyn Standard Union*, 2/6/24, p. 1; "Victims Say Young Girl May Be Thief," *Brooklyn Citizen*, 2/6/24, p. 1.

62 **Bobbed Haired Bandit:** "Two Bobbed-Haired Women Held for Police Line-Up," *New York Evening Post*, 2/6/24, p. 1; "Girl Bandit Again Busy in Brooklyn," *New York Evening Post*, 2/7/24, p. 3.

62 **Daniel Carey himself:** "Bobbed-Haired Girl Held as Boro Bandit in Crime Roundup," *Brooklyn Eagle*, 2/6/24, p. 1.

63 **Rose go home:** "Two Bobbed-Haired Women Held for Police Line-Up," p. 1.

63 **without an escort:** "Hold Bobbed Haired Girl as Pal of Alleged Bandits," *Brooklyn Eagle*, 2/7/24, p. 2.

64 **to stay there:** Ibid.

NOTES TO CHAPTER 8

64 *Brooklyn Eagle:* "Forget Sex — Shoot!" Order in New War on Girl Bandit," *Brooklyn Eagle*, 2/10/24, p. A19.

64 **looting of the store:** "Gunmiss Strafes Brooklyn with New Holdup," *New York Daily News*, 2/7/04, n.p.

64 **BUSY IN BROOKLYN:** "Girl Bandit Again Busy in Brooklyn," *New York Evening Post*, 2/7/24, p. 3.

64 **two revolvers:** Bobbed Bandit Repeats Visit," *New York American*, 2/7/24, p. 3.

65 **three weeks before:** "Bobbed-Haired Girl Bandit Gives Druggist Return Call," *Brooklyn Standard Union*, 2/7/24, p. 1.

65 **tam-o'-shanter:** "Woman Thief Again Robs Drug Store," *Brooklyn Citizen*, 2/7/24, last page.

65 **honest druggists:** Bobbed Bandit Repeats Visit," p. 3.

65 **Bobbed Haired Bandit:** Ibid.; "Girl Bandit Again Busy in Brooklyn," p. 3.

66 **metropolitan banditry:** "Bobbed Bandit Repeats Visit," p. 3.

66 *somewhat* **in error:** Ibid.; emphasis added.

66 **her tall companion:** "Bobbed Haired Bandit Worries Detectives," *New York Herald*, 2/8/24, p. 3.

67 **also be "scrutinized":** Ibid.

67 **streets of Brooklyn:** "Girl Bandit Gives Druggist Return Call," p. 16.

67 **description of her:** Ibid.

67 **opposing a super-criminal:** "Girl Bandit Now Sought outside City," *Brooklyn Citizen*, 2/8/24, p. 5.

67 **of the investigation:** "Enright Takes Charge of Girl Bandit Hunt," *Brooklyn Citizen*, 2/8/24, p. 1.

67 **efforts to capture her:** "Enright to Direct Hunt for Daring Woman Bandit," *Brooklyn Standard Union*, 2/8/24, p. 1.

67 *Brooklyn Eagle:* "Forget Sex — Shoot!" p. A19.

68 **has to be stopped:** "Two Stores Robbed by New Holdup Gang; Bob-Hair Girl Busy," *Brooklyn Standard Union*, 2/11/24, p. 16.

68 **Bobbed Haired Bandit:** "Detectives Confer on Bobbed Bandit," *New York American*, 2/10/24, p. 1.

68 **DETECTIVES OF BROOKLYN:** "Shakeup Seen for Detectives of Brooklyn," *Brooklyn Citizen* 2/9/24, p. 1.

68 **hunting criminals:** "'Shoot to Kill Order' to Gungirl Hunters," *Brooklyn Standard Union*, 2/10/24, p. 22.

68 **street duty in uniform:** "Shakeup Seen for Detectives of Brooklyn," p. 1.

68 **and done thoroughly:** "Two Stores Robbed by New Holdup Gang; Bob-Hair Girl Busy," p. 16.

68 **your life or hers:** "'Get Girl Bandit Dead or Alive,' Carey Orders," *Brooklyn Standard Union*, 2/9/24, n.p.

68 **probably more so:** "Forget Sex — Shoot!" p. A19.

69 **searching eyes tonight:** "'Shoot to Kill Order' to Gungirl Hunters," p. 22.

69 **until dawn:** "Forget Sex — Shoot!" p. A19.

69 **with bobbed hair:** "'Get Girl Bandit Dead or Alive,'" n.p.

69 **of a chain store:** "'Shoot to Kill' Edict Fails; Girl Bandit Strikes Again," *Brooklyn Standard Union*, 2/10/24, p. 1.

69 **New Robbery:** "Brooklyn Holdups Net Bandits $3,900," *New York Herald*, 2/10/24, p. 3.

70 **on her tail:** Ibid.

70 **driven out:** "Two Stores Robbed by New Holdup Gang; Bob Hair Girl Busy," p. 16.

70 **confidence in the police:** "Crime Wave Rampant; Big Shakeup Impends," *Brooklyn Standard Union*, 2/14/24, p. 1.

70 **over the past decade:** "Crime Cut 40% Enright Tells His Men," 1/7/24, *New York Evening Journal*, n.p.

70 **decrease or increase:** *Annual Report of the Police Department*, 1924, New York Police Department, pp. ii, iii.

70 **crime sells newspapers:** Andie Tucher, *Froth and Scum* (Chapel Hill: University of North Carolina Press, 1994), p. 9.

71 **to protect himself:** "Bobbed Hair Bandits Again," *Brooklyn Eagle*, 2/14/24, p. 1.

71 **her "tall" companion:** "Bobbed Hair Bandit Gives New Mystery," *New York Evening Post*, 2/16/24, n.p.

71 **saying little else:** Ibid.

72 **across the bridge:** Elizabeth Smith, "Who Is the Girl Bandit? Ask the Police; They Don't Know," *New York Telegram and Evening Mail*, 2/15/24, p. 7.

73 **know much about her:** Ibid.

74 **at the cops all day:** Tom W. Jackson, "The Periscope," *Boston Standard Union*, 2/11/24, p. 10.

74 **carnival of crime:** "57 Crimes of Violence and Theft . . ." *Brooklyn Eagle,* 2/17/24, n.p.

74 **skyscraper of felonies:** Nelson Harding, "Skyscrapers," cartoon, *Brooklyn Eagle,* 2/18/24, editorial page.

74 **to haul it away:** "6 Bandit Gangs in Boro Roundup Confess Crimes," *Brooklyn Eagle,* 2/18/24, pp. 1, 6.

75 **remember you now:** Ibid.

75 **fit for exhibition:** Ibid.

76 **his daily worries:** Ibid., p. 1.

76 **he was arrested:** "2 Girls Captured with 8 Suspects in Bandit Roundup," *Brooklyn Eagle,* 2/19/24, p. 1.

77 **summoned to headquarters:** Ibid.; "Woman Held as Possible Girl Bandit," *Brooklyn Citizen,* 2/19/24, p. 1; "Eighteen Bandit Suspects Held . . ." *Brooklyn Standard Union,* 2/19/24, p. 1.

77 **two months ago:** "Police Take Three as Hold-up Aids to Bob-Haired Girl," *New York Evening Post,* 2/18/24, n.p.

NOTES TO CHAPTER 9

81 *True Detective Mysteries:* George Spelvin, "The Mystery of the Bobbed-Haired Bandit," *True Detective Mysteries,* May 1924, pp. 58–60, 91.

81 **to do his bidding:** "Bobbed-Hair Girl Bandit Keeps the Town Guessing," *Brooklyn Standard Union,* 2/11/24, p. 3.

82 **submit to arrest:** Ibid.

82 **what she gets is HERS:** Mabel Abbot, "Is Dread Bob-Haired Bandit Female Dr. Jekyll–Mr. Hyde?" *New York World,* 4/13/24, pp. 1, 2, 5.

84 **a new dress:** Ibid.

84 **by night:** Captain Carey was quoted months earlier as stating that the Bobbed Haired Bandit was a "female Dr. Jekyll and Mr. Hyde who consorts with bandits at night and probably lives respectably during the daytime," in "Girl Bandit Gives Druggist Return Call," *Brooklyn Standard Union,* 2/7/24, p. 16.

84 **traditional subservience:** Abbot, "Is Dread Bob-Haired Bandit Female Dr. Jekyll–Mr. Hyde?" pp. 1, 2, 5.

85 **occasion required:** "Bobbed Haired Bandit May Be a Boy," *Brooklyn Eagle,* 2/3/24, p. 4a.

85 **weaker sex:** Ibid.

85 **unprintable and torrid:** Ibid.

85 **"coarse" and "ordinary":** "Bobbed-Hair Girl Bandit Keeps the Town Guessing," p. 3.

86 **to the Tombs:** "Denies Bob-Haired Charge," *New York Evening Post,* 3/1/24, p. 3; "Bobbed-Haired Man Dressed as Woman . . ." *Brooklyn Eagle,* 3/1/24, p. 2; "Bobbed Hair Bandit May Prove a Man," *New York American,* 3/1/24, p. 18.

86 *New York American:* "Bob Hair Hid Shaven Necks," *New York American,* 3/3/24, p. 13.

86 **favorite territory:** "Hold Two in Girls Dresses as Bandits," *New York Telegram and Evening Mail*, 3/2/24, pp. 1, 2.

87 **before his eyes:** "Two Bob-Haired Humorists Lose Skirts and Locks," *New York Tribune*, 3/2/24, p. 5.

87 **usual chauffeur type:** "Two Arrested as Bob-Haired Bandit," *New York Telegram and Evening Mail*, 3/2/24, p. 2.

87 **They're dicks:** "Bob Hair Hid Shaven Necks," p. 13.

88 **eleven o'clock at night:** Ibid.

88 **Leo Weinstein:** "Two Arrested as Bob-Haired Bandit," p. 2.

89 **to jail:** "Hold Two in Girls' Dresses as Bandits,"p. 1.

89 **lost sight of:** "Two Arrested as Bob-Haired Bandit," p. 2.

90 **carnival of crime:** "Citizens Demand More Police as Banditry Grows," *Brooklyn Eagle*, 3/3/24, p. 3.

90 **"Palais Royal" costume:** "Two Arrested as Bob-Haired Bandit," p. 2.

90 **feminine disguise:** "Bob-Haired Boys Deluged with Love Notes, Police Find," *Brooklyn Eagle*, 3/6/24, p. 14.

91 **suspended sentence:** "Man, Disguised as Woman, Fools Cops until Hat Falls Off; Then Arrest Follows," *Brooklyn Eagle*, 3/6/24, p. L1.

93 **purchase the beverage:** "Three "Cake Eaters" Sought in Holdup," *Brooklyn Standard Union*, 1/12/24, p. 1.

93 **jazz orchestra:** Ibid., last page.

94 **Whisks Pair Away:** "Brooklyn's Fair Gunmiss Merrily Pursues Career," *New York Daily News*, 1/23/24, p. 3; "Bobbed Hair Girl Holds up Grocer," *New York Herald*, 1/23/24, p. 2.

94 **pretty and intelligent:** "Bobbed Hair Girl Holds up Grocer," p. 2.

94 **well dressed:** "Girl Bandit and Aide Strike Again . . ." *Brooklyn Citizen*, 1/23/24, p. 2.

94 **leave the place:** "Bobbed-Hair Girl Bandit Keeps the Town Guessing," p. 3.

94 **kicked him vigorously:** "New York Gun Girl Stages a Hold-Up," *New York Times*, 2/25/24, p. 1.

95 **she had vanished:** Ibid.

95 **Amazonian world:** "This Amazonian World," *New York Telegram and Evening Mail*, 2/26/24, p. 10.

95 **hold-up yarn:** "Invented Park Girl Bandit, *New York Times*, 2/26/24, p. 5.

96 **World War:** Marjorie Dorman, "The Bobbed-Hair Bandit Is a Revolt," Sunday *Eagle* Magazine, 3/16/24, p. 5.

96 **back to the corset:** Ibid.

NOTES TO CHAPTER 10

96 *New York Daily News:* Bill B., "Voice of the People," *New York Daily News*, 4/5/23, p. 13.

97 **business-like fashion:** "Bobbed Haired Girl Bandit Emerges, Gets $60,

Vanishes," *Brooklyn Standard Union*, 2/24/24, p. 1. Note: Her "familiar turban" was, in fact, pink. The black fur hat was a new addition.

97 **through the pocket:** "2-Gun, Bob-Haired Bandit Holds up 6 in Boro Store," *Brooklyn Eagle*, 2/24/24, p. 1.

98 **her small hands:** "Seven Held up by Girl Bandit," *New York Telegram and Evening Mail*, 2/24/24, p. 1; "Girl Bandit Comes back after Rest," *Brooklyn Citizen*, 2/24/24, p. 1.

98 **had escaped:** "2-Gun, Bob-Haired Bandit Holds up 6 in Boro Store," p. 1.

98 **'Two-Gun' Woman:** "Girl Bandit Comes back after Rest," p. 1.

98 **used a horse:** "Bobbed Hair Girl Bandit Keeps the Town Guessing," *Brooklyn Standard Union*, 2/11/24, p. 3.

98 **woman's clothing:** "Seven Held up by Girl Bandit," p. 1; "2-Gun, Bob-Haired Bandit Holds up 6 in Boro Store," p. 1.

99 **Poplar Street:** Tom W. Jackson, "The Periscope," *Brooklyn Standard Union*, 2/28/24, p. 10.

99 **important at all:** "150 Brooklyn Detectives Meet behind Closed Doors," *New York American*, 2/27/24, p. 6.

100 **cause of the meeting:** "Bob-Haired Bandit Invites a Shooting," *New York Evening Post*, 2/27/24, p. 2.

100 **"bobbed-hair" squad:** "Detectives Here Organized 'Bobbed Hair Bandit Squad,'" *Brooklyn Standard Union*, 2/28/24, p. 1.

100 **the gungirl's holdups:** List of Bob Squad detectives from William Casey and Allan Van Hoesen, "How We Caught the Bobbed-Haired Bandit," *True Detective Mysteries*, July 1924, pp. 17–24.

100 **all the robberies:** "Detectives Here Organized 'Bobbed Hair Bandit Squad,'" p. 1.

100 **the *Tribune* noted:** "Good Looks and Bobbed Hair Unlucky Charms in Brooklyn," *New York Tribune*, 3/8/24, p. 6.

100 **proved futile:** "Detectives Here Organized 'Bobbed Hair Bandit Squad,'" p. 1.

102 ***New York Evening Post:*** "1500 More Police Wanted by Enright," *New York Evening Post*, 3/1/24, p. 4.

102 **must go forward:** Ibid.

102 **Tammany Hall:** Ibid.

103 **field of battle:** Ibid.

103 **maze of streets:** Ibid.

103 **associates and dupes:** Ibid.

103 **wealth and property:** Ibid.

103 **dangers of a pestilence:** Ibid.

104 **the city ever had:** "Al, the Supersmith, Peeks into the Future," *New York Times*, 3/4/24, p. 19.

104 **returns to his desk:** "Mayor to Return Quietly," *New York Telegram and Evening Mail*, 3/1/24, n.p.

104 **back in the harness:** "Hylan, Brisk and Fit after Long Illness, Back Ready to Work," *New York Times*, 3/5/24, p. 1.

104 *New York Evening Post:* "Two Bullets Miss Bob-Haired Bandit," *New York Evening Post*, 3/5/24, p. 3.

104 **Louis Pfeiffer:** "Bobbed-Hair Bandit and Male Companion Targets for Victim," *Brooklyn Standard Union*, 3/5/24, p. 1.

104 **March 5th:** "Two Bullets Miss Bob-Haired Bandit," p. 3.

105 **in his stomach:** "Bob-Hair Bandit Gets $1485," *New York Telegram and Evening Mail*, 3/5/24, p. 2.

105 **into a pistol barrel:** "Two Bullets Miss Bob-Haired Bandit," p. 3.

105 **three or four scratches:** "Girl Bandit and Aide in New Holdup," *Brooklyn Citizen*, 3/5/24, p. 1.

105 **was waiting:** "Bobbed Bandit Takes $2000 from an Armed Man," *Brooklyn Eagle*, 3/5/24, p. 1.

105 **"Dick, pick me up!":** "Two Bullets Miss Bob-Haired Bandit," p. 3.

105 **return the fire:** "Bobbed-Hair Bandit and Male Companion Targets for Victim," p. 1.

105 **of the bandits:** "Two Bullets Miss Bob-Haired Bandit," p. 3.

105 **short distance away:** "Bob-Hair Bandit Gets $1485," p. 2.

105 **she has terroized:** Ibid.

106 **but failed:** "Bobbed Bandit Takes $2000 from an Armed Man," p. 1; "Two Bullets Miss Bob-Haired Bandit," p. 3; "Girl Bandit and Aide in New Holdup," p. 1.

106 **don't know anything:** "Blonde Bandit Enters Replaces Noted Sister," *Brooklyn Standard Union*, 3/6/24, last page.

106 **progress and righteousness:** "Hylan, Back in Harness after Six Months . . ." *Brooklyn Standard Union*, 3/5/24, p. 1.

107 **bandit on sight:** "Bobbed Bandit Robs while Police Hunt," *New York American*, 3/6/24, p. 1.

107 **"some stunt":** "Bobbed-Hair Bandit's Own Story," VIII, *New York American*, 5/6/24, p. 3.

107 *New York American:* "Bobbed-Hair Bandit's Own Story," VIII, *New York American*, 5/6/24, p. 3.

107 **"Stick 'em up":** Ibid.

108 **sweet joke:** Ibid.

108 **looked empty:** "Gun Girl Robs Store as 250 Police Hunt Her," *New York Tribune*, 3/6/24, p. 1.

108 **Celia recalled:** "Bobbed-Hair Bandit's Own Story," VIII, p. 3.

108 **immediate neighborhood:** "Bobbed Bandit Robs while Police Hunt," *New York American*, 3/6/24, p. 1.

109 **in my right:** "Bobbed-Hair Bandit's Own Story," VIII, p. 3.

110 shaking and crying: Ibid.

110 little social party: Ibid.

110 cautioned her charges: "Gun Girl Robs Store as 250 Police Hunt Her," p. 1.

110 with a gun: "Comb City for Bold Girl Bandit after Most Daring Raid," *Brooklyn Eagle*, 3/6/24, p. 3.

110 said Celia: "Bobbed-Hair Bandit's Own Story," VIII, p. 3.

111 women that night: Ibid.

111 remained silent: "Bobbed Bandit Holds up 6 More," *New York Telegram and Evening Mail*, 3/6/24, pp. 2, 6.

111 drawers of the safe: "Blonde Bandit Enters Replaces Noted Sister," p. 1.

111 for the Cooneys: "Comb City for Bold Girl Bandit after Most Daring Raid," p. 3.

111 Jefferson avenue: "Girl Bandit and Pal Stage New Holdup," *Brooklyn Citizen*, 3/6/24, p. 3.

112 except ours: "Bobbed-Hair Bandit's Own Story," VIII, , p. 3.

112 in the neighborhood: "Comb City for Bold Girl Bandit after Most Daring Raid," p. 3.

112 notorious couple: Bobbed Bandit Robs while Police Hunt," p. 1.

112 walked home safe: "Bobbed-Hair Bandit's Own Story," VIII, p. 3.

112 PURGED OF DISHONESTY: Front page headline, *New York Tribune*, 3/6/24.

112 dead or alive: "Bobbed Bandit Holds up 6 More," pp. 2, 6.

112 was back: "Gun Girl Robs Store as 250 Police Hunt Her," p. 1.

112 of her career: "Comb City for Bold Girl Bandit after Most Daring Raid," p. 3.

112 bold bobbed one: Ibid.

113 left the store: "Bobbed Bandit Holds up 6 More," pp. 2, 6.

113 "leisurely departed": "Bobbed Bandit Robs while Police Hunt," p. 1.

113 three-quarter length: "Blond Bandit Now Joins Noted Sister," *Brooklyn Standard Union*, 3/6/24, p. 18.

113 blue tam o' shanter: "Bobbed Bandit Holds up 6 More," pp. 2, 6.

113 cute little blonde: "Bobbed-Hair Bandit's Own Story," VIII, p. 3.

114 "high pitched" and "excited": "Gang of Bobbed-Haired Bandits Here, 2-Gun Blonde Cultured, Brunette Nervy," *Brooklyn Eagle* 3/7/24, p. 3.

114 might be the reason: Ibid.

115 "Hold up your hands.": "Girl Bandit Ubiquitous," *Brooklyn Citizen*, 3/8/24, p. 4.

115 Bobbed Haired Bandit: F. Scott Fitzgerald, "Echoes of the Jazz Age," 1931, in *The Crack-Up*, Edmund Wilson, ed. (New York: New Directions, 1993), p. 21 We found no newspaper reports confirming Fitzgerald's claims. However, if Zelda was merely pulled over and not arrested as Fitzgerald remembered seven years later, this event could well have gone unnoticed. Given their relations with the press at this time, the police would certainly not publicize such a high-profile mistake.

115 under her coat: "Beware the Bobs," *New York Daily News*, 3/8/24, p. 11.

116 **in her lair:** Albert F. Mullady, "That Bobbed-Haired Bandit," *Brooklyn Eagle*, 3/6/24, p. A4.

116 **blue uniform:** "Police Told to Get Bob-Haired Girl," *New York Times*, 3/9/24, p. 16.

118 **and Her Accomplices:** Ibid.

NOTES TO CHAPTER 12

119 *Brooklyn Eagle:* "A Word for the Yegg," *Brooklyn Eagle*, 4/3/24, p. 6.

119 **Bobbed-Haired Bandit:** "Bobbed-Hair Bandit's Own Story," IX, *New York American*, 5/7/24, p. 7.

120 **Sing Sing:** "28 Gunmen to Face Long Prison Terms in County Court," *Brooklyn Eagle*, 3/9/24, p. 24A.

120 **bobbed-haired banditry:** "Bobbed-Haired Bandit and Male Companion Targets for Victim," *Brooklyn Standard Union*, 3/5/24, p. 1.

120 **drawing power:** "Bobbed Hair Bandit Invades Manhattan, Holding up Store," *New York World*, 3/20/24, p. 1; "Bobbed-Hair Girl Indicted as Bandit," *New York Evening Post*, 3/28/24, p. 2.

121 **MOTORCAR WRECKED:** "Bullets Fly after Bobbed Haired Girls; Motorcar Wrecked," *Brooklyn Eagle*, 3/24/24, p. 1.

121 **early today:** "Own Car Wrecked, Bob-Haired Girl's Pals Steal Taxi," *Brooklyn Eagle*, 3/31/24, p. 3.

121 **Brooklyn police:** "Bob-Haired Bandit Steals a Taxi Cab," *New York Telegram and Evening Mail*, 3/31/24, p. 3.

122 **with the roads:** " "Bobbed Hair" Girl out of Luck on Long Island," *Brooklyn Eagle*, 3/8/24, p. 2.

122 **'bobbed-haired bandit':** "Girl Bandit Victims Go to Manhattan for Look at New Suspect," *Brooklyn Citizen*, 3/21/24, p. 1.

122 **under his overcoat:** "Bob-Haired Blonde Is Seized in Store When 2 Men Rob It," *New York World*, 3/21/24, p. 1.

122 **knocking the bolt over:** "Girl Bandit Victims Go to Manhattan for Look at New Suspect," p. 1.

123 **blocked traffic:** "Bob-Haired Blonde Is Seized in Store When 2 Men Rob It," p. 1.

124 **through curiosity:** "Girl Bandit Victims Go to Manhattan for Look at New Suspect," p. 1.

124 **sober up:** "Girls Would Love to See Real Bandit but a Woozy Woman Hater Is Enough," *New York American*, 3/2/24, p. 1.

125 **"all the time worried":** "Bobbed-Hair Bandit's Own Story," IX, p. 7.

125 **head off a horse:** Ibid.

125 **she recalled:** "Bobbed-Hair Bandit's Own Story," VIII, *New York American*, 5/6/24, p. 3.

125 **out West:** "Bobbed-Hair Bandit's Own Story," IX, p. 7.

126 **Celia was game:** Ibid.

129 *Brooklyn Standard Union:* Tom W. Jackson, "The Periscope," *Brooklyn Standard Union*, 1/19/24, p. 6.

129 **"all planned out":** "Bobbed-Hair Bandit's Own Story," IX, *New York American*, 5/7/24, p. 7.

129 **ready cash:** "Baby Causes Capture of Bobbed Bandit and Pal," *Brooklyn Eagle*, 4/21/24, pp. 1, 2.

129 **vindicate ourselves:** "Bobbed Bandit, Due Today . . ." *New York Times*, 4/22/24, pp. 1, 4. Note: The *Times* reported that this conversation happened *after* the Biscuit robbery. Since all other reports agree that Celia and Ed went directly to the steamship from the robbery, we think that this conversation happened before the robbery. The reporter may have been mistaken, or perhaps Mrs. Cooney wanted to mislead the press and police.

131 **with a chauffeur:** "Bobbed-Hair Bandit's Own Story," IX, p. 7.

132 **pulled harder:** Ibid. While it is very likely that Celia did practice tying Ed up in their hotel room, the faint whiff of S&M bondage that permeates the scene might be the ghostwriter, William Seabrook's touch. In his autobiography, *No Hiding Place*, Seabrook extensively details his fetish, recalling a fantasy in which his Grandmother Pliny led him to the woods one summer dawn. There:

> A red velvet carpet stretched toward a great chair or throne on which a girl sat robed in green with red-gold braided hair and feet in golden clogs. Her high golden heels were resting on a leather foot-stool, her ankles bound by shining metal circlets joined by a gleaming metal chain. She smiled and raised her hand to bid us welcome. Encircling and joining her wrists were other bright glittering chains which tinkled like soft bells.
>
> Pliny let go of my hand and I went forward alone to sit by the leather foot-stool and put my arms around the lady's knees. She pressed my head against her knees and stroked my hair. She led my hands down the soft silk folds to her chained feet and pressed them tightly there until my own hand held and drew the chains tighter.
>
> I was trembling with happiness. I clung to her feet, looked up into her green golden eyes and pressed my face against her wrists, which were lifted and outstretched as if in benediction. As she moved here hands to and fro, stroking my hair, the chains were sweet bells ringing.
>
> This vision was my deepest dream come true; was the key to my locked need; was my supremest want fulfilled. For — long before it came, indeed from the beginning in my up-to-then forever — any thought, sight, picture, image, story, tale, or mere suggestion of girl in chains, or with bound hands, had been more desirable than any other image — whether in the objective world of picture books, magazines, statuettes and stories, or in the subjective world of my own childish fantasy. (William B

Seabrook. *No Hiding Place* [New York: J. B. Lippincott, 1942], pp. 24–26)

132 **fur and turban:** There's some disagreement over the color of Ed's hat. The *Brooklyn Standard Union* reports it as brown ("Girl Bandit Shoots Victim of Holdup; Police Get Auto," *Brooklyn Standard Union*, 4/1/24, p. 1); however, the APB that went out later, based on witnesses' descriptions, said Ed's hat was pearl gray.

134 **if they knew:** "Bobbed-Hair Bandit's Own Story," IX, p. 7.

134 **see the manager:** "Gunmiss, Roused, Shoots Man," *New York Daily News*, 4/2/24, p. 3.

134 **Celia's gun:** "Bobbed-Hair Bandit's Own Story," IX, p. 7.

134 **"pistols crossed, cowboy style":** "Girl Bandit Shoots Man and Vanishes; Abducts Chauffer," *New York Evening Post*, 4/1/24, p. 1.

134 **completed the picture:** "Bobbed Bandit and Pal Shoot Cashier, Escape," *New York Herald-Tribune*, 4/2/24, n.p.

136 **still as death:** "Bobbed-Hair Bandit's Own Story," X, *New York American*, 5/8/24, p. 9.

136 **said Ed:** Ibid.

NOTES TO CHAPTER 14

136 *New York Evening Post:* "Girl Bandit Shoots Man and Vanishes," *New York Evening Post*, 4/1/24, p. 1.

136 **both of us:** "Bobbed-Hair Bandit's Own Story," X, *New York American*, 5/8/24, p. 9.

137 **beat it quick:** "Bobbed-Hair Bandit, Home, Unrepentant," *New York Herald-Tribune*, 4/23/24, p. 9.

137 **Celia recalled:** "Bobbed-Hair Bandit's Own Story," X, p. 9.

137 **Eddie asked calmly:** "What the World Didn't Know," *Modern Romances*, April 1940, p. 104.

137 **still running:** "Gunmiss, Roused, Shoots Man," *New York Daily News*, 4/2/24, p. 3.

137 **Atlantic Avenue:** "Bob-Haired Bandit Shoots Cashier," *Brooklyn Eagle*, 4/1/24, p. 1.

137 **shots they heard:** "Girl Bandit Shoots Victim," *Brooklyn Standard Union*, 4/1/24, pp. 1, 6.

137 **"a maze of traffic":** "Bob-Haired Bandit Shoots Cashier," p. 1.

137 **Pacific Street:** Ibid.

138 **on the floor:** "Bobbed Bandit and Pal Shoot Cashier," *New York Herald-Tribune*, 4/1/24, n.p.; "Bobbed Haired Girl Flees," *Brooklyn Citizen*, 4/1/24, p. 1.

138 **would have been another:** "Bobbed-Hair Bandit's Own Story," X, p. 9. It's hard to determine the significance of this lost notebook. Celia says,

cryptically, that it contained "our addresses." The *New York Telegram and Evening Mail* claims that Celia told Assistant District Attorney Hughes:

> When we abandoned the automobile we used that day . . . we purposely left behind a memorandum book, in which had been written the names of a number of stores, to give the police the impression that we were planning to rob these, when as a matter of fact we had made up our minds to quit Brooklyn that day and did so. We did not want the police to think we had left and we thought by leaving the memo book it might throw them off the scent. ("Bobbed Bandit Pleads Guilty," *New York Telegram and Evening Mail*, 4/23/24, p. 2)

The *New York American* reported that the paper contained "ten addresses, mostly of second class hotels and rooming houses. The police found that couples resembling the Cooneys had lived at all of them under various names." ("Bride Is Hunted as Bandit," *New York American*, 4/16/24, p. 5)

The only official mention of the dropped book is in the police commissioner's *Annual Report* for 1924 when the address book is mentioned as one of the pieces of writing matched up to conclude that Ed and Celia Cooney are the Bobbed Haired Bandit and her partner.

If the *Telegram* is correct, then Celia and Ed were having just a bit more fun with the cops, trying to throw them off the scent as they had with their notes and their Mr. and Mrs. Parker of Boston "clew." If the *American* is right, then it gives credence to Detective Casey's later claim that he tracked the Cooneys to Massachusetts — how else would he have located them in Fall River? Or perhaps they were just a list of addresses of New York City hotels that Celia and Ed had looked into before settling on the Claman in Times Square. The mystery remains unsolved.

138 **Ed was right:** "What the World Didn't Know," *Modern Romances*, May 1940, p. 35.

138 **for questioning:** "Bobbed Haired Girl Flees," *Brooklyn Citizen*, 4/1/24, p. 1.

138 **West Forty-third Street:** "Girl Bandit Shoots Victim," pp. 1, 6.

139 **National Biscuit plant:** "Cashier Shot by Bob-Haired Girl Bandit," *New York Telegram and Evening Mail*, 4/1/24, p. 2

139 **two shots:** "Girl Bandit Shoots Victim," pp. 1, 6.

139 **"take a nap":** "Girl Bandit Shoots Man and Vanishes," *New York Evening Post*, 4/1/24, pp. 1, 20.

139 **elevated train:** "Girl Bandit Shoots Victim," pp. 1, 6.

139 **stations on the line:** Ibid.

139 **Borough Hall:** "Cashier Shot by Bob-Haired Girl Bandit," p. 2.

139 **trail ended:** "Gunmiss, Roused, Shoots Man," p. 3.

140 **each holdup:** "Detectives Make Fruitless Search," *Brooklyn Standard Union*, 4/2/24, pp. 1, 18.

140 **put the money in:** "Bobbed-Hair Bandit's Own Story," X, n.p.

140 **biscuit office:** "Bobbed Bandit and Pal Shoot Cashier," n.p.

140 **hard manual labor:** "Detectives Make Fruitless Search," pp. 1, 18.

140 **told the reporter:** "Bob Haired Girl and Pal Change Clothes," *Brooklyn Daily Times,* 4/2/24, p. 1.

140 **stenographer's position:** "Bobbed Bandit and Pal Shoot Cashier," n.p.

141 **GIRL BANDIT HUNT:** "Police Using Radio in Girl Bandit Hunt," *New York Evening Post,* 4/2/24, n.p.

141 **failed to materialize:** "Detectives Make Fruitless Search," *Brooklyn Standard Union,* 4/2/24, pp. 1, 18.

141 **arrayed before them:** Ibid.

141 **attempt yesterday:** "Police Are Baffled by Bob-Haired Bandit," *New York Evening Post,* 4/2/24, p. 3

141 **another hold up:** "Police Using Radio in Girl Bandit Hunt," n.p.

142 **for murder!:** "Bobbed-Hair Bandit's Own Story," X, n.p.

142 **a different spelling):** The *Daily News* and the *Times* spelled his name Mazo; the *Brooklyn Eagle,* Maeze; the *American,* Mazio or Mazzo; the *Brooklyn Standard Union,* Maezo or Mazo; and most other papers spelled it Maizo. The official indictments of Celia and Ed called "Nathan Mazo" as a witness, so we have decided to stick with the spelling "Mazo."

142 **"little hope for . . . recovery":** "Bobbed Haired Girl Flees," *Brooklyn Citizen,* 4/1/24, p. 1.

142 **may cause his death:** "Gunmiss, Roused, Shoots Man," p. 3.

142 **dangerous:** "Girl Bandit Shoots Man and Vanishes," p. 1.

142 **"reported to be dying":** "Cashier Shot by Bob-Haired Girl Bandit," *New York Telegram and Evening Mail,* 4/1/24, pp. 1, 2.

142 **"superficial":** "Bob-Haired Bandit Shoots Cashier," *Brooklyn Eagle,* 4/1/24, p. 1.

142 **may set in:** "Detectives Make Fruitless Search," pp. 1, 18.

142 **going to shoot her:** "Victim Threatens to Kill Girl Bandit — Next Time," *Brooklyn Standard Union,* 4/3/24, p. 1.

143 **who had shot him:** "Bob-Haired Bandit Shoots Cashier Who Rips Her Veil in Holdup of Boro Factory," *Brooklyn Eagle,* 4/1/24, p. 1.

143 **to the floor:** "Gunmiss, Roused, Shoots Man," p. 3.

143 **first time:** Ibid.

143 **"Jessica James":** "Victim Threatens to Kill Girl Bandit — Next Time," p. 1.

143 **yet put over:** "Cashier Shot by Bob-Haired Girl Bandit," pp. 1, 2.

143 **the entire time:** "Bobbed-Hair Bandit's Own Story," X, p. 9.

143 **in the laundry:** Ibid.

143 **stay anyway:** "New York's Bobbed Haired Bandit and Accomplice Taken," *Florida Times-Union* 4/21/24, p. 1.

144 **around a garage:** "Bobbed-Hair Bandit's Own Story," X, p. 9.

144 **there it all was:** Ibid.

144 **"lived quietly":** "Bob-Haired Bandit Says Husband Tried Suicide," *Brooklyn Daily Times,* 4/21/24, pp. 1, 2.

NOTES TO CHAPTER 15

144 *True Detective Mysteries:* Detective William J Casey, as told to Allan Van Hoesen, "How We Caught the Bobbed Haired Bandit, *True Detective Mysteries*, Vol. 1, no. 4, July 1924, pp. 17–24.

145 thirty-dollar-a-week salary: Ibid.

145 Detective Casey: Ibid.

146 had been suspended: Ibid.

146 nearby garage: James M. Wood, "Crime Impulse in Celia Cooney," *Brooklyn Eagle*, 4/21/24, p. 10.

146 in the vicinity: "Girl Bandit Believed Known; Wed and Lived Near Police;" *Brooklyn Standard Union*, 4/15/24, p. 4.

146 29th of March: "Bobbed Bandit and Pal Shoot Cashier," *New York Herald-Tribune*, 4/2/24, n.p.

146 with child: "Think Mrs. Cooney Is Both Brunette and Blond," *New York World*, 4/17/24, p. 1.

147 all had padlocks: "Bobbed Hair Bandit's Mate Located by Police," *Brooklyn Daily Times*, 4/17/24, p. 13.

147 to do with motorcars: "Bobbed Bandit and Mate Near Capture," *Brooklyn Eagle*, 4/17/24, p. 10.

147 1099 Pacific: "Cooney Girl Sought as Bobbed Bandit Caught in Florida," *New York Times*, 4/21/24, p. 1.

147 Times Square: "Bobbed Bandit and Mate Near Capture," p. 10.

147 Hotel Claman: "Bobbed Hair Bandit's Mate Located by Police," p. 13.

147 They all matched: *Annual Report of the Police Department, City of New York*, 1924, n.p.

147 Cooney broadcast: Casey, "How We Caught the Bobbed Haired Bandit," pp. 17–24.

147 throughout the country: "Cooney Is the Name of Bobbed Bandit," *New York Telegram and Evening Mail*, 4/15/24, p. 3.

147 "telephone, telegraph and letter": "Girl Bandit's Name Is Given out by Police," *Brooklyn Citizen*, 4/15/24, p. 1.

147 public buildings: "Cooney Is the Name of Bobbed Bandit," p. 3.

148 gray veil: Ibid.

148 in their possession: Ibid.

148 couple's portrait: "Mystery of the Girl Bandit Solved," *New York World*, 4/16/24, pp. 1, 8.

148 *Standard Union:* "Think Girl Bandit Will Put up Fight," *Brooklyn Standard Union*, 4/16/24, p. 2.

148 came out yesterday: "Stork Hovers, Net Tightening about Gunmiss," *New York Daily News*, 4/16/24, p. 2.

149 cake-eater companion: "Cooney Is the Name of Bobbed Bandit," p. 3.

149 defray the expense: Ibid.

149 'in a good cause': Ibid.

149 **lost his job:** "Bride Hunted as Bob Bandit," *New York American*, 4/16/24, p. 5.

149 **furniture was removed:** "Bob Hair Bandit Mrs. Cooney," *New York Sun*, 4/15/24, n.p.

149 **resorted to banditry:** "Girl Bandit's Name Is Given out by Police," p. 1.

149 **shoot to kill:** Ibid.; the shoot to kill order was reported in "'Forget Sex — Shoot!' Order in New War on Girl Bandit," *Brooklyn Eagle*, 2/10/24, p. A19.

149 **police record:** "Bride Hunted as Bob Bandit," *New York American*, 4/16/24, p. 5. Ed's police record was reported by the 17th of April, but without commentary.

150 **NEAR POLICE:** "Girl Bandit Believed Known . . . ," *Brooklyn Standard Union*, 4/15/24, p. 1.

150 **blatant luxury:** "Girl's Excuse, I Had to Rob," *New York American*, 4/16/24, p. 5.

151 **Fifth avenue on that:** Ibid.

151 **rugs and tapestries:** "Think Mrs. Cooney Is Both Brunette and Blond Bandit," pp. 1, 3.

151 **when they returned:** James M. Wood, "Crime Impulse in Celia Cooney," *Brooklyn Eagle*, 4/21/24, p. 10.

152 **a she devil:** "Bobbed Bandit 'Hard Boiled,' Former Landladies Say," *Brooklyn Eagle*, 4/22/24, pp. 1, 3.

152 **she struck me:** "Bobbed Bandit, Due Here Today, Admits Career of Robbery," *New York Times*, 4/22/24, pp. 1, 4.

152 **you need in life:** Wood, "Crime Impulse in Celia Cooney," p. 10.

152 **life of crime:** "Stork Hovers, Net Tightening about Gunmiss," p. 2.

154 **"unusually attractive":** "Bride Hunted as Bob Bandit," p. 5.

154 **to look at—twice:** "Bobbed Bandit and Mate Near Capture," p. 10.

154 **other times black:** "Think Mrs. Cooney Is Both Brunette and Blond Bandit," pp. 1, 3.

154 **her black locks:** Ibid.

154 **Jack," he said:** "Mystery of Girl Bandit Solved," *New York World*, 4/16/24, pp. 1, 8.

154 **You'll get hurt.:** "Bobbed Bandit and Mate Near Capture," p. 10.

154 **bring results:** Ibid.

155 **Bobbed Hair Bandit:** "Coughlin Credits the World," *New York World*, 4/22/24, p. 1.

155 **right cheek:** "Red Rash on Face . . ." *New York World*, 4/18/24, p. 28.

155 **as cooks:** "Bobbed Bandit aboard Rum Ship," *Brooklyn Daily Times*, 5/20/4, n.p.

155 **from a bootlegger:** Ibid.

156 **NEAR CAPTURE:** "Bride Hunted as Bob Bandit," p. 5; "Bobbed Bandit and Mate Near Capture," p. 10.

NOTES TO CHAPTER 16

156 *New York American:* "Bobbed-Hair Bandit's Own Story," X, *New York American*, 5/8/24, p. 9.

156 **any time soon:** "Think Mrs. Cooney Is Both Brunette and Blond Bandit," *New York World*, 4/17/24, pp. 1, 3.

156 **far away:** "Bob Hair Bandit Mrs. Cooney," *New York Sun*, 4/15/24, n.p.

157 **Ed's location:** Detective William J. Casey, as told to Allan Van Hoesen, "How We Caught the Bobbed Haired Bandit," *True Detective Mysteries*, July 1924, pp. 17–24.

In this account Casey claims that the Parkers/Cooneys were in Massachusetts *before* the Nabisco robbery. We believe this is a mistake either Casey or Van Hoesen made in the chronology of events. *True Detective* is not the "paper of record," and Casey's account is full of other inconsistencies. In addition, no other newspaper or official accounts mention either the police sojourn to Massachusetts or report that the Cooneys were out of state before their last robbery.

But what if that is what happened?

However unlikely, there is another theory that explains the trail of the Parkers to Massachusetts, one that fits with this early date (it also dovetails with one of the theories about the lost address book).

Perhaps Celia and Ed, knowing that every cop and every storeowner in New York City was on the lookout for the Bobbed Hair Bandit, beat it up to the Boston area to pull off a couple of quick holdups to raise money for the hotel and taxi fare necessary for the Biscuit job and the steamship tickets for the escape down to Jacksonville. If she did not wear her sealskin coat and signature bobbed hair tucked under her turban, Celia could have held up all the groceries and drugstores she desired in Massachusetts. Without these tell-tale signs, and in a different context, there would be little to connect stickups around Boston with New York's famous Bobbed Hair Bandit. Or, because Celia was far into her pregnancy at that point, perhaps Ed did the jobs himself. Again, a lone gunman sticking up stores in 1924 was not a newsworthy event. If this happened, then it makes sense that this little trip was left out of Celia's memoirs. The last thing that Celia would have wanted to admit while writing from a jail cell before sentencing was that she and Ed had committed robberies that would bring them new charges in another state. Another true detective mystery.

157 **mental force:** "Crime Impulse in Celia Cooney . . . ," *Brooklyn Eagle*, 4/20/24, p. 10.

157 **simply a tool:** Ibid.

158 **precede motherhood:** Ibid.

158 **ever lived in:** Ibid.

158 **is a fool:** Ibid.

159 **a new life:** Ibid.

159 **rather have died:** Ibid.

159 **take me away:** Ibid.

160 **on its way:** "What the World Didn't Know," *Modern Romances,* May 1940, p. 37.

160 **talcum powder:** "Bobbed-Hair Bandit's Own Story," X, p. 9.

160 **did not improve:** Ibid.

160 **mother's milk:** "What the World Didn't Know," p. 37.

160 **have a chance:** "Bobbed-Hair Bandit's Own Story," X, p. 9.

160 **daughter died:** There's a fair amount of confusion as to exactly when the baby was born and died, but the most common dates are April 10th or the early morning of the 11th for the baby's birth and the 12th for her death. See "Bobbed Hair Bandit Captured with Husband after Child Dies," *Brooklyn Standard Union,* 4/21/24, p. 1; "Newborn Child Dead, Girl and Husband Give up to Police," *Brooklyn Citizen,* 4/21/24, n.p.; and the paper closest to the source: "New York's Bobbed Haired Bandit and Accomplice Taken, " *Florida Times-Union,* 4/21/24, p. 1.

160 **later reasoned:** "Bobbed-Hair Bandit's Own Story," X, p. 9.

160 **Ocean Avenue:** "Bobbed Bandit on Way Back; Trapped by Baby's Death," *New York Telegram and Evening Mail,* 4/21/24, p. 3.

160 **and the undertaker:** "Bobbed-Hair Bandit's Own Story," X, p. 9.

160 **first train South:** Casey, "How We Caught the Bobbed Haired Bandit," pp. 17–24.

161 **outguessed them:** "Girl Bandit Takes All Blame, Says She Influenced Husband," *New York Sun,* 4/21/24, n.p.

161 **from New York:** "Bobbed Hair Bandit Captured with Husband after Child Dies," p. 1; "Bobbed Bandit, Due Today," *New York Times,* 4/22/24, pp. 1, 4.

161 **arrived in Florida:** "New York's Bobbed Haired Bandit and Accomplice Taken," pp. 1, 7. Only one New York paper, the *World,* backed up Casey's accounting of events — and then only in a vague and contradictory way, mentioning that the Jacksonville police wired up, and then later in the paragraph stating that the NYPD had intercepted Ed's letter. "Bobbed Bandit Confesses," *New York World,* 4/22/24, pp. 1, 2.

162 **Frank Gray:** "Girl Bandit Takes All Blame, Says She Influenced Husband," n.p. The 1923 arrest date is also supported by the official alienists' report on Ed. See John Meagher and Siegfried Black, *Commission Report on Edward Cooney,* May 5, 1924, New York Municipal Archives. The *New York World* and the *Brooklyn Daily Times* report Ed's previous arrest date as November 17th, 1922, a little more than a year earlier. This is doubtful, but even if they are correct, it does not change the fact that Casey would have known that Ed had a record.

162 *True Detective:* Casey, "How We Caught the Bobbed Haired Bandit," p. 17.

162 **enough to eat:** "Bobbed-Hair Bandit's Own Story," X, p. 9.

162 **were caught.):** "Police Arrest Brooklyn Girl Robber in South," *New York Sun,* 4/21/24, p. 1; "Bobbed Bandit, Due Today . . . ," pp. 1, 4; "Bobbed Bandit and Husband Confess Guilt," *New York Evening Post,* 4/21/24, n.p.

162 **a hundred dollars:** Celia remembers sending the letter before their baby was born, but most of the newspapers report that the letter was sent after she had died. The commissioner's *Annual Report* also states that the letter was intercepted the 19th of April, nine days after her baby was born. "Bobbed-Hair Bandit's Own Story," X, p. 9.

162 **hold their mail:** "Bobbed Hair Bandit Captured with Husband after Child Dies," p. 2.

162 **return address:** *Annual Report of the Police Department, City of New York,* 1924, report on the capture of the "'Bobbed-Hair' Bandit," n.p.; "watchful authorities" in "Baby Causes Capture of Bandit and Pal," *Brooklyn Eagle,* 4/21/24, pp. 1, 2.

163 **went to work:** Casey, "How We Caught the Bobbed Haired Bandit," pp. 17–24.

163 **trace the Cooneys:** "New York's Bobbed Haired Bandit and Accomplice Taken," *Florida Times-Union,* 4/21/24, pp. 1, 7.

163 **Monroe Street address:** Ibid.

163 **in their sights:** "Bob Haired Bandit Says Husband Tried Suicide as Sleuths Came," *Brooklyn Daily Times,* 4/21/24, p. 1.

NOTES TO CHAPTER 17

164 *New York Daily News:* "Mob Surges to Bobbed Bandit," *New York Daily News,* 4/23/24, p. 3.

164 **East Jacksonville:** "New Born Child Dead, Girl and Husband Give up to Police," *Brooklyn Citizen,* 4/21/24, p. 1.

164 **surrounded the place:** "Baby Causes Capture of Bobbed Bandit and Pal," *Brooklyn Eagle,* 4/21/24, p. 1.

164 **dog barked:** "Many Scan Train for Free Glimpse of Bobbed Bandit," *New York World,* 4/23/24, p. 6.

164 **name of the law:** Ibid.; William J. Casey, as told to Allen Van Hoesen, "How We Caught the Bobbed Haired Bandit," *True Detective,* July 1924, pp. 17–24; "Bobbed-Hair Bandit's Own Story," XI, *New York American,* 5/9/24, p. 9.

164 **behind the door:** "Bobbed-Hair Bandit's Own Story," XI, p. 9.

164 **Celia remembered:** Ibid.

164 **shuffling their feet:** "Many Scan Train for Free Glimpse of Bobbed Bandit," p. 6; "Bobbed-Hair Bandit's Own Story," XI, p. 9.

165 **going to do?:** "Baby Causes Capture of Bobbed Bandit and Pal," p. 1.

165 **before they break in:** "Bobbed-Hair Bandit's Own Story," XI, p. 9.

165 **we were through:** Ibid.

166 **either of us alive:** "Baby Causes Capture of Bobbed Bandit and Pal," p. 1.

166 **to be killed:** "Bobbed-Hair Bandit's Own Story," XI, p. 9.

166 **with a bang:** Casey, "How We Caught the Bobbed Haired Bandit," p. 18.

166 **would surrender:** "Bobbed Bandit and Husband Confess Guilt," *New York Evening Post*, 4/21/24, pp. 1, 5.

167 **he was through:** "Bobbed-Hair Bandit's Own Story," XI, p. 9.

167 **trouser pocket:** "Many Scan Train for Free Glimpse of Bobbed Bandit," p. 6.

167 **from the neighborhood:** Casey, "How We Caught the Bobbed Haired Bandit," p. 18.

167 **he muttered:** "Many Scan Train for Free Glimpse of Bobbed Bandit," p. 6.

167 **the baby died:** Casey, "How We Caught the Bobbed Haired Bandit," p. 18.

167 **in the extreme:** "Baby Causes Capture of Bobbed Bandit and Pal," p. 1.

168 **beaded bag:** Ibid.; "New York's Bobbed Haired Bandit and Accomplice Taken," *Florida Times-Union*, 4/21/24, pp. 1, 7.

168 **have hesitated:** "New York's Bobbed Haired Bandit and Accomplice Taken," pp. 1, 7.

168 **living up to it:** "What the World Didn't Know," *Modern Romances*, May 1940, p. 93.

168 **of telling you:** "Bobbed-Hair Bandit's Own Story," XI, p. 9.

168 **She's sick.:** Ibid.

169 **blame himself:** Ibid.

169 **series of confessions:** "Bobbed Gun Girl Back Today," *New York Daily News*, 4/22/24, p. 3.

170 **genuine footpad:** Ibid.

170 **stick it out:** "Girl Bandit Here; Spurns Legal Aid," *New York World*, 4/23/24, p. 6.

170 **Bobbed Haired Bandit:** "Baby Causes Capture of Bobbed Bandit and Pal," *Brooklyn Eagle*, 4/21/24, p. 1.

170 **Florida Times-Union:** "Men Who Trailed Cooneys," *Florida Times-Union*, 4/22/24, p. 22.

170 **of the confession:** "Bobbed Bandit and Husband Confess Guilt," *New York Evening Post*, 4/21/24, p. 1.

171 **BANDIT EPISODE:** "Brooklyn Police Now Believe It Is Their Turn to Snicker over Bob-Hair Bandit Episode," *Brooklyn Citizen*, 4/21/24, p. 2.

171 **front-page news:** "What the World Didn't Know," p. 95.

171 **New York papers:** "Bobbed Bandit on Way Back," *New York Telegram and Evening Mail*, 4/21/24, p. 3.

171 **page one:** *Washington Post*, 4/21/24, p. 1; *Chicago Tribune*, 4/21/24, p. 1; *San Francisco Chronicle*, 4/21/24, p. 1; *Los Angeles Times*, 4/21/24, p. 1.

171 **felt fine:** "Bobbed-Hair Bandit's Own Story," XI, p. 9.

171 **waived extradition:** "Newborn Child Dead," *Brooklyn Citizen*, 4/21/24, p. 1; "Bobbed Gun Girl Back Today," *New York Daily News*, 4/22/24, p. 3.

172 **loosen them for her:** "Bobbed-Hair Bandit's Own Story," XI, p. 9.

172 *Washington Post:* "Captured, Bobbed-Hair Bandit Still Smiles," *Washington Post*, 4/22/24, p. 3.

172 **"glum and nervous":** "Bobbed Bandit, Due Here Today," *New York Times*, 4/22/24, p. 1.

172 **reporters and people:** "Many Scan Train for Free Glimpse of Bobbed Bandit," p. 6; "Bobbed-Hair Bandit's Own Story," XI, p. 9.

172 **hands together:** "Bobbed-Hair Bandit's Own Story," XI, p. 9.

173 **across from them:** Ibid.; "Bandit Cool; Curls Hair on Train," *New York Evening Post*, 4/22/24, p. 17.

173 **particular interest:** "Bandit Cool; Curls Hair On Train," p. 17.

173 **Citizen's headline:** "Special Guard to Keep Girl Bandit's Husband from Taking His Life," *Brooklyn Citizen*, 4/22/24, p. 1.

173 **stared at:** "Many Scan Train for Free Glimpse of Bobbed Bandit," p. 6; Mary Mallon, "Missing the Circus Frets Bandit Celia," *New York Evening Post*, 4/23/24, pp. 1, 9.

173 **girl bandit:** "Girl Bandit Here; Wants No Lawyer; Crowds Greet Her," *New York World*, 4/23/24, p. 1.

174 **locking behind her:** "'Doesn't Pay,' Says Gun Girl," *New York American*, 4/23/24, p. 1.

174 **free hand at them:** Ibid.

174 **damn quick:** "Bobbed-Hair Bandit's Own Story," XI, p. 9.

174 **went on to comment:** "Ten Crimes in Brooklyn Admitted by Girl Bandit," *New York Daily News*, 4/23/24, p. 12.

175 **their stickups:** "Bobbed-Hair Bandit, Home, Unrepentant," *New York Herald-Tribune*, 4/23/24, p. 1.

175 **four inches on you:** Mallon, "Missing the Circus Frets Bandit Celia," pp. 1, 9.

176 **engagement ring:** Ibid.

176 **ankle strap shoes:** "Baby Causes Capture of Bobbed Bandit and Pal," *Brooklyn Eagle*, 4/21/24, p. 1; "Bobbed Bandit Confesses Shooting Clerk in Hold-Up," *New York World*, 4/22/24, p. 1.

176 **was first cut:** "Ten Crimes in Brooklyn Admitted by Girl Bandit," p. 12.

176 **an automatic in it:** "Girl Bandit Here; Wants No Lawyer; Crowds Greet Her," p. 1.

176 **really was bobbed:** "Police Arrest Brooklyn Girl Robber in South," *New York Sun*, 4/21/24, n.p.

177 **lining showing:** "Many Scan Train for Free Glimpse of Bobbed Bandit," p. 6.

177 **weary smile:** "Police Arrest Girl Robber in South," *New York Sun*, 4/21, n.p.

177 **the baby died:** Mallon, "Missing the Circus Frets Bandit Celia," pp. 1, 9. This report of Celia claiming that her baby had lived eight days is at odds with the other newspapers, which agreed that Katherine had lived only one or two days. See note 19 in the previous chapter.

178 **in a subhead:** "Bobbed Hair Bandit, Home, Unrepentant," pp. 1, 9. Interestingly enough, the other bobbed haired bandit article in the *Herald-Tribune*

that day, "Robbed to Get Home for Baby Girl, Bandit Says," as the title
suggests, was remarkably sympathetic to Celia.

178 **a big laugh:** Mallon, "Missing the Circus Frets Bandit Celia," p. 9.

178 **BEFORE IT CLOSES:** "Bobbed Hair Bandit, Home, Unrepentant," p. 1.

178 **awful lot to them:** Mallon, "Missing the Circus Frets Bandit Celia," p. 9.

179 **powder puff:** Ibid.

179 **than I do now:** "Bobbed Hair Bandit, Home, Unrepentant," p. 1.

179 **the best I got:** Ibid., p. 9.

179 **watched her and laughed:** "'Doesn't Pay' Says Gun Girl," *New York American*,
4/23/24, p. 1; "Bobbed-Hair Bandit's Own Story," XI, p. 9.

180 **Mrs. Edward Cooney:** "Excited Mob Meets Bob Hair Bandit Here," *New York
Telegram and Evening Mail*, 4/22/24, p. 1.

180 **April 22nd:** "Girl Bandit Here; Wants No Lawyer; Crowds Greet Her," p. 1.

180 **to meet him:** "Bobbed-Hair Bandit's Own Story," XII, *New York American*,
5/10/24, p. 9.

NOTES TO CHAPTER 18

183 **Brooklyn Citizen:** Mitzi Kolisch, "Celia Cooney Calm While Mate Wilts,"
Brooklyn Citizen, 4/23/24, p. 1.

183 **"jeer" the bandit:** "Proud Girl Bandit Describes 10 Crimes," *New York Times*,
4/23/24, p. 4.

183 **of the nation:** "Bob-Haired Bandit and Husband Plead Guilty—Are Jailed,"
Brooklyn Eagle, 4/23/24, p. 2.

183 **page one:** "Girl Bandit Cheered on Arrival," *New York Evening Journal*,
4/23/24, p. 1.

183 **outnumbered men:** *New York Telegram and Evening Mail*, *New York Evening
Post*, *New York Sun*, all on 4/22/24, p. 1; and *Brooklyn Eagle* and *New York
Herald-Tribune*, 4/23/24, p. 1. Estimates varied from one to ten thousand, to
"thousands."

183 **just to see her:** "Excited Mob Meets Bob Hair Bandit Here," *New York
Telegram and Evening Mail*, 4/22/24, p. 1.

183 **the train level:** "Girl Bandit Here; Wants No Lawyer; Crowds Greet Her,"
New York World, 4/23/24, p. 1.

183 **and kiss her:** Ring Lardner, "Valuable Hints to Bobbed Bandit," *New York
American*, 5/11/24, p. 5E.

183 **"jammed the platform":** "Riotous Throngs Block Path of Bobbed Bandit," *New
York Evening Post*, 4/22/23, p. 1.

184 **most talked about bandit:** "Robbed to Get Home for Baby Girl, Bandit Says,"
New York Herald-Tribune, 4/23/24, p. 9.

184 **someone called:** Kolisch, "Celia Calm While Mate Wilts," p. 1. The "Wolf of
Wall Street" was the popular nickname for stock trader Jesse Livermore.
Already notorious in 1924, he would gain further infamy in 1929 when he

made one hundred million dollars selling short and was personally blamed for bringing on the great crash.

184 **bobbed-hair bandit:** "Ten Crimes in Brooklyn Admitted by Girl Bandit," *New York Daily News*, 4/23/24, p. 12.

184 **were riding:** "Riotous Throngs Block Path of Bobbed Bandit," p. 1.

184 **were not enough:** "Bobbed Haired Bandit Arrives," *New York Sun*, 4/22/24, n.p.

184 **back stairway:** "Robbed to Get Home for Baby Girl, Bandit Says," p. 9; "Excited Mob Meets Bob Hair Bandit Here," p. 1.

186 **like a cannonade:** "Robbed to Get Home for Baby Girl, Bandit Says," p. 9.

186 **onto the platform:** "Proud Girl Bandit Describes 10 Crimes," *New York Times*, 4/23/24, p. 4.

186 **reporters and cameramen:** "Bobbed Haired Bandit Arrives," n.p.; "Bobbed-Hair Bandit's Own Story," XII, *New York American*, 5/10/24, p. 9.

186 **wildest excitement:** "Excited Mob Meets Bob Hair Bandit Here," p. 1.

186 **was a ballgame:** "Bobbed-Hair Bandit's Own Story," XII, p. 9.

186 **for a good view:** "Excited Mob Meets Bob Hair Bandit Here," p. 1.

186 **Bobbed Haired Bandit:** "Bobbed-Hair Bandit's Own Story," XII, p. 9.

186 **Pennsylvania Railroad police:** "Excited Mob Meets Bob Hair Bandit Here," p. 1; "Bobbed Haired Bandit Arrives," n.p.

186 **four o'clock:** "Excited Mob Meets Bob Hair Bandit Here," p. 1.

187 **Celia remembered:** "Bobbed-Hair Bandit's Own Story," XII, p. 9.

187 **through the crowd:** "Robbed to Get Home for Baby Girl, Bandit Says," p. 9.

187 **clear a passageway:** "Excited Mob Meets Bob Hair Bandit Here," pp. 1–2.

187 **Casey and Gray demanded:** "Bobbed-Hair Bandit's Own Story," XII, p. 9.

187 **criminal fraternity:** Robert Leibowitz, telephone conversation, 6/13/02.

187 **shooting rap:** Robert Leibowitz, *The Defender: The Life and Career of Samuel S. Leibowitz 1893–1933* (Englewood Cliffs, NJ: Prentice Hall, 1981), pp. 35–76.

187 **critical information:** Leibowitz, telephone conversation.

187 **middle initial "I":** Samuel S. Leibowitz's name is even misspelled Samuel I. Leikowitz in the *Washington Post* and *Los Angeles Times*, 4/23/24.

188 **"we believed them":** "Bobbed-Hair Bandit's Own Story," XII, p. 9.

188 **"without delay":** "Bobbed Bandit, Due Here Today, Admits Career of Robbery," *New York Times*, 4/22/24, p. 1

188 **resolution vanished:** "Bobbed-Hair Bandit's Own Story," XII, p. 9.

188 **Captain McCloskey:** "Bobbed Haired Bandit Arrives and Refuses Aid of Counsel," *New York Sun*, 4/22/24, n.p.

188 **reluctantly agreed:** "Excited Mob Meets Bob Hair Bandit Here," *New York Telegram and Evening Mail* 1, 4/22/24, pp. 1–2. The judge that issued the writ was Justice Levy.

188 **could sweat them:** "Girl Bandit Arrives and Refuses Counsel," n.p.

189 **in handcuffs:** "Excited Mob Meets Bob Hair Bandit Here," p. 1.

189 in the first place: "Riotous Throngs Block Path of Bobbed Bandit," *New York Evening Post*, 4/22/24, p. 1.

189 their lawyer at all: "Bobbed-Hair Bandit's Own Story," XII, p. 9.

189 took command: "Excited Mob Meets Bob Hair Bandit Here," pp. 1–2.

189 Brother Tom.: "Girl Bandit Here," *New York World*, 4/23/24, pp. 1, 6.

189 "appeared confused": Ibid.

189 ambiguous "undecided": "Excited Mob Meets Bob Hair Bandit Here," pp. 1–2.

190 untrained as it is: Kolisch, "Celia Cooney Calm While Mate Wilts," p. 1.

190 was decisive: "Girl Bandit Here," pp. 1, 6.

190 "but Leibowitz": "Bobbed-Hair Bandit's Own Story," XII, p. 9.

190 lawyer "stunned": "Excited Mob Meets Bob Hair Bandit Here," pp. 1–2.

190 *Brooklyn Citizen*: Kolisch, "Celia Cooney Calm While Mate Wilts," p. 1.

190 two thousand persons: "Excited Mob Meets Bob Hair Bandit Here," pp. 1–2.

192 was "filled": Ibid.

192 they hang her: "Bobbed-Hair Bandit's Own Story," XII, p. 9.

192 couple was caught: Ibid.; "Cooney's Plead Guilty to Robbery Indictment," *Brooklyn Standard Union*, 4/23/24, p. 1.

192 Casey and Gray: "Robbed to Get Home for Baby Girl," *New York Herald-Tribune*, 4/23/24, p. 4. The two other ADAs in the room were George Palmer Jr. and James Cuff.

192 bobbed haired at all: "Bobbed-Hair Bandit's Own Story," XII, p. 9.

192 shooting at a cop: Ibid.

192 in her statements: "Robbed to Get Home for Baby Girl," p. 4.

192 take her punishment: Ibid.

193 writing any others: "Bobbed-Hair Bandit's Own Story," VII, *New York American*, 5/5/24, n.p.

193 stamp drawers: "Girl Bandit Here," pp. 1, 6.

193 Celia replied: "Robbed to Get Home for Baby Girl," p. 4.

193 $30 a week: "Girl Bandit Here," p. 6.

193 rough time I had: "Bobbed-Hair Bandit's Own Story," I, *New York American*, 4/28/24, pp. 1, 3.

193 on this day: "Robbed to Get Home for Baby Girl," p. 4.

193 to hurt him: Ibid.

194 into the office: "Girl Bandit Here," p. 6.

194 'gone straight': "Robbed to Get Home for Baby Girl," p. 4.

194 if she could: Ibid.

194 incumbent expense: Ibid.

194 of a melodrama: "Girl Bandit Proudly Describes 10 Crimes," *New York Times*, 4/23/24, pp. 1, 4.

NOTES TO CHAPTER 19

195 *New York Times:* "Girl Bandit Proudly Describes 10 Crimes," *New York Times*, 4/23/24, pp. 1, 4.

195 Poplar Street: "Girl Bandit Here," *New York World*, 4/23/24, p. 6.

195 Brooklyn Bridge: The Poplar Street station still stands today, but is closed and shuttered. In contrast, Commissioner Enright's magnificent police headquarters in Manhattan has been turned into luxury housing.

195 as did his wife: "Girl Bandit Here," p. 6.

195 so long Eddie: "Bobbed Bandit Smiles in Cell," *New York American*, 4/23/24, p. 3.

195 Christina McPeth: "Bob-Haired Bandit and Husband Plead Guilty—Are Jailed," *Brooklyn Eagle*, 4/23/24, p. 1.

195 help much either: "Bobbed Bandit Pleads Guilty," *New York Telegram and Evening Mail*, 4/23/24, pp. 1–2 ; "Girl Bandit, Mate, Enter Guilty Plea," *Brooklyn Daily Times*, 4/23/24, pp. 3–4.; "Cooneys Identified by Thirteen Victims," *Brooklyn Citizen*, 4/23/24, pp. 1–2; "Cooneys Plead Guilty to Robbery Indictment," *Brooklyn Standard Union*, 4/23/24, p. 1.

196 fit to comment: "Cooneys Identified by Thirteen Victims," pp. 1–2; "Girl Bandit, Mate, Enter Guilty Plea," pp. 3–4.

196 station house: "Girl Bandit, Mate, Enter Guilty Plea," pp. 3–4.

196 was before him: "Bobbed Bandit Pleads Guilty," *New York Telegram and Evening Mail*, 4/23/24, pp. 1–2.

196 of Georgia: "Bob-Haired Bandit and Husband Plead Guilty—Are Jailed," p. 1; "Bobbed-Haired Bandit Pleads Guilty at Once," *New York Sun*, 4/23/24, pp. 1–2.

196 their new heroine: "Bobbed Bandit Pleads Guilty," *New York Telegram and Evening Mail*, 4/23/24, pp. 1–2. PS 8, still functioning, is located at the corner of Poplar and Hicks, twenty yards away from the station house.

196 black masks: "Bobbed-Haired Bandit Pleads Guilty at Once," pp. 1–2.

196 the day began: "Bobbed Bandit Pleads Guilty," pp. 1–2. The *Brooklyn Citizen* reported the Cooneys' recognizing neighborhood detective Owen Carney. "Cooneys Plead Guilty," *Brooklyn Citizen*, 4/23/24, pp. 1–2.

196 smiled too: "Bob-Haired Bandit and Husband Plead Guilty—Are Jailed," p. 1.

198 erupted in laughter: Ibid.

198 $85 from you: "Tamed Gungirl Pleads Guilty," *New York Daily News*, 4/24/24, pp. 3, 8.

198 pants pocket: "Girl Bandit and Husband Plead Guilty," *New York American*, 4/24/24, pp. 1, 3.

198 Herald Tribune: "Bobbed Bandit Pleads Guilty; Teases Victims," *New York Herald-Tribune*, 4/24/24, pp. 1, 6.

198 all a mistake: "Bobbed-Haired Bandit Pleads Guilty at Once," pp. 1–2.

199 how much was meant: "Bobbed Bandit Pleads Guilty; Teases Victims," pp. 1, 6.

199 didn't we?: Ibid.

199 **JEERS VICTIM:** "Tamed Gungirl Pleads Guilty," pp. 3, 8.

199 **still "SAUCY"?:** "Girl Bandit Saucy in Plea of Guilty," *New York World*, 4/24/24, pp. 1, 5.

199 **"feel like dirt":** "Bobbed-Hair Bandit's Own Story," XII, *New York American*, 5/10/24, p. 9.

200 **the Sun reported:** "Bobbed-Haired Bandit Pleads Guilty at Once," pp. 1–2.

200 **assault charges:** "Bobbed Bandit Pleads Guilty; Teases Victims," pp. 1, 6.

200 **first degree:** Indictment nos. 48, 704 A, B, C, and D, records of the Court of General Sessions, Kings County, New York Municipal Archives.

200 **their first sentence:** "Bobbed Bandit Pleads Guilty; Teases Victims," pp. 1, 6.

201 **one little girl:** "Bobbed Bandit East Side Girl," *New York Telegram and Evening Mail*, 4/24/24, p. 2.

201 **to be arraigned:** "Girl Bandit and Husband Plead Guilty," *New York American*, 4/24/24, pp. 1, 3.

201 **Jacob Shientag:** The newspapers at the time report Samuel Leibowitz's partner that day as John Scheverin or Isaac Schaverein. However, as Leibowitz's law partner at the time is confirmed to be Jacob Shientag, and also knowing the newspaper's propensity to misrepresent names, we think it is a safe bet that it was Shientag in court with Leibowitz that day.

201 **not guilty:** "Bob-Haired Bandit and Husband Plead Guilty — Are Jailed," p. 1; "Girl Bandit and Husband Plead Guilty," *New York American*, 4/24/24, pp. 1, 3.

201 **money and influence:** "Governor Urges Ousting of Martin as 'Not Fit' Judge," *New York Times*, 9/7/39, pp. 1–2; "'Preface' to the Charges Judge Martin Faces," *New York Times*, 9/7/39, p. 20; "G. W. Martin Dies," *New York Times*, 11/23/48, p. 30.

201 **dismissed the case:** Robert Leibowitz, *The Defender* (Englewood Cliffs, NJ: Prentice Hall, 1981), pp. 29–30. Detective Frank Gray was also involved in the Acuna trial.

202 **and add purjury:** "Cooneys Plead Guilty," *Brooklyn Standard Union*, 4/23/24, p. 1.

202 **alleged against her:** Ibid.

202 **right now:** Ibid.

202 **don't want any Judge:** "Girl Bandit and Husband Plead Guilty," pp. 1, 3.

202 **kindly retire:** "Cooneys Plead Guilty," p. 1.

202 **for sentencing:** "Girl Bandit and Husband Plead Guilty," pp. 1, 3.

202 **dispatched this case:** "Cooneys Plead Guilty," p. 1.

204 **so long a time:** "Bob-Haired Bandit and Husband Plead Guilty — Are Jailed," p. 1.

204 **by reformers:** "Harry Honeck, 63, Ex-Warden, Dead," *New York Times*, 5/2/34, n.p.; "New $3,000,000 Jail Asked in Brooklyn," *New York Times*, 9/18/30, n.p.; "Brooklyn's Bastille," exhibit on the website of the New York State Correction History Society, www.correctionhistory.org. The Raymond Street Jail was finally torn down in 1963.

204 **for his prisoners:** "Harry Honeck, 63, Ex-Warden, Dead," n.p.

204 **ex-laundry worker:** "Girl Bandit and Husband Plead Guilty," pp. 1, 3.

205 **an awful feeling:** "Bobbed-Hair Bandit's Own Story," I, *New York American*, 4/28/24, pp. 1, 3.

205 **next Tuesday:** "Girl Bandit and Husband Plead Guilty," pp. 1, 3.

205 **in deep trouble might be:** "Gungirl's Happy Jail Life," *New York Daily News*, 4/25/24, final edition cover; "Bobbed Bandit Weeps in Cell," *New York Sun*, 4/25/24, n.p.

205 **to kill himself:** "Cooney's Sanity Is Questioned," *New York Sun*, 4/24/24, n.p.

205 **the entire night:** Ibid. Other papers reporting the same incident have Celia telling the drunk woman that "she ought to be ashamed of herself."

206 **bread and coffee:** "Girl Bandit Cheerfully Waits Fate," *Brooklyn Citizen*, 4/24/24, p. 1.

206 **color of your money:** "Girl Bandit and Husband Plead Guilty," *New York American*, 4/24/24, pp. 1, 3.

206 **cigarette money:** "Alienists to Test Cooney for Sanity," *New York Times*, 4/25/24, p. 6.

206 **PRISON IDOL:** "Girl Bandit Prison Idol," *New York Daily News*, 4/25/24, first edition cover.

207 **quickly agreed:** William B. Seabrook, *No Hiding Place* (New York: J. B. Lippincott, 1942), pp. 216–217; "Bob-Haired Bandit in Cell Writing a Book of Exploits," *Brooklyn Eagle*, 4/25/24, p. 2.

207 **Trigger Finger:** "Bobbed-Hair Bandit's Own Story," I–XII, *New York American*, 4/28/24–5/10/24.

208 **Cecelia Cooney:** Seabrook, *No Hiding Place*. Recalled nearly twenty years after the fact, Seabrook seems to have forgotten that Macfadden's *Graphic* wasn't published until later in 1924.

210 **Deborah Luris' handcuffs:** Ibid., p. 219.

211 **a couple years:** Winifred Van Duser, "Ending Career Packed with Melodrama," *Westminster Democratic Advocate*, November 2, 1945, reprinted in Jay A. Graybeal, "William Buehler Seabrook," *Carroll County Times*, October 28, 2001. Also personal correspondence with Michael G. Sullivan, who is writing a biography of Seabrook. Personal e-mail correspondence, August 4, 2003–August 14, 2003. As all writers on Seabrook — from Van Duser to Sullivan — caution, Seabrook's biographical details, many of them supplied by the author in his autobiography *No Hiding Place*, need to be taken with a good shake of salt.

211 **to pay for it:** Seabrook, *No Hiding Place*, pp. 179, 184–185.

212 **John Haynes Holmes:** Ibid., p. 214.

213 **were taboo:** Ibid., pp. 184–185.

213 **of the *American*:** Ibid., p. 218.

213 **newspapers attest:** The account of Celia's schooling is her own: "Bobbed-Hair Bandit's Own Story," I, *New York American*, 4/28/24, pp. 1, 3. Auburn Prison records also describe Celia as literate.

213 *Argosy-All Story* magazines: "Bobbed Bandit 'Hard Boiled' Former Landladies Say," *Brooklyn Eagle*, 4/22/23, pp. 1, 3.

213 Bandit's Own Story: "Bobbed-Hair Bandit's Own Story," I, pp. 1, 3. Probably the best case for this first of Celia's printed confessions being largely her own words comes from one of her sons, who, reading the *American* series more than seventy-five years later, told us that it sounded like the Celia Cooney he remembered.

214 hair-raising story: "Bob-Haired Bandit in Cell Writing a Book of Exploits," p. 2.

214 as we could: Seabrook, *No Hiding Place*, p. 218.

214 still be ladies: "Bobbed-Hair Bandit's Own Story," I, pp. 1, 3.

215 Ed and me both: Ibid.

215 Irish-American boy: "Girl Bandit Takes All Blame," *New York Sun*, 4/21/24, n.p.

215 red Indian I guess: "Bobbed-Hair Bandit's Own Story," I, pp. 1, 3.

216 the big act: "Jailbirds Envy Bobbed Bandit," *New York Daily News*, 4/25/24, n.p.

NOTES TO CHAPTER 20

216 *Brooklyn Eagle:* "Mrs. Jesse James, New York," Editorial, *Brooklyn Eagle*, 4/25/24, p. 6.

216 brief married life: "Bob-Haired Bandit Decides to Fight," *New York Times*, 4/27/24, p. 17.

217 request was urgent: Ibid.; "Girl Bandit May Set up Temporary Insanity Plea," *Brooklyn Standard Union*, 4/27/24, p. 22.

217 *New York Times* headline: "Bob-Haired Bandit Decides to Fight," p. 17.

217 on previous occasions: "Cooney's Sanity Is Questioned," *New York Times*, 4/24/24, n.p.

217 of poor quality: "Alienists to Test Cooney for Sanity," *New York Times*, 4/25/24, p. 6.

217 A STUDY OF CONTRASTS: "A Study of Contrasts," *New York Daily News*, 4/24/24, p. 3.

217 her criminal career: "Bob-Hair Bandit Faces Sanity Test," *Washington Post*, 4/25/24, p. 1.

218 so much the better: Ring Lardner, "Valuable Advice to Bobbed Hair Bandit," *New York American*, 5/11/24, p. 5E.

218 criminal girlfriends: "Girl Bandit May Set up Temporary Insanity Plea," *Brooklyn Standard Union*, 4/27/24, p. 22; "Girl Bandit Planning Fight for Freedom," *Brooklyn Citizen*, 4/27/24, p. 3.

218 pleaded guilty: "Cooney Opens Fight to Save Bandit Wife," *New York Herald-Tribune*, 4/28/24, p. 1.

219 BANDIT WIFE: Ibid.

220 *Psychosexual Life:* "Bob-Haired Bandit's Sanity Test Ordered," *New York Evening Post*, 4/28/24, p. 2; "Court Appoints Alienists to Test Cooney's Sanity," *New York Herald-Tribune*, 4/29/24, p. 6; John Francis Meagher, *A Study of Masturbation and the Psychosexual Life* (New York: Wood, 1929).

221 **glimpse of the girl:** "Bob-Haired Celia Dodges Cameras in Dash to Van," *Brooklyn Eagle*, 4/29/24, p. 2.

221 **to her fans:** "Bobbed Bandit Happy as She Rides in Van," *New York Telegram and Evening Mail*, 4/29/24, n.p.

221 **Raymond Street Jail:** "Cooney's Talk in Private with Judge Martin," *Brooklyn Daily Times*, 4/29/24, n.p.

221 **plea of guilty:** "Bob-Haired Bandit Decides to Stick to Guilty Plea," *Brooklyn Eagle*, 4/30/24, p. 1.

221 **this latest turn:** "Court Appoints Alienists to Test Cooney's Sanity," p. 6.

221 **of a lawyer:** Tom W. Jackson, "The Periscope," *Brooklyn Standard Union*, 4/25/24, p. 14.

222 **to folow acquittal:** Lardner, "Valuable Advice to Bobbed Hair Bandit," p. 5E.

222 **to the testimony:** Ibid.

222 **Kings county:** "Cooneys Plead Guilty," *Brooklyn Standard Union*, 4/23/24, p. 1.

223 **and her mate:** "Let Law Exact Pound of Flesh Say Shopkeepers," *New York Daily News*, 4/27/24, n.p.

224 **make the community safer:** Ibid.

224 **law abiding citizens:** "Girl Bandit May Get Ten Years," *Brooklyn Daily Times*, 5/1/24, pp. 1–2.

224 **in his sentencing:** Ibid.

225 **not being crazy:** "Bobbed-Hair Bandit's Own Story," XII, *New York American*, 5/10/24, p. 9.

225 **an abnormal mind:** Cecil McCoy and Anna Ralston, *Commission Report on Celia Cooney*, May 5, 1924, New York Municipal Archives, 74/136B.

225 **"no evidence whatever of insanity":** John Meagher and Siegfried Black, *Commission Report on Edward Cooney*, May 5, 1924, New York Municipal Archives, 74/136B.

225 **in his cell:** "Love of Girl Bandit and Husband Touches Heart of Warden Honeck," *Brooklyn Daily Times*, 5/2/24, n.p.

226 **away for life:** Ibid.

226 **the same prison:** "Bobbed Bandit Breaks Down," *New York American*, 5/4/24, n.p.

226 **easy to look at:** "Bobbed Bandit Sentenced; Weeps," *New York Daily News*, 5/7/24, pp. 2–3.

226 **craned their necks:** "Bobbed Bandit and Mate Get 10 to 20 Years," *New York Herald-Tribune*, 5/7/24, pp. 1, 6.

226 **underneath the courtroom:** "Bobbed Hired Thief and Husband Given Long Prison Terms," *Brooklyn Citizen*, 5/6/24, pp. 1, 12.

226 up to the bench: "Cooneys Get 10 to 20-Year Terms," *Brooklyn Daily Times*, 5/6/24, pp. 1–2.

227 a blue tie: "Bobbed Hired Thief and Husband Given Long Prison Terms," pp. 1, 12; "Bob Haired Bandit Gets 10 to 20 Years," *New York Evening Post*, 5/6/24, pp. 1, 7.

227 try and spot her: "10 to 20 Years in Prison Is Girl Bandit's Sentence," *New York World*, 5/7/24, pp. 1, 4.

227 CECILIA COONEY: "Bobbed Bandit Gets Ten Years in Prison," *New York Times*, 5/7/24, pp. 1–2.

227 hand clapping: "Bobbed Bandit Gets 10 to 20 Years," *New York American*, 5/7/24, pp. 1, 7.

227 judge's bench: "10 to 20 Years in Prison Is Girl Bandit's Sentence," pp. 1, 4; "Cooneys Get 10 to 20-Year Terms," pp. 1–2.

229 ten to twenty years: "Bobbed Bandit Gets 10 to 20 Years," pp. 1, 7.

NOTES TO CHAPTER 21

230 *New York Herald-Tribune*: "Bobbed Bandit and Mate Get 10 to 20 Years, *New York Herald-Tribune*, 5/7/24, pp. 1, 6.

230 head held high: "Bobbed Bandit and Husband Sentenced in Presence of Her Parents," *New York Sun*, 5/6/24, n.p.

230 a state occasion: "Cooneys Get 10 to 20-Terms, She in Auburn, He in Sing Sing," *Brooklyn Daily Times*, 5/6/24, p. 1.

230 won the crowd: "Bob-Haired Bandit Gets 10 to 20 Years; Husband the Same," *New York Evening Post*, 5/6/24, p. 1.

230 without a whimper: "Bobbed Bandit Gets 10 to 20 Years," *New York American*, 5/7/24, pp. 1, 7; "Bobbed Bandit Weeps at Sentence," *Washington Post*, 5/7/24, p. 3.

230 went away unsatisfied: "Bobbed Bandit Gets 10 to 20 Years," pp. 1, 7.

230 wrote one suggestively: "Bob-Haired Bandit Gets 10 to 20 Years; Husband the Same," p. 1.

230 mouth was open: Ibid.

230 "sullen" and back: "Bobbed Haired Thief and Husband Given Long Prison Terms," *Brooklyn Citizen*, 5/6/24, p. 1; "Bob-Haired Bandit Gets 10 to 20 Years; Husband the Same," p. 1.

231 Cooney & Cooney: "Bob-Haired Bandit Gets 10 to 20 Years; Husband the Same," p. 1.

231 anyone was watching: "Bobbed Bandit and Mate Get 10 to 20 Years," *New York Herald-Tribune*, 5/7/24, pp. 1, 6; "Bobbed Bandit Gets Ten Years in Prison," *New York Times*, 5/7/24, pp. 1–2.

231 held a revolver: "Bobbed Bandit Gets 10 to 20 Years in Jail," *New York Telegram and Evening Mail*, 5/6/24, p. 2.

231 fixed on the door: "Girl's Parents Hear Sentence — Story Told to Press Untrue," *Brooklyn Citizen*, 5/6/24, p. 2.

232 wasting no tears: "Bob-Haired Bandit Gets Ten-Year Term," *New York Evening Post*, 5/7/24, p. 7.

232 dejected-looking persons: "Cooneys Get 10 to 20-Terms, She in Auburn, He in Sing Sing," p. 1.

232 recognized them at all: "Bobbed Bandit Gets 10 to 20 Years in Jail," p. 2.

233 the kind of man Celia did: "Still Untamed, She Awaits Her Sentence Today," *New York Daily News*, 5/6/24, p. 7.

233 came home and cried: Ibid.

233 ever did before: Ibid.

233 the Russian school: "Bob Haired Bandit Gets 10 to 20 Years," *New York Evening Post*, 5/6/24, pp. 1, 7.

236 case came up: "Bobbed Bandit Gets Ten Years in Prison," *New York Times*, 5/7/24, pp. 1–2; "Probation Officer's Report Shows Parents Neglected Cecelia Cooney," *New York World*, 5/7/24, p. 4.

236 give her a recommendation: "Bobbed Bandit Gets Ten Years in Prison," pp. 1–2.

236 always left open: Ibid.

238 denied their existence: Ibid.

238 harsh sentencing: "Bobbed Bandit Gets Ten Years in Prison," pp. 1–2.

NOTES TO CHAPTER 22

239 *New York World*: Walter Lippmann, "Cecilia Cooney," *New York World*, 5/8/24, p. 10.

239 Low Environment: "Bobbed Bandit Gets Ten Years in Prison; Warns Other Girls," *New York Times*, 5/7/24, p. 1.

239 courage and coolness: "Bobbed Bandit Gets 10 to 20 Years in Jail," *New York Telegram and Evening Mail*, 5/6/24, p. 2.

240 gain by toil: "Movies Lured Cooneys, Says Judge Martin," *Brooklyn Standard Union*, 5/9/24, p. 2.

240 to help him: "Bobbed Bandit Gets Ten Years in Prison," p. 2.

240 on a honeymoon: "The Bobbed-Haired Bandit," *Brooklyn Daily Times*, 4/22/24, p. 6.

240 A. Yes.: "Cooneys Are Sad at Final Parting," *New York World*, 5/9/24, p. 15.

241 terrible accusation: Lippmann, "Cecilia Cooney," p. 10.

242 children in the world: Ibid.

243 her crimes and ours: Ibid.

243 of the century: "Cooneys Are Sad at Final Parting," p. 15.

243 A BETTER CHANCE: "Celia Cooneys of Today Have a Better Chance," *New York Times*, 5/18/24, p. 8.

243 to build on: Joanna C. Colcord, "Cecilia Cooney's Case and the C. O. Society," letter, *New York World*, 5/10/24, p. 6.

244 future "unfortunates": "Cites Girl Bandit as Lesson," *New York Evening Post*, 5/10/24, p. 11.

244 misguided youths: "Prevent Breeding of Criminals, Is Plea by Minister," *New York World*, 5/10/24, p. 15.

245 birth control: Ibid.

246 the human race: "Girl Bandit's Fall Is Laid to Liquor," *Brooklyn Standard Union*, 5/12/24, p. 9.

246 years in prison: Ibid.

247 to the streets: "Mrs. Catt Draws a Lesson from Bobbed Bandit's Story," *New York American*, 5/8/24, n.p.

247 a jungle product: "Exit to a General Amen," *Brooklyn Eagle*, 5/7/24, n.p.

247 prison sentence: A. A., "Not an Amen for Bobbed Bandits," letter, *Brooklyn Eagle*, 5/15/24, p. A7.

247 life of drudgery: Fair Play, "The Case of Cecilia Cooney," letter, *New York World*, 5/12/24, p. 10.

248 study of Socialism: Julius Lichtenfeld, "Try Socialism," *New York World*, 5/14/24, p. 10.

248 numerical superiority: R. H. Towner, "In Defense of Society," letter, *New York World*, 5/12/24, p. 10.

249 not society: John A. Cutter, "The Individual Sinner," letter, *New York World*, 5/12/24, p. 10.

249 make this world better: E. S., "Schools, Crime and Punishment," letter, *New York Telegram and Evening Mail*, 5/15/24, p. 12.

249 night and day: L. R., "Child of Misfortune," letter, *New York Daily News*, 5/20/24, p. 13.

249 the editors concluded: "The Only Banditry Cure," *Brooklyn Standard Union* 5/7/24, p. 8.

252 themselves and society: "A Closed Career," *Brooklyn Daily Times*, 5/8/24, p. 6.

252 regarding their case: "Setting a Good Example," *New York Telegram and Evening Mail*, 5/7/24, p. 10.

253 have suffered: "No 'Bandit,' Only a Deluded Woman," *New York American*, 5/3/24, n.p.

253 safety of society: "Criminals, Class A," *New York World*, 5/10/24, p. 6.

253 shopmen's tills: Ibid.

254 alike to steal: "The Majesty of the Law," *Nation*, 5/28/24, p. 602.

253 baby at home: "Cooneys Dubbed Rank Amateurs in Underworld's View of Exploit," *New York World*, 5/11/24, p. 15.

253 at an end: Editorial, *New York Evening Post*, 5/7/24, p. 10.

254 prison guard: Jane Dixon, "Poor Pay," *New York Telegram and Evening Mail*, 5/9/24, p. 15.

255 in the matter: "That Girl 'Bandit,'" *New York American*, 5/17/24, n.p.

255 he concluded: William L. Barnhart, "The Six Deadly Pitfalls," *Washington Post*, 12/21/24, p. SM1.

NOTES TO CHAPTER 23

259 *New York Daily News:* "Bobbed Bandit Sentenced; Weeps" *New York Daily News,* 5/7/24, pp. 2–3.

259 **ten-minute egg:** "Bobbed Bandit and Mate Get 10 to 20 Years," *New York Herald-Tribune,* 5/7/24, p. 1.

259 **sealskin coat:** "10 to 20 Years in Prison Is Girl Bandit's Sentence," *New York World,* 5/7/24, pp. 1, 4.

260 **Raymond Street Jail:** Ibid.; "Bobbed Bandit Gets Ten Years in Prison," *New York Times,* 5/7/24, pp. 1–2; "Bobbed Bandit and Mate Get 10 to 20 Years," pp. 1, 6; "Bob Haired Bandit Gets 10 to 20 Years," *New York Evening Post,* 5/6/24, pp. 1, 7; "Bobbed Bandit Gets 10 to 20 Years in Jail," *New York Telegram and Evening Mail,* 5/6/24, p. 1.

260 **head in arms:** "Bobbed Bandit Gets Ten Years in Prison," pp. 1–2.

260 **in the laundry:** "Bobbed Hair Bandit's Own Story," XI, *New York American,* 5/10/24, p. 9.

260 **and the mangle:** Ibid.

260 **detective stories:** "Cooney's Still in Jail," *New York Times,* 5/8/24, p. 17.

261 **when we get out:** "Bobbed Bandit Gets Ten Years in Prison," pp. 1–2.

261 **and be respectable:** "Bobbed Hair Bandit Weeps at Sentence," 5/7/24, *Washington Post,* p. 3.

261 **"imminent collapse":** "Girl Bandit May Not Say Good-Bye to Her Husband," *Brooklyn Standard Union,* 5/7/24, p. 1.

261 **happy to see them:** "Girl Bandit in Tears Bidding Ed Good-By," *New York Evening Post,* 5/8/24, n.p.

261 **her mother:** Ibid.

261 **and she left:** "Gungirl's Parents Hid in Woe," *New York Daily News,* 5/6/24, pp. 1, 7.

261 **see her parents:** "10 to 20 Years in Prison Is Girl Bandit's Sentence," *New York World,* 5/7/24, pp. 1, 4.

261 **both in tears:** "Girl Bandit in Tears Bidding Ed Good-By," n.p.

261 **who played bandit:** "Celia Cooney Tearful and Shaky," *Brooklyn Citizen,* 5/9/24, p. 1.

262 **a gush of tears:** "Girl Bandit in Tears Bidding Ed Good-By," n.p.

262 **with a smile:** "Cooneys, in Tears, Separate in Jail," *New York Times,* 5/9/24, p. 12; "Girl Bandit in Tears Bidding Ed Good-By," n.p.

262 **Celia said wistfully:** "Celia Cooney Tearful and Shaky," p. 1.

262 **is against me:** "Girl Bandit Jokes Leaving for Prison," *New York Evening Post,* 5/9/24, n.p.; Bobbed Bandit off for Auburn," *New York Sun,* 5/9/24, n.p.

264 **eroded their numbers:** "Celia Cooney Tearful and Shaky," p. 1.

264 **rush hour crowd:** "Bobbed Girl Goes in Tears to Auburn," *New York World,* 5/10/24, p. 11.

264 **page eleven:** Ibid.; the line quoted is the subhead.

264 **no longer big news:** "Bobbed Bandit off for Auburn," n.p.

264 Edward Cooney: "Bobbed Girl Goes in Tears to Auburn," p. 11; "Cooney Bandits Serving Terms," *New York Sun*, 5/10/24, n.p.

264 in the book: 75, 907: "Cooney Bandits Serving Terms," n.p.

265 out of trouble: Ibid.

265 head width: 14.7+: Bertillion Register, Auburn Prison, B0054: New York State Prison for Women, Female Inmate Identification File, New York State Archives.

265 handle a gun: "Bobbed Bandit Sings in Prison," *Brooklyn Eagle*, 5/11/24, n.p.

265 so lonely then: "What the World Didn't Know," *Modern Romances*, June 1940, pp. 45, 84.

266 until six: Ibid.

266 songs in her cell: "Bobbed Bandit Sings in Prison," n.p.

266 for Sing Sing: "Cooney Too 'Hard' for Sing Sing" *Brooklyn Eagle*, 6/22/24, p. 22.

267 "model prisoner": Ibid.; "Cooneys Win Praise," *New York Sun*, 1/31/25, n.p.

267 sympathetic ear: "Bob-Haired Bandit Visits with Hubby," *Brooklyn Eagle*, 7/21/24, n.p.; "What the World Didn't Know," p. 84.

267 wiping the tears away: "What the World Didn't Know," p. 84.

267 give each other courage: Ibid.; see also: "Bob-Haired Bandit Visits with Hubby," n.p.

268 prison hospital: "Edward Cooney Loses 4 Fingers in Prison Accident," *Brooklyn Eagle*, 8/21/24, n.p.

268 was a success: "Bandit Edward Cooney Here with Prison-Mangled Arm," *Brooklyn Eagle*, 1/13/26, n.p.; "State Pays Cooney for Loss of Hand," *New York Evening Post*, 12/24/31, n.p.

268 from his wife: "State Pays Cooney for Loss of Hand," n.p.; "Bob-Haired Bandit Free Soon," *New York Sun*, 10/16/31, n.p.

268 every week: Mildred Lovell, "Cupid Frees Gungirl and Mate to Love," *New York Daily News*, 1/12/30, n.p.

268 prison school: Ibid.; "'Bob Haired' Bandit Gets Parole in November," *New York Herald-Tribune*, 10/17/24, n.p.

269 Brooklyn bandit: "Candidates and Campaigns Draw Gridiron Club Satire," *Washington Post*, 4/27/24, p. 1.

269 bob it or bandit: *Life*, 7/10/24, p. 23.

270 Bandit and Society: "Religious Services" listings, *New York Times*, 5/10/24, p. 17.

270 return to New York: "Gossip of Vaudeville," *New York Times*, 5/11/24, p. E4.

270 on the circuit: "Theater and Resorts," *Washington Post*, 8/21/24, p. 16.

270 lion's mouth: Shelton Brooks, "Throw Dirt in Your Face," recorded 2/17/26, *Ethel Waters*, 1925–1926, Melodie Jazz Classic.

271 Marry 'Em: "Buffalo Bobbed Bandit," *New York Herald-Tribune*, 5/12/24, p. 1; "Bobbed Hair Bandit Sticks up Chicagoan," *New York World*, 5/4/24, p. 1; "Catches 5 'Baby' Bandits," *New York Times*, 5/30/24, n.p.; "China's Bobbed Hair Bandits Steal Wealthy Young Men and Marry 'Em," *New York American*, 5/11/24, p. 1.

271 the money the next: "Post and Paddock," *New York Times*, 5/3/25, p. 25.

271 literature and baseball: Lovell, "Cupid Frees Gungirl and Mate to Love," n.p.

271 made regular use of: "What the World Didn't Know," p. 84.

271 in her books: Lovell, "Cupid Frees Gungirl and Mate to Love," n.p.

271 correspondence courses: "What the World Didn't Know," p. 85.

273 better housekeeper: Ibid., p. 84.

273 Celia Cooney's Case: "Will Prison Reform Girl Bandit?" *New York Daily News*, 5/25/24, n.p.

273 priest's advice: "Celia Cooney and Mate Bid Crime Adieu," *New York Daily News*, 11/7/31, n.p.

273 never bob it again: "Celia Cooney, Bandit, No Longer Bobs Hair," *New York American*, 2/16/25, n.p. Other than the long *News* feature in 1930, this 1925 *American* story was the only one we found that followed up on Celia's prison life.

273 Celia insisted: Lovell, "Cupid Frees Gungirl and Mate to Love," n.p.

273 she loves a man: Ibid.

273 same machine: "Celia Cooney Testifies in Husband's Suit," *Brooklyn Eagle*, 4/24/31, p. 1.

275 neatly pinned up: "Convict Suing State," *New York Sun*, 4/23/31, n.p.; "State Pays Cooney for Loss of Hand," *New York Evening Post*, 12/24/31, n.p.; "$12,000 to Cooney for Injury in Jail," *New York Sun*, 12/24/31, n.p.

NOTES TO CHAPTER 24

275 Christmas Day: "Cooney, Hurt at Prison Task, to Get $12,000," *New York American*, 12/25/31, n.p.

275 with the safe: Mildred Lovell, "Cupid Frees Gungirl and Mate to Love," *New York Daily News*, 1/12/30, n.p.

276 as his wife: "Crowds Unaware as Celia Cooney Arrives in City," *New York Herald-Tribune*, 10/7/31, n.p.

276 to be confidential: Minutes of Meetings by Board of Parole, Oct. 1931, Auburn Prison, New York State Archives.

276 to avoid publicity: "Celia Cooney Free," *New York Sun*, 11/6/31, n.p.; "Celia Cooney and Mate Bid Crime Adieu," *New York Daily News*, 11/7/31, n.p.

276 dismissed in 1932: Indictment No. 48704 A-D, *The People vs. Edward Cooney and Celia Cooney*, Court of General Sessions, Kings County, NY, New York Municipal Archives.

276 to Syracuse: "Celia Cooney Is Freed," *New York Times*, 11/7/31, n.p.

276 New York Central: "Celia Cooney, Bobbed-Hair Bandit, Freed," *New York Herald-Tribune*, 11/6/31, n.p.

277 between 1924 and 1931: "What the World Didn't Know," *Modern Romances*, June 1940, p. 86.

277 crowd of thousands: "Crowds Unaware as Celia Cooney Arrives in City," n.p.; "What the World Didn't Know," p. 86.

277 **crowds of the city:** "Crowds Unaware as Celia Cooney Arrives in City," n.p.

277 **seems to be different:** "Celia Cooney and Mate Bid Crime Adieu," *New York Daily News*, 11/7/31, n.p.

277 **887 Dean Street:** "Crowds Unaware as Celia Cooney Arrives in City," n.p..; "Celia Cooney Comes to First Real Home," *Brooklyn Eagle*, 11/7/31, n.p.

278 **the couple's return:** "Celia Cooney Comes to First Real Home," n.p.

278 **well-deserved skepticism:** "Celia Cooney Leaves to Live with Aunt," *Brooklyn Eagle*, 11/8(?)/31, n.p.

278 **they drifted off:** "The Cooney's Have Gone to a Farm," *New York Sun*, 11/7/31, n.p.

278 **isn't any Santa Claus:** "Cooney, Hurt at Prison Task, to Get $12,000," n.p. It's unclear why Celia would risk violating the terms of her parole by granting such an interview. Considering the *American* had paid for access to Celia before, it is tempting to speculate that a little Christmas "gift" changed hands.

279 **in the end:** Earl Sparling, "Bob-Haired Bandit Loses Home She Won by Prison Term," *New York World-Telegram*, 9/5/36, n.p.

279 **to New York:** "Celia Cooney and Mate Bid Crime Adieu," n.p.; "Bob Haired Bandit Free Soon" *New York Sun*, 10/16/31, n.p.; Edward Cooney Jr., personal correspondence, 12/9/02.

282 **went on relief:** Sparling, "Bob-Haired Bandit Loses Home She Won by Prison Term," n.p.; Warren Hall, "Death Claims Mate of First Bobbed Bandit," *New York Daily News*, 5/30/36, pp. 3, 8.

282 **second billing:** Sparling, "Bob-Haired Bandit Loses Home She Won by Prison Term," n.p.; Hall, "Death Claims Mate of First Bobbed Bandit," pp. 3, 8; "Cooney Dead: Husband of 'Bobbed Hair Bandit,'" *New York Herald-Tribune*, 5/30/36, n.p.; "Celia Cooney, Broke, Plans New Life Here," *Brooklyn Eagle*, 12/6/36, n.p.; Cooney Jr., personal correspondence. Taking care of her husband, Celia also contracted TB. Fortunately, it was treated and arrested.

282 **"former occupation":** "Celia Cooney, Broke, Plans New Life Here," n.p.

282 **come out on top:** Sparling, "Bob-Haired Bandit Loses Home She Won by Prison Term," n.p.

283 **said it all:** "Ex-'Girl Bandit,' Going Straight, Loses All in Fire," *New York Mirror*, 4/22/39, n.p.

284 **about the Tips:** *Modern Romances*, March–June 1940, table of contents.

284 **this big world:** "What the World Didn't Know," May 1940, p. 96.

285 **asking for me:** Ibid., March 1940, p. 85.

285 **"quiet obscurity":** Ibid., April 1940, p. 32.

285 **It was true.:** Ibid., March 1940, p. 20.

285 **sordid and cheap:** Ibid., May 1940, p. 94.

286 **I was born in:** Ibid., March 1940, p. 21.

287 **I am human:** Ibid., June 1940, p. 88.

NOTES TO CHAPTER 25

287 *Modern Romances:* "What the World Didn't Know," *Modern Romances,* June 1940, pp. 87–88.

288 **Bobbed Haired Bandit:** All information and quotes attributed to Patrick and Edward Cooney, personal interviews, 10/17/01 and 10/10/01, respectively, and personal correspondence, Edward Cooney, 12/9/02.

292 **from a jewelry store:** "Girl Bandit's Brother Shot," *New York Herald Tribune,* 3/16/27, n.p.

292 **Casey and Gray:** "Celia Cooney's Kin Held as Robber," *New York World,* 6/21/25, n.p.

NOTES TO THE EPILOGUE

297 **"greeted with laughter":** "Tammany Leaders Laugh at Hylan for Third Term," *New York Times,* 5/11/24, p. 1.

297 **Al Smith:** Ibid.

297 **number of votes:** "City Pays Homage to Ex-Mayor Hylan," *New York Times,* 1/13/36, p. 1.

298 **purposes:** "Secret Crime Lists Taken by Enright," *New York Times,* 1/6/26, p. 1.

298 **for that matter:** "McLaughlin Ends Honorary Posts," *New York Times,* 1/24/26, p. 1.

298 **"Square Deal" party:** "Square Deal Party Seeks Subway Seat," *Christian Science Monitor,* 9/6/29, p. 2.

298 **proved right:** George Creel, "No 'Crime Wave' in New York City, Police Commissioner Richard E. Enright Responds to His Critics" (New York: Bureau of Printing, Police Department, 1921). Originally from *New York Times,* 1/23/21.

298 **'crook stuff':** "Movies and Literature Beckon to Enright," *New York Times,* 10/31/25, n.p. The reporter is quoting Malcolm Strauss, a movie producer, on Enright.

298 **enticing, irresponsible:** Richard E. Enright, *Vultures of the Dark* (New York: Brentano's Publishers, 1924), p. 3.

299 **into retirement:** "J. D. Coughlin Dies, Police Ex-Official," *New York Times,* 10/01/51, n.p.; "W. J. Lahey Dead, Retired Inspector," *New York Times,* 4/3/33, n.p.; "Lahey and Coughlin Rose Fast on Force," *New York Times,* 12/20/28, n.p.

299 **Captain John McCloskey:** "Roll of Honor," *Annual Report of the Police Department,* 1924, n.p.; "Ex-Capt. D. J. Carey, Policeman 41 Years," *New York Times,* 4/26/50, n.p.

299 **until his retirement:** "Charles Dodd, 74, Ex-Justice, Is Dead," *New York Times,* 7/25/47, n.p.

299 **seven years after that:** "Governor Urges Ousting of Martin as 'Not Fit' Judge," *New York Times,* 9/7/39, pp. 1–2; "'Preface' to the Charges Judge Martin

Faces," *New York Times*, 9/7/39, p. 20; "G. W. Martin Dies," *New York Times*, 11/23/48, p. 30.

300 **Riker's Island:** "Honeck Is Shifted in Prison Shake-Up," *New York Times*, 7/20/33, n.p.; "Harry Honeck, 63, Ex-Warden, Dead," *New York Times*, 5/2/34, n.p.

300 **with the bottle:** Winifred Van Duser, "Ending Career Packed with Melodrama," *Westminster Democratic Advocate*, November 2, 1945, reprinted in Jay A. Graybeal, "William Buehler Seabrook," *Carroll County Times*, October 28, 2001. Also personal correspondence with Michael G. Sullivan, who is writing a biography on Seabrook. Personal e-mail correspondence, August 4, 2003, and August 14, 2003.

300 **of a young woman:** Robert Leibowitz, *The Defender: The Life and Career of Samuel S. Leibowitz 1893–1933* (Englewood Cliffs, NJ: Prentice Hall, 1981), pp. 35–76.

300 **East Harlem street:** Ibid., pp. 170–181.

300 **and was executed:** Robert Leibowitz, telephone conversation, 6/13/02.

301 **death sentence:** "Scottsboro Case," in *The Reader's Companion to American History*, Eric Foner and John A. Garraty, eds. (Boston: Houghton-Mifflin, 1991), pp. 971–972.

301 **"new Moses":** "Leibowitz in Harlem Stirs 4,000 by Plea," *New York Times*, 4/14/34, p. 5.

301 **they could find:** Frank Luther Mott, *American Journalism* (New York: Macmillan, 1942), p. 669. Macfadden's *Daily Graphic* folded in 1932 after losing millions for the publisher.

301 **Ed left prison:** Ronald Steel, *Walter Lippmann and the American Century* (Boston: Little, Brown, 1980), pp. 269–280.

302 **two hundred dailies:** Ibid.

Acknowledgments

This book, like all histories, would not have been possible without the assistance of many librarians and archivists. We acknowledge the generous help we received at the New York State Library, where we "discovered" Celia Cooney. We also found valuable sources with the help of the staff at the New-York Historical Society, the Brooklyn Historical Society, the New York State Archives, and the Museum of the City of New York. In particular we thank the staff in the microfilm room of the New York Public Library for retrieving all those reels, Joy Holland and Susan Aprill of the Brooklyn Collection of the Brooklyn Public Library, Ken Cobb at New York Municipal Archive, Maja Keech at the Library of Congress, Lauren Gurgiolo and Pete Smith at the Harry Ransom Humanities Research Center at the University of Texas at Austin, Angela Troisi at the *New York Daily News*, and Leila Mattson at the Great Neck Public Library. We especially thank Ms. Billie Aul, Mr. Paul Mercer, and Mr. Jim Corsaro of the New York State Library for assisting us in this, as well as other projects over the years. Other people who have been instrumental in the making of this book include Bruce Bennett, Sofia Contreras, Tom and Patricia Glynn, Robert Leibowitz, Peter H. Mattson, Thomas McCarthy of the New York Correction History Society, Graham Rayman, Thomas Reppetto, David Sandlin, William Sites, Bob Stratton, Maryellen Strautmanis, Michael Sullivan, Leila Walker, and Tsana Yu. Sally, David, and Jane Duncombe, Julie Glynn, and Jean Railla also provided invaluable editing advice. Assistant editor Emily Park, production manager Charles Hames, and managing editor Despina Papazoglou Gimbel of NYU Press transformed the manuscript into a real book. Our friend Stewart Cauley of Pollen Design helped us in a hundred different ways to make this book special. Many thanks go out to Stuart and Liz Ewen and Rosalyn Baxandall for kindling our passion in media history, Caleb Carr and Suzanne Gluck for believing in us back when this project began, and Eric Zinner who is everything we wanted in an editor. The advice, support, and patience of our growing families — Julie, Natalie, Nora, and Ella; Jean, Sydney, and Sebastien — was critical over the long haul of this book. And finally we extend a very special thanks to Patrick and Edward Cooney Jr. for sharing their stories — and their mother — with all of us.

Index

Page numbers in italics refer to illustrations.

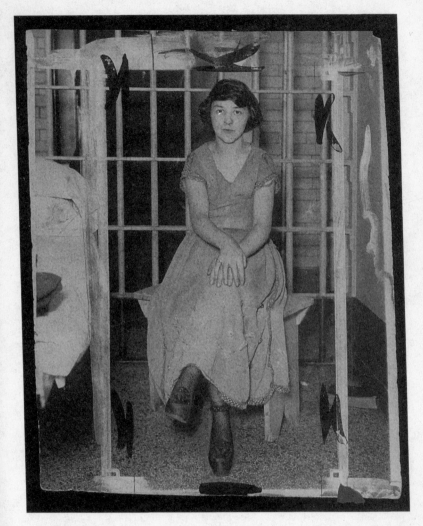

Celia Cooney (Harry Ransom Humanities Research Center)

About the Authors

STEPHEN DUNCOMBE and ANDREW MATTSON met when they were both students at the Graduate Center of the City University of New York. Since that time they have coedited a fanzine of historical primary documents, cohosted a show on a pirate radio station, cowritten scholarly articles, and taught together. Duncombe currently teaches the history and politics of media at the Gallatin School of New York University, and Mattson teaches American Studies and Media Communications at the State University of New York at Old Westbury. They both live in New York City.